S0-BFA-665

TRAUMA
and Its
WAKE

VOLUME I: The Study
and Treatment of
Post-traumatic Stress Disorder

Brunner/Mazel Psychosocial Stress Series
Charles R. Figley, Ph.D., Series Editor

1. Stress Disorders Among Vietnam Veterans
   Edited by Charles R. Figley, Ph.D.
2. Stress and the Family, Volume 1: Coping with Normative Transitions
   Edited by Hamilton I. McCubbin, Ph.D., and Charles R. Figley, Ph.D.
3. Stress and the Family, Volume II: Coping with Catastrophe
   Edited by Charles R. Figley, Ph.D., and Hamilton I. McCubbin, Ph.D.
4. Trauma and Its Wake
   Edited by Charles R. Figley, Ph.D.
5. Post-traumatic Stress Disorder and the War Veteran Patient
   Edited by William E. Kelly, M.D.

Editorial Board

BRUNNER/MAZEL PSYCHOSOCIAL STRESS SERIES NO. 4

TRAUMA and Its WAKE

VOLUME I: The Study and Treatment of Post-traumatic Stress Disorder

Edited by

Charles R. Figley, Ph.D.

BRUNNER/MAZEL, *Publishers* • New York

Library of Congress Cataloging in Publication Data
Main entry under title:

Trauma and its wake.

   (Brunner/Mazel psychosocial stress series)
   Includes bibliographies and index.
   1. Post-traumatic stress disorder. I. Figley,
Charles R., 1944-   . II. Series. [DNLM: 1. Stress
Disorders, Post-Traumatic. WM 170 T777]
RC552.P67T73   1985   616.85'21   84-29344
ISBN 0-87630-385-8

Copyright © 1985 by Charles R. Figley

Published by

BRUNNER/MAZEL, INC.
19 Union Square West
New York, New York 10003

MANUFACTURED IN THE UNITED STATES OF AMERICA

10 9 8 7 6 5 4 3

Dedicated to
Laura Reeves Figley

Editorial Note

Recently the American Psychiatric Association, on the eve of a national epidemiological study of post-traumatic stress disorders (PTSD), solicited my input regarding the future revision of their *Diagnostic and Statistical Manual of Mental Disorders* (Third Edition). Assembled were the national leaders in the study, measurement, and treatment of PTSD. Though there were lively exchanges, the near consensus was that 1) PTSD is a viable and appropriate diagnostic category; 2) generating a precise definition of what causes PTSD would be impossible at this point in the science of traumatic stress; 3) delayed reactions are rare; when each so-called delayed PTSD is carefully examined, it is apparent that the disorder was detectable soon after exposure to the traumatic event or catastrophe; 4) the symptom profile changes over the course of the disorder; 5) depression and substance abuse are frequently observed associated features of PTSD. Other more minor issues were described. What all these observations and the subsequent draft of a revised description of PTSD represent is the emergence of a more sophisticated understanding of the immediate and long-term psychosocial consequences of traumatic events.

Trauma and Its Wake, Volume I: The Study and Treatment of Post-Traumatic Stress Disorder is part of the Brunner/Mazel Psychosocial Stress Series. Its topic is psychosocial stress—human response to alarming events. The purpose of the Series is to develop and publish books with potential for making a significant contribution to our understanding of psychosocial stress. Of special interest are books applicable to either preventing or ameliorating ineffective coping. The first book in this Series, *Stress Disorders Among Vietnam Veterans: Theory, Research, and Treatment*, for example, was among several which helped shape the current thinking about traumatic stress, including the PTSD category in DSM-III. Moreover, it has been published and translated internationally. As the first volume, it sets the tone for the Series: a medium for conceptualizing and solving emotional problems associated with alarming events, although the book deals almost exclusively with war veterans and their families.

The next two books published in the Series focus on the context of the family for both generating and processing psychosocial stress. *Stress and the Family, Volume I: Coping With Normative Transitions* deals systematically with methods families utilize to cope with normative changes and transitions through the life cycle. In contrast, *Stress and the Family, Volume II: Coping With Catastrophe* focuses on extraordinary circumstances (e.g., rape, unemployment, illness) and the methods families utilize to cope.

Trauma and Its Wake: The Study and Treatment of Post-Traumatic Stress Disorder is the fourth book in the Series. This volume shifts the focus back to both systemic *and* individual functioning. This will be the inaugural volume of a series within the Series, which will publish a volume each year making available the most important unpublished work in the growing area of traumatic and post-traumatic stress studies. As with a journal, the Series Editorial Board will review each paper considered for the *Trauma and Its Wake* volumes. This refereed publication may someday emerge into an international journal when this field requires one.

This present volume provides a rich selection of the latest research findings and theoretical and clinical innovations associated with post-traumatic stress disorder. Twelve separate traumatic events are discussed (e.g., war combat, childhood incest, rape, natural disasters, and crime victimization). But the emphasis throughout this and subsequent volumes is toward development of a generic view of traumatic stress: identifying common features among a wide variety of catastrophes and individuals and systems that experience them.

Those interested in submitting either a book proposal for the Series or a manuscript for the *Trauma and Its Wake* volumes should write the Editor of the Series, % the Family Research Institute, 525 Russell Street, Purdue University, W. Lafayette, Indiana 47906.

Charles R. Figley
Series Editor

Contents

Acknowledgments

With such an ambitious project to produce this volume involved many people whose contributions were critical. Certainly the early scholars noted in Chapter 1 deserve special recognition. It is their initial insights and published works which provide the critical foundation for this volume.

The Editorial Board for this volume and book series represents all sectors of the human sciences and are listed on a separate page along with their affiliations. They assisted with the initial screening of the more than 125 papers considered for inclusion in this and subsequent volumes. Moreover, they provided detailed and systematic reviews of those which were eventually selected, significantly improving the scholarship and readability of the volume. They were joined by others who served as reviewers for specific works. They include: Joan Jurich, Orville Lips, Chris Hatcher, Shirley Smith, Marvin McDonald, Gary Ladd, Barbara Segal, Gail Melson, Marcie Kaplan, Robert McFarland, Elaine Alvarey, Michael Jackson, David Spiegel, Walter Schumm, and William Southerly.

Certainly the contributors to this volume deserve special recognition apart from their separate chapters. They were forced to endure the endless correspondence from the editor asking for just one more modification, however slight.

My Purdue University colleagues in the Department of Child Development, including the Department Head, Robert Lewis, and Clinical Program Director, Wallace Denton, deserve my acknowledgment for their encouragement and support. I am especially indebted to the University's Agricultural Experiment Station's support of my research, along with the Director, Dr. Billy R. Baumgardt. My students Shirley Ann Segal, G. Richard Kishur, Sandra K. Burge, Kathleen Gilbert, and C. J. Harris deserve special praise. In their own way and to varying extents they reviewed many of the manuscripts, reacted to my changing ideas regarding traumatic stress, and offered creative insights and suggestions. Certainly my secretary, Alice Benner, was a constant source of encouragement and support in all phases and aspects of this project.

Finally, my family was my source of inspiration. My wife, Dr. Marilyn Reeves and daughter, Jessica, though confused about why it was taking so long, were always supportive and interested companions in the wake of this trauma.

Contributors

Mary E. Bender, Ph.D.
Assistant Clinical Professor, Department of Psychiatry, University of California-Irvine, Irvine, California.

Connie L. Best, Ph.D.
Assistant Clinical Professor, Department of Psychiatry and Behavioral Sciences, Medical University of South Carolina, Charleston, South Carolina.

Ann Wolbert Burgess, R.N., D.N.Sc., F.A.N.N.
The van Ameringen Professor of Psychiatric Nursing, University of Pennsylvania School of Nursing, Philadelphia, Pennsylvania.

Juesta M. Caddell, M.S.
Program Coordinator, Veterans Administration Medical Center, Jackson, Mississippi.

Yael Danieli, Ph.D.
Director, Group Project for Holocaust Survivors and their Children, New York.

Robert C. Davis, Ph.D.
Director of Research/Systems, Victim Services Agency, New York.

Mary Ann Donaldson, M.S.W., A.C.S.W.
Clinical Instructor, Division of Psychiatry-Behavioral Science, Department of Neuroscience, University of North Dakota School of Medicine, Fargo, North Dakota.

Spencer Eth, M.D.
Assistant Professor, Department of Psychiatry and the Behavioral Sciences, University of Southern California, Los Angeles.

John A. Fairbank, Ph.D.
Director, Behavioral Consultation Program, Veterans Administration Medical Center, and Assistant Professor, University of Mississippi Medical Center, Jackson, Mississippi.

Charles R. Figley, Ph.D.
Professor and Director, Traumatic Stress Research Program, Department of Child Development and Family Studies, Purdue University, West Lafayette, Indiana.

Ellen Frey-Wouters, Ph.D.
Professor, Center for Policy Research and Department of Political Science, Graduate Center/Brooklyn College, City University of New York.

Lucy N. Friedman, Ph.D.
Executive Director, Victim Services Agency, New York.

Mark S. Gallops, Ph.D.
Senior Research Associate, Center for Policy Research, Department of Sociology, Columbia University, New York.

Russell Gardner, Jr., M.D., F.A.P.A.
Professor and Chairman, Division of Psychiatry-Behavioral Science, Department of Neuroscience, University of North Dakota School of Medicine, Fargo, North Dakota.

Bonnie L. Green, Ph.D.
Associate Professor and Co-Director, Traumatic Stress Center, Department of Psychiatry, University of Cincinnati College of Medicine, Cincinnati, Ohio.

Carol R. Hartman, R.N., D.N.Sc.
Associate Professor and Coordinator, Graduate Psychiatric-Mental Health Nursing Program, Boston College, Chestnut Hill, Massachusetts.

Donald M. Hartsough, Ph.D.
Associate Professor, Department of Psychological Sciences, Purdue University, West Lafayette, Indiana.

Ronnie Janoff-Bulman, Ph.D.
Associate Professor, Department of Psychology, University of Massachusetts, Amherst, Massachusetts.

Suzanne K. Johnson
Graduate student, Department of Psychology, Cleveland State University, Cleveland, Ohio.

Terence M. Keane, Ph.D.
Chief, Psychology Service, Veterans Administration Medical Center, and Associate Professor, University of Mississippi Medical Center, Jackson, Mississippi.

Dean G. Kilpatrick, Ph.D.
Professor, Department of Psychiatry and Behavioral Sciences, Medical University of South Carolina, Charleston, South Carolina.

Robert S. Laufer, Ph.D.
Associate Professor, Center for Policy Research and Department of Sociology, Brooklyn College/Graduate Center, City University of New York.

Jacob D. Lindy, M.D.
Associate Clinical Professor and Co-Director, Traumatic Stress Center, Department of Psychiatry, University of Cincinnati College of Medicine, Cincinnati, Ohio.

Erwin Randolph Parson, Ph.D.
Clinical Psychologist in private practice, Uniondale, New York, and Regional Manager, Medical Region I, Readjustment Counseling Service, Montrose, New York.

Robert S. Pynoos, M.D., M.P.H.
Assistant Professor, Department of Psychiatry and the Behavioral Sciences, University of California at Los Angeles.

E. L. Quarantelli, Ph.D.
Director, Disaster Research Center, and Professor, Department of Sociology, University of Delaware, Newark, Delaware.

Jeffrey C. Savitsky, Ph.D., J.D.
Associate Professor, Department of Psychological Sciences, Purdue University, West Lafayette, Indiana.

Raymond M. Scurfield, D.S.W., L.C.S.W.
Assistant Director of Counseling, Readjustment Counseling Service, Veterans Administration, Washington, D.C.

W. Ken Smith
Graduate student, Department of Psychology, Cleveland State University, Cleveland, Ohio.

Michael R. Trimble, M.R.C.P., F.R.C.Psych.
Consultant Physician in Psychological Medicine, and Senior Lecturer in Behavioural Neurology, The National Hospital, Queen Square, London, England.

Lois J. Veronen, Ph.D.
Assistant Clinical Professor, Department of Psychiatry and Behavioral Sciences, Medical University of South Carolina, Charleston, South Carolina.

John P. Wilson, Ph.D.
Professor, Department of Psychology, Cleveland State University, Cleveland, Ohio.

Rose T. Zimering, Ph.D.
Research Associate, Veterans Administration Medical Center and University of Mississippi Medical Center, Jackson, Mississippi.

Introduction

This volume is about the immediate and long-term psychosocial consequences of extraordinarily stressful events. The last decade has included an extraordinary increase in attention to these matters. News reports of various catastrophes, tragedies, and violent episodes included an analysis of victims' responses as well as the circumstances which caused the victimization. Responses, for example, of crime victims, such as President Reagan; Vietnam war veterans; terrorist hostages, such as those held in Iran; the Holocaust survivors and their children; natural and man-made disaster survivors, such as those evacuated from around the Three Mile Island nuclear reactor, were described and analyzed.

Simultaneously, the social science and psychotherapy literatures have focused attention on these and other types of victims and survivors. Some attempts were made to synthesize these literatures, and will be discussed throughout this volume. Yet, for the most part, scholars and clinicians have focused on individual types of stressors (e.g., war combat, rape, family violence). Rarely, for example, have rape researchers tested and applied the findings of researchers studying other types of victimization, such as other violent crimes. It is equally rare, moreover, that clinicians reporting on work with specific types of victims discuss similar reports on other types of victims.

Compiled here is a collection of reports which together transcend this traditional, single-stressor approach. The purpose of this book is three-fold: First, we hope to provide a comprehensive overview of the current scientific literature on traumatic stress. Second, by this effort, we hope to advance the knowledge based in this area through the contributions in historical analysis, theoretical conceptualizations, research findings, and treatment and policy innovations. Third, in the process, we especially hope to develop a unified or generic theory of the psychosocial consequences of traumatic stress. Early explorers and pioneers in new territory relied on maps to guide their efforts and continually improved their accuracy as new discoveries were made. The "maps" presented here are the initial attempts to guide us and our colleagues to discoveries about the special psychosocial consequences of extraordinarily stressful situations. It is a beginning.

BASIC CONCEPTS

The 17 chapters of this volume include numerous concepts which, together, provide the material for building our "map" or generic theories of traumatic stress. The most central of these, however, is the concept of "trauma." It is important in the beginning of this volume, to provide a clear definition of this and related concepts.

Trauma

The term trauma can be traced to the Greek meaning of "wound." Relying on a psychoanalytic (Crowe's) conceptualization, Bullock and Stallybrass (1977) note that:

> The trauma is supposed to break through the individual's defenses, and in the absence of normal abreaction (i.e., Josef Breuer's notion of the process of discharges of repressed emotions by revising and reliving painful experiences that have been buried in the unconscious . . . a discharge of tension) to cause a foreign-body reaction—the mental equivalent of the process whereby the tissues of the body wall off a foreign body lodged in them. Subsequently emotional arousal may reawaken early traumatic experiences, resulting in an attack on defense mechanisms from inside and outside simultaneously. (pp. 644-645)

In this volume, we use the concept of trauma to represent *an emotional state of discomfort and stress resulting from memories of an extraordinary, catastrophic experience which shattered the survivor's sense of invulnerability to harm.*

Catastrophe

A catastrophe, the situational prerequisite for the emergence of a trauma, is defined here as *an extraordinary event or series of events which is sudden, overwhelming, and often dangerous, either to one's self or significant other(s).*

Traumatic Stress Reaction

The natural consequent behaviors and emotions of a trauma *during* a catastrophe is the *traumatic stress reaction* and can be defined as *a set of conscious and unconscious actions and emotions associated with dealing with the stressors of the catastrophe and the period immediately afterwards.*

Some have described this as, for example, in more pathological terminology, panic reaction, hysterical reaction, acute grief, and outcry. Traumatic stress reactions are the first indication of the presence of a trauma. They occur in the initial wake of a traumatic event or catastrophe. It is like the initial wake created by casting a pebble into a pond.

Post-traumatic Stress Reaction

While traumatic stress reactions are those natural behaviors and emotions which occur during the catastrophe, post-traumatic stress reactions are defined as *a set of conscious and unconscious behaviors and emotions associated with dealing with the* memories *of the stressors of the catastrophe and immediately afterwards.*

In the analogy of the pond, as traumatic stress reactions can be represented by the initial wake created by the pebble, post-traumatic stress reactions are the subsequent ripples which may last long after the pebble penetrates the surface of the pond.

A post-traumatic stress *disorder* is the clinical manifestation of problems associated with trauma induced during the catastrophe and represented by the post-traumatic stress reactions.

In terms of our pond analogy, post-traumatic stress disorder could be viewed as the destruction resulting from the waves initially created by the pebble landing in the pond.

POST-TRAUMATIC STRESS DISORDER

The diagnosis of post-traumatic stress disorder (PTSD) emerged from the latest version of the American Psychiatric Association's manual of mental disorders, the Diagnostic and Statistical Manual of Mental Disorders, third edition (DSM-III) (1980).

TABLE 1
Diagnostic Criteria for
Post-traumatic Stress Disorder*

A. Existence of a recognizable stressor that would evoke significant symptoms of distress in almost anyone

B. Reexperiencing of the trauma as evidenced by at least one of the following:
    (1) recurrent and intrusive recollections of the event
    (2) recurrent dreams of the event
    (3) sudden acting or feeling as if the traumatic event were reoccurring, because of an association with an environmental or ideational stimulus

C. Numbing of responsiveness to or reduced involvement with the external world, beginning some time after the trauma, as shown by at least one of the following:
    (1) markedly diminished interest in one or more significant activities
    (2) feeling of detachment or estrangement from others
    (3) constricted affect

D. At least two of the following symptoms that were not present before the trauma:
    (1) hyperalertness or exaggerated startle response
    (2) sleep disturbance
    (3) guilt about surviving when others have not, or about behavior required for survival
    (4) memory impairment or trouble concentrating
    (5) avoidance of activities that arouse recollection of the traumatic event
    (6) intensification of symptoms by exposure to events that symbolize or resemble the traumatic event

The *Longman Dictionary of Psychology and Psychiatry* (Goldenson, 1984) defines PTSD as:

An anxiety disorder produced by an uncommon, extremely stressful event (e.g., assault, rape, military combat, flood, earthquake, death camp, torture, car accident, head trauma), and characterized by (a) reexperiencing the trauma in painful recollections or recurrent dreams or nightmares, (b) diminished responsiveness (emotional anesthesia or numbing), with disinterest in significant activities and with feelings of detachment and estrangement from others, and (c) such symptoms as exaggerated startle response, disturbed sleep, difficulty in concentrating or remembering, guilt

*Reprinted with permission from the American Psychiatric Association. *Diagnostic and Statistical Manual of Mental Disorders*, Third Edition. Washington, D.C.: APA, 1980, p. 238.

about surviving when others did not, and avoidance of activities that call the traumatic event to mind. (p. 573)

Table 1 is the diagnostic criteria for PTSD which is taken directly from DSM-III (American Psychiatric Association, 1980). It should be noted that the disorder includes two subtypes. Acute PTSD occurs when the onset of symptoms is within six months of the catastrophe or traumatic event, but the duration of symptoms is less than six months. Chronic or Delayed PTSD occurs when either or both of the following are found: 1) the duration of symptoms is six months or more (chronic); 2) the onset of symptoms was at least six months after the trauma (delayed).

The DSM-III conceptualization of PTSD also notes its "associated features," which have important implications for both diagnosis and treatment. DSM-III suggests that symptoms of depression and anxiety are common and may be severe enough to deserve additional diagnoses. Moreover, sporadic and unpredictable explosions of aggressive behavior may also be associated with PTSD, along with other impulsive reactions (e.g., sudden trips, unexplained absences, changed life-styles and residences).

There are, of course, many unanswered questions which are not addressed in DSM-III. These include, for example:

1) What constitutes a "psychologically traumatic event"?
2) Among those who are exposed to such an event, who will experience a trauma in contrast to those who will not?
3) Among those who will, how many will experience an acute reaction and how many will experience either a delayed or chronic reaction?
4) How long will the latter reactions last?
5) Is PTSD "curable" or is it a lifelong disorder which can only be controlled, such as diabetes?
6) Among those who may be exposed to a traumatic event is it possible to detect who is most vulnerable to PTSD and who is least vulnerable?
7) What is it about the circumstances of a catastrophe, the survivor, and the aftermath which lead to both the induction of a trauma as well as its maintenance and resistence to recovery?
8) How do we know, for sure, who has PTSD apart from those who are malingering?
9) How do we know when a person who has been diagnosed with PTSD has recovered?

These are among the many questions which are either answered or raised by this volume.

ORGANIZATIONAL STRUCTURE AND
SUBSTANTIVE ISSUES

Trauma and Its Wake is organized into three sections. Each section focuses on a separate area of inquiry: theoretical, empirical, and clinical.

Section I: Theory

This section includes four chapters which attempt to advance the theory of traumatic stress, either directly or indirectly. Chapter 1, "Post-traumatic Stress Disorder: History of a Concept," is written by Michael R. Trimble, an English neuropsychiatrist, and is based, in part, on his highly acclaimed volume, *Post-traumatic Neurosis* (1981). The chapter traces the history of PTSD from its current conceptualization back to its origins in the late 19th century. The chapter includes a discussion of such issues as shell shock and other war-related stress syndromes including malingering, secondary gain and compensation "neurosis," predisposition to stress reactions; and anatomical versus psychological origins of symptoms of traumatic stress.

Chapter 2, "The Aftermath of Victimization: Rebuilding Shattered Assumptions," is written by Ronnie Janoff-Bulman, a social psychologist who has written extensively about the cognitive processes of victims representing a variety of catastrophes. Her chapter presents convincing evidence that PTSD is the result of "the shattering of basic assumptions victims hold about themselves and their world." Three assumptions are especially important: personal invulnerability, meaningfulness of the world, and positive self-concept. Among the natural coping tendencies associated with recovery is self-blame, found to be surprisingly adaptive in reestablishing shattered assumptions.

The shattered world of children of a murdered parent is the backdrop of Chapter 3, "Developmental Perspective on Psychic Trauma in Childhood," written by Spencer Eth and Robert S. Pynoos. Both are child psychiatrists who have studied and written extensively about this special population of children. Their chapter presents a developmental schema for understanding childhood PTSD, including a delineation of the specific developmental characteristics of children at various ages. They argue that recognition of these phase-salient differences is critical for understanding and treating childhood PTSD.

An interdisciplinary team of researchers has collaborated on Chapter 4, "Conceptualizing Post-traumatic Stress Disorder: A Psychosocial Framework," written by two psychologists, Bonnie L. Green and John P. Wilson, and a psychiatrist, Jacob D. Lindy. They present a model of viewing the myriad variables associated with the development, maintenance, and eventual recovery from the disorder. Their "Working Model of Processing a Catastrophic Event" includes five major conceptual groups: the catastrophic experience, the post-traumatic cognitive processing, individual characteristics, the recovery environment, and adaptation.

Section II: Research

The second section of the volume includes five chapters which report on recently completed, original research projects. Each makes an important contribution to the expanding knowledge about traumatic stress.

Chapter 5, "Traumatic Stressors in the Vietnam War and Post-traumatic Stress Disorder," was written by an interdisciplinary team of researchers at the New York-based Center for Policy Research. Sociologists Robert S. Laufer and Mark S. Gallops, and political scientist Ellen Frey-Wouters report on a portion of the results of a national survey of 1,342 men grouped by the degree to which they were exposed to the Vietnam War. They conclude, among other things, that the nature of catastrophe, or the nature of the traumatic situation, needs more careful analysis. This conclusion is based, in part, on their findings that factors other than the stressors of traditional combat contributed to the development of PTSD.

Although not specifically focused on PTSD, Chapter 6, "The Emotional Aftermath of Crime and Violence," reports on a unique study of survivors of crime and their social support system. Psychologists Robert C. Davis and Lucy N. Friedman, who serves as Executive Director of the Victim Service Agency in New York City, reports that "practically all the victims suffered severe emotional distress that often endured at least four months and that included components of PTSD, particularly sleep disturbances, constricted affect, feelings of estrangement from others, recurrent thoughts about the incident, and avoidance of situations that reminded them of the traumatic event." All of these symptoms are closely associated with the symptoms of PTSD.

A special group of crime victims, survivors of rape, are the focus of Chapter 7, "Factors Predicting Psychological Distress Among Rape Victims," written by psychologists Dean G. Kilpatrick, Lois J. Veronen, and Connie L. Best. Among other things, the researchers found that initial levels of distress among a sample of 125 rape victims were the best predictors of psychological functioning three months to four years post-rape. These findings suggest that indicators of acute PTSD, and perhaps even traumatic stress, may identify those who are at risk of developing chronic PTSD.

Psychologist John P. Wilson and his students, W. Ken Smith and Suzanne K. Johnson, wrote Chapter 8, "A Comparative Analysis of PTSD Among Various Survivor Groups." They report a recent study of 409 people who have survived one or more catastrophes. It was predicted and found that the degree of loss of a significant other and life-threat were predictive of PTSD.

Chapter 9, "An Assessment of Conflicting Views on Mental Health: The Consequences of Traumatic Events," by sociologist E. L. Quarantelli, reviews the divergent views of the psychological consequences of community disasters. In contrast to "a minority" that argues that mental health effects are widespread, deep, persistent, and dysfunctional, he finds that most investigators come to a different conclusion. He suggests that most psychological effects of disasters are non-persistent, of short duration, and are often beneficial to the survivors.

Section III: Treatment

This section includes seven chapters which, together, provide a useful primer for clinicians interested in either preventing or ameliorating PTSD. Each chapter, except for the last one, addresses the difficult issues of assessment and treatment outcome.

Chapter 10, "Post-trauma Stress Assessment and Treatment: Overview and Formulations," by Raymond M. Scurfield, a social worker, provides a generic view of clinical intervention with survivors of catastrophic events who are exhibiting symptoms of PTSD. In addition to a brief critique of the literature on assessment and treatment, Scurfield offers five principles of individual treatment and a discussion of the critical elements related to group and family therapy.

This team of investigators has made important research contributions and, in Chapter 11, "A Behavioral Approach to Assessing and Treating Post-traumatic Stress Disorder in Vietnam Veterans," they describe a systematic behavioral treatment program. The team includes Terence M.

Keane, John A. Fairbank, Juesta M. Caddell, Rose T. Zimering, and Mary E. Bender, clinical psychologists at the VA Medical Center, Jackson, Mississippi. Also described are their methods of assessment and theoretical orientation.

Chapter 12, "The Treatment and Prevention of Long-term Effects and Intergenerational Transmission of Victimization: A Lesson from Holocaust Survivors and Their Children," is written by clinical psychologist Yael Danieli who was born in a concentration camp. For the last decade she has studied and treated the children of the survivors of the Holocaust. In the chapter she describes both her theoretical orientation to and treatment of survivor children. In addition, she describes her program, The Group Project for Holocaust Survivors and Their Children.

In Chapter 13, "Ethnicity and Traumatic Stress: The Intersecting Point in Psychotherapy," psychologist Erwin Randolph Parson addresses a topic rarely addressed by clinicians: the role of the client's ethnic origin. Parson asserts that the intersecting point of ethnicity and traumatic stress needs to be understood in its synergistic impact upon the client, as well as on the therapeutic process. He asserts that clinicians must be aware of the client's "cultural behavioral norms" and views as well as their own ethnocentric views to successfully treat clients of differing ethnic origin than the clinicians'.

Nationally known nurse scholars have collaborated on Chapter 14, "Illness-related Post-traumatic Stress Disorder: A Cognitive-Behavioral Model of Intervention with Heart Attack Victims." Carol R. Hartman and Ann Wolbert Burgess present a treatment model which adopts the principles of cognitive and behavioral treatment strategies, especially neuro-linguistic programming, found to be successful in working with heart attack survivors. The model is especially applicable during the acute recovery phase and is relevant to other medically debilitated populations as well.

Social worker, Mary Ann Donaldson and psychiatrist, Russell Gardner, Jr., wrote Chapter 15, "Diagnosis and Treatment of Traumatic Stress Among Women After Childhood Incest," based on their clinical work with 26 adult women who had experienced incest as children. Their approach is based on Horowitz's concept of stress response syndrome and appears to be applicable to survivors of other childhood traumas.

Chapter 16, "Use of the Environment and the Legal Impact of Resulting Emotional Harm," written by psychologists Donald M. Hartsough and Jeffrey C. Savitsky, also an attorney, approaches treatment from a social policy perspective. They review the legal impact of negative emotions resulting from "land use projects," such as the Three Mile

Island nuclear power plant. They conclude that concern about the psychological health of those affected by these projects must be tempered with the limitations of their assessments. They predict, however, that such issues will have growing importance in assessing the overall environmental impact of such projects.

The final chapter by the editor, "From Victim to Survivor: Social Responsibility in the Wake of Catastrophe," serves both as a summary statement for the volume and our current understanding of the immediate and long-term consequences of catastrophes. It is argued that a society rich in knowledge and material wealth should shoulder a greater share of the responsibility for the emotional suffering of its citizens which result from man-made causes. Moreover, the chapter suggests that the distinction between victim and survivor is critical to an appreciation of the full recovery from traumatic events. A victim explains his or her inability to cope based on being victimized by a catastrophe, while a survivor explains why he or she is able to cope so effectively based on surviving a catastrophe.

Together, these chapters represent a new generation of thought and scientific inquiry regarding human reactions to overwhelmingly stressful experiences. It is the first volume to attempt to synthesize in a systematic way the views and approaches of scholars and clinicians from so many different disciplines, areas of interest and application. It will certainly not be the last.

REFERENCES

American Psychiatric Association, *Diagnostic and statistical manual of mental disorders,* third edition. Washington, D.C.: American Psychiatric Association, 1980.

Bullock, A., & Stallybrass, O. *The Fontana dictionary of modern thought.* London: The Chaucer Press, 1977.

Goldenson, R.M. *Longman dictionary of psychology and psychiatry.* New York: Longman, 1984.

TRAUMA
and Its
WAKE

The Study and

Treatment of

Post-traumatic Stress Disorder

SECTION

I

INTRODUCTION AND CONCEPTUAL-IZATION

1

Post-traumatic Stress Disorder: History of a Concept

MICHAEL R. TRIMBLE

Although the DSM-III (APA, 1980) has neatly sanctioned post-traumatic stress disorder in its umbrella of diagnoses, this relatively common human problem has been known for many hundreds of years, although under different names. In this chapter the history of post-traumatic neurosis is briefly reviewed, and the introduction of the new term examined alongside other concepts. It is concluded that post-traumatic stress disorder will be extremely useful in bringing further clarity to the concept that is envisaged by the term, and that it will lead to greater interest in and research of the condition.

INTRODUCTION

To this British observer, the term "post-traumatic stress disorder" springs from the pages of the DSM-III like some newly found tropical flower, previously undescribed, yet clearly present in its full-blooded maturity for any onlooker to see. The more established term "post-traumatic neurosis" is lost. Indeed, the term "neurosis" is omitted from the new classification, despite its use in medicine for over 200 years. The explanation for the omission is that Freud apparently used the term "psychoneurosis" both descriptively and etiologically (APA, 1980), as if the history of the subject had started with the well-known man from Vienna.

In fact, the history of neurotic disorders is better traced back to some of the great men in the seventeenth and eighteenth centuries, in other parts of Europe, including Willis, Sydenham, Boerhaave, Whytt, Cheyne and Cullen (Trimble, 1981). It should be noted in passing that disenchantment with the term neurosis has previously led to its temporary disappearance. During the second half of the nineteenth century, with the increased emphasis on pathological anatomy and an anatomico-clinical medicine, the term and concept of neurosis became unpopular in Britain and disappeared from the medical writings of the country (Lopez Pinero, 1983). Its reappearance, with a brightly polished handle "psycho" and the emphasis of the Freudian School on psychodynamic mechanisms in pathogenesis, a trend continually emphasized during the first half of the twentieth century, may well have led to the present disenchantment. However, if history is anything to go by—and anyone interested in the concept of post-traumatic neurosis or in a patient suffering from that condition will be most interested in history—then as Lewis (1975) said of hysteria, the term is likely to outlive its obituarists and reappear.

Post-traumatic Neurosis

Indeed, the concept that following an accident a person may develop symptoms, mainly subjective and usually not associated with any clearly defined somatic pathology, is an old one. Many of the descriptions come to us from the war setting. Taken from Shakespeare's *King Henry IV*, for example, is:

Oh, my good lord, why are you thus alone?
For what offence have I this fortnight been
A banish'd woman from my Harry's bed?
Tell me, sweet lord, what is't that takes from thee
Thy stomach, pleasure, and thy golden sleep?
Why dost thou bend thine eyes upon the earth,
And start so often when thou sit'st alone?
Why hast thou lost the fresh blood in thy cheeks,
And given my treasures and my rights of thee
To thick-eyed musing and cursed melancholy?

These lines, uttered by Lady Percy, are followed by a description of nightmares from which Hotspur was suffering, particularly dreams of war. Thus, she said of his actions while asleep:

And heard thee murmur tales of iron wars;
Speak terms of manage to thy bounding steed;
Cry "courage! to the field!" . . .

A good civilian account has recently been described by Daly (1983) from Samuel Pepys' Diary, in which Pepys described the effects of the Great Fire of London. The Diary's account of this begins on September 2, 1666, and outlines the gradual progression of the fire toward his home, the terror that he sees in other people, unable to protect their property, and his own preparations for the transportation of his valuables. He subsequently developed "dreams of the fire and falling down of houses." Six months later he was writing that he was still unable to sleep "without great terrors of fire" and in his diary referred to the sequelae of the disaster for others, including attempted suicide.

Another diarist who left a testament for us was Charles Dickens. He was involved in a railway accident at Staplehurst in Kent on June 9, 1865, and in a letter, described the horrifying scene of "two or three hours work . . . amongst the dead and dying surrounded by terrific sights. . . ." Although that in itself was enough to render his "hand unsteady," it was some time after the accident that he wrote: "I am not quite right within, but believe it to be an effect of the railway shaking. . . ." There is no doubt of the fact that, after the Staplehurst experience, the diary tells more and more about it (railway shaking, that is) instead of, as one might expect, less and less. He developed a phobia of railway traveling but summed up the sequelae as: "I am curiously weak—weak as if I were recovering from a long illness. . . ." (Forster, 1969).

Two important human activities toward the end of the last century led to an explosion of literature and interest in the concept of post-traumatic disorders (Trimble, 1981). First, there were the wartime experiences, mainly the American Civil War, and later the First World War. Second, there was the development of workmen's compensation acts in many countries which, for the first time, provided some financial compensation for those injured during the course of work.

The experience gained by physicians dealing with such trauma syndromes prompted speculation regarding their etiology. From the war point of view, the concept that the symptoms were due to micro-structural lesions in the central nervous system arose and several monographs on the subject appeared. Mott (1919) coined the term "shell shock" and suggested that the condition was due to a physical lesion of the brain, brought about in some manner by carbon monoxide or changes in atmospheric pressure. Others, however, disagreed. Myers (1940) who had experience with over 2,000 cases of shell shock divided the problem into shell concussion and shell shock. The latter gave rise to hysteria, neurasthenia, or even psychiatric illness, and could occur in soldiers not exposed to exploding missiles, if they were subject to emotional stress. He concluded that the term shell shock was ill-chosen and generally had little to do with carbon monoxide or atmospheric pressure but that psychical causes were involved in the vast majority of cases, which were precipitated by horror and fright.

Indeed, neurologists dealing with casualties in such wars accepted a psychological approach both to the etiology and treatment of these neuroses, and techniques, such as suggestion or hypnosis, were widely used. Kardiner (1941) suggested that war created only one syndrome, and that this was essentially no different from traumatic neuroses in peacetime. For him, shell shock, battle neurosis, battle fatigue and combat exhaustion all meant the same thing. "They all refer to the common acquired disorder consequent on war stress." Further, the suggestion that symptoms were interlinked with gain became readily ingrained in the literature.

The term "compensation neurosis" was introduced by Rigler in 1879 following an increase in invalidism reported after railway accidents with the introduction of compensation laws in Prussia in 1871. Railways, although they had been in use for some time, in particular for the haulage of goods from one place to another, began to see extensive use as a means of passenger travel in the mid-nineteenth century. The advent of steam engines, the use of iron rails rather than wood, and the needs of the Industrial Revolution led to the widespread development of the railway system, against much initial opposition.

As the traffic began to grow, so did the number of accidents, and the railway companies, clearly identifiable industrial megaliths, were seen as an easy target for compensation. Physicians, of course, were called upon to examine potential litigants, and an influential book appeared in 1882 entitled *On Concussion of the Spine: Nervous Shock and Other Obscure Injuries of the Nervous System in their Clinical and Medico-legal Aspects*, by John Eric Erichsen. He was Professor of Surgery at University College Hospital, London, and made his intention clear on the first page of his introduction, namely ". . . to direct attention to certain injuries of the spine that may arise from accidents that are often apparently slight, from shocks to the body generally, as well as from blows inflicted directly upon the back."

Such injuries were seen frequently in patients "subject to the violent shock of railway collision" and Erichsen's general thesis was that "concussion of the spine" was a recognized clinical entity, which led to physical symptoms in patients subject to accidents. The term "railway spine" became part of medical language, and Clevenger (1889), a consultant physician from Chicago, actually wrote a book on the subject which was subtitled "Erichsen's Disease." He invoked disturbance of "molecular condition" as the organic pathology for these conditions, and speculated that sympathetic action of the nervous system with interference of the vascular supply of the spinal cord might be the underlying pathogenesis.

The disorder, and its accompanying pathology were seized upon by litigants, and one author wrote of "clinical and pathological possibilities that were before this undreamed of. . . . Erichsen's little volume became a guidebook that might lead the dishonest plaintiff, if he felt so disposed, to set upon a broad road of imposture and dissimulation with the expectation of getting a heavy verdict" (Hamilton, 1907).

It was not long before defense came to the railway companies. Herbert Page, surgeon to the London and North West Railway, published his book entitled *Injuries of the Spine and Spinal Cord Without Apparent Mechanical Lesion* in 1885. It was essentially a rebuttal of Erichsen's ideas and in its subtitle used the term "nervous shock." Page (1885) introduced this concept as follows:

> Nervous shock in its varied manifestations is so common after railway collisions, and the symptoms thereof play so prominent a part in all cases which become the subject of medico-legal inquiry, whether they be real or feigned, that we are almost sure to meet with the symptoms of it associated with pains and points of tenderness along the vertebral spinal processes. . . . We cannot help thinking that it is this combination of the symptoms of general nervous prostration or shock and pains in the back which has laid the foundation of the views—erroneous views as we hold them to be—so largely entertained of the nature of these common injuries of the back received in railway collisions.

Page was unable to find any evidence that railway spine in the majority of cases was associated with organic disease, and believed that the symptoms were essentially psychological in origin.

Several others around this time supported these views of Page. For example, the *Boston Medical and Surgical Journal* carried a series of articles exploring the issues. In one, Putnam (1881) acknowledged the "special service which Mr. Page has rendered" and made the point that at least some of the cases were "examples of that important neurosis which is called hysteria."

The central feature of many of these arguments in relationship to railway accidents, of course, was to what extent patients were malingering for their own personal gain. Indeed, this subject is the bitter kernel found at the center of the whole issue of post-traumatic disorders in general. Erichsen dismissed the topic of malingering in a few pages, but Page devoted a whole chapter to it, and clearly the term "compensation neurosis" had been introduced with malingering in mind. The discussion of malingering was extended much further with the introduction of workmen's compensation acts, the first of which in the U.K. was passed in 1880. This provided for compensation to workmen who received injury in the course of their employment, provided that the injury was not the direct result of negligence on their part. However, as time progressed, such restrictions were removed, and in 1906 anyone in the U.K. who entered into a contract of service or apprenticeship with an employer was covered. Within a few years of the passing of the 1906 act the number of reported accidents and injuries rose by 44%, despite the fact that the number of people at work remained the same. Compensation paid in respect to these accidents rose by 64%. Not surprisingly, some skepticism was reflected by such authors as Collie (1917) who said: "Workmen have a great tendency now to make what they think is the best of an injury which befalls them—that is, to get the most money out of it."

The concept of malingering has been the subject of many papers over the last 100 years. Some authors have sought to explain it in medicopsychological terms. The fact of the matter is, however, that in many legal cases, opinion is split between those who are called by and would support an insurance agency paying compensation and suggest that malingering is frequent, and those who are more likely to represent the victims and who feel it is rare. In truth, detection of malingering is difficult and several authors have added confusion to the literature by invoking unconscious mechanisms in its production (cf. Trimble, 1981).

Miller (1961) was one of the more outspoken of those who believed malingering was a major problem:

Many of those intimately concerned with compensation work—and here I refer to trade union and insurance officers as well as to judges, barristers and solicitors—are convinced that it [malingering] is far from uncommon in these cases, and deplore the inability of doctors to recognise the condition or their hesitancy in expressing an opinion in this connection, to which they will freely admit in private conversation.

His own conclusions were based on a review of 47 patients selected from 200 consecutive head injury referrals with psychoneurotic symptoms. The vast majority of these were referred by insurance companies, but Miller's findings were that such complaints were twice as common with industrial as opposed to road accidents. This was especially true if employers were large industrial organizations or nationalized industries. Moreover, 1) it was twice as common in men as it was in women; 2) there was an inverse relationship between the neurosis and severity of the injury or the duration of any unconsciousness; and 3) it was more prevalent in patients in lower social classes. He concluded that such symptoms were related to "lack of social responsibility. . . ." In follow-up, Miller noted the majority of patients recovered following settlements, implying "accident neurosis [the term he preferred] is not the result of the accident but a concomitant of the compensation and a manifestation of the hope of financial gain."

The concept of gain, either conscious financial personal gain or a more subtle "unconscious" gain, was clearly entwined in the literature of post-traumatic neurosis. In the battle setting it was well recognized. Kardiner (1941) said:

We know of the secondary gain in the form of compensation for illness after the war but there is another equally important secondary gain in the form of legitimate escape from duty. The compensation issue then does not in these terms actually create the neurosis but is more a source of resistance in treatment and rehabilitation.

Today, in any courtroom where a patient is complaining of post-traumatic symptoms, and legal settlement of compensation is being decided, the strains of this dichotomy between what is "genuine" and what is malingering will persistently be heard. However, the concept has widened far beyond the war setting, railway trains, and accidents at work. Several environmental disasters have been the subject of medical study, including the Aberfan Disaster in 1966 (Lacey, 1972), the Bristol floods of 1968 (Bennet, 1970) and the Buffalo Creek Disaster of 1972 (Newman,

1976). The phenomenon of "nervous shock" is frequently seen in those who are involved in and survive major disasters, where compensation is not an issue.

The conceptualization of traumatic stress has been varied. Authors are writing about the "survivor syndrome," referring to the long-term psychological sequelae of survivors from Nazi persecution, or more simply to survival of other extreme situations, such as hijack or hostage (Kijak & Funtowicz, 1982), even naming variants such as the "rape-trauma syndrome" (Burgess & Holmstrom, 1974). Indeed, the variety of names associated with sequelae of accidents, which has been used throughout the literature, is clearly enormous. It is in this context, perhaps, that we should view the development of post-traumatic stress disorder in the DSM-III.

There can be little doubt that, in spite of the long history of this condition as indicated, the Korean and then the Vietnam War focused the attention of the American public and professionals to this particular problem. Clearly, the condition is not limited to short-term neurotic syndromes occurring mainly at the battle front or in close proximity to action. Particularly since the Vietnam War, more and more reports of the longer-term chronic and delayed sequelae of this are being reported in the literature (cf. Figley, 1978). The appelation "post-Vietnam syndrome," like the term shell shock, perhaps detracts from forming an appropriate concept of a wider variety of disorders which are seen in response to stress. Thus the reification of "post-traumatic stress disorder," sanctioned so neatly by the DSM-III, clearly has both conceptual and medico-legal implications.

Officially the designation 309.81 refers to "the development of characteristic symptoms following a psychologically traumatic event that is generally outside the range of human experience" (APA, 1980). The particular symptoms are referred to elsewhere in this volume, but one of the essential features is reexperiencing the traumatic event, either through dreams, nightmares, daydreams, or "dissociative states." Withdrawal and depressive symptoms are common, as are depersonalization and anxiety. Two subtypes are recognized, one in which the onset of symptoms occurs within six months of the trauma, and the duration of symptoms is usually less than six months, and one in which the onset of symptoms is delayed. This implies some difference in pathogenesis for the two, although there is little in the literature to support such a clear-cut demarcation.

The concept that the traumatic event should be outside the range of usual human experience is limiting. Accidents at work, or following car accidents are common and well within the range of usual human experience, yet the symptoms produced may be identical, and the subsequent morbidity substantial.

The loss of the epithet "neurosis," as emphasized in the introduction, is likely to be a temporary respite. However brief, the respite will certainly provide relief to many psychiatrists and others in medico-legal practice who appear on behalf of the plaintiff, in the sense that the term neurosis is misunderstood by the lay public and the legal profession and mere mention of the term immediately hints of malingering and prejudices a financial settlement. More clearly, as a recognized syndrome, "DSM-III, 309.81 Post-traumatic Stress Disorder" will give a great deal of leverage to those seeking compensation and the counting off of symptoms in checklist fashion will become routine practice in many a lawyer's office.

CONCLUSION

The etiology and pathogenesis of post-traumatic stress disorder, in spite of its new suit of clothes, remains, as those of the king in Hans Christian Andersen's famous story, invisible. As has been pointed out elsewhere (Trimble, 1981), the history of post-traumatic neurosis forms a paradigm for understanding shifting concepts of disease in medicine over the past 200 years. Ideas in the literature reflect the zeitgeist of the communities in which they are written. Generally northern Europe and the Western World have undergone a periodicity with regard to the extent to which they allow classical or romantic ideas to sustain the dominant vein of thought. The organic speculations of Erichsen reflected the increased tendency toward anatomico-pathological medicine in the middle of the last century, itself a reaction to the earlier phase of the romanticism of Naturphilosophie. This response reappears, to some extent, in the neoromantic period, which was dominated by the widespread influence of psychoanalysis in the early part of this century. In time, this led to the rediscovery of neurosis, renamed *psycho*neurosis.

In spite of these whims of medical thought, it is through changing ideas that hypotheses are formulated and used to construct investigations to advance knowledge. At least the clear designation by the authors of the DSM-III of the concept *post-traumatic stress disorder* has highlighted a most important part of psychiatric practice, and a caveat in our understanding of a most frequent, yet clearly misunderstood aspect of human experience. It is hoped that it will lead to research in this important area. Moreover, it may diminish the tiresome arguments that are continually noted between protagonists of different schools when cases suffering from post-traumatic stress disorder are presented.

REFERENCES

American Psychiatric Association. *Diagnostic and statistical manual of mental disorders* (3rd ed.). Washington, DC: American Psychiatric Association, 1980.

Bennet, G. Bristol Floods in 1968. *British Medical Journal*, 1970, *3*, 454-456.

Burgess, A.W., & Holstrom, L.L. The rape-trauma syndrome. *American Journal of Psychiatry*, 1974, *131*, 981-986.

Clevenger, S.V. *Spinal concussion*. London: F.A. Davies, 1889.

Collie, J. *Malingering and feigned sickness*. London: Edward Arnold, 1917.

Daly, R.J. Samuel Pepys and post-traumatic stress disorder. *British Journal of Psychiatry*, 1983, *143*, 64-68.

Erichsen, J.E. *On concussion of the spine: Nervous shock and other obscure injuries of the nervous system in their clinical and medico-legal aspects*. London: Longmans, Green and Company, 1882.

Figley, C.R. (Ed.). *Stress disorders among Vietnam veterans*. New York: Brunner/Mazel, 1978.

Forster, J. *The life of Charles Dickens*. Volume 2. London: J.M. Dent and Sons, 1969.

Hamilton, A.M. *Railway and other accidents*. London: Baillière Tindall, 1906.

Kardiner, A. The traumatic neurosis of war. *Psychosomatic Medicine Monographs 2-3*. New York: Paul B. Hoeber, 1941.

Kijak, M., & Funtowicz, S. The syndrome of the survivor of extreme situations. *International Review of Psychoanalysis*, 1982, *9*, 25-33.

Lacey, G.N. Observations on Aberfan. *Journal of Psychomatic Research*, 1972, *16*, 257-265.

Lewis, A. The survival of hysteria. *Psychological Medicine*, 1975, *5*, 9-12.

Lopez Pinero, J. *Historical origins of the concept of neurosis* (G. Berrios, Trans.). New York: Cambridge University Press, 1983.

Miller, H. Accident neurosis. *British Medical Journal*, 1961, *1*, 919-925, 992-998.

Mott, F.W. *War neuroses and shell shock*. London: Oxford Medical Publications, 1919.

Myers, C.S. *Shell shock in France, 1914-18*. Cambridge: Cambridge University Press, 1940.

Newman, C.J. Children of Disaster: Clinical observations at Buffalo Creek. *American Journal of Psychiatry*, 1976, *133*, 306-310.

Page, H. *Injuries of the spine and spinal cord without apparent mechanical lesion*. London: J. & A. Churchill, 1885.

Putnam, J.J. Recent investigations into patients of so-called concussion of the spine. *Boston Medical and Surgical Journal*, 1881, *109*, 217.

Trimble, M.R. *Post-traumatic neurosis*. Chichester: Wiley, 1981.

CHAPTER

2

The Aftermath of Victimization: Rebuilding Shattered Assumptions

RONNIE JANOFF-BULMAN

It is proposed that post-traumatic stress following victimization is largely due to the shattering of basic assumptions victims hold about themselves and their world. The impact of victimization on three particular assumptions (i.e., the belief in personal invulnerability, the perception of the world as meaningful, and the perception of oneself as positive) is discussed. Coping with victimization is presented as a process that involves rebuilding one's assumptive world. Specific coping strategies are discussed in terms of how they help rebuild particular assumptions; there is a focus on the phenomenon of self-blame, a coping strategy that is surprisingly adaptive in terms of reestablishing shattered assumptions.

The experience of victimization lasts far longer than the actual victimizing incidents, for such extreme events as violent criminal acts, acci-

---

This chapter is a revised and expanded version of a paper that first appeared in the *Journal of Social Issues* (Janoff-Bulman & Frieze, 1983).

dents, serious illnesses, and disasters exact a tremendous psychological toll. The emotional responses of victims are generally immediate, intense, and often surprisingly long-lived. Unfortunately, the literature on victims is comprised of more or less distinct areas, each reflecting the study of a particular type of victim (e.g., rape victim, incest victim, cancer victim) or a particular category of victim (e.g., crime victim), and there is a tendency to try to understand psychological responses within each category rather than across victimizations. The literature on victims maximizes the likelihood of perceiving differences across victimizations rather than of recognizing similarities. Yet, a reading of these distinct literatures suggests that there are common psychological experiences shared by a wide variety of victims. Emotional reactions that appear to cross a wide range of victimizations include shock, confusion, helplessness, anxiety, fear, and depression (cf. Bard & Sangrey, 1979; Burgess & Holmstrom, 1974, 1976, 1979; Ellis, Atkeson, & Calhoun, 1981; Frank, Turner, & Duffy, 1979; Frederick, 1980; Krupnick, 1980; Krupnick & Horowitz, 1980; Maguire, 1980; Notman & Nadelson, 1976; Ochberg & Spates, 1981; Symonds, 1975, 1976). Even relatively "minor" victimizations such as burglary or robbery can result in a great deal of suffering and disruption.

The recognition of commonalities in reactions across victim types has been furthered by the American Psychiatric Association's (1980) most recent diagnostic system, DSM-III. There now exists a newly defined classification—the post-traumatic stress disorder—that describes characteristic symptoms that may follow "a psychologically traumatic event that is generally outside the range of usual human experience" and "would evoke significant symptoms of distress in most people" (American Psychiatric Association, 1980, p. 236). While post-traumatic stress disorder is often readily associated with military combat, and particularly the problems manifested by veterans of the Vietnam War (Figley, 1978), it also aptly describes the reactions of individuals who have experienced other traumatic events such as serious crimes (e.g., rape, kidnapping), accidents (e.g., car accidents with serious physical injury, airplane crashes), and disasters (e.g., floods, large fires). What, then, are the characteristic features of this syndrome?

Apart from the existence of a recognizable stressor, post-traumatic stress disorder entails two primary symptoms: 1) reexperiencing the traumatic event, commonly through repetitive, intrusive recollections or recurrent dreams of the event; and 2) numbing or reduced responsiveness to the outside world, commonly evidenced by diminished interest in previously enjoyed significant activities, a feeling of detachment from others, or constricted affect. In addition, at least two of the following symptoms are present: hyperalertness, sleep disturbance, survivor guilt, impairment of memory or concentration, avoidance of activities that arouse recollection of the event, and intensification of symptoms by exposure to events resembling the traumatic incident (American Psychiatric Association, 1980). Clearly, these symptoms are indicative of the tremendous distress suffered by victims, who are psychologically unprepared for such extreme, unusual occurrences. The resources of victims are taxed; experience has not provided them with automatic "adaptive" responses (Lazarus & Cohen, 1978). More important, their victimization does not conform to the expectations and assumptions they have held about themselves and their world; their "cognitive baggage," representing years of prior experience, has been severely challenged and may no longer be viable. Much of the psychological trauma produced by victimizing events derives from the shattering of very basic assumptions that victims have held about the operation of the world.

VICTIMS' SHATTERED ASSUMPTIONS

From day to day, we all function on the basis of assumptions and personal theories that allow us to set goals, plan activities, and order our behavior. Several psychologists have addressed the significance of such conceptual systems which develop over time and provide us with viable expectations about ourselves and our environment. For example, Epstein (1980) writes, "Whether we like it or not, each of us, because he has a human brain, forms a theory of reality that brings order into what otherwise would be a chaotic world of experience. We need a theory to make sense out of the world. . . ." (p. 34). Epstein (1973, 1979, 1980) suggests that there are two subtheories—a theory about oneself and a theory about the world—that comprise one's overall theory of reality. Further, these subtheories are hierarchically organized into major and minor postulates, representing relatively broad versus narrow generalizations, respectively, about the self and the world. Parkes (1971, 1975) also writes about the existence and importance of people's basic assumptions. He maintains that individuals' views of reality constitute their "assumptive world," which is "a strongly held set of assumptions about the world and the self which is confidently maintained and used as a means of recognizing, planning and acting. . . . Assumptions such as these are learned and confirmed by the experience of many years" (1975, p. 132). These views are consistent with parallel conceptions by

Bowlby (1969), who writes of "world models," and by Marris (1975), who discusses "structures of meaning." They also closely resemble Kuhn's (1962) notion of "paradigm" in his philosophy of science. Paradigms provide scientists with ways of seeing and organizing their work; they provide the framework within which to conduct "normal science," in the same way that assumptive worlds or theories of reality provide the framework within which to conduct "normal" (i.e., day to day) living (Janoff-Bulman & Timko, in press).

In general, we operate on the basis of this conceptual system without awareness of its central postulates (Epstein, 1980); our basic assumptions are implicit, rather than explicit, and in general are "relatively inaccessible to introspection" (Parkes, 1971). Nevertheless, there are particularly impactful events in our lives that force us to recognize, objectify, and examine our basic assumptions (cf. Parkes, 1975, discussion of "psychosocial transitions"). These events, which include victimizations such as disasters, serious diseases, criminal acts, and accidents, produce tremendous stress and anxiety, for the victim's experience cannot be readily assimilated; the assumptive world, developed and confirmed over many years, cannot account for these extreme events. The old assumptions and theories of reality are shattered, producing psychological upheaval (cf. Kuhn's, 1962, discussion of the crisis in science resulting from the discovered inadequacy of a paradigm). The stress syndrome described by post-traumatic stress disorder is largely attributable to the shattering of victims' basic assumptions about themselves and their world.

The number and extent of assumptions that are shattered, or at least seriously challenged, by the experience of victimization, is no doubt largely dependent upon the individual involved. However, based on the literature cited above, there appear to be three types of assumptions, shared by most people, that are especially affected. The three are highly related to one another and are presented here as discrete beliefs for ease of discussion rather than to indicate something about the actual structure of our conceptual systems. The three assumptions are: 1) the belief in personal invulnerability; 2) the perception of the world as meaningful and comprehensible; and 3) the view of ourselves in a positive light. Victimization calls into question each of these primary postulates of our assumptive world, and by doing so destroys the stability with which we are ordinarily able to function. As Bard and Sangrey (1979) write, victims experience a "loss of equilibrium. The world is suddenly out of whack. Things no longer work the way they used to" (p. 14). Victims' perceptions are now marked by threat, danger, insecurity, and self-questioning.

The Assumption of Invulnerability

We all seem to recognize that crimes are common, cancer will strike a high proportion of the population, and car accidents do happen. However, we simultaneously believe that "It can't happen to me." In our day-to-day existence we operate on the basis of an "illusion of invulnerability" (Janoff-Bulman & Lang-Gunn, in press; Perloff, 1983). Weinstein (1980; Weinstein & Lachendro, 1982) has demonstrated that people overestimate the likelihood of their experiencing positive outcomes in life and underestimate the likelihood of experiencing negative events. People see themselves as less likely than others to be victims of diseases, crimes, and accidents (Perloff, 1983).

The self-perception of invulnerability can be maladaptive if it keeps people from engaging in effective preventive behaviors (e.g., wearing seat belts, stopping smoking; Janis, 1974; cf. Tyler, 1981), or causes them to be slow to recognize that a crime is taking place (Greenberg, Ruback, & Westcott, 1983). An example of this was reported by Lejeune and Alex (1973), who found that mugging victims first defined the event in a non-threatening way, such as a practical joke, perhaps because of their disbelief that a crime was really happening to them. In general, the illusion of invulnerability protects us from the stress and anxiety associated with the perceived threat of misfortune.

The experience of victimization shatters the assumption of invulnerability. One is no longer able to say, "It can't happen to me." Researchers working with victims of crime (Bard & Sangrey, 1979; Krupnick, 1980; Notman & Nadelson, 1976), disease (Weisman, 1979; Wortman & Dunkel-Schetter, 1979), and disasters (Lifton & Olson, 1976; Titchener, Kapp, & Winget, 1976; Wolfenstein, 1957) have discussed the sense of vulnerability that pervades the perceptions of victims. As Wolfenstein (1957) writes, a victim feels a sense of "helplessness against overpowering forces . . . and apprehension that anything may now happen to him. He feels vulnerable . . . " (p.159). Feelings of intense anxiety and helplessness accompany the victim's lost sense of safety and security. The victim's new perception of vulnerability frequently manifests itself, in part, in the victim's preoccupation with the fear of recurrence. A primary emotional response of rape victims is the fear of future rapes (Burgess & Holmstrom, 1974). People who have been robbed report being more afraid of another robbery than are their neighbors (Stinchcombe, Adams, Heimer, Scheppele, Smith, & Taylor, 1980). Cancer patients are tremendously fearful of recurrence and interpret any new symptoms, no

matter how minor, as indicative of cancer (Burdick, 1975). Once victimized, it is relatively easy to see oneself in the role of victim once again;
the experience is now "available" and one sees oneself as "representative" of the subsample of people who are victimized (Kahneman &
Tversky, 1973).

Victims no longer perceive themselves as safe and secure in a benign
environment. They have experienced a malevolent world. In human-
induced victimizations, such as criminal assaults, this is particularly
distressing, for the victim is no longer able to feel secure in the world
of other people. "The crime victim has been deliberately violated by
another person. The victim's injury is not an accident; it is the direct
result of the conscious, malicious intention of another human being.
Some people can't be trusted—again we all know that, but the victim
is confronted with human malevolence in a very graphic way" (Bard
& Sangrey, 1979, pp. 14-15). Interestingly, the DSM-III notes that post-
traumatic stress disorder is "apparently more severe and longer lasting
when the stressor is of human design" (American Psychiatric Association, 1980, p. 236). To the victim, the world is a threatening place; not
only is there malevolence (e.g., crime, disaster), but such malevolence
is now vivid and undeniable, for it has struck home.

The World as Meaningful

Our assumption of invulnerability rests, in part, on a basic belief that
events in our world are comprehensible and orderly (Antonovsky, 1979).
Our world "makes sense," for we have constructed social theories that
enable us to account for specific occurrences. One way for us to make
sense of our world is to regard what happens to us as controllable
(Seligman, 1975). For example, we believe we can prevent misfortune
by engaging in sufficiently cautious behaviors (Scheppele & Bart, 1983).
At a fundamental level, we also believe we are protected against misfortune by being good and worthy people. According to Lerner's (1970,
1980) just-world theory, we believe people deserve what they get and
get what they deserve. People appear to operate on the basis of such
just-world assumptions even when they verbally deny a belief in such
a "social law" (Lerner & Ellard, 1983). The justice motive is apparently
very strong, and events that counter our expectation of what we deserve
are extremely problematic. In regarding the world as just and controllable, we have constructed a view of the world as optimally benign. It
is a meaningful world, for we know what to expect and why negative
events occur.

The world does not appear meaningful to victims who feel they have been cautious and good people (Scheppele & Bart, 1983; Silver & Wortman, 1980). The victimization simply does not make sense. It does not fit with the "social laws" one has held about the operation of the world. The inability to make sense of the world was acutely present among survivors of the Holocaust. Following his experience in Auschwitz, Victor Frankl (1963) posited the need for meaning as a fundamental human motivation. Frankl maintained that in order to survive, individuals had to see meaning and purpose in their suffering. The search for an explanation and a sense of world-order was pervasive among survivors of Hiroshima as well. As Lifton (1967) wrote, "The dropping of the atomic bomb in Hiroshima annihilated a general sense of life's coherence as much as it did human bodies" (p. 525). The lack of meaning does not necessarily derive from a victim's inability to see a purpose in the victimization. Instead, finding a purpose in the victimization is one way of coping with a world that makes little sense. In a study of accident victims by Bulman and Wortman (1977), one paraplegic said that he was paralyzed because God needed his legs for someone else, and another indicated God wanted to teach him a lesson about the importance of one's mind rather than one's legs. The lack of meaning derives from the inability to understand the event in light of one's prior theories about the operation of the world.

In the case of serious crimes, accidents, and diseases, the problem of loss of meaning often seems to focus not on the question, "Why did this event happen?" but on the more specific question, "Why did this event happen *to me*?" It is the selective incidence of the victimization that appears to warrant explanation. One can explain rape by pointing the finger at a society that encourages socialized differences in the sexes or by pointing the finger at a psychotic rapist; one can explain cancer by invoking a theory of stress and immunological breakdown. Such explanations, however, do not account for why the event happened to the particular victim. They explain the phenomenon in general, but not the victim's lot in particular (Janoff-Bulman & Lang-Gunn, in press). Victims often feel a total lack of comprehension regarding the whys and wherefores of their misfortune. Particularly if they regard themselves as decent people who take good care of themselves and are appropriately cautious, victims are apt to find themselves at a loss to explain why they were victimized.

Positive Self-perceptions

People generally operate under the assumption that they are worthy, decent people; that is, they maintain a relatively high level of self-esteem.

The experience of being victimized leads to a serious questioning of these self-perceptions. The trauma of victimization activates negative self-images in the victim (Horowitz, Wilner, Marmar & Krupnick, 1980). Victims see themselves as weak, helpless, needy, frightened, and out of control (Krupnick, 1980). Bard and Sangrey (1979) note that one essential component of an individual's equilibrium is the sense of autonomy, and crime victims invariably experience a profound threat to their autonomy. The victimization is neither expected nor intended by them. They perceive themselves as powerless and helpless in the face of forces beyond their control (Peterson & Seligman, 1983). This sense of helplessness "can serve as a catalyst for revision of one's self-concept, leading to a loss of self-esteem" (Krupnick & Horowitz, 1980, p. 45). In addition to weakness and powerlessness, victims are apt to experience a sense of deviance. After all, they have been singled out for misfortune and this establishes them as different from other people. The self-perception of deviance no doubt serves to reinforce negative images of oneself as unworthy and weak (Coates & Winston, 1983).

COPING WITH VICTIMIZATION

As a result of their victimization, victims' views of the world and of themselves are seriously challenged, and the assumptions that formerly enabled them to function effectively no longer serve as guides for behavior. The state of disequilibrium that results is marked by intense stress and anxiety, and characteristic symptoms are often those described by post-traumatic stress disorder. To a great extent, coping with victimization involves coming to terms with these shattered assumptions and reestablishing a conceptual system that will allow the victim to once again function effectively. The parts of the conceptual system that have been shaken will have to be rebuilt, and the coping process will involve coming to terms with a world in which bad things can and do happen—and to oneself. While victims are not likely to ever again view the world as wholly benevolent, or themselves as entirely invulnerable, they will still need to work on establishing a view of the world as not wholly malevolent and of themselves as not uniquely vulnerable to misfortune. The victim will also face the tasks of reestablishing a view of the world as meaningful, in which events once again make sense, and regaining a positive self-image, including perceptions of worth, strength, and autonomy.

In an important way, then, the coping process following victimization entails the establishment of an assumptive world which incorporates one's experiences as a victim. This perspective is similar to that presented by Horowitz (1980, 1982), who focused on the role of intrusive and repetitive thoughts in trauma victims. Among the individuals studied by Horowitz were people who suffered as a result of accidents, violence, or illness. Intrusive, repetitive thoughts about their victimizations were almost universally reported by these victims, thereby validating this criterion of post-traumatic stress disorder. Horowitz takes a functional perspective on these symptoms and regards the intrusions and repetitions as the mind's effort to process new information. He maintains that people have a "completion tendency," which is an "important tendency to integrate reality and schemata" (Horowitz, 1980, p. 249). Before the new information is integrated, it is stored in active memory; when "completion" occurs, the information becomes part of "long-term models and inner schemata." At this point, repetitions and intrusions cease. Horowitz (1982) writes that events such as victimization "will eventually change inner models. . . . The models change, and reality and models of reality reach accord" (p. 727).

Incorporating one's experience as a victim involves reworking one's assumptions about oneself and the world so that they "fit" with one's new personal data. Certainly, the nature and strength of prior theories of reality will have a significant impact on the extent of trauma and the success of coping efforts following victimization. To the extent that particular assumptions are held with extreme confidence and have not been challenged, they are more likely to be utterly shattered, with devastating results for the victim. In the area of attitudes and persuasion, McGuire's (1964) work on inoculation against persuasion provides a useful analogy. McGuire found that cultural truisms (i.e., beliefs so widely accepted that people are unpracticed in defending them) are "highly vulnerable to influence" because people have no counterarguments to use in resisting persuasive messages. Similarly, basic assumptions that have not been questioned may shatter most easily and lead to the greatest psychological disruption. Thus, if an individual strongly believes that the world is truly a benevolent place (e.g., he or she has never been confronted with situations that would lead one to at least admit the possibility of malevolence in the world), this assumption will be easily destroyed by the experience of victimization, and the process of rebuilding is apt to be a difficult one. In the case of perceived vulnerability, Perloff (1983) maintains that those who feel most invulnerable prior to the victimization are likely to have the greatest adjustment problems following the victimization (cf. Wortman, 1983). And Wolfenstein (1957) has written,

There is likely to be more emotional disturbance following the event on the part of those who beforehand warded off all anxiety, and denied the reality of the threat, than on the part of those who were able to tolerate some anticipatory alarm and to acknowledge that the disaster could happen. (pp. 25-26)

Similarly, Scheppele and Bart (1983) found that those women who felt safest prior to being raped were also those who suffered the greatest psychological disturbance ("total fear reaction") following the rape experience. These women felt secure either because they believed the attack situation was entirely safe (e.g., they were with someone they trusted or in a place they believed to be totally safe, such as their locked home) or because they were following the "rules of rape avoidance" (i.e., were engaging in precautionary behaviors believed to ensure against rape). The rape experience invalidated their prior assumptions about personal safety and invulnerability, and their victimization now had to be integrated into a new, viable assumptive world. For victims, the assumptive realms of vulnerability, meaning, and self-esteem (cf. Taylor, 1983) are particularly subject to examination, alteration, and reexamination. A number of coping strategies are available that appear to help victims rebuild their theories of reality about themselves and their world.

COPING STRATEGIES

Victims' coping strategies seem to fall roughly into two categories of response: intrapsychic/cognitive modes and direct action. In order to provide a sense of the range of strategies used by victims, several coping responses are presented in the first part of this section. This list is not intended to be exhaustive, but rather is meant to convey a general sense of coping possibilities. The second part of this section will be a more in-depth look at one particular and frequently misunderstood coping reaction that often follows victimization—the phenomenon of self-blame.

Some Coping Possibilities

Redefining the event. One important way of reacting to victimization is to redefine the event so as to be consistent with and, thus, minimize the threat to one's assumptive world. By redefining the event, the victim maximizes the possibility of maintaining his or her prior theories of reality; the event is not evaluated as an instance of harsh victimization, and the threat to one's assumptive world is minimized. Taylor, Wood, and Lichtman (1983) addressed the process of redefining victimization through attempts to minimize the perceived impact of the victimizing event. They proposed five mechanisms that victims use in selectively evaluating their victimization: comparing with less fortunate others; comparing on the basis of a favorable attribute; creating hypothetical worse worlds; construing benefit from the experience; and manufacturing normative standards of adjustment. These self-enhancing strategies are effective for reducing the likelihood of perceiving oneself as a victim.

In their research with rape victims, Scheppele and Bart (1983) also addressed the issue of redefinition, or cognitive appraisal (see Lazarus, 1966) of victimization. Although all the women they studied were victims of acts legally defined as rape, those who were subjected to non-phallic sexual acts were likely to have labeled themselves as having escaped rape (Bart & Scheppele, 1980). It was not the severity of the attack (in terms of violence) that distinguished the women who defined themselves as rape victims from those who felt they were avoiders. Those who felt they had avoided rape had the mildest reactions to the event. Apparently, how one evaluates (i.e., cognitively appraises) the victimization affects the extent to which the victimization functions as a stressor and threat. To the extent that the victimization itself is minimized in the mind of the victim, basic assumptions about oneself and one's world are less likely to be seriously challenged.

Finding meaning. Once having defined themselves as victims, individuals who attempt to cope with their victimization are apt to include other cognitive or intrapsychic modes of response. An important aspect of the coping process is the attempt to make sense of one's experience, to search for meaning in the victimization (Bulman & Wortman, 1977; Silver & Wortman, 1980). In a recent study of incest victims, Silver, Boon, and Stones (1983) found that those women who were able to make sense of their experience were less psychologically distressed and better socially adjusted than those who were unable to make sense of the event. Further, those who were unable to make sense of their incest experience reported greater intrusive thoughts, indicating, according to Horowitz (1980, 1982), that they had not yet integrated the experience with their "inner models."

One way of making sense of an event is to find some purpose in it (Frankl, 1963). If the victimization can be viewed as serving a purpose, the victim will be able to reestablish a belief in an orderly, comprehen-

sible world. Victims can reestablish this same view of the world, however, without invoking teleological explanations for the event. They can
explain their victimization by making causal attributions which provide
an explanation for what happened and thereby satisfy the need to reestablish a view of the world in which events "make sense." Victimizations are apt to bring about spontaneous attributions, for they are
negative, intense, personally important, unexpected, and stressful
(Brickman, Rabinowitz, Karuza, Coates, Cohn, & Kidder, 1982; Wortman & Dintzer, 1978). One type of attribution—self-blame—may be particularly helpful in enabling the victim to rebuild his or her assumptive
world, and is discussed in greater detail below.

Changing behaviors. Once individuals have defined themselves as victims and the situation as a victimization, they may engage in particular
actions to adapt to the changes wrought by these new definitions. Crime
victims, for example, often become obsessed with preventive behaviors
(Bard & Sangrey, 1979). Robbery victims not only put new locks on their
doors and bars on their windows, but some also refrain from going out
at night, move to a new residence, or change their place of employment
(Cohn, 1974). Similar responses have been reported for mugging victims
(Lejeune & Alex, 1973). Rape victims, too, often engage in behavior
changes. Burgess and Holmstrom (1979) found that those rape victims
who engaged in actions such as changing their residence or obtaining
an unlisted phone number were also those women to recover faster from
the rape. Behavior changes can remove the victim from daily confron-
tations with the scene of one's victimization (e.g., one's home, neighborhood, or place of employment), thereby removing constant physical
reminders of the victimization. More important, direct actions can provide victims with a sense of environmental control which can serve to
minimize their newfound perception of vulnerability and help reestablish a view of the world that is not wholly unresponsive to one's own
efforts. This awareness of perceived control not only helps victims rebuild assumptions about their own relative invulnerability, but also helps
reestablish a positive self-image, including perceptions of personal
strength and autonomy.

    To the extent, then, that direct actions following victimization foster
a sense of personal control and safety, the effect on the victim will be
positive. Taylor (1983) has discussed the beneficial impact of assuming
control over aspects of one's cancer care. For victims of criminal assaults
and muggings, formal training in self-defense may be an effective route
to minimizing vulnerability and maximizing positive self-perceptions.

Kidder, Boell, and Moyer (1983) have conducted research demonstrating the positive impact of self-defense training and assertiveness training on women's perceptions of fear, helplessness, and the right to resist. By building up women's self-confidence, such training helps to eliminate the sense of helplessness that often follows victimization (Peterson & Seligman, 1983).

Seeking social support. Victims engage in other types of behaviors in an attempt to cope with their experience and rebuild shattered assumptions. A common response to victimization is to turn to others for emotional as well as other forms of help. Other people, however, may not be as helpful as one might expect. Although one might predict that Judeo-Christian ethics and a general tendency to help the powerless would lead us to be compassionate toward victims, this is clearly not always the case. Instead, people tend to see victims as responsible for their fate (Lerner, 1970; Ryan, 1971) and are thereby able to maintain their own beliefs in personal invulnerability (Janoff-Bulman, 1982; Lerner, 1980; Shaver, 1970). Or victims may simply be ignored (Reiff, 1979) because they are seen as losers (Bard & Sangrey, 1979), or because of fears of guilt by association (Frederick, 1980; Weis & Weis, 1975). Another reason for avoiding victims is that they are often depressed and most people prefer not to be around unhappy people (Coates, Wortman, & Abbey, 1979). As a consequence, victims may be socially isolated at a time when social supports are especially important (Coates & Winston, 1983; Symonds, 1980).

A number of researchers (Bard & Sangrey, 1979; Burge & Figley, in press; Cobb, 1976; Kutash, 1978; Sales, Baum, & Shore, 1984; Silver & Wortman, 1980) have maintained that positive social support following victimization helps the victim reestablish psychological well-being, largely by enhancing self-esteem. Friedman, Bischoff, David, and Person (1982) reported that the more supporters victims had, the sooner they recovered from the post-traumatic stress of victimization. Evidence is now accumulating to indicate that support from family, friends, the helping and legal professions, and the community-at-large is vital to the recovery and adjustment of crime victims (Bard & Sangrey, 1979; Burgess & Holmstrom, 1976; Krupnick & Horowitz, 1980; Symonds, 1980). Supportive others not only provide the victim with an opportunity to talk about the event and vent his or her emotions (Coates, Wortman, & Abbey, 1979; Silver & Wortman, 1980), but also assist the victim in problem-solving (Gottlieb, 1979; Hirsch, 1980).

When social supports from family and friends are inadequate a victim may seek therapeutic help. In recent years, an increasing number of people have turned for help to peer support groups comprised of individuals who have experienced a similar life crisis or problem. According to Coates and Winston (1983), peer support groups are therapeutic in that they reduce the victim's self-perception of deviance. They therefore serve to enhance a victim's positive self-image, which generally needs to be rebuilt following victimization. Professional efforts involving therapy with victims also attempt to address the important issue of rebuilding positive self-perceptions (Krupnick, 1980).

Although the primary impact of social support may be to enable victims to reestablish basic assumptions about their own esteem and worth, it is also likely that such support also helps victims reestablish a more benevolent view of the world. Victims need to know that social supports are unconditionally available; if they are unavailable or negative in tone, the victim may find this more distressing than the initial victimizing experience (Gittleson, Eacott, & Mehta, 1978). However, to the extent that others are concerned, available, positive, and caring, the victim is confronted with an immediate social world that is safe and secure. In the end, this experience will no doubt help the victim reestablish a sense of relative invulnerability by directly challenging his or her newfound perception of the world as malevolent and threatening.

A Focus on Self-blame

Self-blame is a surprisingly common reaction following victimization (Janoff-Bulman & Lang-Gunn, in press; Wortman, 1976). It is a common response of victims of rape (Burgess & Holmstrom, 1974; Janoff-Bulman, 1979; Medea & Thompson, 1974), battering (Frieze, 1979, 1983; Hilberman & Munson, 1978; Walker, 1978, 1979), disease (Abrams & Finesinger, 1953; Bard & Dyk, 1956; Davis, 1963; Friedman, Chodoff, Mason, & Hamburg, 1977), and accidents (Bulman & Wortman, 1977). Survivor guilt following group disasters (Lifton, 1967, 1971; Wolfenstein, 1957) can also be regarded as instances of self-blame. Self-blame does not reflect a veridical perception of the victim's actual role in the victimization, for victims blame themselves far more than would appear warranted by the actual circumstances of the victimizing events. Why, then, is self-blame a common reaction? Could there be some adaptive value to this attributional response?

In their study of paralyzed accident victims, Bulman and Wortman (1977) examined the relationship between victims' attributions and coping (as assessed by nurses and social workers who worked with the victims) and found that while blame of others was associated with poor coping, self-blame was a predictor of good coping. This finding regarding the adaptiveness of self-blame was consistent with conclusions reached by Chodoff, Friedman and Hamburg (1964) in their study of coping by parents of children with leukemia. Nevertheless, this view of self-blame as adaptive directly contradicts the more popular conception of the phenomenon and the view held by depression theorists such as Beck (1967), who regard self-blame as maladaptive, a symptom of depression. How, then, can these perspectives be reconciled?

In an attempt to resolve these inconsistencies, Janoff-Bulman (1979) proposed that there are actually two distinct types of self-blame, one representing an adaptive response, the other a maladaptive response. "Behavioral self-blame" involves blaming one's own behavior and is adaptive, whereas "characterological self-blame" involves attributions to one's enduring personality characteristics and is maladaptive (cf. Miller & Porter, 1983). Thus, the rape victim who believes she should not have hitchhiked or should not have walked alone is engaging in behavioral self-blame, whereas the rape victim who believes she is a bad person or a poor judge of character is engaging in characterological self-blame. The primary distinction between these two self-attributions is the perceived modifiability and controllability of the factor blamed; behaviors are generally regarded as modifiable through one's own efforts, whereas personality or character traits are generally regarded as stable and relatively unchangeable. It is primarily the modifiability of behavior that renders behavioral self-blame adaptive, for this attribution enables the victim to believe in the future avoidability of the victimization. Victims can believe that by altering their behavior, they will avoid being victimized in the future and can exert personal control over future misfortunes. While the behavioral self-blamer is concerned with the future and the avoidability of misfortune, the characterological self-blamer focuses on the past and the question of deservedness rather than avoidability.

Characterological self-blame is associated with depression (Janoff-Bulman, 1979; Peterson, Schwartz, & Seligman, 1981) and presumably represents the type of self-blame discussed by depression theorists. It is important to note that behavioral self-blame is apt to coexist with characterological self-blame, for it is difficult to believe, for example, that one is a stupid person but does not do stupid things. Thus, behavioral self-blame is adaptive only when it exists in the absence of characterological self-blame (e.g., I did a stupid thing but am not a stupid person). In a survey of rape crisis centers, Janoff-Bulman (1979) found that the

overwhelming majority of rape victims (69%) blamed themselves behaviorally rather than characterologically (19%). There appears to be
some evidence, then, that victims' self-attributions are behavioral in
nature, rather than characterological, and may therefore represent adaptive coping strategies. Recent research with cancer patients (Timko &
Janoff-Bulman, 1984) and victims of technological disaster at Three Mile
Island (Baum, Fleming, & Singer, 1983) provides support for a positive
relationship between behavioral self-blame and coping outcome among
victimized populations.

From the perspective of rebuilding a viable assumptive world following victimization, behavioral self-blame may be a particularly effective
strategy, for it addresses three major areas in which assumptions have
been shattered: personal invulnerability, the world as meaningful, and
positive self-perceptions. As presented above, behavioral self-blame enables the victim to believe in his or her own control over future victimizations by modifying the "blamed" behavior, and as a result is likely
to help the victim reestablish a belief in relative invulnerability. At the
same time, behavioral self-blame is also likely to help the victim rebuild
a positive self-image involving control and autonomy. This self-attri-
bution specifically does not involve attributions to negative character
traits or personality dispositions and thus minimizes the victim's negative self-perceptions. In addition to helping in the areas of vulnerability
and esteem, behavioral self-blame also provides the victim with a means
of making sense of the event. The incomprehensibility of victimization
is largely reflected in the question "Why me?"; this question would
naturally lead victims to turn to themselves in order to provide a personally satisfying response. Behavioral self-blame appears to explain
why the event happened to the victim in particular—because of something he or she did or failed to do. While characterological self-blame
would also be a satisfactory way to respond to "Why me?," this self-
attribution would be detrimental to the rebuilding of assumptions about
personal invulnerability and positive self-esteem. Overall, behavioral
self-blame can help the victim rebuild shattered assumptions in three
important domains: *invulnerability*, *meaning*, and *esteem*. It is not particularly surprising, then, that such attributions are relatively common
following the experience of victimization. Behavioral self-blame is adaptive in spite of the fact that victims are generally not to blame for their
victimization. It is not the accuracy of the attribution, but rather its
impact on the victim's perceptions and assumptions that render it beneficial to the coping process.

CONCLUSION

Throughout this chapter, the term "victim" has been used to describe individuals who have had the misfortune of experiencing such extreme events as criminal acts, serious accidents, disasters, and serious diseases. While clearly there are problems with the term, I nevertheless believe it is a useful label, for it serves to relieve victims of responsibility for their victimization. The suggestion that victims are not responsible for what happened, however, does not imply that they are not capable of ameliorating their situation. Brickman and his colleagues (1982) made an important point when they noted that there is a difference between responsibility for a problem (i.e., victimization) and responsibility for a solution (i.e., recovery). Similarly, helplessness in the face of victimization differs from helplessness in the face of recovery. The weakness and powerlessness often associated with the term victim represent an unfortunate generalization of helplessness from the victimizing event to the recovery process. People can be powerless in preventing their own victimization and powerful in coping with it. In using the term victim I wish to recognize both the victim's lack of responsibility in bringing about the victimization and the victim's tremendous strength in coping with the experience. The coping task confronting victims is a remarkably difficult one. Basic assumptions about themselves and their world, built over years of experience, have been shattered, and a new assumptive world—one that incorporates the experience of victimization—must be rebuilt.

REFERENCES

Abrams, R.D., & Finesinger, J.E. Guilt reactions in patients with cancer. *Cancer*, 1953, *6*, 474-482.

American Psychiatric Association. *Diagnostic and statistical manual of mental disorders* (3rd ed.). Washington, D.C.: American Psychiatric Association, 1980.

Antonovsky, A. *Health, stress, and coping.* San Francisco, CA: Jossey-Bass, 1979.

Bard, M., & Dyk, R.B. The psychodynamic significance of beliefs regarding the cause of serious illness. *Psychoanalytic Review*, 1956, *43*, 146-162.

Bard, M., & Sangrey, D. *The crime victim's book.* New York: Basic Books, 1979.

Bart, P.B., & Scheppele, K.L. *There ought to be a law: Women's definitions and legal definitions of sexual assault.* Paper presented at the Meeting of the American Sociological Association, New York, August 1980.

Baum, A., Fleming, R., & Singer, J.E. Coping with victimization by technological disaster. *Journal of Social Issues*, 1983, *39*, 119-140.

Beck, A.T. *Depression: Clinical, experimental, and theoretical aspects.* New York: Harper & Row, 1967.

Bowlby, J. *Attachment and loss* (Vol. 1: Attachment). London: Hogarth, 1969.

Brickman, P., Rabinowitz, V.C., Karuza, J., Coates, D., Cohn, E., & Kidder. L. Models of helping and coping. *American Psychologist*, 1982, *37*, 368-384.

Bulman, R., & Wortman, C.B. Attributions of blame and coping in the "real world": Severe accident victims react to their lot. *Journal of Personality and Social Psychology*, 1977, *35*, 351-363.

Burdick, D. Rehabilitation of the breast cancer patient. *Cancer*, 1975, *36*, 645-648.

Burge, S.B., & Figley, C.R. The Social Support Scale: Development and initial estimates of reliability and validity. *Family Process*, in press.

Burgess, A., & Holmstrom, L. Rape trauma syndrome. *American Journal of Psychiatry*, 1974, *131*, 981-985.

Burgess, A., & Holmstrom, L. Coping behavior of the rape victim. *American Journal of Psychiatry*, 1976, *133*, 413-417.

Burgess, A., & Holmstrom, L. Adaptive strategies and recovery from rape. *American Journal of Psychiatry*, 1979, *136*, 1278-1282.

Chodoff, P., Friedman, S.B., & Hamburg, D.A. Stress, defenses, and coping behavior: Observations of children with malignant diseases. *American Journal of Psychiatry*, 1964, *120*, 743-749.

Coates, D., & Winston, T. Counteracting the deviance of depression. *Journal of Social Issues*, 1983, *39*, 171-196.

Coates, D., Wortman, C.B., & Abbey, A. Reactions to victims. In I.H. Frieze, D. Bar-Tal, & J.S. Carroll (Eds.), *New approaches to social problems: Applications of attribution theory*. San Francisco: Jossey-Bass, 1979.

Cobb, S. Social support as a moderator of life stress. *Psychosomatic Medicine*, 1976, *38*, 300-314.

Cohn, Y. Crisis intervention and the victim of robbery. In I. Drapkin, & E. Viano (Eds.), *Victimology: A new focus* (Vol. 2). Lexington, MA; Lexington Books, 1974.

Davis, F. *Passage through crisis: Polio victims and their families*. Indianapolis, IN: Bobbs-Merrill, 1963.

Ellis, E., Atkeson, B., & Calhoun. K. An assessment of long-term reaction to rape. *Journal of Abnormal Psychology*, 1981, *90*, 263-266.

Epstein, S. The self-concept revisited: Or a theory of a theory. *American Psychologist*, 1973, *28*, 404-416.

Epstein, S. The ecological study of emotions in humans. In P. Pliner, K.R. Blanstein, & I.M. Spigel (Eds.), *Advances in the study of communication and affect* (Vol.5). New York: Plenum Press, 1979.

Epstein, S. The self-concept: A review and the proposal of an integrated theory of personality. In E. Staub (Ed.), *Personality: Basic issues and current research*. Englewood Cliffs, NJ: Prentice-Hall, 1980.

Figley, C.R. (Ed.). *Stress disorders among Vietnam veterans*. New York: Brunner/Mazel, 1978.

Frank, E., Turner, S.M., & Duffy, B. Depressive symptoms in rape victims. *Journal of Affective Disorders*, 1979, *1*, 269-277.

Frankl, V.E. *Man's search for meaning*. New York: Washington Square Press, 1963.

Frederick, C. Effects of natural vs. human-induced violence. *Evaluation and Change*, 1980, 71-75.

Friedman, K., Bischoff, H., Davis, R., & Person, A. Samaritan blues. *Psychology Today*, 1982, July, 26-28.

Friedman, S.B., Chodoff, P., Mason, J.E., & Hamburg, D.A. Behavioral observations on parents anticipating the death of a child. In A. Monat, & R. Lazarus (Eds.), *Stress and coping*. New York: Columbia University Press, 1977.

Frieze, I.H. Perceptions of battered wives. In I.H. Frieze, D. Bar-Tal, & J.S. Carroll (Eds), *New approaches to social problems: Applications of attribution theory*. San Francisco: Jossey-Bass, 1979.

Frieze, I.H. Investigating the causes and consequences of marital rape. *Signs*, 1983, *8*, 532-553.

Gittleson, N.L., Eacott, S.E., & Mehta, B.M. Victims of indecent exposure. *British Journal of Psychiatry*, 1978, *132*, 61-66.

Gottlieb, B.H. The primary group as supportive milieu: Applications to community psychology. *American Journal of Community Psychology*, 1979, *7*, 469-489.

Greenberg, M.S., Ruback, R.B., & Westcott, D.R. Seeking help from the police: The victim's perspective. In A. Nadler, J.D. Fisher, & B. Depaulo (Eds.), *Applied perspectives on help-seeking and receiving*. New York: Academic Press, 1983.

Hilberman, E., & Munson, K. Sixty battered women. *Victimology*, 1978, *2*, 460-471.

Hirsch, B.J. Natural support systems and coping with major life changes. *American Journal of Community Psychology*, 1980, *8*, 159-172.

Horowitz, M.J. Psychological response to serious life events. In V. Hamilton & D. Warburton (Eds.), *Human stress and cognition*. New York: Wiley, 1980.

Horowitz, M.J. Stress response syndromes and their treatment. In L. Goldberger & S. Breznitz (Eds.), *Handbook of stress*. New York: Free Press, 1982.

Horowitz, M.J., Wilner, N., Marmar, C., & Krupnick, J. Pathological grief and the activation of latent self-images. *American Journal of Psychiatry*, 1980, *137*, 1137-1162.

Janis, I.L. Vigilance and decision-making in personal crises. In G.V. Coelho, D.A. Hamburg, & J.E. Adams (Eds.), *Coping and adaptation*. New York: Basic Books, 1974.

Janoff-Bulman, R. Characterological versus behavioral self-blame: Inquiries into depression and rape. *Journal of Personality and Social Psychology*, 1979, *37*, 1798-1809.

Janoff-Bulman, R. Esteem and control bases of blame: "Adaptive" strategies for victims versus observers. *Journal of Personality*, 1982, *50*, 180-192.

Janoff-Bulman, R., & Frieze, I.H. A theoretical perspective for understanding reactions to victimization. *Journal of Social Issues*, 1983, *39*, 1-17.

Janoff-Bulman, R., & Lang-Gunn, L. Coping with disease and accidents: The role of self-blame attributions. In L.Y. Abramson (Ed.), *Social-personal inference in clinical psychology*. New York: Guilford, in press.

Janoff-Bulman, R., & Timko, C. Working with victims: Changes in the researcher's assumptive world. In A. Baum, & J. Singer (Eds.), *Advances in environmental psychology* (Vol. 5). Hillsdale, NJ: Erlbaum, in press.

Kahneman, D., & Tversky, A. On the psychology of prediction. *Psychological Review*, 1973, *80*, 237-251.

Kidder, L.H., Boell, J.L., & Moyer, M.M. Rights consciousness and victimization prevention through personal defense training and assertiveness training. *Journal of Social Issues*, 1983, *39*, 155-170.

Krupnick, J. Brief psychotherapy with victims of violent crime. *Victimology*, 1980, *5*, 347-354.

Krupnick, J., & Horowitz, M. Victims of violence: Psychological responses, treatment implications. *Evaluation and Change*, 1980, 42-46.

Kuhn, T.S. *The structure of scientific revolutions*. Chicago: University of Chicago Press, 1962.

Kutash, I. Treating the victim of aggression. In I. Kutash, & L. Schlesinger (Eds.), *Violence: Perspective on murder and aggression*. San Francisco: Jossey-Bass, 1978.

Lazarus, R. *Psychological stress and the coping process*. New York: McGraw-Hill, 1966.

Lazarus, R., & Cohen, J. Environmental stress. In I. Altman & J. Wohlwill (Eds.), *Human behavior and environment* (Vol. 1). New York: Plenum Press, 1978.

Lazarus, R., & Launier, R. Stress-related transactions between person and environment. In L. Pervin & M. Lewis (Eds.), *Perspectives in interactional psychology*. New York: Plenum Press, 1978.

Lejeune, R., & Alex, N. On being mugged: The event and its aftermath. *Urban Life and Culture*, 1973, *2*, 259-287.

Lerner, M. The desire for justice and reactions to victims: Social psychological studies of some antecedents and consequences. In J. Macaulay & L. Berkowitz (Eds.), *Altruism and helping behavior*. New York: Academic Press, 1970.

Lerner, M.J. *The belief in a just world*. New York: Plenum Press, 1980.

Lerner, M.J., & Ellard, J. *The justice motive: How people define and react to victimization.*

Unpublished manuscript, University of Waterloo, 1983.

Lifton, R.J. *Death in life: Survivors of Hiroshima*. New York: Simon and Schuster, 1967.

Lifton, R.J. *History and human survival*. New York: Vintage Books, 1971.

Lifton, R.J., & Olson, E. Death imprint in Buffalo Creek. In H.J. Parad, H.L.P. Resnick, & L.G. Parad (Eds.), *Emergency and disaster management*. Bowie, MD: Charles Press, 1976.

Maguire, M. Impact of burglary upon victims. *British Journal of Criminology*, 1980, *20*, 261-275.

Marris, P. *Loss and change*. Garden City, NY: Anchor/Doubleday, 1975.

McGuire, W.J. Inducing resistance to persuasion: Some contemporary approaches. In L. Berkowitz (Ed.), *Advances in experimental social psychology* (Vol. 1). New York: Academic Press, 1964.

Medea, A., & Thompson, K. *Against rape*. New York: Farrar, Straus, & Giroux, 1974.

Miller, D.T., & Porter, C.A. Self-blame in victims of violence. *Journal of Social Issues*, 1983, *39*, 141-154.

Notman, M., & Nadelson, C. The rape victim: Psychodynamic considerations. *American Journal of Psychiatry*, 1976, *133*, 408-412.

Ochberg, F., & Spates, R. Services integration for victims of personal violence. In S. Salasin (Ed.), *Evaluating victim services* (Vol. 7). Beverly Hills, CA: Sage, 1981.

Parkes, C.M. Psycho-social transitions: A field for study. *Social Science and Medicine*, 1971, *5*, 101-115.

Parkes, C.M. What becomes of redundant world models? A contribution to the study of adaptation to change. *British Journal of Medical Psychology*, 1975, *48*, 131-137.

Perloff, L.S. Perceptions of vulnerability to victimization. *Journal of Social Issues*, 1983, *39*, 41-61.

Peterson, C., Schwartz, S.M., & Seligman, M.E.P. Self-blame and depressive symptoms. *Journal of Personality and Social Psychology*, 1981, *41*, 253-259.

Peterson, C., & Seligman, M.E.P. Learned helplessness and victimization. *Journal of Social Issues*, 1983, *39*, 105-118.

Reiff, R. *The invisible victim: The criminal justice system's forgotten responsibility*. New York: Basic Books, 1979.

Ryan, W. *Blaming the victim*. New York: Vintage Books, 1971.

Sales, E., Baum, M., & Shore, B. Victim readjustment following assault. *Journal of Social Issues*, 1984, *40*, 117-136.

Scheppele, K.L., & Bart, P.B. Through women's eyes: Defining danger in the wake of sexual assault. *Journal of Social Issues*, 1983, *39*, 63-81.

Seligman, M.E.P. *Helplessness: On depression, development, and death*. San Francisco, CA: Freeman, 1975.

Shaver, K. Defensive attribution: Effects of severity and relevance on the responsibility assigned for an accident. *Journal of Personality and Social Psychology*, 1970, *14*, 101-113.

Silver, R.L., Boon, C., & Stones, M.L. Searching for meaning in misfortune: Making sense of incest. *Journal of Social Issues*, 1983, *39*, 83-103.

Silver, R.L., & Wortman, C.B. Coping with undesirable life events. In J. Garber & M.E.P. Seligman (Eds.), *Human helplessness*. New York: Academic Press, 1980.

Stinchcombe, A.L., Adams, R., Heimer, C.A., Scheppele, K.L., Smith, T.W., & Taylor, D.G. *Crime and punishment: Changing attitudes in America*. San Francisco: Jossey-Bass, 1980.

Symonds, M. Victims of violence: Psychological effects and aftereffects. *American Journal of Psychoanalysis*, 1975, *35*, 19-26.

Symonds, M. The rape victim: Psychological patterns of response. *American Journal of Psychoanalysis*, 1976, *36*, 27-34.

Symonds, M. The "second injury" to victims. *Evaluation and Change*, 1980, 36-38.

Taylor, S. Adjustment to threatening life events: A theory of cognitive adaptation. *American Psychologist*, 1983, *38*, 1161-1173.

Taylor, S.E., Wood, J.V., & Lichtman, R.R. It could be worse: Selective evaluation as a response to victimization. *Journal of Social Issues*, 1983, *39*, 19-40.
Timko, C., & Janoff-Bulman, R. *Attributions, vulnerability, and coping: The case of breast cancer.* Manuscript submitted for publication, 1984.
Titchener, J.L., Kapp, F.T., & Winget, C. The Buffalo Creek syndrome: Symptoms and character change after a major disaster. In H.J. Parad, H.L.P. Resnick, & L.G. Parad (Eds.), *Emergency and disaster management*. Bowie, MD: Charles Press, 1976.
Tyler, T.R. Perceived control and behavioral reactions to crime. *Personality and Social Psychology Bulletin*, 1981, *7*, 212-217.
Walker, L.E. Battered women and learned helplessness. *Victimology*, 1978, *2*, 525-534.
Walker, L.E. *The battered woman*. New York: Harper & Row, 1979.
Weinstein, N.D. Unrealistic optimism about future life events. *Journal of Personality and Social Psychology*, 1980, *39*, 806-820.
Weinstein, N.D., & Lachendro, E. Egocentrism as a source of unrealistic optimism. *Personality and Social Psychology Bulletin*, 1982, *8*, 195-200.
Weis, K., & Weis, S. Victimology and the justification of rape. In I. Drapkin & E. Viano (Eds.), *Victimology: A new focus* (Vol. 3). Lexington, MA: Lexington Books, 1975.
Weisman, A.D. *Coping with cancer*. New York: McGraw-Hill, 1979.
Wolfenstein, M. *Disaster: A psychological essay*. Glencoe, IL: Free Press, 1957.
Wortman, C.B. Causal attributions and personal control. In J.H. Harvey, W.J. Ickes, & R.F. Kidd (Eds.), *New directions in attribution theory* (Vol. 1). Hillsdale, NJ: Erlbaum, 1976.
Wortman, C.B. Coping with victimization: Conclusions and implications for future research. *Journal of Social Issues*, 1983, *39*, 197-223.
Wortman, C.B., & Dintzer, L. Is an attributional analysis of the learned helplessness phenomenon viable? A critique of the Abramson-Seligman-Teasdale reformulation. *Journal of Abnormal Psychology*, 1978, *87*, 75-90.
Wortman, C.B., & Dunkel-Schetter, C. Interpersonal relationships and cancer: A theoretical analysis. *Journal of Social Issues*, 1979, *35*, 120-155.

CHAPTER

3

Developmental Perspective on Psychic Trauma in Childhood

SPENCER ETH and ROBERT S. PYNOOS

This chapter will present a developmental schema for children exposed to psychic trauma. We begin by describing our research with children who have witnessed the homicide of a parent. Our observations of the child's early efforts at trauma mastery indicate important developmental influences on behavior, cognition, and emotion. Similarities between our findings and those of other investigators enable us to present a general phenomenology of the post-traumatic syndrome in childhood. We then delineate the specific developmental characteristics of the pre-school, school-age, and adolescent-age groups. Recognition of these phase-salient differences is critical for the understanding of traumatic effects on personality and the implementation of developmentally sound treatment strategies.

TRAUMA RESEARCH

There has been a recent intensification of interest in the consequences of psychic trauma during childhood (Ayalon, 1983; Black, 1982; Newman, 1976). Several case reports suggest that the DSM-III criteria for

36

post-traumatic stress disorder, as validated for adults (Horowitz, Wilner, Kultreider, & Alvarez, 1980), can be directly applied to children who have been physically abused (Green, 1983), kidnapped (Senior, Gladstone, & Nurcombe, 1982), and bitten by a dog (Gislason & Call, 1982). Some authors have stressed the common traumatic elements that can be found across all age groups or have emphasized the continuum of the response to trauma from the infantile to the adult form. For instance, after studying survivors of Hiroshima and the Buffalo Creek Flood, Lifton and Olson (1976) observe, "if the stress is great enough it can produce strikingly similar psychological disturbances in virtually everyone exposed to it" (p. 16). Terr (1979), writing about the children of Chowchilla abducted in their school bus, comments: "Since the age range was five to 14, one might expect to find important differences in their responses to trauma based on their stages of development. Such, surprisingly, was not the case. There was an amazing similarity of response across the entire age range" (p. 616). However, from our own research and analysis of the literature, we have clarified distinct, phase-specific features. We will first outline the similarities and then the age-dependent differences of the post-traumatic syndrome in childhood.

During the past three years we have investigated the early responses of children who personally witnessed the homicide of a parent. We have been able to see children referred by the police and social agencies within days or weeks of the crime. To date we have examined over 40 children fairly equally divided among preschool, school-age, and adolescent-age groups. This work has provided a unique opportunity to study psychic trauma in a most extreme form. Our goal is to offer consultation to the child and family about the acute impact of the trauma. Since these children were forced to contend with severe traumatic anxiety, a full range of reactions was readily observable. During the pilot stage of our clinical research, we developed a thorough, semi-structured interview technique which facilitates spontaneous and full descriptions by the children of their subjective experiences. Before speaking to a child, we obtain information from the referral source and family about the circumstances of the homicide and the child's responses.

There are three phases to the interview proper. First, we engage the children by having them draw and tell a story about a picture of their choice. Often the content of the event is spontaneously displayed. This opening phase alerts the therapist to the child's current means of coping and defensive maneuvers to minimize traumatic anxiety. Second, in the trauma phase, the interviewer fully explores the child's view of the violent event. Attention is directed to the child's perceptual and affective experiences, issues of human accountability and impulse control, and past traumatic incidents. We may ask the child to draw or play-act the central action, a fantasy of revenge, or some other significant element of the trauma. Third, during the closing phase, we review the child's present and future life concerns. Time is allotted to support the children in their mourning work. Finally, we review the interview with the child, invite reactions, and effect a separation. We always arrange to be available to the child and family for follow-up consultation. If significant psychopathology, either antedating or arising from the traumatic incident, is noted, appropriate referral for formal psychiatric evaluation and treatment is initiated. A complete description of this interview technique can be found in Pynoos and Eth (in press).

PSYCHIC TRAUMA

Psychic trauma occurs when an individual is exposed to an overwhelming event resulting in helplessness in the face of intolerable danger, anxiety, and instinctual arousal. Our data establish that the witnessing of a parent's homicide constitutes a psychic trauma. The viewing is painful, frightening, and distressing, and is usually followed by a constellation of psychiatric symptoms (Pynoos & Eth, 1984). Besides observing catastrophic violence, other events of high personal impact, especially those affecting a child's immediate family, can be traumatic. In particular, we are impressed with the similarities between the most severely affected children of divorce and our own subjects (Kelly & Wallerstein, 1976; Wallerstein & Kelly, 1974, 1975, 1976). Since "the central event of the divorce process for most children is the parental separation" (Kelly & Wallerstein, 1976, p. 4), it is likely that the moment of a parent leaving the home is experienced by some children as traumatic. Wallerstein (1983) describes the "core memory" of that event as extremely long-lasting and detailed: "The poignant, vivid sense of recall is reminiscent of that of bereaved people, or of people who have lived through a natural disaster" (p. 278). We will, therefore, refer in this chapter to relevant findings from their longitudinal research as well as from our own child interviews.

Terr's many papers on the Chowchilla school-bus kidnapping provide a wealth of material concerning the child victims' responses to that horrifying crime (1979, 1981a, 1981b, 1983a, 1983b, 1983c). Her work is particularly valuable in helping to identify the common post-traumatic symptomatology. In addition we reviewed the child psychiatry literature for descriptions of children facing a variety of single traumatic events, including a tornado (Bloch, Silber, & Perry, 1956), a severe winter storm (Burke, Borus, Burns, Millstein, & Beasley, 1982), the non-fatal attack of a parent by a wild animal (Maclean, 1977; Waelder, 1967), and the killing of a parent (Bergen, 1958; Pruett, 1979; Schetky, 1978). Work with the children of the Holocaust documents the devastating consequences of the concentration camp experience and focused early attention on the effects of observing human-induced lethal violence directed against a parent. However, the accounts present a confusing picture of physical and psychic trauma inflicted over a prolonged period of time (Klein, 1974; Krystal, 1971). Similarly, articles about youth in London during the Blitz make reference to the children's heightened sensitivity to war stress when a parent had been absent, injured, or under physical threat. But these articles are confounded by the children's exposure to multiple rather than discrete trauma (Carey-Trefzer, 1949; Glover, 1942). The concept of "cumulative trauma" (Khan, 1963) differs from our definition of the term trauma in that it primarily addresses cases of attenuated insult or emotional deprivation in parent-child interactions. The use of this less restrictive form of "trauma" has added considerable confusion to the literature and will be omitted from further discussion in this chapter.

Technically, psychic trauma is a process initiated by an immediate situation which confronts an individual with an acute, overwhelming threat (Freud, 1917). That event propels the individual into a traumatic state lasting the brief period of time needed for psychic equilibrium and the stimulus barrier to be reestablished (Furst, 1978). The susceptibility of a particular child to psychic trauma is a function of several factors, including: genetic, constitutional and personality makeup; past life experiences; state of mind and phase of development; and the content and intensity of the event (Furst, 1967; Kelman, 1945; Moses, 1978).

Children in a traumatic state of regression and helplessness have been variously described as:

1) exhibiting paralysis and immobilization, ranging from numbness to an emotional storm; disorganized feelings, thoughts and behavior; and physical symptoms reflecting autonomic dysfunction (Solnit & Kris, 1967);
2) appearing frozen, pale, infantile, submissive or frenzied, and panicked (Furst, 1967); and
3) resulting in aimless, frenzied overactivity, sometimes culminating in tantrums or rage, or a shock-like, stunned reaction,

presenting various degrees of unresponsiveness, inactivity or torpor (Greenacre, 1967).

Although of theoretical and clinical interest, the immediate, brief traumatic state itself cannot be studied in vitro. Further, the child's later accounts are influenced by the subsequent course of development and therefore fall victim to retrospective elaboration, distortion, and suppression. Therefore, we attempt to focus on the early responses, which are determined by the pre-trauma factors, the nature and meaning of the event, and the subsequent conditions which can exacerbate morbidity or assist trauma mastery (Chamberlain, 1980; McCubbin, Joy, Cauble, Comeau, Patterson & Needle, 1980).

GENERAL FEATURES

In "Moses and Monotheism," Sigmund Freud (1939) distinguished positive from negative effects of trauma. Positive effects consist of attempts to bring the trauma into operation again by remembering, repeating and reexperiencing. Negative effects serve to keep the forgotten event from being repeated, and as such are the defensive reactions of avoidance, inhibition, and phobia. Today it is recognized that these symptoms will frequently coalesce into the pattern of a post-traumatic stress disorder as defined by the DSM-III (American Psychiatric Association, 1980). Although the diagnostic criteria are intended for adults, they can be fulfilled by children demonstrating this disorder as well. The symptoms include: recurrent and intrusive recollections of the event; anxiety dreams; psychic numbing with markedly diminished interest in activities; feelings of detachment and constricted affect; fear of repeated trauma and renewed anxiety resulting in hypervigilant or avoidant behavior; decline in cognitive performance; startle reactions; and persistent feelings of guilt out of proportion to personal responsibility (American Psychiatric Association, 1980).

Other characteristics of the post-traumatic syndrome have been identified as common in children. These phenomena involve: increased misperception of the duration and sequencing of time and events (Terr, 1983a); retrospective presifting or premonition formation (Ayalon, 1983); reenactments or unknowing performance of acts similar to the traumatic occurrence (Terr, 1983c); repetitive, unsatisfying play involving traumatic themes (Terr, 1981b); pessimistic expectations for the future, including foreshortened lifespan (Terr, 1983b); and marked, enduring personality changes (Gislason & Call, 1982). We have found that the traumatic event may alter the recognition and tolerance of the affect of fear, contributing to inhibition or counterphobic behavior. The studies published to date have failed to find evidence of stress-induced amnesia in children, in contrast to its frequency in traumatized adults (Grinker & Spiegel, 1943). None of the children we have interviewed expressed having felt any disbelief about the reality of what they had seen. The children do exert efforts to reverse the traumatic helplessness and anxiety, often in the form of what Lifton (1982) has referred to as an inner plan of action. As we have observed, these fantasies may seek to alter the precipitating events, to undo the violent act, to reverse the lethal consequences, or to minimize future risks.

In summary, children's early responses to psychic trauma generally involve deleterious effects on cognition (including memory, school performance, and learning), affect, interpersonal relations, impulse control and behavior, vegetative function, and the formation of symptoms. Our interviews and literature review lead us to conclude that developmental phase contributes to the specific constellation of findings in a particular child. We will now outline how age helps shape the children's experience of trauma and their subsequent reactions. We have divided the developmental period into three groups: preschool, school-age, and adolescent-age. We believe that there are sufficient differences in each group to render it distinct, and so would disagree with Krystal's (1978) contention that there is a gradual transition of trauma from the infantile to the adult form.

PRESCHOOL

Due to their limited cognitive resources, young children are quite sensitive to traumatic situations. They feel the most helpless and passive when confronted by overwhelming danger, and require the most assistance from the outside in order to reestablish psychic equilibrium (Wolfenstein, 1965). In the face of fear from external threat they feel defenseless, being unable to imagine ways by their own action to prevent or alter the trauma. They may choose to flee or remain, to look or turn away, to be attentive or try to sleep; but these are all the choices of an observer, not a participant.* Occasionally, young children can imagine

---

*For example, even though a four-year-old was warned to stay under the blankets while his mother was being beaten to death, he courageously took a "big look" at the assailant.

superhero powers protecting them from attack or fantasize aid from an older sibling or relative. In their play they may ask the interviewer to assume this role and, for instance, repair a parent's injury. By so doing the therapist can offer some relief of the child's passivity and helplessness associated with trauma.

More than any other age group, preschoolers can initially appear withdrawn, subdued, or perhaps mute. Glover (1942) wrote of a four-year-old girl who, during a London air raid, "sat for several days on the exact spot where her mother had left her, would not speak, eat or play and had to be moved around like an automaton" (p. 34). We interviewed a three-year-old who had sat next to her slain mother for eight hours before she was discovered by a returning roommate. Many children will maintain a stance of silent aloofness, choosing not to speak of the traumatic occurrence. This should not be mistaken for amnesia or disavowal of the event, as the child may, after some delay, describe the details to a trusted person. A week after her mother's brutal death, the same little girl spontaneously told her great-grandmother of the killing, implicating her father as the murderer. A boy, aged two years three months, watched as his mother was shotgunned to death by her estranged second husband. One year later he spoke vividly of the tragedy for the first time with his recently acquired language. In Bergen's (1958) case report of an analysis of a four-year-old who witnessed the aftermath of her mother's fatal stabbing, the girl first confided her memory to her analyst many months after the event.

Preschool children commonly engage in reenactments and play involving traumatic themes. Bergen (1958) described how her patient carefully painted her hands red and acted out a game of stabbing herself with a paint brush. Maclean (1977) refers to the "play reenactments" of a three-and-a-half-year-old boy seen in treatment following an attack by a leopard. Disregarding other details, these young children focus on the central action. For example, we interviewed a three-year-old boy who, in all of his accounts, repeatedly acted out the phrase, "Daddy squished Mommy's neck." Wallerstein and Kelly (1975) surmise that this form of play is burdened, constricted, and joyless. Their preschool children of divorce illustrated an unsatisfying play theme when they endlessly searched for and then fitted together small objects.

Children under four years of age are notably dependent on their parents, and they commonly react to trauma with anxious attachment behavior (Bowlby, 1977). There may be an intensification of separation and stranger anxiety, or a return to former transitional objects. The younger child will frequently become visibly nervous, with whining, crying, clinging, and tantrum behaviors. Elizur and Kaffman (1982) characterize this cluster of symptoms as an "overanxious-dependent" reaction.* Other regressive behaviors also emerge in the traumatized, young child. Some children will experience a partial loss of toilet training, the reappearance of open autoerotic activity, or the abandonment of previously learned skills (Bloch, Silber, & Perry, 1956). Scharl (1961) compared the reactions of eight- and five-year-old sisters to the sudden death of their father. She observed that regression was more prominent in the younger child, perhaps because the older sibling was able to draw upon more elaborate defenses.

Two authors (Pruett, 1979; Schetky, 1978) independently reported two sets of siblings under the age of four years who saw their fathers murder their mothers. Both psychiatrists commented on the incidence of posttraumatic nightmares and sleep disturbances in this age group. We have also noted the frequency of stage four sleep disorders, including somnambulism, sleep talking, and pavor nocturnus (night terror), in traumatized youngsters. Burke et al.'s (1982) survey of preschool children before and after a severe winter storm documented a significant increase in aggressive conduct scores. Increased levels of anxiety, new fears and avoidance behavior have been widely observed by us and others (Bloch, Silber, & Perry, 1956; Newman, 1976; Terr, 1981b).

Many of the children we examined equated the parent's killing with the moment of hurt or separation. Even without fully appreciating the permanence of death (Lonetto, 1980), they will identify the traumatic event as unique, for instance the beating "when Mommy never got up." These young children long for confirmation of what they saw as a validation of external reality. When preschoolers are secure in their belief of their parent's physical death, they will speak openly of their grief. However, young children exhibit a "short sadness span" (Wolfenstein, 1966), reflecting a limited ability to sustain dysphoric affect. The mourning process is also complicated by associations to the traumatic death. A few of our children complained that changes in daily routines, such as bedtime stories, reminded them of the lost parent and evoked upsetting memories of the violent event.

When feeling sad, young children are apt to rely on the various forms of denial, including denial in fantasy, denial in action, and denial of affect, to ease the pain of the traumatic consequences (Freud, 1966). One boy poignantly expressed his sorrow that his murdered mother had not

---

*A little girl, who was three when the Buffalo Creek flood struck, was still sleeping each night in her mother's bed two years later (Newman, 1976).

attended his fifth birthday party and would not be present at his sixth or seventh as well. But, moments later when the phone rang, he animatedly asked if it were his mother calling. Elizur and Kaffman (1982) demonstrated that young Israeli children, whose fathers died in war, tended to expect their fathers' return during the first year of bereavement. Bergen (1958) related that for her preschool patients, fantasies of mother living elsewhere and returning someday coexisted with an accurate appraisal of the events and knowledge of bodily destruction.

SCHOOL-AGE

The school-age child has a far larger repertoire of cognitive, behavioral and emotional responses to psychic trauma. In the cognitive domain, school-age children may display many of the features of cognitive constriction described in adults, including general dullness, obtuseness, and a concomitant lowering of intellectual function. The cognitive effects are most apparent in the corresponding decline in school performance. Nearly every account of trauma in childhood makes reference to the onset or exacerbation of school difficulties related to the child's decreasing ability to concentrate in class. Gardner (1971) hypothesized that impairment of aggressive learning is a consequence of experiencing violence. We believe that school problems derive from: 1) the intrusion of memories and thoughts connected to the traumatic event causing the child to be distracted from an academic task; 2) the evolution of a cognitive style of forgetting associated with an inhibition of spontaneous thought, which serves to dispel reminders of the traumatic event; and 3) the interference of a depressed affect on mental processes. As one second grade girl lamented: "I hear everything at school, and then it's just gone. What happened to my mommy comes right back to me."

Having greater cognitive maturity, these children no longer act as mere witnesses to a parent's homicide; they can be participants, if only in fantasy. They can imagine calling the police, locking the doors, grabbing the gun, providing aid, or even capturing the assailant. These wishful inner plans of action may reflect the magical invulnerability of this age group and frequently involve fantasies of rescuing the parent or victim. Waelder (1967) tells of a boy of seven who watched his father's bloody goring by a stag. The traumatized child stood crying in helpless panic. For weeks the boy reenacted the scene in his play. While in reality he had been a passive, terrified onlooker, in play he became the hero who kills the stag and rescues his desperate father. A twelve-year-old girl interviewed by us imagined herself successfully treating her mother's fatal wound.

School-age children are somewhat aware of the irreversibility of death (Lonetto, 1980), and may no longer anticipate the parent's return after the homicide. They also sense the impossibility of restoring or being forgiven by the deceased parent. Instead these children can imagine ways to alter the fatal outcome through denial in fantasy. For example, an 11-year-old pointed the gun in a direction where it would have fired harmlessly.

School-age children will also devise inner plans of action covering a period of time after the traumatized event. Children who have seen a parent murdered may fantasize executing revenge on their own, without the aid of police, courts, or prisons. An eight-year-old boy, who learned that his parent's killer had been captured, exclaimed to his friends, "Let's get some bats and play baseball with his head." An eleven-year-old girl hoped to get rich so that she could afford to pay a "hit man" one million dollars to assassinate her mother's murderer. These fantasies may also have the effect of relieving the child's guilt over not having done more to protect the parent at the time of the violent death.

Some school-age children, relying on the obsessional defenses of latency, spend an inordinate time discussing the details of the traumatic event. The child may be temporarily protected from the coexisting feelings of anxiety and grief by isolation of affect. This ploy can become a form of fixation on the trauma when it leads to unemotional, journalistic accounts of the event, which is symptomatic of the failure of trauma mastery. For instance, one eight-year-old would always introduce himself by saying, "I'm Tommy, my father killed my mother." The reverse is also possible. These children remain in a constant state of anxious arousal, as if to prepare for further danger. The terms pseudophobia (Krystal, 1978) or traumatophobia (Rado, 1942) similarly refer to the dread of a recurrence of the traumatic experience or its associations. We have discovered that in children, this hypervigilant alertness serves to replace memories of the actual traumatic event with self-initiated fantasies of future danger. A seven-year-old, who saw his father murdered by a stranger, expressed his persistent fear that he would be kidnapped from his front yard. By dwelling on his dreaded loss of personal security, he avoided discussing the actual violence that had afflicted his family.

School-age children display a diversity of behavioral alterations following the experience of psychic trauma. Relatives and teachers have complained that the children seem both different and inconsistent. Otherwise well-behaved youngsters can become irritable, rude, and argumentative. Frequently, peer relationships suffer as a result. Normally exuberant children can turn passive, inhibited, and unspontaneous. The same child may vacillate between unprovoked outbursts of aggression and prominent avoidance of conflictual situations. This can be readily apparent in the schoolyard or in team sports where physical contact is commonplace. For example, an eight-year-old boy told us that he became nauseated and ran to the lavatory when a fight erupted in the playground. This incident occurred two weeks after he saw his father stabbed by a stranger. A few children have voiced their concern that since their parent's homicide they find it harder to control their own behavior and are less trusting of adult restraint.

Reenactments and play sequences become more elaborate and sophisticated as the child grows older. School-age children may involve their friends in redramatizations and trauma-related games. A seven-year-old girl, whose father strangled her mother and then carried the body to the bedroom, forces all her friends to play the mommy game. In the mommy game, "you play dead, and I'll pick you up." Bloch et al. (1956) similarly allude to the "Tornado games" of the children in his study. However, the older child is able to communicate more extensively with words and depends less on actions to recreate the traumatic situation.

Traumatized school-age children can undergo an intense perceptual experience. For the child witnessing a parent's homicide all sensory modalities are involved: the sight, sound and smell of gunfire, the screams or sudden silence of the victims, the splash of blood on the child's clothes, the grasp of a dying parent, and the sirens of the arriving police. In addition, the child is aware of autonomic arousal and other bodily sensations. As one boy proclaimed, "My heart hurt; it was beating so loud." Children in this age group are especially susceptible to the development of psychosomatic complaints, such as stomach aches, headaches, and other bodily discomforts. Krystal (1978) attributes the high incidence of these symptoms to a post-traumatic regression in affects resulting in dedifferentiation,* deverbalization, and particularly resomatization of affect. Others point to children's propensity for identifying with the victim's physical pain (Nagera, 1970). We would suggest that the school-age child's greater awareness of and investment in body image increases the likelihood of linking anxious affect with autonomic perceptions in a recurring way.

---

*A form of thought disorganization and primitivization.

ADOLESCENT-AGE

The manifestation of adolescent trauma begins to resemble the composite of the adult post-traumatic syndrome. In fact, a principle reaction of traumatized adolescents is a precipitation of a premature entrance into adulthood or a premature closure of identity formation. It is easy to appreciate how the abrupt loss of a parent can propel an adolescent into a false sense of readiness to leave the home and community. Further, feelings of rage, shame, and betrayal can erode the teenager's position with the social group, leading to an anxious search for new horizons (Wallerstein & Kelly, 1974).

All too often the adolescent will embark upon a period of post-traumatic acting-out behavior characterized by school truancy, precocious sexual activity, substance abuse, and delinquency (Newman, 1976). Family members and teachers describe these adolescents as more rebellious and are dismayed by unusual antisocial acts. One day after her mother was shot, a 13-year-old stole a piece of jewelry from her aunt, only to return it the next day. Because of their access to automobiles and weapons, poor impulse control and reenactment behavior can be life-threatening to the adolescent. One mother shot her estranged husband in self-defense in the presence of their 17-year-old son. On the first anniversary, the boy became enraged and attempted to shoot his mother. Many adolescents will explain their use of illicit drugs as a means by which they can relieve their dysphoria arising from the traumatic event (Newman, 1976).

These actions can be understood as a form of the defense mechanism of turning against the self (Freud, 1966). It seems that because they are too old to engage in play reenactments and denial in fantasy, adolescents must use directly self-destructive behavior as a way to distract themselves from anxiety and painful memories and to expiate their guilt. Adolescent Holocaust survivors manifested chronic identity diffusion, interpersonal difficulties, and poor work values attesting to the potentially devastating consequences on personality of trauma during this developmental period (Koenig, 1964).

Though capable of giving a full account of the episode, adolescents may present as uncooperative, suspicious, and guarded in an interview. While discussing the homicide they show relatively less interest in the act of killing and more closely scrutinize the overall participation of the assailant, victim, themselves and others. Adolescents are alert to the issue of human accountability. They seem compelled to judge the courage of their own actions and reluctant to criticize the behavior of the murdered parent. Unlike school-age children who may, in fantasy, mis-interpret the cause of the trauma as their own behavior, adolescent participants can accurately identify how their actions figured in the chain of events and then inflate their own guilt feelings. One 13-year-old boy berated himself as a coward because he had been too terrified to approach his mortally wounded mother.

In spousal homicide, culpability becomes intensely painful to the adolescent. Horrified at having implicated his father as a murderer, one boy ended the police interview by stating, "But I love him." These children may have strong allegiances toward a particular parent. They understand that they can ignore or report certain facts, causing one parent to seem more at fault. For example, two siblings, residing with different parents colored their accounts accordingly. The boy neglected to mention having seen his father load the gun, while his sister's account included this fact, but omitted her mother's defiant taunt, "OK, show them what a big man you are—shoot." However, in recounting the traumatic event, adolescents are more likely to emphasize their own action or inaction on behalf of the victim or assailant. For example, the brother warned his mother not to go up to the house because his angry father stood there with a loaded shotgun, while his sister bitterly regretted her failure to unload the gun two weeks earlier when she had the chance.

Adolescents have the capacity for an abstract understanding of motivation, alternative action, and the sequencing of events over a longer duration of time. They are fully capable of anticipating how the trauma will personally affect their lives. Unlike their younger counterparts, they no longer conceive of themselves as invulnerable. On the contrary, they are exquisitely sensitive to their own imperfections and are painfully cognizant of what others might think, often fearing being stigmatized by their peer group. Adolescents specifically dread the evolution of a shared outcome with a parent victim. Many have confided to us that they plan never to marry or have children because of their belief that tragedy will repeat itself. Krystal (1971) highlights the "inhibition against assuming the function of a wife and mother" (p. 24). Anniversary responses to the trauma prompt a reaffirmation of their conviction not to tempt fate.

CONCLUSION

Previous research tended to focus on childhood risk factors associated with vulnerability or resilience to psychic trauma (Garmezy, 1983). We believe that in cases of a catastrophic psychosocial stressor, attention is more properly directed toward the course of the almost inevitable post-traumatic reaction. In particular four developmental considerations warrant close examination. First, the symptom presentation and content of a post-traumatic stress disorder may vary according to age, although the general phenomenology is often similar. We have noted that the affective and ego constriction so evident in adults may go undetected in the younger child. The specific nature of the traumatic occurrence and its meaning to the child serve as another variable. Sigmund Freud (1926) was the first to propose a developmental sequence of intrapsychic danger situations consistent with his interest in the fantasy life of children. Much more work is needed to elucidate the differential responses of children to various types of real events, from floods to murders, during each developmental phase.

Second, children's early efforts to cope with traumatic anxiety and helplessness are a function of maturity. This can be clearly seen in their evolving capacity to regulate intense affects and formulate cognitive reappraisals such as inner plans of action. Each particular traumatic incident generates its own agenda of specific tasks. As we found, witnessing physical injury to a parent results in efforts to reconstitute the parent's bodily integrity. Parental death adds a considerable burden by contaminating grief with unwelcomed violent imagery. Currently, there are no available taxonomies of childhood coping similar to those conceptualized for adults.

The third consideration is the developmental influence that can enhance or impede trauma resolution. Children, according to age, are more or less susceptible to the effects of intrapsychic, familial, and societal pressures. Phase-salient psychosexual conflicts can also interfere with the child's inner resourcefulness. In addition, any preexisting psychopathology will complicate efforts at trauma mastery. The child's reliance on the family for cognitive information and emotional support changes with age. Further, the child's ability to address issues of accountability can be seriously compromised by perceived conflicts of parental loyalty. Children and their families are embedded in a broad social network. In natural disasters the consequences of a loss of communality have been underscored (Erikson, 1976). Often overlooked are the community disruptions caused by acts of personal violence. Children and adolescents have differing sensitivities to issues of media notoriety, stigma, open court appearances and other forms of public recognition.

The fourth developmental concern is the interplay of the processes of trauma resolution and other childhood tasks. Immediately, schoolwork, play, and interpersonal relationships are hampered. The child's growing ability to assume an active role in addressing issues related to changes in current life circumstances may be eroded by traumatic anxiety. Over time, the child's progression across the individual developmental lines (Freud, 1965) may show modifications. There can be accentuations, retardations or fixations in certain areas. For instance, one adolescent may leave home prematurely, while another remains interminably. Of great concern is the danger posed by a selective deviation of impulse control and neutralization of aggression. The continued reworking of traumatic memories may cause enduring effects on cognition and learning. Persistent changes in the child's affective life can alter the perception, nature and stability of human relationships. And there may be powerful influences on the child's future orientation as reflected in major life decisions such as the choice of a spouse or a career.

We have offered a beginning approximation of the developmental perspective on psychic trauma in childhood. Future treatment strategies designed to alleviate the symptoms and minimize the pathological consequences of psychic trauma should be developmentally based. Our work so far suggests the following three guidelines: 1) Early intervention for the child to prevent maladaptive trauma resolution; 2) Professional contact to assist the family in more fully attending to the child's psychological needs; and 3) Therapeutic efforts of mental health professionals enhanced by the acquisition of special interview techniques to explore thoroughly the child's experience of the traumatic occurrence. Ultimately, longitudinal studies are required to establish the natural history of the traumatic process and the effectiveness of any specific intervention.

REFERENCES

American Psychiatric Association. *Diagnostic & statistical manual of mental disorders* (3rd ed.). Washington, DC: American Psychiatric Association, 1980.

Ayalon, O. Coping with terrorism. In D. Meichenbaum, & M. Jaremko (Eds.) *Stress reduction and prevention*. New York: Plenum Press, 1983.

Bergen, M. Effect of severe trauma on a 4-year-old child. *Psychoanalytic Study of the Child*, 1958, *13*, 407-429.

Black, D. Children and disaster. *British Medical Journal*, 1982, *285*, 989-990.

Bloch, D.A., Silber, E., & Perry, S.E. Some factors in the emotional reaction of children to disaster. *American Journal of Psychiatry*, 1956, *113*, 416-422.

Bowlby, J. The making and breaking of affectionate bonds. *British Journal of Psychiatry*, 1977, *130*, 201-208 & 421-431.

Burke, J.D., Borus, J.F., Burns, B.J., Millstein, K.H., & Beasley, M.C. Changes in children's behavior after a natural disaster. *American Journal of Psychiatry*, 1982, *139*, 1010-1014.

Carey-Trefzer, C.J. The results of a clinical study of war-damaged children who attended the child guidance clinic, The Hospital for Sick Children, Great Ormand Street, London. *Journal of Mental Science*, 1949, *95*, 535-559.

Chamberlain, B.C. The psychological aftermath of disaster. *Journal of Clinical Psychiatry*, 1980, *41*, 238-244.

Elizur, E. & Kaffman, M. Children's bereavement reactions following death of the father: II. *Journal of the American Academy of Child Psychiatry*, 1982, *21*, 474-480.

Erikson, K.T. Loss of communality at Buffalo Creek. *American Journal of Psychiatry*, 1976, *133*, 302-305.

Freud, A. *Normality and pathology in childhood.* London: Hogarth Press, 1965.

Freud, A. *Ego and mechanisms of defense.* New York: International Universities Press, 1966.

Freud, S. (1917) Introductory lectures on psychoanalysis XVII. In J. Strachey (Ed.), *Standard edition, 16,* London: Hogarth Press, 1963.

Freud, S. (1926) Inhibitions, symptoms and anxiety. In J. Strachey (Ed.), *Standard edition, 20.* London: Hogarth Press, 1959.

Freud, S. (1939) Moses and monotheism. In J. Strachey (Ed.), *Standard edition, 23.* London: Hogarth Press, 1964.

Furst, S.S. A Survey. In S.S. Furst, (Ed.), *Psychic trauma.* New York: Basic Books, 1967.

Furst, S.S. The stimulus barrier and the pathogenicity of trauma. *International Journal of Psychoanalysis*, 1978, *59*, 345-352.

Gardner, G.E. Aggression and violence-enemies of precision learning in children. *American Journal of Psychiatry*, 1971, *128*, 445-450. :

Garmezy, N. Stressors of childhood. In N. Garmezy, & M. Rutter (Eds.), *Stress, coping and development in children.* New York: McGraw-Hill, 1983.

Gislason, I.L., & Call, J.D. Dog bite in infancy: Trauma and personality development. *Journal of American Academy of Child Psychiatry*, 1982, *21*, 203-207.

Glover, E. Notes on the psychological effects of war conditions on the civilian population. III. The "Blitz." *International Journal of Psychoanalysis*, 1942, *23*, 17-37.

Green, A. Dimensions of psychological trauma in abused children. *Journal of the American Academy of Child Psychiatry*, 1983, *22*, 231-237.

Greenacre, P. The influence of infantile trauma in genetic patterns. In S.S. Furst (Ed.), *Psychic trauma.* New York: Basic Books, 1967.

Grinker, R.R., & Spiegel, J.P. *War neuroses in North Africa: The Tunisian campaign.* The Air Surgeon, Army Air Forces, NY: Josiah Macy Foundation, September, 1943.

Horowitz, M.J., Wilner, M., Kultreider, N., & Alvarez, W. Signs & symptoms of post-traumatic stress disorder. *Archives of General Psychiatry*, 1980, *37*, 85-92.

Kelly, J.B. & Wallerstein, J.S. The effects of parental divorce: Experience of the child in early latency. *American Journal of Orthopsychiatry*, 1976, *46*, 20-32.

Kelman, H. Character and the traumatic syndrome. *Journal of Nervous and Mental Disease*, 1945, *102*, 121-153.

Khan, M.M.R. The concept of cumulative trauma. *Psychoanalytic Study of the Child*, 1963, *18*, 286-306.

Klein, H. Child victims of the holocaust. *Journal of Clinical Child Psychology*, 1974, Summer 1974, 44-47.

Koenig, W.K. Chronic or persisting identity diffusion. *American Journal of Psychiatry*, 1964, *120* 1081-1084.

Krystal, H. Trauma: Considerations of its intensity and chronicity. *International Psychiatry Clinics*, 1971, *8*(1), 11-24.

Krystal, H. Trauma and affects. *Psychoanalytic Study of the Child*, 1978, *33*, 81-116.

Lifton, R.J. Psychology of the survivor and the death imprint. *Psychiatric Annals*, 1982, *12*, 1011-1020.

Lifton, R.J., & Olson, E. The human meaning of total disaster: The Buffalo Creek Experience. *Psychiatry*, 1976, *39*, 1-18.

Lonetto, R. *Children's conceptions of death.* New York: Springer, 1980.

Maclean, G. Psychic trauma and traumatic neurosis: Play therapy with a four-year-old boy. *Canadian Psychiatric Association Journal*, 1977, *22*, 71-76.

McCubbin, H.I., Joy, C.B., Cauble, A.E., Comeau, J.K., Patterson, J.M. & Needle, R.H.

Family stress and coping: A decade review. *Journal of Marriage and the Family*, 1980, 42, 855-871.

Moses, R. Adult psychic trauma: The question of early predisposition and some detailed mechanisms. *International Journal of Psychoanalysis*, 1978, 54, 353-363.

Nagera, H. Children's reactions to the death of important objects: A developmental approach. *Psychoanalytic Study of the Child*, 1970, 25, 360-500.

Newman, C.J. Children of disaster: Clinical observations at Buffalo Creek. *American Journal of Psychiatry*, 1976, 133, 306-312.

Pruett, K.R. Home treatment for 2 infants who witnessed their mother's murder. *Journal of the American Academy of Child Psychiatry*, 1979, 18, 647-657.

Pynoos, R., & Eth, S. Witness to violence: The child interview. *Journal of the American Academy of Child Psychiatry*, in press.

Pynoos, R.S. & Eth, S. Child as criminal witness to homicide. *Journal of Social Issues*, 1984, 40, 87-108.

Rado, S. Psychodynamics and treatment of traumatic war neurosis. (traumatophobia). *Psychosomatic Medicine*, 1942, 4, 362-368.

Scharl, A. Regression and restitution in object loss. *Psychoanalytic Study of the Child*, 1961, 16, 47-58.

Schetky, D.H. Preschoolers' response to murder of their mothers by their fathers: A study of 4 cases. *Bulletin of the American Academy of Psychiatry and Law*, 1978, 6, 45-47.

Senior, N., Gladstone, T., & Nurcombe, B. Child snatching: A case report. *Journal of the American Academy of Child Psychiatry*, 1982, 21, 579-583.

Solnit, A.J., & Kris, M. Trauma and infantile experience. In S.S. Furst (Ed.), *Psychic trauma*. New York: Basic Books, 1967.

Terr, L. Children of Chowchilla: Study of psychic trauma. *Psychoanalytic Study of the Child*, 1979, 34, 547-623.

Terr, L. "Forbidden games": Post-traumatic child's play. *Journal of the American Academy of Child Psychiatry*, 1981a, 20, 741-760.

Terr, L. Psychic trauma in children. *American Journal of Psychiatry*, 1981b, 138, 14-19.

Terr, L. Chowchilla revisited: The effects of psychic trauma four years after a school bus kidnapping. *American Journal of Psychiatry*, 1983a, 140, 1543-1550.

Terr, L. Life attitudes, dreams and psychic trauma in a group of "normal" children. *Journal of the American Academy of Child Psychiatry*, 1983b, 22, 221-230.

Terr, L. Time sense following psychic trauma: A clinical study of ten adults and twenty children. *American Journal of Orthopsychiatry*, 1983c, 53, 244-261.

Waelder, R. Trauma and the variety of extraordinary challenges. In S.S. Furst (Ed.), *Psychic trauma*. New York: Basic Books, 1967.

Wallerstein, J.S. Children of divorce: Stress and developmental tasks. In N. Garmezy, & M. Rutter (Eds.), *Stress, coping, and development in children*. New York: McGraw-Hill, 1983.

Wallerstein, J.S., & Kelly, J.B. The effects of parental divorce: The adolescent experience. In E.J. Anthony & C. Koupernik (Eds.), *The child in his family: Children at psychiatric risk, Vol. 3*. New York: Wiley, 1974.

Wallerstein, J.S., & Kelly, J.B. The effects of parental divorce: Experiences of the preschool child. *Journal of the American Academy of Child Psychiatry*, 1975, 14, 600-616.

Wallerstein, J.S., & Kelly, J.B. The effects of parental divorce: Experiences of the child in later latency. *American Journal of Orthopsychiatry*, 1976, 46, 256-269.

Wolfenstein, M. Introduction. In M. Wolfenstein,& G. Kliman (Eds.), *Children and the death of a president*. Garden City, NY: Doubleday, 1965.

Wolfenstein, M. How is mourning possible. *Psychoanalytic Study of the Child*, 1966, 21, 93-123.

4

Conceptualizing Post-traumatic Stress Disorder: A Psychosocial Framework

BONNIE L. GREEN, JOHN P. WILSON, and
JACOB D. LINDY

The present chapter delineates the authors' conceptualization of how catastrophic events are processed at an individual level. The model presented emphasizes individual differences in psychological outcome as a function of the nature of the person's experience. Psychological processing of the event is seen to interact with and be influenced by both long-standing characteristics of the individual, and by characteristics of the recovery environment. Case examples from a number of catastrophic events are presented which illustrate the similarities and differences across events in the manifestations of PTSD, and which focus on the variables in the model as they are illustrated in the specific cases.

INTRODUCTION

For millennia people have witnessed and been involved in extraordinarily stressful life experiences that extend well beyond the normal exigencies of day-to-day existence. From earliest times to the present day there have been wars, earthquakes, tornadoes, floods, volcanic eruptions, devastating accidents, as well as other life-threatening events of a similar magnitude which leave lasting psychic effects in the lives of ordinary people. Perhaps the breadth and pervasiveness of disaster situations can be more fully appreciated when it is noted that from 1947 to 1973 there were over 836 major disasters reported worldwide in which over 100 persons were injured or killed or which resulted in one million dollars in damages (Gleser, Green, & Winget, 1981). In approximately that same span of time (1940–1975), the United States was involved in three wars which resulted in over 10 million dead and over a million injured as a direct result of combat or civilian involvement in the wars.

As an outgrowth of the medical and psychological studies on the effects of these experiences on the survivors (Figley & Leventman, 1980; Gleser, et al., 1981; Lifton, 1967; Titchener & Kapp, 1976), it has been recognized that catastrophically stressful events can produce long-term stress responses. More recently, studies concerned with the psychological consequences of the Vietnam War have indicated that as many as 500,000 combat veterans currently suffer from stress disorders (Egendorf, Kadushin, Laufer, Rothbart, & Sloan, 1981; Figley, 1978; Wilson, 1978). From these various studies of civilian and military disasters it would appear that the incidence of such disorders may be higher than has been previously suspected. Such findings indicate that stress disorders constitute a pervasive mental health problem which requires the attention and understanding of professionals in the field.

The purpose of this chapter is to outline our conceptualizations of post-traumatic stress disorder, and to delineate the factors which affect the onset, manifestation, and course of the disorder. This is followed by case summaries from various civilian disasters and the Vietnam War, which highlight these factors of the model and some manifestations of the PTSD syndrome.

THE CLINICAL ENTITY

In the DSM-III (APA, 1980), post-traumatic stress disorder was acknowledged as a clinical entity which could arise in response to a stressful event and which could be either acute, chronic, or delayed. Defining the parameters of such a clinical response to stress has provided a point of embarkation for theoreticians, clinicians, and researchers alike in the understanding and treatment of persons who have been through traumatic experiences, either individually or collectively.

The central feature of PTSD is that the survivor reexperiences elements of the trauma in dreams, uncontrollable and emotionally distressing intrusive images, and dissociative mental states. Alternately, the victim feels numb (psychic numbing), experiences a loss of normal affect and emotional responsiveness, and exhibits less interest and involvement in work and interpersonal relationships. The reexperiencing of the trauma and the emotional constrictedness are assumed to coexist in the same individual and may occur in cycles, although one phase may predominate in a given individual or time period. Secondary symptoms occurring with the disorder may include excessive autonomic nervous system arousal, startle response, hyperalertness or hypervigilance, memory impairment, depressive symptoms, survivor guilt, avoidance of stimuli with trauma-related associational value, explosiveness, and a loss of capacity for intimacy.

Consistent with other DSM-III diagnoses, PTSD is presented descriptively as a set of symptoms which, taken together, characterize the disorder. This syndrome can also be seen as reflecting a dynamic process by which a survivor attempts to integrate a traumatic event into his or her self-structure. The process itself is a natural one and is not labeled as pathological (i.e., as a disorder) unless it is prolonged, blocked, or exceeds a tolerable quality (Zilberg, Weiss, & Horowitz, 1982). It might also be argued that in order to be considered pathological this process must interfere with regular functioning to a significant extent.

In order to explain the phenomenology of the alternating intrusion-numbing cycles of both pathological and non-pathological processing, Horowitz (1976, 1979) has proposed an information-processing model which assumes that a major aspect of human cognitive processes is the *completion tendency* in which "the mind continues to process important new information until the situation or the models change, and reality and models reach accord" (Horowitz, 1979, p. 249). Until a traumatic life event can be assimilated and successfully integrated into existing schemata, the psychological elements of the event will remain in active memory storage. They will produce thought representations of the traumatic event on all levels of cognitive functioning, which sometimes break through as emotionally upsetting, intrusive, and uncontrolled images of the event. According to Horowitz (1976), "repeated episodes of intensely conscious representation occur because 1) active memory tends toward repeated representations and 2) because representations of stress-related information are recognized as important and as hard to process to completion" (pp. 103–104). The numbing cycle of the disorder is seen as a defense against the breakthrough of these intrusive images, where the individual consciously or unconsciously wards off the memory and the meaning of the experience. It serves the function of reducing cognitive processing, thus reducing the anxiety associated with the intrusive representations. "As assimilation and accomodation occur, there is a gradual reduction in the intensity, preemptoriness and frequency of the repeated representations" (1976, p. 104). In his model, Horowitz attempts to integrate both the classical explanation of stress syndromes, i.e., the psychoanalytic theory of repetition compulsion, with more current psychological explanations which are based more on the way in which cognitive mechanisms mediate or process the stressful events (Janis, 1969; Lazarus, 1966).

Viewing the process from the perspective of psychological control mechanisms, the two poles of the process can be viewed, according to Horowitz (1979), as follows:

> Excessive controls interrupt the process, change the state of the person to some form of denial and may prevent complete processing of the event. Failures of control lead to excessive levels of emotion, flooding and retraumatization, causing entry into intrusive states. Optimal controls slow down recognition processes and so provide tolerable doses of new information and emotional responses. (p. 249)

Eventually, if working through occurs, the new external information is incorporated into the preexisting internal model and, gradually, information storage in active memory will terminate. At completion, the experience is integrated so it is a part of the individual's view of the world and of him- or herself, and it no longer needs to be walled off from the rest of his or her personality. Until this working through has occurred, the individual can be viewed as experiencing psychic overload, a state in which the immensity of the experience(s) is not understandable in the context of the existing model of reality. The normal ego-defensive and coping mechanisms have been overwhelmed and are not adequate to deal with the trauma (Horowitz, 1979).

As explicated in the next section, if conditions are favorable, the working through process may take place naturally, and an end state which is adaptive may occur. If conditions are not favorable, the individual may require help in the working through process to modulate intrusions and the defenses against them. In the most unfavorable circumstances, the working through may not occur at all, and some form of psychopathology will be the ultimate outcome. It has not yet been empirically determined whether there is a critical point beyond which it is difficult or impossible to go back and work through a traumatic experience in a successful way. However, it has been proposed that the passage of time may be inversely related to the ease with which such working through may occur, due to the rigidity that defensive structures may acquire over time (Titchener & Kapp, 1978).

Some individuals may not experience psychic overload in the first place, depending on the nature of their particular experience. In these cases, the individual would be able to assimilate the traumatic event in such a way that it does not become part of active memory storage but is integrated in a congruent manner into existing cognitive schemata (Antonovsky, 1979).

FACTORS INFLUENCING POST-TRAUMATIC STRESS DISORDER

The preceding section has focused on the phenomenology of the stress response as it manifests itself following a variety of individual and group traumatic events. However, not all people develop a formal stress disorder. It is, therefore, of interest from both a clinical and research standpoint, which factors lead to psychic overload and a final adaptation in terms of psychological response. To address this question, one must develop a conceptual model of the process by which a particular traumatic event leads to a particular psychological process, and finally to some symptomatic or functional outcome. This model must take into account characteristics of a particular individual (survivor) and characteristics of the environment in which that individual experiences and attempts to recover from the trauma.

A working model was developed to guide clinical work and empirical investigations and is depicted in Figure 1. The primary sequence in this model is the occurrence of a catastrophic event of which the person has his or her particular experience; the cognitive (conscious and unconscious) processing of that event; and a final (positive or negative) adaptation in terms of functioning. The processing of the event (it's

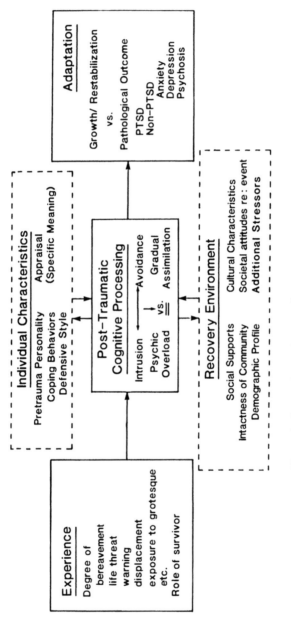

Figure 1. Processing a Catastrophic Event: A Working Model

appraisal, alternations between intrusion and avoidance, and whether it reaches a point of psychic overload) takes place within an individual and a social context. Thus, whether a person is able to assimilate the trauma gradually and restabilize is dependent on what individual characteristics he or she brings to bear when perceiving, understanding, and dealing with the event. It is also dependent on the social environment in which the event and the working through take place. These three constructs are briefly delineated below. First, however, it should be noted that the model proposed is one which describes processing of an event at an *individual* level. Thus, it focuses on the person's particular experience of an event and how that ultimately influences a final adaptation. This notion implies that different people who are present at the *same event* will have different outcomes because, not only will their experiences differ, but the individual characteristics they bring to bear upon the psychological processing are different, and this processing may take place in differing recovery environments.

Catastrophic events themselves may also be conceptualized as varying along a number of dimensions which, in collective situations, would affect their psychological impact in terms of the number of people affected. However, this level of analysis is a group level and is not really relevant here. A review of dimensions of disaster and comparisons among disasters with regard to psychological impact can be found in an earlier review (Green, 1982).

Person's Experience of the Event

Although a relatively recent development, there is a growing literature which is attempting to relate specific aspects of a person's experience during a catastrophic event to their later psychological functioning. There is some beginning evidence that certain experiences are empirically connected with long-term functioning. Some of these experiences, examined within collectively stressful circumstances (disasters, war), and shown to be related to outcome, include the following: bereavement (Gleser, et al., 1981; Green, Grace, & Gleser, in press; Green, Grace, Lindy, Titchener, & Lindy, 1983); displacement (Gleser, et al., 1981; Huerta & Horton, 1978); life-threat (Adler, 1943; Gleser, et al., 1981; Green et al., in press); exposure to grotesque sights (Green et al., in press; Taylor & Frazer, 1982); and combat stress (Foy, Sipprelle, Rueger & Carroll, 1984; Penk, Robinowitz, Roberts, Patterson, Dolan & Atkins, 1981). An additional variable that we would like to suggest is that the particular role taken by the survivor may also be important. Thus, being a patron at a nightclub that burns to the ground may be a very different experience than being a rescue worker who arrives on the scene after the fire is burning. Issues of preparation and suddenness would probably be important here. Likewise, whether a person is a passive victim in such a situation, or takes a role which could be considered more active (an *agent* role), we feel could also be important. The person who convinced a group to attend the nightclub where the fire occurred and where members died would probably be at higher risk than the person who just happened to be in attendance on a particular night. Likewise, a soldier in combat not only has experiences happen to *him*, but he acts on the environment as well and may be involved in killing or injuring others. We feel that such circumstances would increase the risk for later impairment.

Individual Characteristics

The extent to which personality characteristics affect response to stress is still being debated. At this point, however, most writers take an interactional approach, assuming that neither individual characteristics nor aspects of the stressful event solely determine outcome (Wilson, Smith, & Johnson, 1984). Early expressions of this interaction can be found in Hocking (1970) and Saul & Lyons (1961). Lazarus and his colleagues (Lazarus, Averill, & Opton, 1974) have developed a model of the coping process that takes into account not only the stressor itself, but the person's *appraisal* of that stressor based on his or her prior experience. DSM-III suggests that *preexisting psychopathology* predisposes individuals to develop PTSD. This has not yet been empirically investigated. There is some evidence that prior characteristics of the individual do predict post-traumatic adjustment (Helzer, Robins, Wish & Hesselbrock, 1979). Relative to preexisting personality is the notion of *prior stressful events* that may make a person more vulnerable and/or affect his or her appraisal of the situation. These have been related to outcome in such situations as well (Green, et al., in press). *Coping mechanisms* of the individual have also been studied in this context. This variable has clearly been empirically demonstrated to mediate the relationship between a stressful experience and its outcome (Anderson, 1976; Gleser et al., 1981; Weisman & Worden, 1977).

Recovery Environment

Less emphasized in the disaster literature have been those aspects of the social environment which may contribute to the person's ultimate adaptation. The most often examined variable in this group is that of *social supports* and, not surprisingly, more supportive environments tend to be associated with a better adjustment to stress (Andrews, Tennant, Hewson & Vaillant, 1978; Burge & Figley, in press; Green, et al., in press). This variable may be viewed as either an individual characteristic or as a characteristic of the social system, i.e., more supports may be available in a particular recovery environment and some people may make better use of such supports than others. The other variables which we see as falling into this category have been less well-conceptualized and studied. Lindy, Grace, & Green (1981) discussed the potential impact of cultural characteristics on the particular way in which survivors respond. Thus survivors who come from a midwestern, middle- to upper-class setting might be expected to perceive and respond to the same event in a way that is potentially quite different than those from a lower class Appalachian culture. Lindy et al. (1981) also discussed an aspect of the recovery environment that they called *trauma membrane*, a phenomenon which played an important role in efforts to reach out to a disaster population in order to study, educate, and treat the survivors. We found that family and friends of survivors often formed a sort of membrane around the survivors which functioned to protect them from people and circumstances that threatened to be further traumatic. To penetrate the membrane (for study or therapeutic intervention) one had to be screened in some fashion and ultimately viewed as helpful, not harmful. The extent to which this membrane was ultimately helpful to the survivor, or served to keep him or her from getting help, could not be determined.

An additional set of variables contributing to the appraisal and working through of a traumatic experience are what we usually call *demographic characteristics* (e.g., age, social class, level of education) (Lumsden, 1975). These factors would represent the groups with which a person is identified within a particular society. For example, better educated people seem to make a better adjustment following a disaster (Gleser et al., 1981; Green et al., in press).

Finally, an aspect of the recovery environment which is just recently beginning to receive attention involves the *attitudes of the society*, and of family and friends within that society toward the traumatic event. This variable is receiving the most attention with regard to returning veterans from the Vietnam War (Figley, 1978; Figley & Leventman, 1980). "Homecoming" for these individuals is being increasingly focused on, since it appears that in some cases, the return to an environment hostile to the traumatic event (the war) and to those who participated (and were traumatized) at the least exacerbates the psychological effects of combat, and may well account directly for some of the negative effects. There are other experiences (e.g., rape) in which the victim may be "blamed" that would also fall into this general category.

CASE ILLUSTRATIONS

Following are four brief case histories of individuals who endured four separate disasters. They illustrate the clinical integrity of the syndrome, post-traumatic stress disorder, as it expresses itself following differing disasters. The working model is used to guide the presentations. The individual case presentations emphasize the relationship between the experience of the event and the clinical picture. The combined discussion additionally highlights how individual and social factors noted in the model influence the form and the intensity of the outcome.

Case 1—Buffalo Creek

> *Mr. A. was a 40-year-old Caucasian man, married, father of two children, ages 11 and 17, who was interviewed alone and together with his family two years after the Buffalo Creek Dam collapse and flood of 1972 (Titchener & Kapp, 1976).*
>
> *He was a clerical employee of the coal company which was responsible for building the collapsed dam. He and his family had been in Appalachia for more than five generations and he had lived his entire life in the hollow of Buffalo Creek. He was a participant in the class action suit against the coal company.*
>
> *Mr. A. minimized his emotional response to the disaster. There was "nothin' wrong with my head." He did, however, admit to "nerves," by which he was referring to a diffuse anxiety state, and observed that "my body just hasn't been the same," referring here to vague epigastric distress and more diffuse muscle aches throughout his body. He argued that these physical symptoms were the cause of his inability to sleep, which had persisted for the past two years. On closer questioning, he reported recurrent nightmares in which black water was carrying away trees and people. He was particularly struck by the repetitive image of children's bodies floating downstream while men stood by on nearby housetops, helplessly watching. Mr. A. also observed that between 2:00 and 4:00 a.m., he had a habit of leaving the upstairs bedroom and sleeping on the couch where he looked out a front bay window in the direction from which*

the flood came. His son, who also had difficulty sleeping, would return from pacing the living room to his bedroom at about the time father would come out to watch. Mr. A. had been listless in his peer relationships and in his relationships with the family: "I keep thinking this is the time I would put in our garden, but not this year. I don't seem to have the energy. Besides nothing will grow here anymore."

When the dam burst, Mr. A. remembers being panic-stricken. As the tidal waters ripped through the valley, Mr. A. climbed to the attic of his house, closed his eyes and prayed. He failed to secure property, failed to be of comfort to his wife and younger child, and particularly lost face in front of his teenage son, who went about the business of bolting the house and moving valuables when possible to safe locations. From the attic he helplessly watched as the careening body of water ripped apart most of the environment around him, leaving his home standing but permanently damaged. In the aftermath, Mr. A. temporarily fled the valley, not participating in the process of digging out his belongings. Later, he passively complied with regulations and was now living in temporary housing quarters supplied by Housing and Urban Development (HUD). Two years after the disaster, none of the community organizations which had been so prevalent in his life previously were functional.

In summary, Mr. A. was exposed to the traumas of the slag dam burst, flood, and aftermath. His life was threatened, he lost his home, his community, and many relatives (none in the immediate family). Two years later, Mr. A. had nightmares, sleep disturbance, and unconscious hypervigilance. He also had somatic preoccupations, withdrawal from close relationships, and excessive guilt and shame. His dominant affect was depressed. Mr. A. met DSM-III criteria of PTSD.

Case 2—Wichita Falls

In June, 1978, a tornado devastated a mile-wide strip through the city of Wichita Falls, Texas. Mr. B., a 35-year-old married man, with two small children, was seen four weeks after the tornado. Mr. B. had grown up in Wichita Falls, as had his parents. He was an administrator. He and his wife had recently bought a new home in a pleasant suburb. Mr. B. was a non-practicing Baptist. Mr. B. had a premonition that the full impact of the tornado experience had yet to hit him. He reported sleeplessness for one week following the *tornado, but since that time had been doing better. There were no nightmares. He became diffusely anxious whenever dark clouds appeared in the sky. He was at this point actively engaged in the community's response to remove the debris from the devastation and to mobilize community efforts in the rebuilding process. Mr. B. found himself almost driven to find and perform acts of community and social good will. He had been helping neighbors and friends day in and day out since the tornado and had taken little time for himself or his immediate family.*

Mr. B. described his experience in the tornado as being initially calm, not suspecting that the visible tornado in the distance would come as close as it did. Like others in his community, he listened to instructions by TV and radio and climbed into the bathtub with his two young children and wife, one mattress underneath and one on top of them. The sound of the tornado was like one thousand locomotives and the experience of enduring it was one of confronting imminent death. Hearing the devastation about them, Mr. B. waited long minutes, and removed the mattress to find his house totally obliterated.

Mr. B. was exposed to a major tornado. He lost his new house. He and his family suffered minor injuries. Four weeks later he was experiencing trigger anxiety (dark clouds), intense activity in community rebuilding, increased irritability, and some minor sleep disturbances. Mr. B. did not meet DSM-III criteria of PTSD.

Case 3—Beverly Hills Fire

In May, 1977 (Memorial Day weekend), a supper club with a crowd of more than 3,000 people burned to the ground. One hundred sixty-five patrons and employees were killed in the fire.

Mr. C., a 57-year-old member of the supper club orchestra, was first interviewed six months after the fire which killed two of his closest friends and destroyed the center of his social and economic life. Mr. C.'s family had been in the area for generations and were actively practicing Catholics.

Mr. C. was housebound at the time of the interview, save for rare occasions. He had given up playing his musical instrument, and was preoccupied and glum. Intrusive images of his dead friends and of the fire interfered with waking hours, and nightmares in which he fled in panic from encroaching flames were recurrent. He was preoccupied with guilt with regard to the death of his two friends, one of whom he felt certain he could have saved. Mr. C. became anxious about smoke, as at barbecue picnics, as well as claustrophobic. Mr. C. held the conviciton that he, rather than his friends, should have died in the fire.

Mr. C. was one of the last people to leave the building alive. In his haste, he failed to warn a close friend whom he thought was directly behind him. In addition, Mr. C. searched through stacks of asphyxiated and charred bodies in an effort to establish whether or not his friend was dead.

In summary, Mr. C. barely escaped with his life at the Beverly Hills fire, where he lost two of his closest friends, his place of work and much of his social life. Six months later, he experienced intrusive images, nightmares, trigger anxiety (smoke), excessive shame and guilt. He had severely withdrawn from interpersonal investments, a decreased libido, and was overtly depressed. Mr. C. met criteria for PTSD with an underlying premorbid depression.

Case 4—Vietnam

Mr. D. was a 34-year-old man who was interviewed 13 years after his return from his second tour of combat duty in Vietnam. Mr. D. was a third generation midwesterner. He grew up in a working class environment, attended a Protestant church, was a strong advocate of midwest values, including hard work, integrity, and patriotic ideals.

Mr. D. was prone to fits of rage during which he would get into fights with friends or strangers or strike his wife. He frequently carried a gun with him for protection. Mr. D. was agitated and tense most of the time, and particularly sensitive to harmful errors made by people in authority.

Mr. D. continued to have dreams which woke him at night. The dreams repeated episodes of his war experience, particularly being overrun on a hill where he was looking about him and seeing his friends die, an image of a Vietcong boy whom Mr. D. killed by smashing his forehead with his rifle, and images of women and children whom he saw in body counts and who in fact may have died from his bullets or napalm. Mr. D. had hyperalert responses to certain noises, particularly backfiring of automobiles and firecrackers on the Fourth of July. He was obsessed with the fear that his home was being encroached upon by unruly, vulgar neighbors who deserved to be "wasted."

Mr. D.'s experience in Vietnam was that of a marine in combat.

He saw action in search and destroy missions. His unit was overrun twice. He was one of two survivors on one occasion. In search and destroy missions, he fired on the supposed enemy, many of whom were women and children.

In summary, Mr. D. was repeatedly exposed to ambush situations as a marine. His unit was overrun, his best friend killed. He probably killed many women and children in search and destroy missions. Mr. D., 13 years later, had recurrent nightmares, intrusive images, hypervigilance, irritability and rage attacks, in which there was unconscious repetition of earlier traumatic experiences. Major affects were suspicion and rage. Mr. D. met DSM-III criteria for PTSD.

Discussion of Cases

Of particular interest in these cases is the linkage between specific symptoms and the traumatizing experience. Mr. A.'s sleep disturbance suggested an unconscious lookout for further flood damage. The loss of his hobby of gardening symbolically condenses the damaged environment and damaged self. The content of traumatic dreams repeats the circumstances of the flood, in particular the segments in which he felt that he failed to act "like a man."

Although Mr. B. did not have a diagnosis of PTSD, he did exhibit some symptoms which indicated a linkage with his specific disaster experience. Specifically, he experienced anxiety with regard to weather conditions reminiscent of the tornado.

Mr. C.'s specific symptoms were also related to the nature of his individual experience in the fire. His giving up playing his musical instrument was related to guilt over the death of his best friend, a musician of superior talent. The specific intrusive images contained the affects of shame and guilt with regard to his perceived unheroic functioning during the fire itself. The trigger symptom of barbecue fires was directly related to smelling burning flesh in the fire.

On an individual level, Mr. D. continued to be symptomatic with his irritation and rage at incompetent and dangerous authority in ways which directly related to his experience in Vietnam. The specific intrusive images and nightmare representations of children and women contained the nucleus of his shame and guilt in connection with search and destroy missions in which he killed civilians. His most troublesome current symptom of the fear of being encroached upon by unruly neighbors is both a repetition of his ambush position and a direct transposition and projection of the circumstances in which he, as an American marine, harassed, encroached upon and made impossible the lives of civilians, including children, in Vietnam.

Individual characteristics such as coping during the catastrophe, influence subsequent adaptation. During the days immediately after the slag dam flood at Buffalo Creek, Mr. A. withdrew. He had been acutely ashamed of his behavior, sought isolation, and ultimately arranged temporary housing outside the valley. As a result, he failed to join teams of volunteers who literally dug out the mud-filled towns. In retrospect, survivors who took on this task did better. Such helping activity shortly after the disaster turned out to be a moderating variable in terms of decreasing overall long-term pathology (Gleser et al., 1981).

Mr. C., at the scene of the fire, chose to examine the bodies of burned and asphyxiated patrons one by one in an effort to find the body of his friend. In retrospect, this activity (probably because of its traumatic imagery) turned out to be predictive of increased psychopathology one year later (Green et al., in press.)

Social factors also affect subsequent adaptation. Culturally, Mr. A., like many dwellers in Buffalo Creek, was a fifth-generation Appalachian, while Mr. C. and Mr. D. were from typical midwestern backgrounds, possibly influencing the particular types of symptoms (e.g., somatic complaints) manifested. Mr. D., like others in Vietnam, was 19 years old during his major exposure to trauma; other survivor populations are more likely to be evenly spread throughout the life span. Mr. B. (Wichita Falls), who was doing fairly well, was a survivor of a natural disaster (tornado); the others who were doing worse clinically experienced manmade disasters, suggesting a potentially important distinction between traumatic events. Also, the survivors of Buffalo Creek, Beverly Hills, and Wichita Falls were largely passive victims of forces beyond their control. In contrast, Mr. D., like his counterparts in combat in Vietnam, was an agent of trauma and death as well as a victim.

Finally, in terms of recovery environment, Mr. A. and Mr. B. remained in communities that were massively destroyed. But Buffalo Creek's social fabric remained disrupted for more than two years, while Wichita Falls was remobilizing within three months. On the other hand, Mr. C. and Mr. D. returned to homes untouched by the trauma. Mr. C. was greeted acceptingly, while Mr. D. was rejected along with the war he fought. All of these distinctions are potentially relevant when it comes to the form and intensity of the post-trauma syndrome.

REFERENCES

Adler, A. Neuropsychiatric complications in victims of Boston's Coconut Grove disaster. *Journal of the American Medical Association*, 1943, *123*, 1098-1101.

American Psychiatric Association. *Diagnostic and statistical manual of mental disorders* (3rd ed.). Washington, DC: American Psychiatric Association, 1980.

Anderson, C.R. Coping behaviors as intervening mechanisms in the inverted U stress performance relationship. *Journal of Applied Psychology*, 1976, *61*, 30-34.

Antonovsky, A. *Health, stress and coping.* San Francisco: Jossey-Bass, 1979.

Burge, S.B., & Figley, C.R. The Social Support Scale. Development and initial estimates of reliability and validity. *Family Process*, in press.

Egendorf, A., Kadushin, C., Laufer, R. Rothbart, G., & Sloan, L. Legacies of Vietnam: Comparative adjustment of veterans and their peers. Washington, DC: U.S. Government Printing Office, 1981.

Figley, C.R. (Ed.). *Stress disorders among Vietnam veterans: Theory, research and treatment.* New York: Brunner/Mazel, 1978.

Figley, C.R., & Leventman, S. (Eds.). *Strangers at home: Vietnam veterans since the war.* New York: Praeger, 1980.

Figley, C.R., & Southerly, W.T. Psychosocial adjustments of recently returned veterans. In C.R. Figley & S. Leventman (Eds.), *Strangers at home: Vietnam veterans since the war.* New York: Praeger, 1980.

Foy, D.W., Sipprelle, R.C., Rueger, D.B., & Carroll, E.M. Etiology of post-traumatic stress disorder in Vietnam veterans: Analysis of premilitary, military, and combat exposure influences. *Journal of Consulting and Clinical Psychology*, 1984, *52*, 88-96.

Gleser, G.C., Green, B.L., & Winget, C.N. *Prolonged psychosocial effects of disaster: A study of Buffalo Creek* New York: Academic Press, 1981.

Green, B.L. Assessing levels of psychological impairment following disaster: A consideration of actual and methodological dimensions. *Journal of Nervous and Mental Disease*, 1982, *170*, 544-552.

Green, B.L., Grace, M.C., & Gleser, G.C. Identifying survivors at risk: Long-term impairment following the Beverly Hills Supper Club Fire. *Journal of Consulting and Clinical Psychology*, in press.

Green, B.L., Grace, M.C., Lindy, J.D., Titchener, J.L., & Lindy, J.G. Levels of functional impairment following a civilian disaster: The Beverly Hills Supper Club Fire. *Journal of Consulting and Clinical Psychology*, 1983, *50*, 573-580.

Helzer, J., Robins, L.N., Wish, E., & Hesselbrock, M. Depression in Vietnam veterans and civilian controls. *American Journal of Psychiatry*, 1979, *136*, 526-529.

Hocking, F. Psychiatric aspects of extreme environmental stress. *Diseases of the Nervous System*, 1970, *31* 542-545.

Horowitz, M.J. *Stress response syndromes* (pp. 104-105). New York: Jason Aronson, 1976.

Horowitz, M.J. Psychological response to serious life events. In V. Hamilton, & D.M. Warburton (Eds.), *Human stress and cognition.* New York: Wiley, 1979.

Huerta, F. & Horton, R. Coping behavior of elderly flood victims. *The Gerontologist*, 1978, *18*, 541-546.

Janis, I.L. *Stress and frustration.* New York: Harcourt, Brace, Jovanovich, 1969.

Lazarus, R.S. *Psychological stress and coping.* New York: McGraw-Hill, 1966.

Lazarus, R.S., Averill, J.R., & Opton, E.M. Jr. The psychology of coping: Issues of research and assessment. In G.V. Coelho, D.A. Hamburg, & J.E. Adams (Eds.), *Coping and adaptation.* New York: Basic Books, 1974.

Lifton, R.J. *Death in life: Survivors of Hiroshima.* New York: Random House, 1967.

Lindy, J.D., Grace, M.C., & Green, B.L. Survivors: Outreach to a reluctant population. *American Journal of Orthopsychiatry*, 1981, *51*, 468-478.

Lumsden, D.P. Towards a systems model of stress: Feedback from an anthropological study of the impact of Ghana's Volta River project. In I.G. Sarason & C.D. Spielberger (Eds.), *Stress and anxiety, Vol. 2*. Washington, DC: Hemisphere, 1975.

Penk, W.E., Robinowitz, R., Roberts, W.R., Patterson, E.T., Dolan, M.D., & Atkins, H.G. Adjustment differences among male substance abusers varying in degree of combat experience in Vietnam. *Journal of Consulting and Clinical Psychology*, 1981, *49*, 426-437.

Saul, L.J., & Lyons, J.W. Acute neurotic reactions. In F. Alexander, & H. Ross (Eds.), *The impact of Freudian psychiatry*. Chicago: University of Chicago Press, 1961.

Taylor, A.J., & Frazer, A.G. The stress of post-disaster body handling and victim identification work. *Journal of Human Stress*, 1982, *8*, 4-12.

Titchener, J.L. & Kapp, F.T. Family and character change at Buffalo Creek. *American Journal of Psychiatry*, 1976, *133*, 295-299.

Titchener, J.L., & Kapp, F. Post-traumatic decline. Presented at the American Psychoanalytic Association Meeting, New York, 1978.

Weisman, A.D. & Worden, J.W. *Coping and vulnerability in cancer patients*. Boston: Harvard Medical School, 1977.

Wilson, J.P. *Identity, ideology and crisis: The Vietnam veteran in transition, Vol. II*. Washington, DC: Disabled American Veteran, 1978.

Wilson, J.P., Smith, W.K., & Johnson, S.K. A comparative analysis of post-traumatic stress syndrome among survivors exposed to different stressor events. In C.R. Figley (Ed.), *Trauma and its wake*. New York: Brunner/Mazel, 1985.

Zilberg, N.J., Weiss, D.S., & Horowitz, M.J. Impact of event scale: A cross-validation study and some empirical evidence supporting a conceptual model of stress response syndromes. *Journal of Consulting and Clinical Psychology*, 1982, *50*, 407-414.

RECENT RESEARCH FINDINGS

CHAPTER

5

Traumatic Stressors in the Vietnam War and Post-traumatic Stress Disorder

ROBERT S. LAUFER, ELLEN FREY-WOUTERS,
and MARK S. GALLOPS

In this chapter we examine the relationship between experiential and subjective indicators of war stress among 326 Vietnam veterans from the Legacies of Vietnam study. Our findings show that experiential indicators of war stress are more consistent predictors of PTSD symptoms. However, we found several subjective indicators of war stress which were also significantly related to PTSD symptoms and disorder. The most consistent relationship was between denial of war stress and subsequent intrusive imagery and numbing symptoms. We conclude that veterans' descriptions of their responses to war trauma are impor-

The findings presented in this chapter are part of the Vietnam Veterans and Controls Study at the Center for Policy Research. Funding for this study has been provided by NIMH grant RO1MH26832-06, and Veterans Administration Contracts V101(134) P-610 and V101 (134) P130. We wish to express our appreciation for the support of this study by both NIMH and the VA. The authors are solely responsible for the findings and conclusions.

73

tant to understanding the enduring relationship between war stress and PTSD.

INTRODUCTION

The literature on traumatic stress disorders covers a broad range of events which are concerned with experiences outside the realm of everyday life. In all such events, whether they be natural disasters or events created by human actions such as war and terrorism, one of the central problems facing researchers is the specification of the stressors and their measurement. The problem of the specification of stress is especially important because of its inclusion in the post-traumatic stress disorder (PTSD) diagnosis in *Diagnostic and Statistical Manual*, 3rd Edition (DSM-III) (American Psychiatric Association, 1980). One key research question is how to differentiate elements of stressful experiences. There are two major components of the problem. First, there is the issue of the experiential indicators of the trauma, i.e., what kinds of stress arise from particular types of objectively defined experience. Second, there is the issue of how individuals cope with this stress. The ability of humans to deal with stress is in large part a function of the initial psychological reactions it produces. These reactions should determine whether long-term stress reactions develop. Once we have established the responses of individuals to traumatic stress, we can determine to what extent they significantly predict long-term symptomatological responses to the stressors, and whether they add to the effects of traumatic experiences.

The literature on the Vietnam War has demonstrated that there are several dimensions of war stress which must be examined in analyzing the incidence and prevalence of PTSD in Vietnam veterans. There is general agreement that combat experience is a central element in estimating the effects of the war experience (Card, 1983; Figley, 1978; Harris, 1980; Laufer, Yager, Frey-Wouters, & Donellan, 1981; Wilson, 1978). But combat exposure is not the sole traumatic experience in a war situation. Other research has demonstrated that there are additional aspects of war stress which need to be incorporated into a conceptualization of traumatic war experiences. In his Vietnam experience scale, Foy (1980) suggested that atrocities were likely to contribute to post-traumatic stress disorder. Other research reports (Laufer, Brett & Gallops, 1983a, 1983b; Laufer, Gallops & Frey-Wouters, 1984) have demonstrated that exposure to abusive violence does contribute to post-traumatic stress disorder independently of the effect of combat. Wilson's (Wilson & Krauss, 1982) work suggests that the physical environment, e.g., the terrain and weather, and subjective reports of stress in combat also play important roles in long-term response to the trauma. The accumulating evidence indicates that there are a range of independent traumatic stressors implicated in post-traumatic stress disorder among Vietnam veterans.

In this chapter we will examine the above issues in the context of Vietnam veterans' responses to the stress of the war through an analysis of data collected in the Legacies of Vietnam study (Egendorf, Kadushin, Laufer, Rothbart, & Sloan, 1981). We will describe the major forms of war stress, discuss the relationships between experiential and subjective indicators of war stress, examine their relative power in predicting long-term post-traumatic stress symptomatology and finally interpret the implications of our findings for understanding the general relationship between stressors and PTSD.

THE SAMPLE

The Legacies of Vietnam study was commissioned by the Veterans Administration to study the physical, psychological, and behavioral impact of military service on veterans who served during the Vietnam War. The sample was constructed of civilians, Vietnam era veterans, and Vietnam veterans so that comparisons could be made across veteran status groups. The sample was collected in 10 sites and stratified on the basis of race and age, as well as veteran status. Telephone screening identified eligible respondents who were then interviewed personally (Rothbart, Fine, & Sudman, 1982). These interview sessions took from three to five hours in which both close- and open-ended information was obtained, the latter being taped and later transcribed. The data for the study were collected in two waves. Respondents in the New York areas sites* were interviewed in 1976 and 1977. Respondents in the other seven sites** were interviewed in 1978 and 1979 (Rothbart, 1981).

The full sample contained 1,342 men who were non-institutionalized at the time of the interview; thus, those in prisons, hospitals, or men still in the military were excluded from the sample. The sample contained 350 Vietnam veterans, 363 Vietnam era veterans and 629 non-veterans.

---

*The three New York area sites were Brooklyn and Westchester, New York, and Bridgeport, Long Island.
**These sites were: 1) Atlanta, GA, 2) Columbus, GA, 3) the rural area outside Columbus, 4) Chicago, IL, 5) South Bend, IN, 6) the rural area outside South Bend, and 7) Los Angeles, CA.

This chapter will deal exclusively with the men in the sample who had service experience in Vietnam. From this group we excluded a special subsample of 24 Chicano veterans who were interviewed in Los Angeles because they do not represent the general Hispanic and Latino population of the country. The sample of Vietnam veterans examined consists of 226 whites and 100 blacks. +

VARIETIES OF WAR STRESS

Combat

Combat is a generally recognized indicator of war stress. The combat scale used here (Laufer et al.,1981) is essentially a measure of the extent to which the veteran's life was threatened, and the range of experiences also provides a latent measure of the frequency of exposure to life-threatening situations.* A number of studies also include whether or not the veteran was in a situation where he actually killed someone. Because of the moral and psychological implications of this act the experience of killing is treated separately.

Respondents commonly reported that general combat exposure led, over time, to psychological impairment and dysfunctioning. The following comments were made by an army helicopter pilot who had heavy exposure.

+Because the sample is stratified, artifically changing the demographic balance of the groups from that of the population from which it was drawn, a weighting factor was constructed to make each local sample representative of the population of that site. All descriptive statistics (means, percentages, and correlations) are based on weighted data. The regression analyses, used to allow multiple controls to be introduced in testing relationships, are based on the unweighted data. Using the multiple regression technique allowed for all factors involved in the stratified sampling design to be controlled. All significance tests reported refer to analysis of the unweighted data.

*The Combat scale is composed of ten items. They are: 1) Served in an artillery unit which fired on the enemy; 2) Flew in an aircraft over Vietnam; 3) Stationed at a forward observation post; 4) Received incoming fire; 5) Encountered mines or booby traps; 6) Received sniper or sapper fire; 7) In a patrol which was ambushed; 8) Engaged VC or NVA in a firefight; 9) Saw Americans or Vietnamese killed; and 10) Was wounded. The scale was coded in an additive fashion. Items 1 through 6 were given a value of 1 if true, items 7 though 10 were given a value of 2 if true. The value of each experience was added cumulatively. The maximum range on the scale was from (0), Had none of these experiences, to (14) Had all of these experiences. The effective range of the scale in our sample was (0) to (13). The mean of the scale was 5.9; the median 5.7; and the standard deviation 4.1 (the characteristics of the weighted data). Nine percent of the sample saw no combat, 33% saw low combat (values 1 through 4), 31% moderate combat (values 5 through 9), and 27% saw heavy combat (values 10 through 13).

I started going crazy. I could not seem to handle the kinds of pressure I was under. I started getting hallucinations. I could not sleep. . . . I was waking up all the time. We flew extraordinarily long missions every day. This problem I had got worse and worse. The flight surgeon there said, "Take these tranquilizers but only at night because it is illegal to fly under the influence of a drug. They should calm you down." I did that and I still got worse. . . . I continued flying . . . I was aware that I was starting to disintegrate. My nerves were going and I could not sleep and I was losing weight. Those were typical symptoms of a high degree of an emotional conflict. It was tearing me apart and I knew it.

Participation in and Witnessing of Abusive Violence

Another type of experience which has been linked to PTSD symptomatology and disorder is exposure to abusive violence directed against non-combatants.* The stress of war in a guerrilla campaign differs in kind from that experienced in conventional conflicts. Our narratives show that many of the strains placed on conventional forces in a guerrilla campaign stem from the inability of these forces to distinguish between non-combatants and the enemy. This problem is, for the most part, absent in a conventional conflict. Guerrilla warfare creates pressures which lead to and sanction acts of brutality against civilians and prisoners of war. The American experience in Vietnam saw a significant number of such episodes by the North Vietnamese, Vietcong, South Vietnamese

---

*In measuring exposure to abusive violence we used a set of open-ended questions in which the veteran was asked whether he experienced the dirty side of war and to describe the events in this category. We required that veterans had at least witnessed the event or to have seen its consequences soon after its commission and to have clearly known who had carried it out. In order to make the measure an indicator of objective experiences we eliminated any events of which they had heard secondhand. In our sample roughly a third (31%) reported they were directly exposed to at least one episode. These episodes varied in character but the most often cited were: the torture of prisoners, including pushing them from helicopters; the physical mistreatment of civilians; the use of napalm, white phosphorous or cluster bombs on villages; death or maiming by booby trap; and the mutilation of bodies. Most of the men who reported episodes described cases in which U.S. regulars were involved (78% of those exposed). Less than a third mentioned ones in which the Vietcong or NV regulars were involved (31% of those exposed). Another 13% reported cases in which ARVN or Korean (ROK) forces were involved. (These three figures do not sum to 100% since over a third of those exposed mentioned more than one episode.)

In previous work we differentiated the effects of exposure to abusive violence by the perpetrator of the act. Our findings suggest that the traumatic quality of the experience is the imagery associated with it; the issue of who initiated the action was not significant if the veteran had only witnessed the event and did not participate in it personally.

and American forces. In our transcripts we found three general types of episodes described: actions against civilians, actions against prisoners of war, and the use of cruel weaponry. In our study, 22% of the Vietnam veterans were exposed to abusive violence and 9% participated in such actions.

Exposure to abusive violence put pressure on soldiers, in addition to the stress produced by the struggle to survive. Men were exposed to arbitrary and immoral acts of violence which ignored the value of human life and the rules of human relations. The reflections of one Army infantryman on his experience of the abuses to which Vietnamese civilians were exposed suggest the long-term depressing and disorienting impact of these experiences.

> These acts make you think there is no God. It destroys a whole lot of young men . . . because when they come home they are not the same anymore. They cannot do the things that everybody might want to do . . . the simple things . . . play ball or go bowling . . . stuff like that. All of that is dead. The prisoners of war, they walked them off to the bushes and they killed them. Girls got raped. . . . The animals, buffalo, they [the farmers] need to farm their land [were shot]. The GI's know they need them but they kill them just to give them a hard time. I could not understand that.

Killing the Enemy

Finally, we examined the effects of whether or not the veteran reported he killed someone in Vietnam. We treated this measure separately because the moral issues involved in killing another human being may have profound psychological implications for the soldier. The imagery surrounding the experience often stays with the man for years in dreams and memories. The reflections of an army paratrooper show the long-term significance this experience had for him.

> We had just moved into a new area that was controlled by the Vietcong. A squad of us went out beyond our perimeter to check and we came under fire. We saw Vietnamese in this grass shack and we started firing. Suddenly a figure moved through the bushes out the back of the grass shack. I shot and it fell. I did not feel anything at first because it was a natural thing to do. We were under fire and it is just instinct. . . . But there were a lot of repercussions after I got out of the service. I had dreams. I still have dreams occasionally. Not just the killing of [this] guy you know,

[but] the whole thing in general, all the people I killed. It was sickening. I began to realize they were human beings.

SUBJECTIVE REACTIONS TO WAR STRESS

In addition to the experiences veterans had during the Vietnam War, veterans' reactions to their war experiences were also explored. Reactions to these experiences represent a means for those exposed to internalize and deal with them. Some response patterns, we believe, are more likely than others to be related to long-term psychological difficulty and disorientation. In the following discussion we concentrate on subjective responses to the death and dying which accompany war. We asked our repondents to tell us their reactions to seeing Americans killed, to seeing Vietnamese killed, and to their combat experience.* From these questions several subjective responses to war trauma emerged. Although we use the language of the respondents in describing how they dealt emotionally with the trauma of war, several distinct response categories are evident. Table 1 shows the most common responses.

Seventy-two percent of the respondents reported experiencing a reaction to seeing Americans killed, while 74% of the respondents reported a reaction to seeing Vietnamese killed. Only for general combat experience was the general response rate low, 51%, but the response rate varied by level of combat exposure. Of those with low exposure only 20% described their reactions to combat, while 58% of moderate combat veterans did so, and 72% of heavy combat veterans.

Reactions to these experiences are fairly evenly distributed across the categories. There are two exceptions. Feeling sadness is the dominant reaction to seeing American deaths (42%), and it is also the dominant reaction to seeing Vietnamese deaths (36%). No category clearly dominates as the chief reaction to combat even though we found in our sample that Vietnam veterans felt the most important thing to them was surviving and getting home alive.

---

*Responses to these experiences were tapped by open-ended questions in which the respondents were asked: 1) "How did you feel about things that happened during combat?"; 2) "What was your reaction to the death of Americans or your buddies?"; and 3) "What was your reaction to (seeing Vietnamese killed)?" A subsample of the interviews were content-analyzed to determine the responses most frequently given. Response categories were chosen which produced an intercoder reliability of .9. The subsample was placed back into the sample and the responses of each veteran were then coded on these questions. Since it was possible for respondents to mention more than one reaction the sum of proportions across the possible reactions is greater than the proportion who reported a reaction to the experience, as seen in Table 1. The reaction categories should thus not be seen as mutually exclusive.

TABLE 1
Subjective Reactions to Traumatic Experiences

Group Which Saw Americans Killed (N = 189)		Group Which Saw Vietnamese Killed (N = 204)		Group Which Experienced Combat (N = 317)	
Felt Anger Seeing Americans Killed	21%	Felt Death of Vietnamese Was Justified	22%	Felt Fear in Combat	17%
Felt Sadness Seeing Americans Killed	42%	Felt Indifferent to the Death of Vietnamese	28%	Concerned with Self-Preservation in Combat	20%
Felt Shock Seeing Americans Killed	24%	Felt Sadness Seeing Vietnamese Killed	36%	Had No Feelings in Combat	20%
Had No Feelings Seeing Americans Killed	14%	Felt Fear Seeing Vietnamese Killed	3%	Felt Frustrated by Constraints in Combat	6%
Accepted the Deaths of Americans	12%				
Reported a Reaction to This Experience	72%	Reported a Reaction to This Experience	74%	Reported a Reaction to This Experience	51%

For the discussion here the importance of these reactions is in their impact on the likelihood and level of long-term symptomatology which was rooted in the war experience.

EFFECTS OF WAR STRESS AND SUBJECTIVE REACTIONS ON PTSD

In an earlier series of analyses we demonstrated that combat and exposure to and participation in abusive violence systematically contribute to increasing PTSD symptomatology and disorder (Laufer et al., 1981; Laufer et al., 1983a,b; Laufer et al., 1984b; Yager, Laufer, & Gallops, 1984). Although some complex interaction effects exist between war stress and factors such as period of service and race on PTSD, there is no question that these behavioral measures consistently enhance our ability to specify the relationship between traumatic stress in war and patterns of post-traumatic stress.

Our three experiential measures of war stress—combat, witnessing of and participation in abusive violence—exhibit a consistent patterned relationship to post-traumatic stress symptomatology and disorder.* In a multiple regression analysis it was found that combat exposure and witnessing abusive violence contribute to higher rates of Intrusive Imagery. Combat also has the effect of elevating the scores on the Hyper-

---

*We developed six measures of Post-traumatic Stress Disorder in our analysis (Laufer et al., 1983a, b). These measures are all derived from a stress scale (Boulanger, Kadushin, & Martin, 1981) used in *Legacies of Vietnam*. The earlier stress scale was composed of 22 items chosen on the basis of their frequent appearance (75% of the time) in a review of the literature on traumatic neuroses and stress disorders, and preliminary drafts of DSM-III criteria. The scale measured the number of symptoms the respondent experienced in the 12 months prior to the interview. Four subscales were created from the larger stress scale. Two of the subscales, Intrusive Imagery and Hyperarousal, measure reexperiencing phenomena. As the names imply, Intrusive Imagery measures the imagic aspect, and Hyperarousal the affective and somatic aspects of repetition. The Hyperarousal subscale consists of: feeling irritable or tense; feeling the impulse to lash out; occasional feeling of losing control; feeling jumpy or easily startled; attacks of sudden fear or panic; and trouble sleeping, staying asleep, or oversleeping. The Intrusive Imagery subscale is composed of the following items: troubling thoughts about experiences in the military; frightening dreams or nightmares; and thoughts of how you might die. The remaining two subscales, Numbing and Cognitive Disruption, measure defenses against reexperiencing phenomena. The items in Numbing are: losing interest in usual activities; feeling that your life isn't meaningful; feeling that what other people care about doesn't make sense; and feeling numb. The items in Cognitive Disruption are: having trouble thinking and having trouble remembering things.

Two measures of disorder were constructed on the basis of the 15 symptoms used to create the four subscales. The Reexperiencing measure of PTSD was based on whether

arousal scale, while participation in abusive violence contributes to symptoms reflecting Cognitive Difficulties. In regard to the measures of disorder both combat and witnessing abusive violence are significantly related to Reexperiencing Disorder, while participation in abusive violence is related to Denial Disorder (Laufer et al., 1983b).

Although transcript evidence suggests that killing others had important psychological consequences for many individuals, we found no statistical association between this experience and stress symptomatology or disorder. Two factors are responsible for this. First, whether an individual took someone else's life in Vietnam is strongly associated with a number of experiences contained in the scale of combat exposure. The correlation between killing and combat exposure is .57, suggesting that the psychological impact of killing is reflected in a range of war-related experiences.

A second factor explaining the lack of a relationship arises from the fact that killing occurred in a number of different contexts in Vietnam. If the individuals killed were enemy combatants or suspected VC collaborators, men often noted it was necessary self-defense. In these cases little doubt is expressed concerning the legitimacy of the action. Consequently, in these cases the psychological impact of the experience is minor. The comments of one marine are typical:

> (I) shot an old lady. She was not supposed to be out after six o'clock. We did not know if (she) was a Vietcong or not so we shot her with a grenade launcher . . . The lady was giving away our position at night . . . we (could have been) overrun the next day, so she got killed. . . . (Another time) a little boy came over with a case of pop and would not open them. There was a booby trap of hand grenades in it so he got killed. Well, it may make it seem like I am awful cold but I'm not. It did not bother me. Things (like that) just did not bother me.

If, however, men killed civilians, whether these civilians were caught in the middle of combat situations, or victimized by tactical designations such as free-fire zones, they often expressed regret, guilt, and a sense of loss. The deaths of Vietnamese in such situations were not taken

---

the respondent reported at least one symptom from the Intrusive Imagery and at least one symptom from the Hyperarousal scales. If the respondent reported the symptoms in this combination he was coded "1" on Reexperiencing PTSD and "0" otherwise. The Denial measure of PTSD was based on whether the respondent reported at least one symptom from Numbing and at least one symptom from Cognitive Difficulties. If the respondent reported the symptoms in this combination he was coded "1" on Denial PTSD, otherwise he was coded "0."

lightly and were not perceived as "justified." In such cases veterans felt strongly their individual responsibility for the deaths and a clear psychological impression was left. The enduring character of this experience is shown in the life of one helicopter gunship pilot who reported an incident where civilians were killed in a firefight with the VC. He noted:

> I felt good about knocking out the machine gun. I felt bad about killing the people. We killed five civilians and the machine gunner. . . . I'm trying to forget the entire incident. But I find that I don't think I can. I wish I had not killed those people. I had dreams about that. It was very surreal you know, I very clearly saw them die and I felt very responsible for it. . . .

The traumatic quality of killing someone varied widely in the sample. It appears, in general, that the impact of killing was conditioned by other aspects of war stress, including general combat exposure and the presence of abusive violence. Consequently, a summary indicator of whether the veteran killed while in Vietnam has limited utility in measuring the long-term impact of this experience on PTSD.

The existence of a pronounced pattern of war-experience effects on stress symptomatology leads to the question of whether the manner in which individuals responded to and dealt with these trauma subjectively affected their long-term propensity to exhibit symptomatology and disorder. Table 2 addresses this question by presenting a multiple regression analysis with six symptom measures as outcomes, and stress experience and subjective reaction measures as predictors.*

As Table 2 shows, the most consistent subjective war stress predictor of post-traumatic stress symptoms and disorder is the feeling that the deaths of the Vietnamese were justified.** We find that those who felt

---

*It should be noted that only four reaction measures were included in the regression, these four proving to be the only ones among the original twelve listed in Table 1 which showed significant effects on any of the six outcome measures.

**The effects of predispositional risk factors were examined to determine whether the effects of experiential trauma or those of subjective reaction could be attributable to pre-service or structural risk factors. The risk factors examined were race, parents' education and occupation, the presence of both parents in the family of upbringing, the individual's history of juvenile problems and truancy, the individual's level of premilitary education, and the period in which the veteran served in Vietnam, before or after the Tet offensive in 1968. Only race was found to have a direct effect on any measure of symptomatology, blacks showing a significantly higher level of Hyperarousal symptomatology. Controlling for these risk factors had no influence on the pattern of significance of either set of stress predictors. The only notable finding concerning the individual's propensity to be exposed to war trauma due to these risk factors was that draftees were significantly less likely than enlistees to have participated in abusive violence while they were in Vietnam.

TABLE 2
The Effects of War Experience and Subjective Reactions on Stress Symptomatology and Disorder

	Intrusive Imagery Symptoms	Numbing Symptoms	Hyperarousal Symptoms	Cognitive Difficulty Symptoms	Denial-Based Disorder	Reexperiencing-Based Disorder
Combat Exposure	.004[a] (.03)[b]	.01 (.05)	.04 (.10)	.01 (.03)	.00 (.04)	.00 (.03)
Witnessing Abusive Violence	.15** (.13)	.08 (.07)	.31 (.07)	.07 (.05)	.08 (.08)	.15** (.15)
Participation in Abusive Violence	-.01 (.01)	-.05 (.03)	.49 (.08)	.27* (.12)	.12 (.09)	-.01 (.01)
Felt Shock Seeing Amer. Killed	.11 (.07)	.20* (.11)	.48 (.08)	.12 (.06)	.17** (.13)	.11 (.07)
Felt Death of Viets Was Justified	.20** (.16)	.23+ (.17)	.37 (.08)	-.04 (.02)	.02 (.02)	.20** (.16)
Felt Sadness Seeing Viets Killed	.08 (.07)	.04 (.03)	.54* (.12)	.04 (.02)	.03 (.03)	.09 (.08)
Felt Fear in Combat	.12 (.09)	-.03 (.03)	.21 (.04)	.25** (.15)	.08 (.08)	.06 (.05)
R^2	.09	.06	.08	.06	.06	.08
N	275	275	275	268	268	275
Mean	.31	.41	1.75	.32	.28	.18
S.D.	.46	.49	1.83	.63	.45	.38

[a] Unstandardized Regression Coefficient
[b] Standardized Regression Coefficient

* Significant at p lt. .10
** Significant at p lt. .05
+ Significant at p lt. .01

the death of Vietnamese was justified currently report higher rates of Intrusive Imagery and Numbing symptomatology, and they also appear to have higher rates of Reexperiencing PTSD. The persistent relationship between this feeling of justification and the presence of symptoms suggests that avoidance or defense against the trauma of witnessing Vietnamese deaths did not serve as an effective coping strategy after leaving Vietnam.

Two types of arguments are presented by Vietnam veterans who emphasized that the killing of Vietnamese that they witnessed was justified. The first line of thought was that the enemy as a whole had to be eliminated, that that was the purpose of the war and of the presence of the U.S. troops. Such an attitude was expressed by a marine sergeant:

I . . . put myself into a state where it (the Vietnamese) is not a person. It is an enemy. The enemy is a threat and it must be eliminated because of their intentions. How could a person be a person (if his) intention is to bring communism about. . . .

This dehumanization of the enemy generally had pronounced ideological and/or cultural elements which emphasized the alienness of the enemy. Another line of thought stressed that the death of Vietnamese was the result of acts of self-preservation by U.S. forces. Vietnamese were killed either as a result of acts of hostility by the VC and NVA or because it was an inevitable consequence of warfare. One veteran who expressed this attitude stated:

(I felt the death of hostile Vietnamese was) vindication for the fact that any Americans had to be there at all. . . . (It was also) retribution for the Vietnamese atrocities on United States servicemen. . . . (It was also an act) of self-preservation. Somebody shot at you, you shot back at them, and the better shot won. (My) prevailing reaction was, here is somebody who is aggressively trying to hurt me. Self-preservation. The enemy was the enemy. Justification was not necessary (for killing them). It was the simple fact of being in the war.

This apparent hardness to the death of Vietnamese is cast into question by the results in Table 2. Seeing Vietnamese killed in "justified" situations still left psychological traces on the witnesses. It is apparent the veterans could not distance themselves from the significance of the Vietnamese deaths.

Veterans who acknowledge that their response to the trauma of combat was fear show evidence of higher levels of Cognitive Difficulties (e.g., inability to concentrate). The disorienting impact of fear is quite marked among many of the veterans. The anticipation of the worst effects of combat was a prevailing concern among many, and as the effect upon current Cognitive Difficulties shows, its impact lasted several years for some. The major element of the fear which men expressed concerned being killed or wounded. The comments of one marine summarized the feelings of many:

> I thought (the possibility of death) was terrible . . . you're afraid of that mostly all the time. . . . Some people say, "Well, it didn't bother me." But, anybody I hear say that, I know they are either a damn fool or a liar. . . . Once you see the guys actually getting killed you think about it. You know, that could be me laying there, or you think about yourself with your head blown off or (being put) in one of them bags.

The fear of death in combat was paralleled by a concern with serious injury resulting in permanent impairment. For some the possibility of this was a stronger basis of fear than the possibility of death.

> A lot of death was all around. (But) most of my friends instead of getting killed got messed up for life. They might step on a booby trap and (get) all that shrapnel. That means this man might have lost his legs or his manhood. In fact, most of the guys I saw hit did not die. They just were hurt bad enough to have lifelong repercussions. In a lot of those cases death might have been a little happier.

We also find a relationship between hyperarousal symptoms and the internalization of feelings of sorrow at the deaths of Vietnamese. This sadness was most often expressed by those sensitive to the plight of the civilians. Civilian casualties were quite high in the war and many veterans had experiences of civilian suffering which were overwhelming. Scenes of civilian carnage which traumatized Vietnam veterans generated not only sadness but also an urge to escape the death and destruction of the war. This impulse was well described by one veteran:

> (The plight of civilians) was a tragedy because people laid in the streets dead. They piled them up on the side (of the road). You would watch them as you went by. It was something that turns your gut. The reaction was that you were there but you do not

know why you were there, and you do not know why everybody was blown apart. . . . You want to get out because there are too many innocent people killed.

These findings indicate that opening the self up to the emotional pain of traumatic stress does not necessarily lead to a remission of long-term symptomatology. However, in our data it does appear that the acknowledgment of the trauma is not associated with higher prevalence rates of either reexperiencing or denial stress disorders.

Veterans who reported feeling shock when they saw Americans killed reported higher levels of numbing symptoms and also were more likely to exhibit denial-based disorder. For some veterans it appears the death of Americans, particularly of close friends and unit buddies, was overwhelming. The immediacy of the loss prevented the veteran from accepting the episode in abstract terms regarding the nature of warfare and the arbitrariness of fate. Those who experienced shock were generally too close to the victim to simply respond, "His number was up." An army infantryman discussed the death of one friend:

We were on patrol and ran into a firefight. We were moving up one at a time and when (name) started to move up he got his head blown off. . . . He was dead on the spot. . . . At first I was concerned with staying alive and couldn't do much about it but after everything died down and we'd picked him up and taken him to the rear, it all kind of hit me at once. It was just the most atrocious thing I'd ever seen. A friend of mine, somebody I grew up with, and here he is dead with half his head missing. I started thinking about his parents, about the things we did when we grew up together. . . . I was maybe ten feet from him. . . . It hurt.

The tie of this reaction to numbing symptomatology suggests that numbing is a reflexive psychological mechanism for dealing with such a rupturing of intimate personal ties. It is striking that the Numbing symptomatology associated with these experiences persists even to the time of the interview, which in some cases was 10 years after the period of service.

As seen in Table 2, the effects of the subjective reactions to stress have eliminated a number of the direct effects of the stress experience variables. Combat exposure no longer significantly effects the level of Hyperarousal symptoms nor does it contribute to Numbing or Intrusive Imagery symptoms or Reexperiencing disorder. Participation in abusive violence loses its effect on Hyperarousal symptoms and its effect on Cognitive Difficulties is also somewhat diminished. In addition, its effect on Denial-based disorder disappears. Only witnessing abusive violence maintains its effects on post-service symptomatology when subjective reactions to traumatic experiences are taken into account. Witnessing continues to contribute to Intrusive Imagery symptoms and Reexperiencing disorder.

The weakening of war experience effects indicates that how the veteran reacted to, internalized, and dealt with his experience at the time is extremely important in helping us understand the enduring relationship between experiential indicators of war stress, subjective reactions to them and long-term psychological adjustment. Symptomatology and disorder appear most pronounced in the stressed population which develops specific psychological reaction patterns.

CONCLUSION

Our findings have general applicability to the question of the relationship between traumatic stress and PTSD. Emotional coping styles appear to be implicated in the effects of cumulative exposure to traumatic experiences, and contribute to long-term PTSD outcomes. Both traumatic experience and types of psychological reaction to it directly affect the presence and level of stress symptomatology.

There are certain differences between traumatic events which are relevant to the measurement of the stressor in PTSD. We would assert that the relationship between the psychological reactions to traumatic stress in war is, for the most part, not applicable to traumatic events of limited duration. There are important differences between traumatic events which involve "career" exposure to trauma and those experiences lasting no more than a day, a few hours, or even moments. The differentiation of traumatic stress is clearly more important in situations where the trauma goes on for an extended period of time. We would expect that the relationship between subjective responses and experiential measures of the trauma would be more characteristic of situations in which trauma persists over time, such as war or child abuse. Only in such instances can patterns of reaction and coping styles develop over time.

In summary, our data suggest that the measurement of stressors in PTSD is a complex problem which requires careful conceptualization of the specific phenomenon under study. The early studies of the effects of the war on PTSD concluded too quickly that combat was the key issue. Future research needs to pay careful attention to the relationships between traumatic experience and patterns of subjective reaction to these experiences, and to develop more systematic measures of this phenomenon than is available in our data. In light of recent research it is clear that a conceptualization of the dimensions of the traumatic experience is central to understanding the relationship between stressors and stress symptomatology and disorder.

REFERENCES

American Psychiatric Association. *Diagnostic and statistical manual of mental health disorders* (3rd ed.). Washington, DC: American Psychiatric Association, 1980.

Boulanger, G., Kadushin, C. & Martin, J. *Legacies of Vietnam, Vol. IV, Long-term stress reactions.* Washington, DC: U.S. Government Printing Office, 1981.

Card, J.J. *Lives after Vietnam: The personal impact of military service.* Lexington, MA: Lexington Books, 1983.

Egendorf, A., Kadushin, C., Laufer, R.S., Rothbart, G., & Sloan, L. *Legacies of Vietnam: Comparative adjustment of veterans and their peers.* Vols. I-IV. Washington, DC: U.S. Government Printing Office, 1981.

Figley, C. (Ed.). *Stress disorders among Vietnam veterans.* New York: Brunner/Mazel, 1978.

Foy, D.W., Supprella, R.C., Rueger, D.B., & Carroll, E.M. Vietnam veterans readjustment research project. (working papers). Brentwood, CA: Veterans Administration, 1980.

Harris, L. *Myths and realities: A study of attitudes toward Vietnam era veterans.* Washington, DC: U.S. Government Printing Office, 1980.

Hough, R.L., Gongla, P., Scurfield, R.M., Corke, T., & Carr, C. The natural history of post-traumatic stress disorder. Anaheim, CA: Paper presented at the American Psychological Association Meeting, 1983.

Laufer, R.S. War trauma and human development: Vietnam. In S. Sonnenberg, A. Blank & J. Talbot (Eds.), *Psychiatric effects of the Vietnam War.* Washington, DC: American Psychiatric Association Press, in press.

Laufer, R.S., Brett, E. & Gallops, M.S. Dimensions of post-traumatic stress among Vietnam veterans. New York: Paper presented at the American Psychiatric Association Meeting, 1983a.

Laufer, R.S., Brett, E., & Gallops, M.S. Patterns of post-traumatic stress disorder among Vietnam veterans exposed to combat and abusive violence. Anaheim, CA: Paper presented at the American Psychological Association Meeting, 1983b.

Laufer, R.S., Frey-Wouters, E., Donnellan, J., & Yager, T. *Legacies of Vietnam, Vol. III, Post-war trauma: Social and psychological problems of Vietnam veterans and their peers.* Washington, DC: U.S. Government Printing Office, 1981.

Laufer, R.S., Frey-Wouters, E., & Gallops, M.S., War stress and post-war trauma. *Journal of Health and Social Behavior,* 1984, *25*, 65-85.

Rothbart, G. General methodology. In *Legacies of Vietnam: Vol II.* Washington, DC: U.S. Government Printing Office, 1981.

Rothbart, G., Fine, M., & Sudman, S. On finding and interviewing the needles in the haystack: The use of multiplicity sampling. *Public Opinion Quarterly,* 1982, *46*, 409-421.

Wilson, J.P. *Identity, ideology and crisis: The Vietnam veteran in transition* (Vol. II). Washington, DC: Disabled American Veterans, 1978.

Wilson, J.P., & Krauss, G.E. Predicting post-traumatic stress syndromes among Vietnam veterans. Coatsville, PA: Paper presented at the 25th Neuropsychiatric Institute, 1982.

Yager, T., Laufer, R.S., & Gallops, M.S. Some problems associated with war experience in men of the Vietnam generation. *Archives of General Psychiatry,* 1984, *41*, 327-333.

CHAPTER

6

The Emotional Aftermath of Crime and Violence

ROBERT C. DAVIS and LUCY N. FRIEDMAN

This chapter reports on the results of a study of the effects of crime on 274 victims of burglary, robbery, and assault. In the study, victims were interviewed twice—once several weeks after the crime and again four months after the crime. The results indicate that victimization initially 1) reduces positive affect; 2) increases negative affect; 3) heightens fear of crime and encourages individuals to take precautions inside and outside their homes; and 4) results in practical problems for the victim. Victims showed substantial improvement on each of these measures over the months following the crime; however, four months after the crime some evidence of the trauma still appeared to be present. Treatment strategies are discussed.

While students of human behavior have long recognized the trauma caused by certain types of human catastrophes, only recently have there been efforts to document and systematize this trauma. Clinicians working with former prisoners of war and survivors of the Holocaust and hostage situations have noted similarities in how people respond to these events. This pattern has been described in the American Psychiatric Association DSM-III (1980) as post-traumatic stress disorder (PTSD).

Evidence has begun to accumulate from researchers and practitioners that serious violent crimes also produce a major, and sometimes lasting, psychological impact on victims. Studies of rape victims, the group on which most research has been conducted, concur that rape causes emotional trauma; Sutherland and Scherl (1970) note anxiety and fear immediately after the assault; Burgess and Holmstrom (1974a, b) reported disorganization and disruption followed by nightmares, phobias, and constriction in life patterns. Frank, Turner, and Duffy (1979) mention depression; Kilpatrick, Veronen, and Resick (1979) and Kilpatrick, Resick, and Veronen (1979) found that victims were significantly more anxious, fearful, suspicious and confused than non-victims for at least a year after the assault.

Counseling staff at the Victim Services Agency* also noted aspects of PTSD in crime victims and families of homicide victims. While to our knowledge no studies have directly analyzed the extent to which rape victims and families of homicide victims suffer PTSD, it is clear that these people do suffer major psychological trauma similar in many respects to victims of other types of catastrophes (Bard & Sangrey, 1979; Figley, 1983; Symonds, 1975).

Even burglary victims are not immune from experiencing adverse psychological effects following the crime. The American Institutes for Research (1978) found that many burglary victims exhibit "crisis behavior" following the incident, and Waller and Okihiro (1978) report that burglary may have long-lasting effects on victims' trust of other people, fear of being alone, and fear of entering their residence.

In 1980, the Victim Services Agency undertook a study which sought to describe the physical, financial, emotional, and social aftermath of crime, and where victims turn for help. In conducting the study, we wanted to know what disturbances to people's lives resulted from the most common crimes—burglary, robbery, and assault. In this chapter, we have excerpted those portions of that study (Friedman, Bischoff, Davis, & Person, 1982, *Victims and Helpers: Reactions to Crime*) which speak to the psychological consequences of victimization.

In our research, we examined a broad range of victim reactions to crime, including practical and emotional problems caused by the incident; changes in positive and negative affective states; increases in fear of crime; precautionary and avoidance behavior aimed at reducing the odds of future victimization; feelings of self-blame; effects on relation-

---

*The Victim Services Agency is a not-for-profit corporation set up in 1978 to provide a wide range of practical and counseling services for crime victims.

ships with others; and efforts of victims to organize with others to combat crime. In addition, we examined to a more limited degree the impact of crime on those persons who lent assistance to victims. While our research was not focused on PTSD, we did cover a number of aspects of PTSD in our questions of victims: recurrent recollections of the incident, feelings of alienation from others, sleep disturbances, affective changes, and avoidance of situations and places. In addition, other evidence of PTSD sometimes emerged unsolicited in the course of our interviews.

THE STUDY

The data we used to determine the extent to which victims of burglary, robbery, and assault suffer emotional problems were generated from interviews with 274 crime victims conducted one to three weeks after the incident, interviews with 182 of the same victims four months after the incident, and interviews with 152 supporters (persons who rendered material or psychological assistance to the victim) named by the victims. Persons interviewed were victims of burglary (63%), robbery (29%), and assault (8%), who had filed criminal complaints with the police in one of three New York City neighborhoods between mid-March and mid-August, 1980.

The neighborhoods chosen for study were diverse to ensure that the results could be generalized to other urban areas. The Fordham section of the Bronx is a high-crime, low-income neighborhood populated predominantly by black and Hispanic residents. Flushing, Queens, is a low-crime, stable neighborhood of single-family homes with primarily white residents with incomes above the City average. Park Slope, Brooklyn, is a mixed-income area in the process of gentrification, transforming decaying buildings into attractive homes for moderate-income, upwardly mobile families. Table 1 provides a detailed description of the sample.

THE RESULTS

Initial Responses to Victimization

On the initial interview, victims were asked about the consequences of the crime. The most common consequences were stolen property

(68%); disruption of daily routine (a range of problems from having to relocate to needing help washing and dressing because of a broken shoulder) (65%); and difficulty sleeping (59%).

In listening to victims describe their problems, we were struck by the degree to which even property loss affected victims emotionally. We therefore categorized victims' answers to questions about crime-related problems according to whether answers mentioned nervousness, shame, anger, or anxiety. According to this scheme, 45% of victims' answers indicated emotional distress. If difficulty sleeping is included as an emotional reaction, three-quarters of the victims experienced emotional stress during the first few weeks after the crime—a surprisingly high figure in a sample in which nearly two in three persons were burglary victims. But even burglary victims experienced fear and anxiety, and a few reported elevated blood pressure. One burglary victim was particularly upset because the incident touched off anxiety about an attempted rape that had happened several months earlier. The daughter of an elderly burglary victim said about her mother that "she keeps going back to the incident. She's very nervous and wants to move."

In contrast to the high proportion of victims who expressed problems in emotional terms, only 32% defined problems in financial terms and 25% in terms of loss of use or enjoyment of a possession stolen in the crime. Even when the victim had no contact with the offender, the fear, anxiety, and tension created by the invasion of a person's private space were more significant than the loss of possessions.

Affect Balance Scale

In addition to the practical problems following victimization, the interviews focused on post-traumatic affective states. Respondents' emotional reactions to victimization were measured by the Affect Balance Scale (ABS). The Affect Balance Scale (Derogatis & Meyer, 1979) is a 40-item checklist of adjectives. The scale is multidimensional, containing four positive (Joy, Contentment, Vigor, and Affection), and four negative (Anxiety, Depression, Guilt, and Hostility) dimensions of mood. The ABS has been used in studies of coping mechanisms among cancer patients (Derogatis, Abeloff, & Melisaratos, 1979), and sexual dysfunction (Derogatis & Meyer, 1979), among others. These studies found that reactions to crisis were more likely to entail a reduction in positive affect than an increase in negative affect. It seemed likely that criminal victimization might produce similar effects.

TABLE 1
Basic Demographics of Sample by Borough

	Fordham n=87	Park Slope n=86	Flushing n=101	Total Sample
Crime Type				
Burglary	59%	70%	59%	62%
Robbery	29%	23%	35%	29%
Assault	13%	7%	6%	8%
Sex				
Male	52%	43%	42%	45%
Female	48%	57%	58%	55%
Age				
18-29 years	34%	45%	22%	33%
30-39 years	22%	27%	22%	23%
40-49 years	13%	9%	19%	14%
50-64 years	22%	12%	23%	19%
65 years +	9%	7%	15%	11%
Income				
0-$4,999	56%	23%	15%	30%
$5,000-$9,999	20%	12%	21%	18%
$10,000-$14,999	12%	30%	15%	19%
$15,000-$19,999	3%	19%	16%	13%
$20,000 +	8%	17%	33%	20%

Education			
Some High School or less	51%	23%	35%
High School or Trade School Graduate	37%	12%	25%
Some College or More	12%	65%	40%
Race			
Hispanic	36%	16%	21%
Black	46%	11%	22%
White	18%	73%	57%
Prior Victimization			
Yes	37%	51%	38%
No	63%	49%	62%
Relationship with Offender			
Yes	40%	14%	19%
No	60%	86%	81%
Time in Neighborhood			
Less than 1 year	14%	16%	13%
1 to 5 years	44%	42%	40%
More than 5 years	42%	42%	48%
Living Situation			
Live Alone	29%	35%	33%
With Others	71%	65%	67%

Table 2 compares mean scores on subscales of the ABS administered at the time of the initial interview with test norms from a sample of college students (norms in the table are weighted to reflect the frequency of male versus female victims in the present study). The table shows that victims scored significantly lower than the test norm on the four positive subscales and significantly higher on the four negative subscales. Although the groups were different, the results at least suggest that victimization impacts on both positive and negative affective states.*

Fear of Crime

Being a victim sharply reduced people's feelings of safety in their homes and neighborhoods. A majority of the sample reported feeling either "very much" less safe (28%), or "somewhat" less safe (35%) in their homes as a result of the crime at the time of the first interview. A smaller, but still sizeable, proportion felt "very much" (18%) or "somewhat" (24%) less safe in their neighborhoods.

A composite "fear of crime" index was constructed by summing responses from the questions on feeling safe at home and in the neighborhood and desire to move.** The scale revealed that victimization reduced women's sense of security to a significantly greater extent than men's (mean score for women on the index was 2.03 compared to 1.63 for men).

The heightened fear among victims is evident in the case of Sam Brown, a 54-year-old man who lived on public assistance. Sam Brown was robbed one night at knifepoint by two youths who broke down the door to his apartment. When he told the youths that he had only $15, they forced him to disclose when he would receive his next check, and said that they would be back on that date. If he didn't have money then, they said they would kill him. As a result of the threat, Sam Brown slept with furniture stacked in front of his door and a large pair of scissors and a can of mace near his bed (Friedman et al., 1982, p. 100).

---

*These data alone cannot rule out the possibility that the victim sample was experiencing greater emotional distress than the norm sample *prior* to victimization. In a following section on readjustment following victimization, additional data are examined that support the contention that reduced positive and increased negative affect in this sample were largely associated with the of victimization experience.

**Two points were given for a response of "very much" and one point for "somewhat" on the first two questions, and a single point for an affirmative answer to the question about wanting to move. Thus, the highest possible score on the scale was five; the mean for the sample was 1.85.

TABLE 2
Comparison of Victims' ABS Scores on Initial Interview With Test Norms

Scales	Victim Sample (n = 200)	Norm Sample (n200)*	Significance
Positive			
Joy	10.1	13.0	t (199) = 8.12**
Contentment	10.1	13.0	t (199) = 9.70**
Vigor	11.0	13.7	t (197) = 8.36**
Affection	12.4	14.1	t (197) = 5.67**
Negative			
Anxiety	9.5	7.2	t (197) = 8.85**
Depression	6.6	4.7	t (196) = 6.91**
Guilt	5.2	3.9	t (197) = 5.06**
Hostility	8.6	5.3	t (197) = 10.89**

* Derogatis and Meyer (1979). Norm means were weighted to reflect frequency of men versus women in the victim sample.
** All t values are significant at the .01 level or better (two-tailed test).

Precautions

Victims were also asked about what they were doing to avoid possible future victimizations. Many people reported taking added precautions after the crime. Sixty percent reported they had installed new locks or bars, had their valuables marked with identification numbers, moved to a safer location, hidden, gotten a dog, or installed an alarm system. Forty-seven percent reported being more cautious about locking doors, and 35% said that they had begun leaving the lights, the television, or the radio on when going out. Several victims volunteered that they had secured weapons to protect themselves.

Victims also increased their precautions outside of their homes: 25% went out less during the day, and 38% less at night compared to before the crime. When they did go out, 39% stated that they were more likely after the crime to avoid particular places, and 45% were more suspicious of people on the street. Mrs. Anderson's story illustrates how crime constricts the lives of its victims.

Mrs. Anderson had been robbed at gunpoint on the way to her car, and had also recently been the victim of a chain-snatch attempt on the subway. She said, "I am scared to walk around by myself. I dread going into the garage. When I come home from work now, I go straight to my apartment and bolt the door. I don't even like being in the hallways. I used to visit neighbors in my building or take my car out at night to visit friends. I don't do that anymore."

Efforts to Organize

Besides taking additional precautions following the crime, 16% of the sample reported that they had tried to organize friends or neighbors to take action to reduce crime in their building or neighborhood. These efforts were directed toward persuading landlords to enhance security in their buildings (by installing locks, intercoms in the lobby, or hiring a doorman), beginning citizen street patrols in their neighborhoods, or encouraging area residents to watch each other's residences. Such efforts may be an effective way to combat the disaffection that sometimes results from the trauma associated with victimization.

Attribution of Responsibility for Victimization

It is well-documented that crime victims often blame themselves for victimization (Burgess & Holmstrom, 1974a). This tendency has been regarded as negative, indicative of depression (Beck, 1967) and detrimental to victims' readjustment (Bard & Sangrey, 1979). Recently, however, Janoff-Bulman and Wortman (1977) found that self-blame among paralyzed victims facilitated coping. Janoff-Bulman (1979) explains this apparently anomalous finding by suggesting that there are two forms of self-blame, characterological and behavioral, the former destructive and the latter constructive. According to Janoff-Bulman:

> Recognizing that self-blame may be both adaptive and maladaptive is a first step towards the conclusion that there are two different types of self-blame . . . individuals can blame themselves for having engaged in (or having failed to engage in) a particular activity, thereby attributing blame to past behaviors; or individuals can blame themselves for the kind of people they are, thereby faulting their character. (1979, p. 1799)

Behavioral self-blame is seen by Janoff-Bulman (cf. Janoff-Bulman, this volume) to be indicative of a belief in personal control over outcomes, a mechanism social psychologists have demonstrated to be advantageous (Bowers, 1968; Dweck,1975; Glass & Singer, 1972).

The victims in our sample were asked if there was anything they felt they could have done to have prevented their victimization. Thirty-six percent responded affirmatively. Many stated that they might have taken greater measures to protect their residence, been more cautious about dangerous areas or carrying valuables, or been more alert. Others felt that they should have behaved differently once confronted by the criminal. One victim said, "We should have given the guys the money." An assault and attempted rape followed the victim's refusal. Another robbery victim expressed the opposite sentiment: "They didn't seem too sure of themselves when they came up to me. If I had yelled at first, they might have run."

Patterns of Response to Crime

We have seen that crime produces a variety of responses. Can any patterns be identified among these responses? Table 3 displays intercorrelations among some of the responses measured in the study. The table reveals that four responses tended to occur together. Victims who reported more extensive or more serious crime-related problems* also

---

*An additive index of crime-related problems was constructed from information about 14 specific problems asked about in the survey. One point was allotted for problems rated as "minor" by the victim and two points for problems rated as "major." Mean score on the scale was 5.66.

TABLE 3
Intercorrelations Among Different Victim Responses to Crime

	Problem Index	Fear of Crime Index	ABS Composite Score	Precautions On Street	Could Have Avoided Crime	Precautions In House
Fear of Crime Index	.39*					
ABS Composite Score	-.26*	-.17*				
Precautions Index: On Street	.38*	.37*	-.18*			
Could Have Avoided Crime	-.12*	-.11	.00	.00		
Precautions Index: In House	.07	.05	.00	.00	.11	
Attempts to Organize	.03	-.02	-.06	.04	.12*	15*

* Significant at the .05 level or better by two-tailed tests.

TABLE 4

Loadings of Victim Response Measures on "General Distress" and
"Instrumental Response" Factors

	General Distress Reaction Factor	Instrumental Response Factor
Problem Index	0.774	−0.022
Fear of Crime Index	0.726	−0.092
ABS Composite Score	−0.502	−0.097
Precautions: On Street	0.712	0.018
Precautions: In-House	0.098	0.636
Attempts to Organize	0.069	0.681
Could Have Avoided Crime	−0.151	0.611

showed a greater increase in fear of crime, exhibited more severe negative affect, and took more precautions on the street. Three other responses—taking efforts to secure one's residence, organizing to fight crime, and the perceiving that victimization could have been avoided—also tended to occur together.

Factor analysis confirmed that responses to crime fell into two distinct groups. Table 4 displays the strength of the relationship between the victim response measures and the two general responses, which we have termed "general distress reaction" and "instrumental response." The general distress reaction is associated with high scores on the problem index, high fear of crime, predominance of negative over positive mood states, and taking precautions on the street (which consists primarily of restricting one's activities, or avoidance responses). An instrumental response is associated with taking precautions at home, organizing with friends and neighbors, and the victim's belief that he or she might have avoided victimization through precautions. This response looks like an effort by the victim to try to establish or reestablish a sense of control over the environment.

Table 5 presents an analysis of subgroups of victims showing that the general distress reaction was more common among women, injured victims, and victims of lower socioeconomic status (those with lower incomes, less education, residents of Fordham and members of ethnic minorities). The instrumental response was more common among younger victims and victims of higher socioeconomic status.

TABLE 5

Association of Victim and Crime Characteristics with "General Distress"
and "Instrumental Response" to Crime

| | Means On: | |
	General Distress Reaction[1]	Instrumental Response[1]
Socioeconomic Status of Victim		
Personal Income		
Less than $5,000	0.28[2]	−0.28[2]
$5,000 to $15,000	0.00	0.01
$15,000 and over	−0.28	0.33
Education		
Did not graduate high school	0.21[2]	−0.33[2]
High school graduate	−0.11	0.15
Employment Status		
Not employed	0.09	−0.18[2]
Employed	−0.05	0.15
Neighborhood		
Park Slope	−0.19[2]	0.14
Fordham	0.26	−0.15
Flushing	−0.06	−0.05
Other Victim Characteristics		
Age		
Under 50	−0.02	0.07[2]
50-64	0.32	−0.23
65 and over	−0.43	−0.27
Sex		
Men	−0.21[2]	−0.03
Women	0.18	−0.01
Ethnicity		
Hispanic	0.18[2]	0.17
Black	0.27	−0.12
White	−0.18	0.11
Prior Victim		
Yes	0.01	−0.10
No	−0.02	0.11
Crime Characteristics		
Offense Type		
Violent Crime	0.13	−0.60[2]
Property Crime	−0.07	0.34
Victim/Offender Relationship		
Strangers	−0.04	0.01
Knew each other before crime	0.20	−0.05
Extent of Injury to Victim		
None	−0.12[2]	0.04

TABLE 5 (cont'd)

Minor (not treated)	−0.34	−0.18
Medical attention sought	0.49	−0.04
Financial Loss		
Under $100	−0.37	0.06
$100-$499	0.15	0.05
$500-$999	−0.02	−0.03
$1,000 and over	0.16	0.01

[1] Variables created from factor scores. Each variable has a range of −1 to 1 and a mean of ø.

[2] Significant at .05 level or better by two-tailed test.

Readjustment After Victimization

The few longitudinal studies that have examined the long-term adjustment of crime victims have largely concentrated on victims of rape (Burgess & Holmstrom, 1974a, 1978; Kilpatrick, Veronen, & Resick, 1979). They have generally found that, over the months following victimization, emotional distress diminishes but that, even years later, victims may still suffer flashbacks, phobic anxieties, recurrent dreams, or other manifestations of post-traumatic stress syndrome.

We did not expect to find such severe or enduring symptoms in our sample, nearly two-thirds of which were victims of burglary. But we were interested in whether the widespread emotional distress observed shortly after victimization would abate or still be evident four months after the crime.

Our results showed that four months after the crime all categories of crime-related problems had declined substantially. The mean score on the composite problem index declined significantly from 5.66 on the first interview to 2.35 on the second (t = −15.64, df = 181, p<.001), or a score roughly equivalent to one "major" or two "minor" problems for each victim. Problems with daily routine, problems resulting from property being stolen, and difficulty sleeping remained the most common problems. But roughly half of the people who reported these problems on the first interview no longer considered them a problem on the second interview.

In light of previous studies, it was anticipated that respondents' scores on the negative subscales of the Affect Balance Scale particularly depression and anxiety, would decrease in the months following victimization. It was also anticipated (although less strongly) that scores on the positive mood scales would increase as time passed.

Table 6 shows that these expectations were confirmed. At the time of the follow-up interview, victims scored significantly lower on three of the four negative mood scales (Depression, Anxiety, and Hostility) than they had at the initial interview. Only the Guilt scale showed little change over time. Moreover, at the time of the follow-up interview, victims scored significantly higher on the positive subscales of the ABS (Affection, Contentment, Joy, and Vigor) than during the initial interview. These results suggest that victimization is associated with both a suppression of positive moods and an augmentation of negative moods followed by a return to more positive and less negative affective states. Significant differences between the victims sampled and the test norm sample still existed on six of the subscales (Contentment, Vigor, Anxiety, Depression, Guilt, and Hostility) at the follow-up interview. These differences may indicate that respondents had not fully recovered four months following victimization, or simply that the victim sample differed from the norm sample of college students prior to victimization.

We do know, however, that the incident continued to be on the minds of many victims. Two in five victims reported that four months after the crime they had spoken with someone about the crime within the past week.

Fear of crime. The increased fear of crime that followed victimization subsided substantially four months after the crime. Scores on our fear of crime index declined significantly from a mean of 1.80 on the initial interview to 1.30 on the four-month follow-up (t = −4.84, df = 1.80, p< .01). By the time of the follow-up interview, women, who had shown a greater increase in fear of crime initially, no longer differed from men on the fear of crime index.

Precautions. We were surprised to find that although the increase in fear of crime that followed victimization had subsided substantially four months later, nearly all respondents continued to take the extra precautions they had begun after victimization. Ninety-eight percent of those who reported initially that they had begun to check doors and windows before going out still did so four months later. Eighty-five percent of those who had begun leaving lights, television, or radio on when going out still did so. Eighty percent of those who had begun avoiding particular areas still did so.

Moreover, in the interval between the first and second interviews, more than half the victims had started taking *additional* precautions. Fifty-three percent reported new precautions such as not going out alone

TABLE 6
ABS Scores:
First and Second Interview Compared

Scale	Initial Mean**	Follow-Up Mean	Significance
Joy	10.1	12.7	t (105) = −4.93**
Contentment	10.1	12.3	t (105) = −4.48**
Vigor	11.0	12.4	t (104) = −3.33**
Affection	12.2	13.7	t (104) = −3.31**
Anxiety	9.5	8.4	t (104) = 2.60**
Depression	6.5	5.5	t (104) = 2.79**
Guilt	5.1	5.0	t (104) = 0.36
Hostility	4.3	3.4	t (104) = 4.48**

* Significant at the .05 level or better (two-tailed test).
** Means differ slightly from those reported in Table 1 because they are based on only those victims who responded to both first and second interviews.

at night and riding in cabs and 52% reported installing new locks on doors or windows. Thus, the measures stemming from heightened fear of crime persisted even after the fear appeared to have subsided.

Victim's feelings about other people. On the four-month follow-up interview, we made an attempt to examine the long-term effects of victimization on respondents' feelings about other people. Sixty-five percent said that being a victim had not changed their relationships with others. But when victimization did affect relationships the effect was usually negative: Thirty-two percent of all victims felt that their relationships were worse while only 3% felt they were improved. Distrust seemed to be the cause for deteriorating relationships. For example, one victim said, "I used to talk to anyone. Now I don't." In other cases, the deterioration seemed to stem from the victim's belief that other people had been unwilling to help. One robbery victim said, "I don't talk to people as much anymore. The only people who helped were my family." Some victims isolated themselves because they felt people did not want to be around them. A man who was mugged said, "I was very depressed, so people didn't want to be near me."

The Experience of Support

In this study, we also looked at the effect of crime on those people who gave the victim assistance. People close to the victim are caught up in an approach-avoidance conflict. They want to help, but may experience costs in doing so. Psychologists have suggested that victims threaten people's belief in a just, orderly world. Lerner (1971) argues that people have a need to believe that the world is a fair place where bad things do not happen to good people. Victims may inadvertently challenge this belief and make others aware of their own fallibility. Studies have suggested that people around the victim frequently experience a heightened fear of crime as well as emotional suffering (Knudten, Meade, Knudten, & Doerner, 1976). Conklin (1971) has referred to these reactions as "secondary victimization."

About half (46%) of the 152 supporters we surveyed reported feeling uncomfortable listening to the victim tell them about the incident. The reasons for the supporters' distress varied. For some, listening to the victim increased their own feelings of vulnerability:

A roommate of a victim who was beaten in an unsuccessful robbery attempt in the hallway of their apartment house arrived home shortly after the attack. She calmed the victim down and got her to call the police. But, as a result of the incident, the roommate was nervous and frightened because, she said, "It could have been me." The supporter-roommate couldn't tell her fears to her parents for fear they would want her to give up her apartment and return home. (Friedman et al., 1982, p. 232)

Some supporters felt uncomfortable because hearing the victim talk about the incident made them feel concerned about the victim's safety. Other supporters reported feeling anger: The son-in-law of an old man who was robbed and then assaulted was upset by "the thought that this would happen to an old man" (Friedman et al., 1982, p. 232). In another case:

A mother witnessed an assault upon her 22-year-old son and subsequently testified in court. As a result of her testimony, she was threatened and her other two sons, who lived with her, were shot at. She reported being uncomfortable listening to her son talk about the incident because it reminded her of the impact that crime had had on all of their lives. She said that none of them saw friends anymore because, "No one wants to be around people who are targets for shooting." (Friedman et al., 1982, p. 232)

Fear of crime and taking precautions among supporters. Data from the supporter interviews confirm previous studies suggesting that knowing a victim enhances fear of crime (Conklin, 1971a, 1971b; Reactions to Crime Project, 1978). Thirty-two percent of supporters reported feeling nervous and frightened as a result of their interaction with the victim. Thirty-nine percent said they were more suspicious of people, while 38% said they felt less safe in their home and 35% felt less safe in their neighborhood. The effects of the original crime were, therefore, multiplied to include those who helped the victims.

As was true among the victim sample, many supporters reported that the increase in fear they felt immediately upon hearing of the victim's experience abated with time. "It affects you for a month or two," one supporter said.

Supporters, like victims, took added precautions following the victim's experience, although at a lower rate than victims. Since helping the victim, 60% of supporters reported becoming more cautious, 19% reported installing new locks or other measures to protect their residences from break-ins, 13% reported going out less at night, and 3% less during the day. One supporter, a neighbor of a burglary victim, reported that she had begun carrying a machete when she went to the mailbox.

We detected that fear and precautions among supporters were strongly affected by the strength of ties between victim and supporter. Increased fear and precautions were more common among supporters who felt close to the victim, supporters who reported frequently discussing problems with the victim, and supporters who were blood relations or lovers of the victim than among supporters with less close ties to the victim (see Table 7). The mother of a victim said that she "never had thought about being robbed" before her daughter's apartment had been burglarized. She added that because her daughter lived in a better area than she did, "It makes me think more."

Supporters who had had a previous victimization themselves were especially sensitive to the dangers of crime. Twenty-nine percent of this group reported taking added precautions in their neighborhoods compared to 12% of other persons who gave support to victims.* Moreover, 54% of supporters who had themselves been victims had scores of three or more on our fear of crime index compared to 42% of supporters who had never been victims.** One supporter of an assault victim (who was also an eyewitness to the incident) had twice been a victim of robbery during the previous year. At the time of the interview, she said, "I don't go out at night. I don't let anyone inside my door unless I know them and they identify themselves. I'm suspicious of everybody."

In spite of the ill effects they often experienced, most supporters did not regret that the victim had turned to them for assistance. One-fifth reported they were brought closer together by the experience, and indeed, only two supporters stated that their relationship was in jeopardy because of the incident. Nine in 10 supporters viewed their contribution to the victim as important. And the overwhelming majority (97%) did not wish that the victim had gone elsewhere for help.

CONCLUSION

This study reports on data collected about crime victims in order to determine whether they suffered from post-traumatic stress. The goal of the inquiry was a better understanding of the emotional aftermath of assault, robbery, and burglary.

The interviews from which the data were drawn did not directly address the symptoms that make up the syndrome of PTSD. However, the

---

*Significant at the .01 level (two-tailed test).
**Significant at the .05 level (two-tailed test).

TABLE 7

Effects of Supporter-Victim Ties on Fear of Crime and Precautions Among Supporters

Supporter-Victim Ties	Proportion of Supporters who:		
	Had Scores of 3 or More on the Fear of Crime Index	Took at Least 1 Precaution in Their Homes	Took at Least 1 Precaution in Their Neighborhood
Live in same neighborhood (n = 78)	53**	73**	26**
Live in different neighborhood (n = 67)	34	54	2
Supporter feels close to victim (n = 120)	47**	69**	17*
Supporter not close to victim (n = 23)	22	39	0
Frequently discuss problems (n = 83)	51**	72**	17*
Occasionally/never discuss problems (n = 67)	36	54	10
Blood relatives/lovers (n = 111)	47	68**	14
Other relationships (n = 39)	33	49	13

* Significant at .05 level or better (two-tailed test)
** Significant at .01 level or better (two-tailed test)

data did reveal that practically all the victims suffered emotional distress that often endured at least four months and that included components of PTSD, particularly sleep disturbances, constricted affect, feelings of estrangement from others, recurrent thoughts about the incident, and avoidance of situations that reminded them of the traumatic event. The latter two reactions are particularly prevalent among crime victims, because they, unlike victims of other traumatic incidents, often have good reason to fear a recurrence of the event. The recurrent thoughts and avoidance behavior among crime victims are probably more related to *anticipation* than to the salience of the trauma in and of itself. The data also indicate that people who assisted the victims suffered some of the same symptoms as the primary victims, suggesting that the trauma may be contagious but that secondary victims suffer a milder case.

The implications of these findings for helping crime victims will increase as knowledge of how best to help PTSD sufferers increases. Fredericks (personal communication, October, 1983) recommends, as do others (see the Introduction to this volume), reenacting the event and revisiting the scene with a sympathetic therapist. Our data indicate that victims did what came naturally: They talked about the crime. The findings that two out of five victims were still talking about the crime four months later suggest that the victims were engaged in a type of self-treatment. However, two other factors might have impeded the victims' emotional recovery. First, victims tended to avoid the place where the crime occurred while perhaps they should have been visiting it frequently. Second, the supporters felt uncomfortable when victims talked about the crime and might have conveyed the message implicitly or explicitly to the victims to stop talking so much about the crime. To the extent that such signals inhibited victims from talking about the crime, the supporters may have unknowingly been doing the victims a disservice. We may need to educate the public about the need to help family and friends who have been victims (Figley & McCubbin, 1983). Rather than encouraging them to shrug off a crime, victims perhaps should be encouraged to dwell on it.

In terms of treatment, the finding that there are different "styles" of reacting to victimization was intriguing. Ways should be explored to encourage those victims who react with fear, negative affect, and avoidance of situations to react instead with measures to regain control over their environment as other victims did. This would include considering ways they might have prevented the incident, securing their homes, and organizing with neighbors to prevent crime.

This study raises additional questions which need more attention from both practitioners and researchers in the future:

- We observed that supporters who had been victims suffered as helpers. Should, therefore, victims' programs focus on preparing former victims to help others so that their trauma is not repeated when they are called on to assist friends or family who have been victimized?
- Do people who respond to crime with an "instrumental response" as opposed to "general distress reaction" cope better in the long run? Is the instrumental response, which involves taking responsibility for the event, a strategy that can be taught?
- If a crime such as burglary can affect people for at least four months, what is the duration of PTSD for victims of catastrophes such as hostage taking?
- If people who assisted victims suffered indirect victimization, what about the family and friends of the victims of more major disasters? What is the psychic cost to supporters of helping family and friends through crises?

REFERENCES

American Institutes for Research. *Crisis intervention: Investigating the need for new applications.* B.B. Bourque, G.B. Brumback, Robert E. Krug, and Louis O. Richardson. March 1978.

American Psychiatric Association. *Diagnostic and statistical manual of mental health disorders* (3rd ed.). Washington, DC: American Psychiatric Association, 1980.

Bard, M., & Sangrey, D. *The crime victim's book.* New York: Basic Books, 1979.

Beck, A.T. *Depression: Clinical, experimental and theoretical aspects.* New York: Harper & Row, 1967.

Bowers, K.S. Pain, anxiety, and perceived control. *Journal of Consulting and Clinical Psychology,* 1968, *32,* 596-603.

Bulman, R.T., & Wortman, C.B. Attributions of blame and coping in the "real world": Severe accident victims react to their lot. *Journal of Personality and Social Psychology,* 1977, *35,* 351-363.

Burgess, A.W., & Holmstrom, L.L. Rape trauma syndrome. *American Journal of Psychiatry,* 1974a, *131,* 981-986.

Burgess, A.W., & Holmstrom, L.L. *Rape: Victims of crisis.* Bowie, MD: Robert J. Brady Company, 1974b.

Burgess, A.W. and Holmstrom, L.L. Recovery from rape and prior life stress. *Research in Nursing and Health,* 1978, *1,* 165-174.

Conklin, J.E. Criminal environment and support for the Law. *Law and Society Review,* November 1971a.

Conklin, J.E. Dimensions of community response to the crime problem. *Social Problems,* 1971b, *18,* 373-384.

Derogatis, L.R., Abeloff, M.D., & Melisaratos, N. Psychological coping mechanisms and survival time in metastatic breast cancer. *Journal of the American Medical Association*, 1979, *242*, 1504-1508.

Derogatis, L.R., & Meyer, J.K. A psychological profile of the sexual dysfunctions. *Archives of Sexual Behavior*, 1979, *8*, 201-223.

Dweck, C.S. The role of expectations and attributions in the alleviation of learned helplessness. *Journal of Personality and Social Psychology*, 1975, *31*, 674-685.

Figley, C.R. Catastrophe: An overview of family reactions. In C.R. Figley & H.I. McCubbin (Eds.), *Stress in the family. Vol. II: Coping with catastrophe.* New York: Brunner/Mazel, 1983.

Figley, C.R. & McCubbin, H.I. Looking to the future: Research, education, treatment and policy. In C.R. Figley & H.I. McCubbin (Eds.), *Stress in the family. Vol. II: Coping with catastrophe.* New York: Brunner/Mazel, 1983.

Frank, E., Turner, S.M., & Duffy, B. Depressive symptoms in rape victims. *Journal of Affective Disorders*, 1979, *1*, 269-297.

Friedman, K, Bischoff, H., Davis, R.C., & Person, A. *Victims and helpers: Reactions to crime.* New York. Victim Services Agency, 1982.

Glass, D.C., & Singer, J.E. *Urban stress: Experiments on noise and social stressors.* New York: Academic Press, 1972.

Janoff-Bulman, R. The two sides of self-blame: Inquiries into depression and rape. *Journal of Personality and Social Psychology*, 1979, *37*, 1798-1809.

Janoff-Bulman, R., & Wortman, C.B. Attributions of blame and coping in the "real world": Severe accident victims react to their lot. *Journal of Personality and Social Psychology*, 1977, *35*, 351-363.

Kilpatrick, D.G., Resick, P.A., & Veronen, L.J. Assessment of the aftermath of rape: Changing patterns of fear. *Journal of Behavioral Assessment*, 1979, *1*(2), 133-148.

Kilpatrick, D.G., Veronen, L.J., & Resick, P. The aftermath of rape: Recent empirical findings. *American Journal of Orthopsychiatry*. 1979, *49*, 658-669.

Knudten, R.D., Meade, A., Knudten, M., & Doerner, W. *Victims and witnesses: The impact of crime and their experience with the criminal justice system.* Report of the Marquette University Milwaukee County Victim/Witness Project, August 15, 1976.

Lerner, M.J. Observer's evaluation of a victim: Justice, guilt and verdical perception. *Journal of Personality and Social Psychology*, 1971, *20*, 127-135.

Reactions to crime project: Responses to perceived fear and insecurity. The results of the preliminary analysis: Findings and new directions. Northwestern University Center for Urban Affairs, April 28, 1978.

Sutherland, S., & Scherl, D.J. Patterns of response among rape victims. *American Journal of Orthopsychiatry*, 1970, *40*(3), 503-511.

Symonds, M. Victims of violence: Psychological effects and aftereffects. *American Journal of Psychoanalysis*, 1975, *35*, 1-26.

Waller, I., & Okihiro, N. *Burglary: The victim and the public.* Toronto: University of Toronto Press, 1978.

CHAPTER

7

Factors Predicting Psychological Distress Among Rape Victims

DEAN G. KILPATRICK, LOIS J. VERONEN, and CONNIE L. BEST

To determine what factors best predict rape-induced psychological distress at three months post-rape, victims were divided into low distress, moderately low distress, moderately high distress, and high distress groups. Information obtained at six to 21 days post-rape was compared across the four distress groups to evaluate if demographic characteristics, previous history, assault characteristics, or initial distress levels were related to three-month post-rape distress. Initial distress was a better predictor of subsequent psychological functioning than other variables. Implications of the findings for assessment and treatment of rape-induced and other types of post-traumatic stress disorder are discussed.

This research was supported by NIMH Grant No. MH29602 from the National Center for the Prevention and Control of Rape.

INTRODUCTION

This chapter describes a study we conducted that investigated the extent to which individual differences in victims' distress three months after a rape experience were related to victims' biographic/demographic characteristics, history prior to the rape, the characteristics of victims' rape experiences, and victims' levels of self-esteem and distress at six-21 days after the rape. The study was part of the Sexual Assault Research Project, a large National Institute of Mental Health-funded clinical research project (Kilpatrick & Veronen, 1984a), that assessed recent rape victims longitudinally at the following post-rape periods: 1) six-21 days, 2) one month, 3) three months, 4) six months, 5) one year, 6) 18 months, 7) two years, 8) three years, and 9) four years. A comparison group of nonraped women matched for age, race, and residential neighborhood was assessed at comparable intervals.

In this chapter, we will review evidence regarding the incidence and prevalence of rape and will argue that the number of rape victims suffering from post-traumatic stress disorder (PTSD) may be much larger than previously estimated. We will briefly summarize research findings regarding major rape-induced problems that victims experience and review such problems from a PTSD perspective. We will describe a learning theory model that explains the development of rape-induced problems, and emphasize that it is important to consider individual differences in response to a stressful event such as rape. Finally, we will describe and present the results of our study that investigated the extent to which individual differences in distress three months after a rape experience were related to a variety of variables.

More specific findings of the Sexual Assault Research Project will be presented subsequently, but a general finding was that acute psychological distress occurs following a rape and manifests itself by the victim's endorsement of nearly every negative symptom possible. At the initial post-rape assessment (six-21 days), victims scored as significantly more disturbed than nonvictims on 34 of 37 dependent measures from a battery of standardized objective psychological tests measuring anxiety, fear, psychological symptomatology, mood state, and self-esteem (Kilpatrick & Veronen, 1984a). There were no differences between the victims' status at six-21 days post-rape and one month post-rape. At three months post-rape, however, victims experienced substantial improvement on many measures, although they remained significantly more disturbed than nonvictims. Importantly, there were no significant differences between victims' scores at three months post-rape and their scores at six months, one year, 18 months, two years, three years, and four years post-rape (Kilpatrick & Veronen, 1983, 1984a). Given the apparent stability of victims' problems and distress after three months post-rape, it seemed appropriate to look at individual differences in distress at three months post-rape since it appeared that victims' distress levels at that point remain fairly consistent for at least three to four years afterward.

Rape is a traumatic event that produces extremely traumatic effects; yet most professionals involved in the assessment and treatment of rape victims have not used the PTSD framework to conceptualize and understand the problems of victims. Similarly, many professionals involved with victims of other types of post-traumatic stress are generally unfamiliar with rape victims and their problems. Thus, prior to describing our study and its results, we will discuss several issues that may help bridge the gap between those interested in rape victims and those interested in victims of other traumatic events.

INCIDENCE AND PREVALENCE OF RAPE

Contrary to popular belief, rape is not a rare event. Obtaining accurate estimates of the incidence and prevalence of rape is difficult since the majority of rape victims do not report to police, receive medical care from hospitals, or seek help from rape crisis centers or other victim service agencies (Kilpatrick, Best, & Veronen, 1983). Thus, examination of police reports, hospital records, or files from victim service agencies provides only a partial estimate of the number of women who have been raped.

Most experts agree that the victimization survey is the best way to estimate incidence and prevalence of major crimes, including rape (McDermott, 1979; Skogan, 1981; Sparks, 1982). Such surveys involve interviewing a sample of the general population about victimization experiences. Those who disclose having been victimized are asked about details of the assault as well as whether or not they reported the assault to police. In some cases, victims are also asked whether they received medical care or sought help from victim service agencies. Information from victimization surveys provides valuable data about incidence and prevalence as well as about the apparent extent of underreporting to police. However, such surveys never identify all victims, so experts agree that victimization rates obtained almost always underestimate true incidence and prevalence.

In a recent article, Koss (1983) noted that one study found that 13% of female college students reported having been raped sometime during their lives, and another found that 22% of adult women in a San Francisco sample had been victims of rape. With support from NIMH, we recently conducted a victimization survey in which a random sample of 2,004 adult female residents of Charleston County, South Carolina, was interviewed via telephone (Kilpatrick & Veronen, 1984c). In this sample, 14.5% of the women disclosed one or more attempted or completed sexual assault experiences. Of these, 5% had been victims of forcible rape and 4% of attempted rape (Kilpatrick, Best, & Veronen, 1983).

According to the 1980 census, there were 75,000,000 adult women in the United States. Thus, application of the 5% prevalence rate of rape obtained in our Charleston County study to the U.S. population of adult women produces an estimate that 3,750,000 adult women have been raped sometime during their lives. Application of the prevalence rates reported by Koss (1983) produces even higher estimates that between 9,750,000 and 16,500,000 women have been raped.*

With respect to the incidence of rape (i.e., number of rapes per year), the FBI Uniform Crime Reports indicate that 81,536 rapes were reported to police during 1981. Because of underreporting, this figure represents a rock-bottom underestimate. For example, in our Charleston County survey, we found that only 29% of the women who had been raped reported to police. Perhaps because of a lack of familiarity with some of the more recent literature, some influential authorities dramatically underestimate the extent to which women are at risk of being raped. Katz and Mazur (1979), after reviewing several studies, the latest of which was published in 1975, concluded that "the estimated chance of a female in the general population being raped is a minute fraction of 1%" (p. 313).

MAJOR RAPE-INDUCED PROBLEMS FROM A
PTSD PERSPECTIVE

Even a cursory examination of the nature of a rape experience, the symptoms of rape victims, and the diagnostic criteria for PTSD listed in

*It is interesting to note that the U.S. population contains more rape victims (3,750,000) than combat veterans (2,480,544) (Veterans Administration, 1980).

the Diagnostic and Statistical Manual of Mental Disorders (DSM-III, American Psychiatric Association, 1980) (see the Introduction of this volume) suggests that many rape victims could be diagnosed as experiencing PTSD. Recent research suggests that a rape experience is viewed as life-threatening by victims (Veronen, Kilpatrick, & Resick, 1979) and that many victims develop clinically significant and persistent rape-induced problems such as fear and anxiety (Kilpatrick, Resick, & Veronen, 1981; Kilpatrick & Veronen, 1983; Kilpatrick, Veronen, & Resick, 1979; Veronen & Best, 1983), depression (Atkeson, Calhoun, Resick, & Ellis, 1982; Frank, Turner, & Duffy, 1979), sexual dysfunction (Becker, Abel, & Skinner, 1979; Becker & Skinner, 1983; Feldman-Summers, Gordon, & Meagher, 1979), and diminished self-esteem (Kilpatrick & Veronen, 1984a; Veronen & Kilpatrick, 1980).

Among the sample of rape victims in our victimization survey (Kilpatrick & Veronen, 1984c), 64% stated they thought they might be killed or seriously injured during the assault. Not surprisingly, women respond to this stressor by experiencing high levels of fear and anxiety. For example, when asked about their emotional and physiological state during the rape, victims in our longitudinal assessment study used the following descriptors: scared (96%), worried (96%), terrified (92%), and helpless (88%). These victims also reported such physiological symptoms as shaking or trembling (96%), heart racing (84%), pain (72%), tight muscles (68%), and rapid breathing (64%) (Veronen et al., 1979). These data clearly document the fact that a rape experience meets the first major DSM-III diagnostic criterion: that it is a sufficiently potent stressor to produce distress in almost everyone (American Psychiatric Association, 1980).

There is clear evidence that most rape victims meet the second major diagnostic criterion for PTSD (APA, 1980), that of reexperiencing the traumatic event. Horowitz, Wilner, and Alvarez (1979) developed the Impact of Event Scale (IES) to measure two important elements of PTSD: event-related intrusion (intrusively experienced ideas, images, feelings, or bad dreams), and avoidance (consciously recognized avoidance of certain event-related ideas, feelings, and situations). We administered the IES to victims at six-21 days, three months, six months, one year, and two years post-rape and found that most victims were experiencing significant levels of rape-related intrusion and avoidance at all assessments (Kilpatrick & Veronen, 1984b). When follow-up was extended to three years post-rape, most victims (88.9%) were still experiencing rape-related intrusion and avoidance (Kilpatrick & Veronen, 1984a).

With respect to the third PTSD diagnostic criterion (APA, 1980) of numbing of responsiveness and reduced involvement with the external world, there is ample evidence that rape victims experience these problems. Our longitudinal research project found that rape-induced fear causes victims to undergo substantial restrictions in their life-style and activities after a rape (Kilpatrick, Veronen, & Resick, 1981). Research conducted by others suggests that victims become more depressed after a rape (Atkeson et al., 1982; Frank & Stewart, 1983). Rape victims have less sexual satisfaction after a rape (Feldman-Summers et al., 1979) and also have less desire to engage in sexual activity (Becker & Skinner, 1983). Victims also describe feeling detached and estranged from other people because of their rape.

The fourth diagnostic criterion for PTSD (APA, 1980) involves having at least two of six symptoms, all of which some rape victims have been shown to experience. For most victims, the most frequent symptoms are avoidance behaviors, hyperalertness, trouble concentrating, and intensification of symptoms when exposed to rape-related cues. Sleep disturbances also occur, although this appears to diminish with time. Guilt about survival is rarely a problem for victims, but guilt over behavior required for survival is sometimes experienced by victims. A much greater guilt-related problem for victims is a frequent tendency to irrationally blame themselves, rather than the rapist, for the assault.

In summary, a comparision of the DSM-III diagnostic criteria for PTSD with the symptoms most frequently experienced by rape victims suggests that rape produces PTSD in many victims.

A LEARNING THEORY MODEL OF THE
ETIOLOGY OF RAPE-INDUCED PROBLEMS

Our work with rape victims predated the current interest in PTSD, a fact that resulted in our not using PTSD as a theoretical construct to explain the etiology of rape-induced problems. Instead, we attempted to predict and explain rape-induced fear and anxiety, depression, and sexual dysfunction on the basis of simple principles derived from learning theory. Our theoretical notions about how rape produces such problems are presented in detail elsewhere (Kilpatrick et al., 1977; Kilpatrick et al., 1982; Veronen & Kilpatrick, 1983) and can be summarized as follows.

We believe that rape victims' fear and anxiety problems are largely acquired through classical conditioning, stimulus generalization, and second-order conditioning. Victims perceive rape as a situation in which their physical well-being and even their lives are in jeopardy. Natural, unconditioned responses to this type of painful, and potentially life-threatening, unconditioned stimuli are feelings of terror and autonomic symptoms of extreme anxiety. As a result, any stimuli associated with the rape become conditioned stimuli that acquire the capacity to evoke fear and anxiety as well. Thus, conditioned stimuli such as people, situations, or events present at the time of the rape acquire the capacity to produce conditioned responses of fear and anxiety through their association with rape-induced terror.

Some stimuli that are present in all rape situations, such as a man and cues associated with sexual intercourse, should be conditioned stimuli for fear and anxiety for practically all rape victims. Other stimuli are more idiosyncratic to each specific rape case, and these stimuli should be conditioned stimuli only in those cases in which they are involved. Thus, if one wished to predict the types of situations most likely to produce fear and anxiety for a particular rape victim, it would be necessary to obtain a detailed description of the stimuli present in her rape situation. For example, a woman awakened from sleep at night and raped by a white man with a gun might develop conditioned anxiety responses to sleeping, being alone at night, white men, and/or guns. The proposed classical conditioning model predicts that a victim's observed fears are related to the particular circumstances of her rape situation. Classical conditioning literature also suggests that fear and anxiety responses can generalize to other stimuli similar to conditioned stimuli present during the rape. Thus, the anxiety response elicited by the stimulus of the rapist might generalize to other men with similar physical characteristics.

Once anxiety symptoms have developed, rape victims often avoid situations because of anticipatory anxiety of being reminded of the rape. Because making an avoidance response is negatively reinforced by the anxiety reduction following the avoidance behavior, avoidance behavior frequently becomes quite resistant to extinction. Moreover, the number of cues precipitating avoidance behavior can be so numerous that the victim's behavior becomes quite restricted. Given that the key element in resolution of a phobia is exposure to the feared object, or extinction, avoidance behavior must be changed if fear responses are to be reduced. In addition, reduced levels of activity produced by avoidance behavior can contribute to the development of depression as well.

We have argued that cognitive events can become conditioned stimuli by their association with the rape experience (Kilpatrick, 1978; Kilpatrick et al., 1982). Thus, thoughts (cognitions) that are associated with the rape experience become conditioned stimuli (cues) for fear and anxiety. An example of this phenomenon is when a rape victim becomes anxious when asked to describe her rape experience to a friend, law enforcement official, crisis counselor, or therapist. In such a case, there are few, if any, physical stimuli to remind the victim of the rape. Rather, it is the cognitive stimuli (cues) that evoke anxiety through their association with the rape experience.

Regardless of whether rape cues are physical or cognitive, their presence will provoke anxiety in the victim. When such a cue produces a conditioned anxiety response, the victim is once more in a state of high arousal and subjective distress. According to the principles of classical conditioning, any stimuli or cues present during this state can become conditioned stimuli for conditioned emotional responses via their association with the original rape cues or conditioned stimuli.

Second-order conditioning is defined as the process in which a previously neutral stimulus, if associated with a conditioned stimulus capable of eliciting a particular response, acquires the capacity to elicit that response. Thus, any stimulus present at the same time as rape-related conditioned stimuli or cues can become a second-order conditioned stimulus that also evokes the conditioned response of fear and anxiety.

Second-order conditioning is important for two reasons. It promotes generalization of rape-induced anxiety to new stimuli and situations. Every time a victim becomes anxious in response to a rape-related stimulus, a whole new set of stimuli and situations become conditioned stimuli. Additionally, there is every reason to believe that it occurs any time a victim experiences anxiety in the presence of those with whom she discusses or thinks about the rape. Thus, such individuals, including therapists, may become stimuli that prompt anxiety and/or avoidance behavior.

PREVIOUS RESEARCH STUDYING INDIVIDUAL
DIFFERENCES IN VICTIM REACTIONS TO RAPE

It is encouraging that many rape researchers have avoided the client uniformity myth; that is, that all rape victims are alike. Rape victims bring to their rape experience differences in biographic/demographic characteristics. A rape experience itself can vary on a variety of dimensions. It is not unreasonable to assume that the psychological distress produced by a rape might vary as a function of the victim's characteristics and the nature of the rape itself. Several investigators have attempted to find predictors of response to rape with mixed results.

With respect to the victim's biographic/demographic characteristics as predictors, McCahill, Meyer, and Fischman (1979) reported that married rape victims currently living with their husbands had greater post-rape adjustment problems than other victims. Ruch and Chandler (1983) found that ethnicity and marital status were important predictors in that married, non-Caucasian women experienced the most trauma after their rapes. In contrast, an examination of differences in recovery rates for black and Caucasian victims in our project found no significant differences attributable to race (Morelli, 1981). McCahill et al. (1979) reported that the victim's age at the time of the rape predicted post-rape adjustment problems, with adult victims having greater problems than adolescent or child victims. These authors also reported that victims' employment status was related to adjustment problems, with victims who were currently employed having greater adjustment difficulties than those who were not.

With respect to the victim's history prior to the rape, Frank, Turner, Stewart, Jacob, and West (1981) found that victims with histories of psychiatric treatment had poorer initial adjustment than those without such histories. Atkeson et al. (1982) reported similar findings in that pre-rape history of anxiety, depression, or physical health problems was modestly predictive of post-rape depression, while the amount of trauma that occurred during the rape itself was not predictive of subsequent depression. The McCahill et al. (1979) study also found that victims with a pre-rape history of adjustment problems had more severe post-rape problems. Ruch, Chandler, and Harter (1980) studied life changes in the year before the rape and how they impacted on ratings of victims' adjustment obtained by social workers during emergency room treatment immediately after the rape. These investigators found a curvilinear relationship between life change and rape impact, with those victims having experienced a moderate amount of life changes faring better than those who had either no changes or a great many changes.

Frank, Turner, and Stewart (1980) studied the effects of several aspects of the rape experience itself on adjustment within the first month post-rape and found no significant differences in individual response as a function of a variety of rape experience characteristics. Similarly, Ruch and Chandler (1983) found no significant effects of the characteristics of the rape upon the amount of psychological trauma experienced afterward. McCahill et al. (1979) also found that the characteristics of the assault made no significant difference in victims' short-term reactions.

However, these investigators found that victims of particularly brutal rapes had greater adjustment problems at one year post-rape.

Norris and Feldman-Summers (1981) examined the effects of several variables upon rape victims using a sample of women whose rapes occurred an average of 3.4 years prior to assessment. On the basis of victim interviews, index scores were derived in each of the following areas: 1) whether the rape was reported to the police and/or a rape center; 2) whether the victim was vulnerable to claims of responsibility for the assault; 3) whether understanding significant others were present after the assault; and 4) the severity of the assault. Impact measures included psychosomatic symptoms, changes in sexual frequency and satisfaction, and changes in reclusiveness. Victims were asked to describe impact within the first six months post-rape. Whether the rape was reported had no effect on impact, but some of the other variables were predictive, although only to a modest degree. For example, when used in multiple regression analyses, the index variables correlated .30 with psychosomatic symptoms, .32 with "going out alone to movies and concerts," and .32 with "going out alone to bars."*

If these studies of individual differences in response to rape are carefully analyzed, it is clear that they are based on some of the following assumptions: First, the victim brings to the rape a certain ability to cope with stress in general and with the stress of a rape situation in particular; second, the ability of the victim to cope with stress is based on her previous life history, certain constitutional factors, and level of psychological functioning at the time of the rape; third, the immediate psychological impact of the rape is a combined function of the potency of the rape as a stressor and the victim's ability to cope with the situation; fourth, the victim's subsequent psychological adjustment to the rape is a function of the rape's immediate impact and the victim's continuing ability to cope with rape-induced distress; and fifth, the victim's post-rape interactions with significant others, family members, friends, law enforcement agencies, hospitals, and/or treatment providers can have either positive, negative, or mixed effects on subsequent psychological adjustment in that they can serve as additional sources of stress, enhancers of coping ability, or some combination of the two.

---

*It is important to remember that the percentage of the variance in impact accounted for by the correlations reported in this study is approximately 10% (r^2).

METHOD

Overview of Study Design

Our Sexual Assault Research Project (SARP) longitudinally assessed recent rape victims and a comparison group of nonvictims matched for age, race, and residential neighborhood. This study produced considerable evidence that rape victims improve substantially from initial assessment to the three-month post-rape assessment. The study also produced evidence that victims continue to have significant rape-related distress for up to four years post-rape and that victims' levels of distress do not decrease significantly after three months post-rape. The present study was conducted to determine the extent to which four types of information are useful in predicting individual differences in victims' distress at three months post-rape.

The four types of information are: 1) victims' biographic/demographic characteristics and history prior to the rape, 2) characteristics of the rape itself, 3) victims' self-esteem six-21 days after the rape, and 4) victims' initial distress at six-21 days post-rape. Based on assessment data collected at three months post-rape, a Distress Index was calculated for each victim. Distress Index scores were rank-ordered and divided into four groups based on quartile splits: 1) low distress, 2) low moderate distress, 3) high moderate distress, and 4) high distress. The pre-rape demographic and background information, the assault characteristics of the rape, the initial post-rape self-esteem, and initial post-rape distress scores of the four distress groups were compared to determine the extent to which each type of information was predictive of level of distress at three months post-rape.

Subjects

Participants were 125 female, recent rape victims, ages 16 or older, who had completed the six-21–day and three-month post-rape assessments as a part of the Sexual Assault Research Project. All victims reported having had an attack that met the following criteria: 1) it occurred without the victim's consent; 2) it involved force or threat of force, and 3) it involved a completed act of oral, anal, and/or vaginal sexual relations.

Victims were recruited from a pool of victims seen by People Against Rape (PAR), a rape crisis center in the Charleston, South Carolina area. PAR provides services to long-term as well as recent victims, but all potential referrals to this study were recent victims seen by PAR at a hospital-based evaluation and treatment center.* PAR counselor advocates obtained verbal permission from victims to be contacted by the SARP staff about participation in the study and then sent a list of potential referrals to SARP. Victims were contacted by a female member of the SARP staff who explained the study and obtained written informed consent from the victims.

The study was described as an investigation of the effects of stressful life events that involved being interviewed and taking paper-and-pencil tests. After volunteering, each victim was informed she would receive seven dollars per hour to partially defray her expenses incurred in participation. Of victims contacted by the project staff, 62.1% agreed to participate in the study.**

Since a major purpose of the study was to investigate if victims' biographic/demographic characteristics predicted distress at three months post-rape, our description of the victim sample on these variables will be presented in the Results section rather than here.

Assessment Instruments

Four sets of assessment instruments were used. The first set was administered at the six-21–day post-rape assessment and collected information about victims' biographic/demographic characteristics, previous history, and potentially stressful life events that happened in the year prior to the rape. This set included the following three instruments:

1) *Biographic/Demographic Data Form.* Using a structured interview format, information was collected about the respondent's age, race, occupational status, current marital status, current living arrangements, religious preference, and number of children. Victims were asked for additional information about length of time in their city and neighborhood at the time of the rape, and where (city and state) they were raped. A sample item from the form is: "What is your current marital status?"

---

*As a part of an official law enforcement protocol, recent rape victims in a three-county area are taken to this hospital center where they undergo a medical-legal rape examination and receive treatment for medical trauma. Volunteer counselor advocates from PAR accompany victims throughout their examination, explain procedures to them, give emotional support, and provide limited crisis counseling to victims.

**Low participation rates represent a major problem in this type of rape victim research, but the 62.1% rate obtained in this study is higher than that reported in several other clinical research studies (Kilpatrick & Veronen, 1984a). No information was available about the 37.9% of victims that did not participate, so it was impossible to compare the characteristics of participants and nonparticipants.

2) *The Life Events Inventory* is a 56-item modification of the Holmes and Rahe (1967) social readjustment rating scale. Victims were presented with a list of life events and changes and requested to indicate whether each event had occurred in the one-year period immediately prior to the rape. In some cases, respondents also provided information about the reasons for and frequency of changes. A sample item from this inventory is: "How many times during the past year have you changed your place of residence?"

3) *The Previous History Inventory* is a structured interview designed to measure the respondent's prior functioning in several areas. The inventory contains 100 items in sections: (a) job history, which measures history of employment-related problems, (b) legal history, which measures history of problems with the criminal justice system, (c) drug or alcohol abuse history, (d) assault history, which measures history of robbery, physical abuse, sexual molestation, attempted rape or rape, and (e) psychological problems and treatment history. A sample item from this inventory is: "Have you ever seen a psychiatrist, psychologist, social worker, or counselor for problems you have had? If yes, when was the most recent consultation?"

The second set of measures was obtained from the Rape Assault Characteristics Checklist, the information for which was gathered by the victim's volunteer counselor/advocate from PAR.

4) *Rape Assault Characteristics Checklist.* This information was included in the clinical case files maintained for each PAR client and included information from victims they worked with about several characteristics of the rape experience itself.* A PAR volunteer reviewed the files of participants and filled out an Assault Characteristics Checklist that included the following information about each victim's rape experience:

1) the number of assailants;
2) the assailant's relationship to the victim (i.e., seen before, known well, total stranger);
3) assailant's use of physical force;
4) assailant's racial status;
5) extent of physical injuries sustained by victim;
6) use of weapon by assailant;
7) location of rape (i.e., in victim's home, other building, automobile, outside location); and
8) type of sexual activity involved in rape (i.e., oral sex, anal sex, and/or sexual intercourse).

---

*The SARP staff did not have access to these clinical case files.

A third set of instruments was administered at the six-21–day post-rape assessment to collect information about the victim's current (at six-21 days) post-rape distress and self-esteem. Instruments included in this set were:

5) *Profile of Mood States Scale* (POMS) (McNair, Lorr, & Droppleman, 1971) is a 65-item, 5-point, Likert-type adjective rating scale that measures six-factor analytically derived dimensions of subjective mood state: tension-anxiety, depression-dejection, anger-hostility, vigor-activity, fatigue-inertia, and confusion-bewilderment. Scores on each dimension are converted to T scores, so a mood profile can be constructed. Participants were requested to rate these items to reflect their moods during the past week. McNair et al. (1971) have established both test-retest and internal consistency reliabilities for the six mood state dimensions. Alpha coefficients ranged from .84 to .95. Test-retest reliability coefficients over an average of 20 days ranged from .65 to .74. With respect to validity, the POMS has been shown to distinguish between rape victims and nonvictims up to one year post-rape (Kilpatrick & Veronen, 1984a). A sample item from the POMS is: "Tense" (item to be rated on a 5-point scale with respect to how descriptive it is of how respondent has been feeling during the past week, including today).

6) *Self-report Inventory* (SRI) (Bown, 1961) is a 48-item measure of self-esteem. Participants are asked to rate each item on a 5-point, Likert-type scale as to how much that item is "like me" or "unlike me." The inventory includes items relating to esteem in a number of settings. The eight subscales are: self, others, children, authorities, work, parents, hope, and reality. The self subscale is said to be most closely related to self-esteem. Total score and subscale scores are obtained. Robinson and Shaver (1973) reported that the subscales have generally good internal consistency, with the exception of the reality subscale (alpha = .28). Alpha coefficients for the self (.78) and total (.87) scales are high. The SRI has been shown to distinguish rape victims from nonvictims for at least one year post-rape (Kilpatrick & Veronen, 1984a). A sample item from this inventory is: "I don't seem to have very much basic respect for myself."

The fourth and final set of instruments were those administered during the three-month post-rape assessment and that contributed to the Distress Index:

7) *The Derogatis Symptom Check List 90-R* (SCL-90-R) (Derogatis, 1977) is a 90-item, self-report symptom inventory designed to reflect psychological symptom patterns of psychiatric and medical patients. Scores are

obtained for nine primary symptom dimensions and three global indices of distress. Three scores from the SCL-90-R were used in the Distress Index: a) anxiety, b) phobic anxiety, and c) Global Severity Index. The anxiety score measures ". . . general signs such as nervousness, tension and trembling . . .[and] panic attacks, feelings of terror, feelings of apprehension, and dread, and some of the somatic correlates of anxiety" (Derogatis, 1977, p. 21). Phobic anxiety measures ". . . a persistent fear response to a specific person, place, object, or situation which is characterized as being irrational and disproportionate to the stimulus and which leads to avoidance or escape behavior" (Derogatis, 1977, p. 23). The Global Severity Index is described as "the best single indicator of the current level or depth of ". . . numbers of symptoms and intensity of perceived distress" (Derogatis, 1977, p. 27).

Derogatis (1977) has established both test-retest reliability and internal consistency for the nine factors of the SCL-90-R. Alpha coefficients range from .77 to .90, and test-retest values range from .78 to .90, with a one-week interval between tests. The SCL-90-R has been shown to discriminate rape victims from nonvictims for at least three years post-rape (Kilpatrick et al., 1979; Kilpatrick et al., 1981; Kilpatrick et al., 1983; Kilpatrick & Veronen, 1984a). A sample item from the SCL-90-R is: "How much were you distressed by feeling afraid to travel on buses, subways, or trains?"

8) *The State-Trait Anxiety Inventory* (STAI) (Spielberger, Gorsuch, & Lushene, 1970) is a 40-item, self-report scale measuring the variables of state and trait anxiety. The trait anxiety score measures how anxious the respondent *generally* is rather than how anxious she or he is at the present time and was used in the Distress Index. An estimate of the internal consistency of this scale yielded an alpha of .89 (Spielberger et al., 1970). The test-retest reliability of the trait anxiety score over a 104-day test interval was .77 for a group of 22 females. The STAI has been shown to distinguish rape victims from nonvictims for at least one year post-rape (Kilpatrick & Veronen, 1984a). A sample item from the trait anxiety scale is: "I worry too much over something that really doesn't matter."

9) *The Veronen-Kilpatrick Modified Fear Survey* (MFS) (Veronen & Kilpatrick, 1980) is a 120-item inventory of potentially fear-producing items and situations. Each item is rated regarding the degree of disturbance it produces. Two MFS scores were used in the Distress Index. The rape subscale score represents ". . . an estimate of the extent to which a woman was disturbed by an aggregate of stimuli and situations selected by a normative group of other rape victims as fear-engendering and rape-related" (p. 388). The second score, the overall MFS score is the sum of fearfulness ratings to all 120 MFS items. Alpha coefficients for

the subscales range from .81 to .94 and is .98 for the overall score. Test-retest values over a 2.5-month interval for subscales range from .60 to .74 and is .73 for the overall score. The MFS has been shown to distinguish rape victims from nonvictims for at least three years post-rape (Kilpatrick et al., 1979; Kilpatrick et al., 1981; Kilpatrick & Veronen, 1983).

Procedure

All victims were individually assessed at six-21 days post-rape and three months post-rape. Assessment data were gathered by one of four female research assistants, all of whom had extensive experience working with rape victims.

After three-month post-rape data were collected, the Distress Index was computed for each victim in the following manner: first, scores on each of the six measures comprising the Index (i.e., SCL-90-R anxiety, phobic anxiety, and Global Severity Index; STAI trait anxiety; and MFS rape and overall scores) were converted to standard scores; second, each victim's standard scores on each of the six measures were summed to yield the total Distress Index for each victim; and third, the Distress Indices for all 125 victims were rank-ordered and divided into quartiles to form the four victim groups: a) low distress (n = 31); b) moderately low distress (n = 32); c) moderately high distress (n = 32); and d) high distress (n = 30).

Four separate sets of data analyses were used to evaluate the extent to which various information sets were related to three-month post-rape distress. First, biographic/demographic data and previous history of the four distress groups were compared. Second, the extent to which the four distress groups had experienced different life changes in the year prior to the rape was studied. Third, the characteristics of the rape assault itself were compared across the four distress groups. Fourth, the four distress groups' initial six-21–day post-rape mood state and self-esteem scores were compared.

RESULTS

Biographic/Demographic and Previous History Data

The continuous variable of age was analyzed using a single-factor analysis of variance and did not differ significantly across the four distress groups. The remaining noncontinuous variables were analyzed via a series of *chi square* analyses. As was the case with age, no significant differences across the four groups were found on the remaining bio-graphic/demographic variables. Although no significant differences oc-curred among groups, the whole victim sample (n = 125) had the following characteristics. Mean age was 26.8 years. With respect to racial status, 53.6% of sample members were white, 44.8% were black, and 1.6% were classified as some other race. With respect to educational status, 30.4% had not completed high school, 32.0% completed high school, 24.8% attended some college, and 12.8% graduated from college. The vast majority of these victims were residents of the state of South Carolina (88.8%), with only 7.2% having lived in the state for less than a year. Of these victims, 44.8% had never married and were not cohab-iting, 22.4% were married, 26.4% were separated or divorced, 2.4% were widowed, and 4.0% were cohabiting.

The five sections of the Previous History Inventory contain 90 items, each of which was analyzed across the four groups via a series of *chi square* analyses. Only three items differed significantly across groups. All items regarding previous psychiatric history and treatment were nonsignificant. Since one would expect to obtain 4.5 significant differ-ences out of 90 analyses using the $p<.05$ level of significance, the three significant findings are best regarded as spurious and will neither be reported nor discussed.

Life Changes Data

Each of the 50 items in the Life Events Inventory was compared across the four groups via a series of *chi square* analyses. Out of the 50 items, seven significant findings occurred, which exceeds the 2.5 that should occur by chance at the .05 level of significance. These items are depicted in Table 1. However, given the relatively low percentage of significant findings, these life event differences among groups should be viewed with great caution. Three of the seven significant findings are particularly interesting. First, a surprisingly large number of victims in all groups reported having been physically assaulted in the year prior to the rape. Second, a relatively large percentage of victims had lost a close family member other than a spouse by death in the year prior to the rape, but considerably fewer of the low distress group had done so. Third, women in the high distress group had a dramatically lower frequency of loving intimate relationships with men in the year prior to the rape than the other groups.

TABLE 1
Life Event Differences Among Distress Groups (n = 123)

1. Experience change in trouble with boss (a lot more or a lot less)?

Group	Yes	No	NA*
Low Distress	9.7%	54.8%	35.5%
Moderately Low Distress	25.0	50.0	25.0
Moderately High Distress	6.5	32.2	61.3
High Distress	20.0	23.3	56.7

2. Placed in jail or on probation?

Group	Yes	No	NA
Low Distress	3.2%	0.0%	96.8%
Moderately Low Distress	0.0	0.0	100.0
Moderately High Distress	16.1	0.0	83.9
High Distress	3.3	0.0	96.7

3. Experienced major business change?

Group	Yes	No	NA
Low Distress	0.0%	45.2%	54.8%
Moderately Low Distress	6.3	53.1	40.6
Moderately High Distress	6.4	19.4	74.2
High Distress	0.0	26.7	73.3

4. Physically assaulted during past year?

Group	Yes	No	NA
Low Distress	25.8%	0.0%	74.2%
Moderately Low Distress	6.2	0.0	93.8
Moderately High Distress	22.6	0.0	77.4
High Distress	23.3	0.0	76.7

5. Who was assailant in physical assault?

Group	Stranger	Relative	Acquaintance	Significant Other	NA
Low Distress	9.7%	3.2%	0.0%	12.9%	74.2%
Moderately Low Distress	0.0	3.1	0.0	3.1	93.8
Moderately High Distress	0.0	9.7	9.7	3.2	77.4
High Distress	3.3	3.3	0.0	16.7	76.7

6. Lost close family member (other than spouse) by death?

Group	Yes	No
Low Distress	12.9%	87.1%
Moderately Low Distress	37.5	62.5
Moderately High Distress	29.0	71.0
High Distress	33.3	66.7

7. Number of times had a loving intimate relationship with a man?

Group	None	1	2	3 or more
Low Distress	13.8%	51.7%	20.7%	13.8%
Moderately Low Distress	16.1	71.0	9.7	3.2
Moderately High Distress	20.0	66.7	10.0	3.3
High Distress	44.4	37.1	18.5	0.0

* NA = Not Applicable

Rape Assault Characteristics Data

The series of *chi square* analyses conducted on the rape assault characteristics data revealed no significant differences across distress groups on any of the rape assault characteristics. That is, there were no differences among distress groups with respect to the number of assailants, the assailants' relationship to the victim, the assailants' racial status, the use of physical force, the use of a weapon, the extent of the victim's physical injuries, the location of the assault, and the type of sexual activity involved in the rape.

Mood State and Self-esteem Data

The six mood state variables and the nine self-esteem scores were compared across groups by a separate analysis of variance for each variable. The mood profiles of the four groups are presented in Figure 1. The mood profile of a comparison group of nonvictims is also included in this figure, although the nonvictims' scores were not used in the analyses of variance. The analyses indicated that significant differences among group means occurred for all of the six mood state variables ($p<.01$). The Duncan multiple range procedure was used to determine which group means differed significantly (Duncan, 1955). For all mood variables except confusion, the low distress group was significantly different from the moderately low, moderately high, and high distress groups. With respect to confusion, the low distress group differed significantly from the moderately high distress and high distress groups, but not from the moderately low distress group. In summary, the initial mood profile of the low distress group was less disturbed than the other three groups.

The mean self-esteem scores of the four groups from the Self-Report Inventory are presented in Table 2. The analyses of variance indicated that significant differences among groups occurred on the self and reality variables. The Duncan multiple range procedure revealed that, on both of these variables, the low distress group was significantly different from the moderately high distress and high distress groups but not from the moderately low distress group.

Post Hoc Analysis of Distress Index, Mood State, and Self-esteem Intercorrelations

The previous analyses indicated that mood state and some aspects of self-esteem at six-21 days post-rape were strongly related to level of

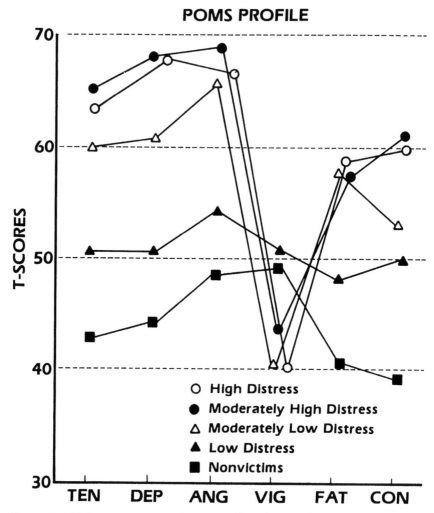

Figure 1. Initial assessment mood state profiles of 3-month post-rape victim and nonvictim groups

distress at three months post-rape. Although the tests used to measure mood state and self-esteem (i.e., POMS and SRI) were not used to construct the three-month post-rape Distress Index, it was possible that these tests may have tapped some of the same distress variables as were tapped by the Distress Index measures (SCL-90-R, STAI, MFS). If the six-21–day post-rape POMS and SRI scores were highly correlated with

TABLE 2
Self-esteem Scores of the Coping Success Groups (n = 123)

Group	SRI Variable								
	Self*	Other	Authority	Child	Work	Reality**	Parent	Hope	Total
Low Distress	17.33	17.79	15.61	18.67	16.63	15.21	15.13	19.29	16.82
Moderately Low Distress	15.68	17.96	15.55	16.91	16.87	15.50	13.50	18.00	16.28
Moderately High Distress	12.75	16.38	14.00	18.75	16.19	13.00	14.70	17.50	15.40
High Distress	13.67	17.83	15.18	20.26	16.37	12.80	14.71	18.05	15.74

* Significant p < .05
** Significant p < .01

the six-21–day post-rape scores on the same SCL-90-R, STAI, and MFS variables used in the Distress Index at three months post-rape, then we would know the extent to which mood state and self-esteem are useful in predicting subsequent distress. Therefore, a series of Pearson product moment correlations was computed to determine the relationships among the six POMS scores, the SRI scores on which significant differences had been found (i.e., self and reality), and the six variables used to compute the Distress Index. *All these scores were obtained at the six-21–day post-rape assessment.* Additionally, correlations were obtained between the three-month post-rape Distress Index itself and the other variables (i.e., POMS Tension, Depression, Anger, Vigor, Fatigue, Confusion; SRI Self & Reality).

The results of these analyses are presented in Table 3. Examination of this intercorrelation matrix reveals that, at the six-21–day assessment, all but two of the 36 correlations between POMS variables and Distress Index variables were statistically significant. Relationships were strongest for the tension and depression variables, with individual correlations ranging from a low of .51 (A-trait, or trait anxiety, and tension) to a high of .71 (GSI and depression). The mood of vigor was negatively related to Distress Index variables, but the correlations were positive between the other mood variables and Distress Index variables. Confusion had the lowest correlation with the Distress Index variables and was not significantly correlated with the two MFS variables. Correlation between self-esteem variables and Distress Index variables were lower than with mood state variables and were negative. The highest correlations were between self and A-trait ($r = -.44$) and between reality and A-trait ($r = -.39$).

Finally, the correlations between each mood and self-esteem variable at six-21 days post-rape and the Distress Index score at three months post-rape were all statistically significant and ranged from a high of .38 for depression to lows of .21 for confusion and of $-.21$ for self. Tension, depression, anger, fatigue, and confusion at six-21 days post-rape were positively related to three-month post-rape distress. Vigor, self, and reality scores at six-21 days post-rape were negatively related to distress at three months post-rape.

DISCUSSION

The major objective of this study was to determine whether there were factors that predicted individual differences in rape victims' distress

TABLE 3
Intercorrelation Matrix (n = 124)

Distress	Index Variables	POMS Variables: 6-21-Day Scores						SRI Variables	
		Tension	Depression	Anger	Vigor	Fatigue	Confusion	Self	Reality
6-21-Day	SCL-90-R								
S	Anxiety	.67	.57	.51	-.30	.55	.42	-.15*	-.13*
C	Phobic Anxiety	.67	.59	.52	-.34	.50	.43	-.22	-.23
O	GSI	.64	.71	.60	-.33	.56	.48	-.30	-.27
R	STAI								
E	A-trait	.51	.66	.41	-.41	.49	.39	-.44	-.39
S	MFS								
	Rape	.54	.57	.52	-.38	.38	.20*	-.22*	-.23*
	Overall	.51	.57	.50	-.44	.35	.19*	-.32	-.23*
At 3 Mos.	Distress Index	.33	.38	.26	-.25	.29	.21	-.21	-.34

* Nonsignificant

at three months post-rape. As noted earlier, in a longitudinal study we found that victims' distress at three months remained stable at four years. Any factors predicting three-month post-rape distress could also be expected to predict chronic distress as well. We found that there were factors that predicted chronic distress, although we also found that several factors identified by other investigators as predictors of post-rape distress were not associated with differing post-rape distress levels in this study. The victims' level of distress at six-21 days post-rape proved to be highly predictive of their level of distress at three months post-rape, and, by inference, of their chronic distress levels for up to four years post-rape.

Thus, we conclude that rape victims do not suffer from a delayed stress reaction, since symptoms at three months were maintained up to four years. The idea that initial distress after a traumatic event is predictive of long-term chronic distress is simple, parsimonious, and at variance with current thinking. Some rape theorists believe, for example, that there is a specific stage in victims' recovery during which victims use massive denial or repression of their rape-induced problems. Sutherland and Scherl (1970) argued that there was such a stage and called it the phase of outward adjustment with denial. Bard and Sangrey (1979) described a recoil stage during which crime victims use a great deal of denial in an attempt to cope with what has happened to them. Proponents of this denial stage might be expected to argue that the victims in our study who reported low distress at three months post-rape were merely denying their problems, rather than actually experiencing less distress. In refutation of this theory, we offer three main points. First, Bard and Sangrey's (1979) and Sutherland and Scherl's (1970) theories regarding a denial stage were based on unstructured, impressionistic, clinical observations, *not* on empirical research. Second, empirical data from longitudinal assessment studies do not indicate that the pattern of recovery for most victims includes a period of low distress followed by a substantial exacerbation of symptoms. Third, without a method by which victims with "genuine" low distress can be empirically distinguished from victims with denial-induced, "false" low distress, the argument that observed low distress ought not be taken at face value appears to be circular, nonscientific, and counterproductive.

Further, our findings suggest that delayed PTSD may not be prevalent among rape victims. Certainly some rape victims who exhibit low distress at three months post-rape will subsequently experience exacerbations that could be labeled as delayed stress. However, we argue that there is little evidence to support a contention that delayed stress is a major problem for most rape victims. In our view, diagnosis of delayed PTSD reactions is probably inappropriate unless: 1) the individual has been carefully assessed longitudinally, beginning shortly after the traumatic event, and 2) the assessment indicates that the individual functioned well immediately after the event and only developed symptoms after a period of good adjustment. In our opinion, much of the current discovery of delayed PTSD among combat veterans may be at least partially an artifact of a failure to carefully assess for PTSD symptoms during and immediately after the veteran's military service. Unlike our colleagues working with combat veterans and others with PTSD, we were able to assess rape victims shortly after their assault, thereby documenting the fact that the nondistressed victim is the exception rather than the rule. Most victims we studied would have to undergo a period of substantial improvement to be capable of developing delayed PTSD reactions.

Synthesis: Profile of Rape Victim Reactions

After contrasting our findings with prevailing views of PTSD victims, let us now describe the characteristics of the rape victim who was low in distress at three months post-rape and how she compared with her counterparts who were initially more distressed.

1) She did *not* differ from more distressed victims on the biographic/demographic characteristics of age, race, educational status, marital status, living arrangements prior to the rape, and religious preference. Our negative findings regarding race, marital status, and living arrangements are in contrast to those reported by McCahill et al. (1979), and Ruch and Chandler (1983).
2) She did *not* differ with regard to most areas of personal history, including previous psychological difficulties and/or treatment for such problems. This finding is in contrast to reports by Frank et al. (1980), Atkeson et al. (1982), and McCahill et al. (1979).
3) She tended to have somewhat fewer life changes in the year prior to her rape, particularly fewer than the high distress victims. She was less likely to have lost a close family member (other than spouse) by death during the previous year, and was more likely to have had loving, intimate relationships with men. The fact that 44.4% of high distress victims lacked such relationships seems particularly noteworthy.
4) The characteristics of her rape experience did *not* differ from the

assaults of the more distressed victims. These findings were consistent with those of other investigators (Atkeson et al., 1982; Frank et al., 1980; McCahill et al., 1979; Ruch & Chandler, 1983).

5) Her self-esteem was significantly higher than that of the other victims. Self-esteem was found to be negatively correlated with distress in that victims with the greatest self-esteem had the least distress and vice versa. Which comes first, the low self-esteem or the distress, is one of those "chicken or the egg" problems which is impossible to answer. In any case, victims with high initial self-esteem were less distressed at three months post-rape than their counterparts with lower self-esteem.

6) Her initial distress was much lower than that experienced by other victims.

Examination of Figure 1 indicates that her mood profile was within normal limits although it was somewhat higher than that of nonvictims.

Treatment Implications for Rape Victims

For those who work with rape victims, our findings suggest that a rape victim's initial distress is an accurate predictor of her subsequent distress. Thus, it is probably unnecessary for therapists to collect a vast array of multivariate information from a victim to predict whether she is likely to be functioning well or poorly in the future. More of the variance in three-month post-rape adjustment was predicted by the single mood score of depression than other investigators have been able to predict using a combination of several variables. Moreover, the measure of mood state used is relatively easy to obtain; it is a paper-and-pencil test. Previous research indicated that initial distress is pervasive (Kilpatrick et al., 1979), so one might be able to use a variety of other measures to tap initial distress as well. The standardized measures of distress in our assessment battery are simple enough to be used by crisis counselors and mental health care delivery professionals. Although it has not been tested empirically, it seems logical that an interview might also be developed that assesses initial distress. Since victims who experience the least distress soon after the rape are the ones who are most likely to be doing well at three months post-rape, this information has important implications for the timing and selection of victims for treatment intervention.

The major implication of our findings for treatment is that we now have ample justification for assuming that victims who need the most help are those whose initial distress is greatest. In contrast, it appears that approximately 25% of recent rape victims are doing reasonably well even at six-21 days post-rape. These victims probably have little need for formal treatment intervention.

Treatment for Other Victims

Our findings may also prove useful to those interested in other victims of trauma, although a lack of well-controlled studies directly comparing the impact of rape with that of other traumatic events suggests that some caution is in order regarding generalization of our findings to victims of other traumatic events. Still, our learning theory model suggests that individuals exposed to equally traumatic events should experience similar difficulties because classical conditioning, stimulus generalization, second-order conditioning, and avoidance learning are basic universal phenomena. Thus, we expect that our theoretical analysis of how PTSD problems develop might prove useful in explaining how other types of traumatic events produce PTSD.

Our findings are most relevant to those dealing with trauma victims in an acute situation. Clinicians who see trauma victims soon after the trauma itself might find it useful to assess initial distress as a method of determining who needs treatment most. Relatively distressed individuals could be given first priority for treatment. Less distressed individuals could be told that they appear to be coping well, given information about "danger signals" of delayed PTSD, and encouraged to seek treatment later if these signals occur.

With respect to treatment for PTSD symptoms induced by other types of traumatic events, we believe that treatment procedures should focus on helping clients understand the etiology of their PTSD symptoms and teaching them skills for coping with PTSD symptoms. In particular, we believe that the cognitive-behavioral treatment package we developed for rape victims might be adapted for use with other types of trauma victims (Veronen & Kilpatrick, 1983; Keane et al., this volume). However, we agree with Bard and Sangrey (1979) that a key element in successful treatment is to help clients put the traumatic event into proper perspective and go on with their lives. Having problems, disappointments, and difficulties is a natural part of the human condition, but many victims of trauma attribute all their problems and difficulties to the traumatic experience. Thus, the combat veteran or rape victim may feel that all their difficulties would not have happened had they not served in Vietnam or been raped. Unless they can learn to transcend the effects of the traumatic event and stop thinking of themselves primarily as "a Vietnam veteran" or "a rape victim," it can be argued that they have not completely recovered from the trauma.

REFERENCES

American Psychiatric Association. *Diagnostic and statistical manual of mental disorders* (3rd ed.). Washington, DC: American Psychiatric Association, 1980.

Atkeson, B.M., Calhoun, K.S., Resick, P.A., & Ellis, E.M. Victims of rape: Repeated assessment of depressive symptoms. *Journal of Consulting and Clinical Psychology*, 1982, *50*, 96-102.

Bard, M., & Sangrey, D. *The crime victim's book.* New York: Basic Books, 1979.

Becker, J.V., Abel, G.G., & Skinner, L.J. The impact of a sexual assault on the victim's sexual life. *Victimology*, 1979, *5*, 229-235.

Becker, J.V., & Skinner, L.J. Assessment and treatment of rape-related sexual dysfunctions. *The Clinical Psychologist*, 1983, *36*(4), 102-105.

Bown, O. The development of a self-report inventory and its function in a mental health assessment battery. *American Psychologist*, 1961, *16*, 402.

Derogatis, L.R. *SCL-90-R: Administration and scoring and procedures manual I.* Baltimore: Clinical Psychometrics Research, 1977.

Duncan, D.B. Multiple range and multiple *T* Tests. *Biometrics*, 1955, *11*, 1-42.

Feldman-Summers, S., Gordon, P.E., & Meagher, J.R. The impact of rape on sexual satisfaction. *Journal of Abnormal Psychology*, 1979, *88*(1), 101-105.

Frank, E., & Stewart, B.D. Treating depression in victims of rape. *The Clinical Psychologist*, 1983, *36*(4), 95-98.

Frank, E., Turner, S.M., & Duffy, B. Depressive symptoms in rape victims. *Journal of Affective Disorders*, 1979, *1*, 269-297.

Frank, E., Turner, S.M., & Stewart, B.D. Initial response to rape: The impact of factors within the rape situation. *Journal of Behavioral Assessment*, 1980, *2*, 39-53.

Frank, E., Turner, S.M., Stewart, B.D., Jacob, M., & West, D. Past psychiatric symptoms and the response to sexual assault. *Comprehensive Psychiatry*, 1981, *22*, 479-487.

Holmes, T.H., & Rahe, R.H. The social readjustment rating scale. *Journal of Psychosomatic Research*, 1967, *11*, 213-218.

Horowitz, M., Wilner, N., & Alvarez, W. Impact of event scale: A measure of subjective distress. *Psychosomatic Medicine*, 1979, *41*(3), 209-218.

Katz, S., & Mazur, M.A. (Eds.). *Understanding the rape victim: A synthesis of research findings.* New York: Wiley, 1979.

Kilpatrick, D.G. *Cognitive repercussions of rape.* Paper presented at the meeting of the Southeastern Psychological Association, Atlanta, March, 1978.

Kilpatrick, D.G., Best, C.L., & Veronen, L.J. *Rape victims: Have we studied the tip or the iceberg?* Paper presented at the meeting of the American Psychological Association, Anaheim, CA, August, 1983.

Kilpatrick, D.G., Resick, P.A., & Veronen, L.J. Effects of a rape experience: A longitudinal study. *Journal of Social Issues*, 1981, *37*(4), 105-122.

Kilpatrick, D.G., & Veronen, L.J. *The aftermath of rape: A three-year follow-up.* Paper presented at the meeting of the Association for Advancement of Behavior Therapy, Washington, DC, December, 1983.

Kilpatrick, D.G., & Veronen, L.J. *Assessing victims of rape: Methodological issues.* Final report, NIMH Grant No. HMH38052, August, 1984a.

Kilpatrick, D.G., & Veronen, L.J. *Rape and post-traumatic stress disorder: A two-year longitudinal study.* Paper presented at the meeting of the American Psychosomatic Society, Hilton Head Island, SC, March, 1984b.

Kilpatrick, D.G., & Veronen, L.J. *Treatment of fear and anxiety in victims of rape.* Final report, NIMH Grant No. HMH29602, February, 1984c.

Kilpatrick, D.G., Veronen, L.J., & Resick, P.A. Responses to rape: Behavioral perspectives and treatment approaches. *Scandinavian Journal of Behavior Therapy*, 1977, 6, 85.

Kilpatrick, D.G., Veronen, L.J., & Resick, P.A. The aftermath of rape: Recent empirical findings. *American Journal of Orthopsychiatry*, 1979, 49(4), 658-669.

Kilpatrick, D.G., Veronen, L.J., & Resick, P.A. *Rape-induced fear: Its effect upon behavior and life style.* Paper presented at the meeting of the Association for Advancement of Behavior Therapy, Toronto, Canada, November, 1981.

Kilpatrick, D.G., Veronen, L.J., & Resick, P.A. Psychological sequelae to rape: Assessment and treatment strategies. In D.M. Doleys, R.L. Meredith, & A.R. Ciminero (Eds.), *Behavioral medicine: Assessment and treatment strategies* (pp. 473-497). New York: Plenum, 1982.

Koss, M.P. The scope of rape: Implications for the clinical treatment of victims. *The Clinical Psychologist*, 1983, 36(4), 88-91.

McCahill, T.W., Meyer, L.C., & Fischman, A.M. *The aftermath of rape.* Lexington, MA: DC Heath, 1979.

McDermott, M.J. *Rape victimization in 26 American cities.* (Analytic Report SD-VAD-6), Department of Justice, Law Enforcement Assistance Administration. Washington, DC: U. S. Government Printing Office, 1979.

McNair, D., Lorr, M., & Droppleman, L. *Manual, profile of mood states.* San Diego: Education and Industrial Testing Service, 1971.

Morelli, P.H. *Comparison of the psychological recovery of black and white victims of rape.* Paper presented at the meeting of the Association for Women in Psychology, Boston, March, 1981.

Norris, J., & Feldman-Summers, S. Factors related to the psychological impacts of rape on the victim. *Journal of Abnormal Psychology*, 1981, 90(6), 562-567.

Robinson, J.P., & Shaver, P.R. *Measures of social psychological attitudes.* Ann Arbor, MI: The University of Michigan, Institute for Social Research, 1973.

Ruch, L.O., & Chandler, S.M. Sexual assault trauma during the acute phase: An exploratory model and multivariate analysis. *Journal of Health and Social Behavior*, 1983, 24, 174-185.

Ruch, L., Chandler, S., & Harter, R. Life change and rape impact. *Journal of Health and Social Behavior*, 1980, 21, 248-260.

Skogan, W.G. *Issues in the measurement of victimization* (NCJ-74682), Department of Justice, Bureau of Statistics. Washington, DC: U.S. Government Printing Office, 1981.

Sparks, R.F. *Research on victims of crime: Accomplishments, issues, and new directions* (DHHS Publication No. (ADM) 82-1091). Washington, DC: U. S. Government Printing Office, 1982.

Spielberger, C.D., Gorsuch, R.L., & Lushene, R.E. *The state-trait anxiety inventory.* Palo Alto, CA: Consulting Psychologists Press, 1970.

Sutherland, S., & Scherl, D. Patterns of response among victims of rape. *American Journal of Orthopsychiatry*, 1970, 40, 503-511.

Veronen, L.J., & Best, C.L. Assessment and treatment of rape-induced fear and anxiety. *The Clinical Psychologist*, 1983, 36(4), 99-101.

Veronen, L.J., & Kilpatrick, D.G. Self-reported fears of rape victims: A preliminary investigation. *Behavior Modification*, 1980, 4(3), 383-396.

Veronen, L.J., & Kilpatrick, D.G. Stress management for rape victims. In D. Meichenbaum & M.E. Jaremko (Eds.), *Stress reduction and prevention.* New York: Plenum, 1983, 341-374.

Veronen, L.J., Kilpatrick, D.G., & Resick, P.A. Treatment of fear and anxiety in rape victims: Implications for the criminal justice system. In W.H. Parsonage (Ed.), *Perspectives on victimology* (pp. 148-159). Beverly Hills, CA: Sage, 1979.

Veterans Administration. *Myths and realities: A study of attitudes toward Vietnam era veterans.* Washington, D.C.: Louis Harris and Associates, July, 1980.

8

A Comparative Analysis of PTSD Among Various Survivor Groups

JOHN P. WILSON, W. KEN SMITH, and
SUZANNE K. JOHNSON

The purpose of the present study was to compare post-traumatic stress syndrome among persons involved in nine different stressor events: combat in the Vietnam War; rape; life-threatening events; divorce; the death of a significant other; critical, near-fatal illness of a significant other; family violence; multiple traumatic events; and no stressful event. To assess the severity of the symptoms which define post-traumatic stress disorder (PTSD), the Impact of Event Scale, the Beck Depression Inventory, the Stress Assessment Scale for PTSD from the Vietnam Era Stress Inventory, and the Sensation Seeking Scale were administered to the participants (N = 409). A person × situation conceptual model of PTSD was presented from which two major hypotheses were tested. As predicted from the model, the loss of a significant other and degree of life-threat were predictive of syndrome-specific symptoms of PTSD. The results of the study strongly support the heuristic value of an interactionist model of PTSD.

The purpose of this chapter is to present a conceptual framework for viewing post-traumatic stress disorder (PTSD) in various survivor groups and to examine empirically the nature and severity of this disorder among persons exposed to nine different traumatic events. The need for a comparative analysis of PTSD among different populations of survivors of unusually stressful life events stems from a number of theoretical and clinical sources.

First, PTSD is now recognized as a distinct mental disorder associated with a variety of traumatic events with explicit diagnostic criteria presented in the *Diagnostic and Statistical Manual* (3rd ed.) (American Psychiatric Association, 1980). Second, despite the new diagnostic category for the stress syndrome, the phenomenon of prolonged stress reactions to catastrophically stressful events has been documented for many decades in medical reports and the psychiatric literature (Lifton, 1983). Third, there is a growing body of empirical research which has begun to identify the antecedent stressor variables that best predict PTSD and its severity in different survivor populations (Figley & Leventman, 1980; Gleser, Green, & Winget, 1981; Wilson & Krauss, 1982). These studies suggest that it is important to construct valid measures of the syndrome in order to obtain precise predictions of the onset, duration, and severity of stress disorders and levels of impairment. Fourth, although there is a core set of features which characterize PTSD, it is likely that the syndrome may vary among survivors depending on 1) predispositional variables, 2) the nature of the traumatic event, and 3) the recovery environment to which the survivor returns (Green, Wilson, & Lindy, this volume).

It is important to focus on both the similarities and differences among various traumatic events in terms of PTSD. Such a comparative analysis of PTSD among survivors of different stressor events is heuristically important since it facilitates an understanding of the dynamic mechanisms which underlie PTSD and their idiosyncratic expression in groups or individuals exposed to qualitatively different life events.

In recent years attempts have been made to develop theoretical models of stress response syndromes and the patterns of adaptation that individuals make to extraordinarily stressful life events (Horowitz, 1976, 1979). In this vein, Green, Wilson and Lindy (this volume) have constructed a preliminary conceptual model to understand PTSD in different survivor groups. Building upon the seminal work of Horowitz (1976, 1979), they propose that it is necessary to consider how *dispositional variables* (e.g., personality traits, premorbid psychopathology, learned ego defenses) and *situational variables* codetermine the specific way in which the trauma is processed cognitively by the survivor. Thus, in order to predict the nature of psychological adaptation to a traumatic event (healthy or pathological), it is necessary to attempt to specify how personological variables *interact* with situational-stressor variables to produce syndrome-specific symptom clusters. Here, we will briefly present a theoretical perspective of the relationship between personality and stressor variables and the development of PTSD.

THE EFFECTS OF STRESSOR VARIABLES ON CORE PERSONALITY PROCESSES

In order to understand the different forms of human adaptation to stressful life events it is necessary to consider how personality processes moderate the perception, evaluation, and cognitive processing of the stressful experience. Clearly, not all persons respond to stressor events in a similar manner, a fact which underscores the need to assess how individual difference variables influence post-trauma adaptation. For the purposes of this chapter we shall present an abbreviated conceptual analysis of the possible role that personality variables play in the development of post-traumatic stress syndrome.

In Table 1, which we will discuss, we present a broad theoretical overview of the effects of stressor variables on core personality processes and the formation of the symptoms that define PTSD. Our goal is to develop a useful way of thinking about the effects of stressor events on some of the core processes of personality functioning. In constructing the table we have selected for discussion those theorists whose work seems most directly applicable to the analysis of PTSD. We shall attempt to discuss the effects of unusually stressful life events from the following theories of personality: 1) *psychosocial development* (Erikson, 1982); 2) *psychoformative processes* (Lifton, 1983); 3) *learned helplessness* (Seligman & Garber, 1980); and 4) *cognitive processing of trauma* (Horowitz, 1979).

Psychosocial Development: The Application of Eriksonian Theory to PTSD

In an earlier paper (Wilson, 1980), we set forth a detailed analysis of stress-producing experiences and their effect on psychosocial development from Erikson's perspective of ego development. We stated that a stressor could impact on psychosocial development in a variety of ways that could lead to PTSD.

First, the stress-producing event could intensify or aggravate the predominant stage of ego development. Thus, the effect produced in terms of PTSD might vary greatly as a function of the stage-specific qualities of ego development. For example, a person in the process of identity formation who experiences a life-threatening event might develop acute or chronic identity diffusion (see Danieli, this volume; Koenig, 1964, for examples in Holocaust victims). As an outcome such a person may manifest ideological confusion, an inability to make commitments to self and others, bisexual confusion, low self-esteem, and a loss of a sense of continuity and self-sameness. In extreme cases, identity diffusion might lead to the formation of PTSD *and* a borderline personality disorder if the disturbance in identity is the predominant clinical symptom.

Second, the stress-producing event can lead to retrogression in ego-development by taxing ego defenses beyond their limits. As a consequence, the survivor may show strong regressive tendencies that are stage-specific in nature. For example, a trauma could produce profound mistrust, a loss of hope and will, feelings of abandonment, a heightened sense of vulnerability, and the need to be nurtured by a protective person. We believe that retrogression occurs to some degree in all cases of PTSD, but is most pronounced and debilitating when there exists either premorbid pathology or a set of specific vulnerabilities that resulted from childhood development (e.g., victim of sexual molestation).

Third, the stress-producing event may lead to acceleration in ego development. We believe that this is an unusual response to a traumatic event, but one which seems to strengthen the survivor by adding greater ego strength through the premature emergence of qualities of awareness centered around generativity and integrity (Wilson, 1980b). In this case, the person is likely to face the paradoxical task of coping with PTSD while experiencing positive alterations in ego identity, values, and beliefs. Wilson (1980) suggested that the psychosocially accelerated person becomes more ethical, altruistic, humanitarian, and self-actualizing.

A traumatic life event can affect psychosocial development in different ways depending on the stage of ego development in the life cycle, the level of personality integration and identity formation (ego strength), and the severity of the trauma itself. Thus, in terms of PTSD, Table 1 indicates that the effects of the stressor on psychosocial development can produce mistrust, a sense of isolation, time confusion, guilt, loss of intimacy, identity diffusion, despair, hopelessness, ideological changes, decreased autonomy, and a lack of goal-directedness. These symptoms would comprise part of the stress syndrome as an overlay to the process of reexperiencing the original event.

Psychoformative Processes

In a modification of Eriksonian theory, Lifton (1983) has attempted to construct a general psychological theory that moves beyond the limitations of instinctual and epigenetic models of personality to one that places emphasis on the self as an active constructor of reality. Briefly, psychoformative theory concerns the ways in which persons conceptualize and symbolize their experiences in life. As an active process, individuals evolve images and forms of their experiences which contribute to a sense of continuity or discontinuity in the self-structure. Specifically, Lifton (1976) proposes that the major focus of experience can be conceptualized as the paradigms of *connection versus separation, movement versus stasis, and integrity versus disintegration.* Thus, when people feel centered in their life experiences, they have a symbolic or actual sense of connection (to people, ideas, space, time), movement (growth, aliveness, creativity), and integrity (psychic wholeness, physical well-being, ego vitality).

However, *immersion in the death experience* can radically alter an individual's sense of continuity and psychoformative processes and lead to traumatic survivor syndromes. Exposure to death, dying, destruction, or the loss of social order may cause the survivor to experience a loss of continuity in psychoformative processes. The individual may struggle in many different ways with a sense of separation, isolation, and a "broken connection" with life as previously experienced. Immersion in the death experience may also lead to a feeling of physical and psychological disintegration—that the self has fragmented into emotional shards that no longer cohere in a meaningful or ordered structure.

In response to these massive changes in psychoformative processes the survivor may become physically numb during the initial stage of adaptation following the trauma. This blunted emotional responsiveness is often coupled with survivor guilt, the recurrence of the death imprint in consciousness, anger, rage, depression (the loss of self, others, and internality in locus of control), and the task of reformulating the experience so as to develop a new sense of the self as alive and growing again. As Table 1 illustrates, psychoformative theory provides a conceptual basis for understanding all aspects of PTSD.

Learned Helplessness

Learned helplessness (Seligman & Garber, 1980) occurs when a person is exposed to an environment in which there are aversive consequences of an uncontrollable and unpredictable nature. It seems to us that learned helplessness is often a core element of PTSD since the survivor of a traumatic event develops cognitions that he or she is a pawn whose destiny is shaped by external forces over which he or she has little or no control. This external locus of attribution in causality may then produce motivational deficits in the form of a loss of ability to initiate adaptive responses. When this occurs, survivors typically begin to see the world as a hostile and threatening place which can inflict more pain and suffering in their lives. Ultimately, the eventual outcome of learned helplessness is depression, withdrawal from the field, isolation, and chronic anxiety associated with the fear that the trauma will recur (Seligman, 1974). If prolonged, this psychological state of being is very likely to lead to illness of a somatoform nature.

Cognitive Processing of Trauma: Horowitz Information Processing Model

In recent years Horowitz (1976, 1979) has attempted to explain the post-traumatic stress syndrome from a cognitive model of information processing. This approach assumes a *completion tendency* in which "the mind continues to process important new information until the situation or the [cognitive] models change, and reality and models reach accord" (Horowitz, 1979, p. 249). Until a traumatic life event can be successfully integrated into the existing self-structure, the psychological elements of the event remain in memory as determinants of intrusive imagery or other stress syndrome symptoms. Further, Horowitz (1979) has found that survivors typically progress through a well-defined sequence of stages when assimilating the trauma: outcry, avoidance, intrusive imagery and reexperience of the event, transition, and integration. However, depending upon the severity of the trauma and the personality of the victim, the survivor may experience a cyclical alternation between the avoidance and intrusion stages. In the process, survivors report feelings of depression, anger, episodic rage, and unconscious reenactment of the event. Thus, Horowitz (1979) has developed a specific model of post-traumatic stress disorder as it affects survivors of different stressor events.

For purposes of a summary, Table 1 illustrates the proposed relationship between stressful life events and the dimensions of personality most likely to be affected by the trauma as derived from the four theoretical positions discussed above. The table also indicates the hypothesized dimensions of PTSD related to core personality processes and to which of the diagnostic criteria in DSM-III the dimensions conform.

TABLE 1

The Effect of Stressor Events on Core Personality Processes: Personological Variables in PTSD

Core Personality Processes: Dimension and Theorist	Dimension of Personality Affected by Stressor Event	PTSD Symptom Related to Personality Process	DSM-III Criteria
Stages of Psychosocial Development (Erikson, 1982)	1) Stage-specific impact on psychosocial development 2) Age-related influences on emergent ego strengths and integrative capacities	Mistrust, isolation, time confusion, identity diffusion, loss of intimacy, decreased autonomy, loss of industry, death anxiety, despair, loss of meaning, ideological changes	Numbing, changes in adaptive behavior
Psychoformative Processes (Lifton, 1983)	1) Decentering and ungrounding of self-structure in modes of psychological experience	Psychic numbing, survivor guilt, rage, depression, loss of continuity in self-structure, symbolic death, search for meaning, denial, loss of intimacy, death guilt	Reexperience, numbing, changes in adaptive behavior
Learned Helplessness (Seligman & Garber, 1980)	1) *Cognitive:* External locus of attribution for causality 2) *Motivational:* Loss of response initiative; loss of goal-directed behavior	Depression, helplessness, intense anxiety, somatic processes, withdrawal, isolation, despair, negative view of world, fear of repetition	Reexperience, numbing, changes in adaptive behavior
Cognitive Processing of Trauma (Horowitz, 1979)	1) Entire self-structure; cognitive process of assimilating trauma into self	Avoidance, denial, dissociation, anxiety, nightmares, intrusive imagery, cognitive constriction, somatic complaints, fear of repetition, rage at source	Reexperience, numbing, changes in adaptive behavior

This framework serves as a basis for our set of testable hypotheses presented in the next section.

THE RELATION OF STRESSOR VARIABLES TO PTSD

A person × situation model of PTSD assumes that there is a predictable relation between personality and situational variables in determining the syndrome-specific dynamics of post-trauma adaptation. Conceptually, three major effects may be discerned regarding post-traumatic adaptation: First, dispositional variables may account for significant degrees of variance in the determination of post-trauma adaptation. For example, an individual with a premorbid personality disorder might manifest more psychopathology after a stressful life event than a matched control subject with no premorbidity. Second, the observed pattern of post-trauma adaptation may be explained by the interaction effect of intrapersonal *and* situational variables. For example, a person with a strong sense of morality and ethics might develop strong survivor guilt as a result of involvement in a situation where he or she fails to act prosocially to help save the life of a victim. Third, the nature of the stressor event itself may constitute the major determinant of the observed pattern of adaptation to the trauma. For example, Lifton (1967) reports that obsessional fear of "atomic-disease poisoning" was a universal symptom among the survivors of the atomic bombing of Hiroshima.

In Table 2 we summarize the hypothesized relationship of different dimensions of stressor events to the development of stress response symptoms. Building upon the stressor dimensions empirically identified in previous research (Gleser et al., 1981), we will discuss ten stressor dimensions and their proposed relationship to the development of PTSD. These dimensions are summarized in Table 2 and include:

1) degree of life-threat;
2) degree of bereavement;
3) speed of onset;
4) duration of trauma;
5) degree of displacement in home community;
6) potential for recurrence;
7) degree of exposure to death, dying, and destruction;
8) degree of moral conflict inherent in situation;

TABLE 2

The Hypothesized Relation of Stressor Variables to the Development of PTSD Symptoms

Nature of Stressor Variable in Trauma	Hypothesized Relation to PTSD Symptoms
Degree of life-threat	Anxiety, intrusive imagery, hypervigilance, hyperalertness, psychic numbing, sensation-seeking tendencies, unconscious reenactment of trauma
Degree of bereavement or loss of significant others	Depression, impacted grief, search for meaning, rage at source, symbolic death, stasis
Speed of onset	Anxiety, helplessness, feelings of chaos, loss of control, externalization of attributions of causality
Duration of trauma	Severity of PTSD, level of psychic numbing and denial, psychosomatic problems, memory impairment, cognitive deficits, alcohol and drug abuse, dissociative states
Degree of displacement in home community	Sense of anomia, rootlessness, loss of community, changes in social bonding and increased social pathology (delinquency, wedlock, drug abuse, child abuse, etc.)
Potential for recurrence	Anxiety, fear of recurrence, mistrust, irritability, hypervigilance, hyperalertness
Degree of exposure to death, dying, and destruction	Intrusive imagery, numbness, survivor guilt, nightmares, rage at the source, humanitarian-prosocial values, fear of loss of loved ones, intimacy conflict, suicidal ideation, fear of isolation
Degree of moral conflict inherent in situation	Moral and survivor guilt, ideological changes in values, somatic complaints, upward shift in moral judgment
Role of person in trauma: agent or victim	*Agent:* Guilt, search for meaning, stigmatization, confusion, ideological change, suicidal ideation, self-recrimination
	Victim: Paranoid ideation, rage at source, feelings of persecution, helplessness
Proportion of community affected by trauma	Loss of a stable social order, illusion of centrality, loss of emotional support systems, rage at source

9) role of person in trauma; and
10) proportion of community affected by trauma.

Degree of Life-Threat

The greater the degree of life-threat, the more likely it is to generate a fear of annihilation and death anxiety (Lidz, 1946). Therefore, this stressor variable is likely to be strongly linked to anxiety, excessive autonomic nervous system arousal as manifested in hyperalertness and hypervigilance, and intrusive imagery.

Degree of Bereavement or Loss of Significant Others

Many studies have shown that bereavement is associated with prolonged stress responses (Gleser et al., 1981). The loss of significant others is most commonly connected to the symptoms of depression, impacted grief, and rage at the source (Horowitz, 1979).

Speed of Onset

The more rapidly a trauma occurs, especially if it is without prior warning, the greater the consequences will be in terms of one-trial learning. Rapid onset of trauma is associated with the formation of intense anxiety, learned helplessness, and external attributions in locus of control over reinforcements (Figley & McCubbin, 1983).

Duration of the Trauma

It is a truism to say that every person has a point of vulnerability to stress. If a trauma persists long enough, no one is immune to its effects. Clearly, the duration of a trauma is expected to strongly correlate with the severity of PTSD, intrusive imagery, psychic numbing, avoidance, memory impairment, dissociative reactions, and physical health problems (Niederland, 1968).

Displacement in Home Community

Displacement from one's home community is most likely to occur when a naturalistic or man-made disaster destroys dwellings, vital resources, and homes. The greater the displacement of persons from their community, the greater will be: 1) various forms of social pathology (e.g., delinquency, drug and alcohol abuse, child abuse, etc.); 2) anomia;

3) need for love, belongingness, and affiliation; and 4) external socio-economic support systems (Gleser et al., 1981).

Potential for Recurrence

The stressor variables which cause PTSD are, by definition, at the extreme end of a continuum. When the potential of recurrence of threatening stimuli is great and unpredictable, it leads to strong feelings of anxiety, mistrust, irritability, and excessive autonomic nervous system arousal (e.g., hypervigilance) (Figley & McCubbin, 1983; Seligman & Garber, 1980).

Exposure to Death, Dying, and Destruction

We believe that in addition to threats on one's life and safety, mere exposure to death, dying, and destruction can cause PTSD. Immersion in death, destruction, and chaos is sufficient to create lasting psychic imprints (Krystal, 1968). The greater the degree of exposure to catastrophic, life-threatening events, the more likely it is that the survivor will develop intrusive imagery, psychic numbing, isolation, survivor guilt, and changes in personality and values (Figley, 1978; Figley & McCubbin, 1983; Lindy et al., 1981).

Degree of Moral Conflict Inherent in Situation

In many traumatic situations the person experiences profound moral conflicts regarding the value of life, property, family, friends, and members of the community. A high degree of moral conflict is likely to cause moral and survivor guilt, fundamental changes in values, and a tendency to develop universal modes of moral reasoning after the trauma (Wilson, 1978). One expression of this change in values is likely to be that the survivor becomes more prosocial and humanitarian in day-to-day life.

Role of Person in Trauma

In many traumatic situations the individual *reacts* to a set of stressor events that impinge on his or her existence. In this sense, the individual can rightly be considered as the victim or object of trauma. However, in other situations (e.g., combat), the person may also be an *agent* who contributes to trauma. Clearly, these different roles can have differential effects in terms of post-trauma cognitive processing (Figley, 1978). While the *agent* role is more likely to be associated with guilt, stigmatization, and self-recrimination, especially if it is difficult to form ideological justification for the act committed, the victim role is to be associated with paranoid ideation, rage at the source, and anxiety (Figley & Leventman, 1980).

Proportion of Community Affected by Trauma

When a traumatic event affects a large portion of a community, the psychosocial consequences are different than if a single person is victimized. If there is widespread destruction of homes and property there is likely to be a sense of a *shared fate*, or what Lifton (1967) has termed the *illusion of centrality*. Although massive destruction produces an immediate change in the survivor's sense of belonging to a stable social order, it may also lead to attributions of the event to an *act of God* which affects everyone in about the same way. Following such an attribution, the psychological consequences are different than if the disaster is attributed to a man-made cause which resulted from malevolence or negligence. Where the survivors perceive that their fate was caused by man-made forces, there is likely to be more rage at the source and a stronger need to restore equity in their lives (c.f. Erikson, 1976; Lindy et al., 1981).

A STUDY OF SURVIVOR GROUPS

We have presented a conceptual framework of PTSD which explicates some of the ways that stressor events affect personality and the development of traumatic stress reactions. The purpose of this chapter is to undertake a pilot study which presents a comparative, empirical analysis of the nature and severity of PTSD among individuals who have been involved in different stressful life events. As such, this research specifically compares stress response symptoms among the survivor groups which include:

1) Vietnam combat veterans;
2) victims of rape, battering, and child abuse;
3) victims of serious life-threats which include auto accidents, armed robbery, and natural disasters;
4) persons divorced;
5) serious, near-fatal illness of a loved one;
6) family trauma, including the effects of alcoholism, mental illness, family break-up;
7) the death of a significant other;

8) victims of multiple traumas; and
9) a control group made up of persons who did not report experiencing stressful life events (see Method section). An additional purpose of this study was to explore the effects of threat and loss of significant others, different stressor variables, or the specific manifestation of the symptom clusters which define PTSD.

METHOD

Subjects

The combat veterans (N = 74) were volunteers who belonged to the Northern Ohio Veterans Association. All subjects had verified combat experience and ranged in age from 31 to 41 with a mean of 35 years. For purposes of statistical comparison, their scores on the assessment instruments were compared with those of a national sample obtained by Wilson and Krauss (1982) of combat veterans participating in the VA's readjustment counseling program. Table 3 indicates that the scores for combat subjects in this study did not differ significantly from those obtained in the national sample and thus appear representative of the larger population of Vietnam combat veterans.

The non-veteran subjects (N = 335) who completed the assessment instruments were drawn from several sources. Approximately 85% were undergraduate students who were attending an urban, state-supported university. These subjects ranged in age from 18 to 50 years with a mean of 21 years. The other subjects were volunteers who worked in abortion or wife-battering centers or other health care agencies located in Cleveland, Ohio. They ranged in age from 21 to 33 years with a mean of 22. In all, 409 subjects (185 females, 214 males) successfully completed the questionnaire. Data on gender were missing for 10 non-veteran subjects.

Assessment Questionnaires

To assess the symptoms of PTSD and other dimensions of personality, the following questionnaires were given to the subjects: The Impact of Events Scale (IES) by Horowitz, Wilner and Alvarez (1979); The Beck Depression Inventory by Beck (1961; 1976); the Stress Assessment Questionnaire for PTSD from the Vietnam Era Stress Inventory (VESI) by Wilson and Krauss (1980); and the Sensation Seeking Scale (SSS) by Zuckerman (1979).

As will be discussed below, these scales were selected because they

TABLE 3
Mean Scores on PTSD Dimensions Classified by Stressful Life Event

PTSD DIMENSION	Vietnam Combat Veterans		STRESSOR CATEGORY							
	National Sample N=114	Northeast Ohio N=74	No Event N=93	Death N=96	Rape N=9	Divorce N=13	Serious Illness N=19	Life-Threat N=62	Family Trauma N=16	Multiple Trauma N=27
VESI										
Depression	121.6	107.58	51.54	58.61	65.11	64.46	60.84	54.00	60.12	63.52
Physical Symptoms	64.8	60.39	35.85	18.74	47.33	42.08	40.74	37.22	42.31	44.96
Stigmatization	42.9	41.69	5.06	5.50	5.33	6.08	5.47	5.02	6.06	7.11
Sensation Seeking	23.4	20.64	10.58	11.38	11.78	12.46	10.79	11.39	12.00	11.59
Rage/Anger	16.8	17.81	10.47	11.44	12.67	13.00	11.53	11.18	12.50	12.04
Intrusive Imagery	27.70	27.55	7.29	7.90	7.33	8.38	7.21	7.85	7.19	8.41
Intimacy Conflict	16.80	16.90	6.71	7.48	9.00	9.46	8.89	6.92	8.12	7.81
Total PTSD	310.9	292.57	127.50	141.05	158.56	155.92	145.47	133.58	148.31	154.81
Sensation Seeking Scale-SSS										
Adventure Seeking	Data Not Available	6.40	6.12	7.42	7.22	7.46	7.00	6.95	6.94	6.22
Experience Seeking	(N/A)	5.53	4.13	4.58	4.56	4.23	5.05	4.22	5.38	5.56
Disinhibition		5.00	4.62	4.76	3.67	3.85	4.63	4.50	3.50	3.74
Boredom Susceptibility		3.55	2.83	2.59	3.56	3.00	2.32	2.89	2.88	2.89
Beck Depression Inventory										
Depression	(N/A)	22.22	5.98	8.58	10.00	10.62	9.32	6.34	8.81	12.04
Impact of Event Scale-IES										
Intrusion	(N/A)	20.32	7.99	15.31	20.00	19.31	14.79	11.58	14.88	17.11
Avoidance		20.42	9.12	16.93	20.78	19.92	15.58	12.87	17.75	18.78
Total		40.74	17.11	32.24	40.78	39.23	30.37	24.45	32.12	35.89

NOTE: Mutually exclusive group membership. No subject who experienced multiple events has been included in any primary stressor category.

contain reliable and valid measures of stress response syndromes. However, several points require clarification. First, since the VESI was originally designed to assess PTSD among Vietnam veterans, the non-veteran subjects marked the items pertaining to combat-related symptoms at the lowest scale point. Similarly, for the subjects who comprised the No Event stressor category, scores on the IES scales correspond to the expected mean (M = 15) for individuals who mark scale point 1, "not at all."

Identification of Stressor Groups

In an adaptation of the IES (Horowitz et al., 1979), subjects were asked to write down the date and nature of any unusually stressful events that had occurred in their lives. More specifically, the question asked:

> Many people experience *unusually stressful events* from time to time in their lives. This includes such things as car accidents, rape, death of a close family member, assault, floods, tornados, fires, airplane accidents, near drowning, witnessing a life-threatening event, military combat, incarceration, child abuse (sexual or physical), wife-beating, sexual assault, robbery, being with someone who is critically ill, etc. If you have had an experience similar to the ones described above, please indicate the approximate date/year——— that you experienced——— (stressful life event).
>
> Below is a list of comments made by people after stressful life events. Please read each item and indicate how frequently these comments were true for you DURING THE PAST SEVEN (7) DAYS by marking the appropriate letter on the computer answer sheet. If they did not occur during that time, please mark the "Not at all" answer.

All events were independently coded by two judges who subsequently agreed on a nine category system of classification with the following operational definitions:

1) *Vietnam Combat Veteran* (N = 74). All veterans had validated combat experience;
2) *No Event* (N = 93). Included here were subjects who indicated that they had not experienced any unusually stressful life events;
3) *Death of Significant Other* (N = 96). This category included subjects who had experienced the death of family members or friends, abortion or miscarriage, or the suicide of a friend or significant other;

4) *Rape/Battering* (N = 9). The subjects were all women who had experienced rape, battering, or severe physical or sexual abuse as children;

5) *Divorce* (N = 13). This category was defined as the termination of a marriage or a long-term, primary love relationship;

6) *Critical Illness of Loved Ones* (N = 19). The events defining this category include the threatened loss of family members or friends due to serious or critical illness, accidents, or attempted suicide;

7) *Life-Threat* (N = 62). Events include serious auto accidents, robbery at gunpoint, natural disasters, fires, explosions, near drowning, and serious medical problems;

8) *Family Trauma* (N = 16). This category includes family alcoholism, divorce, mental illness, and serious legal problems;

9) *Multiple Stressor Events* (N = 27). This category includes persons who had experienced more than one of the stressor events listed above.

A total of 58 different stressor events were listed by these subjects and include: 20 deaths, 10 rapes and batterings, six divorces, seven serious illnesses of significant others, 10 serious life-threats, and five family trauma.

Construct Validity of the Assessment Instrument

The *Beck Depression Inventory (BDI)* was selected for this study as a measure of symptoms similar to traumatic stress reactions (Nace et al., 1978). It consists of 21 categories of symptoms and attitudes which provide a quantitative assessment of the intensity of depression. Each category describes a specific behavior of depression with four to five self-reporting statements about the behavior. The statements range from neutral to maximum severity and are scored zero to three, respectively. For example, item #1 pertains to a person's mood:

A) I do not feel sad   (0) none
B) I feel sad   (1) mild
C) I am sad all the time and I can't   (2) moderate
     snap out of it.
D) I feel that the future is hopeless   (3) severe
     and things cannot improve.

Thus, on the four-point scale the subject's score can range from zero to

63 depending upon severity of depression. Means and standard deviations of the BDI are: 1) no depression $\bar{x}$ = 10.9, SD = 7.7; 2) mild depression $\bar{x}$ = 18.7, SD = 10.2; 3) moderate depression $\bar{x}$ = 25.4, SD = 9.6; 4) severe depression $\bar{x}$ = 30.0, SD = 10.6. A score of 16 and above suggests moderate to severe clinical depression (Beck et al., 1961).

In terms of its psychometric properties, Strober, Green, and Carlson (1981) found that the coefficient alpha was .79 (df = 76). Test-retest reliability of the BDI proved to be highly correlated across time with an $r(76)$ = .69, $p < .001$.

The Impact of Event Scale (IES) or the intrusion-avoidance scale was selected as a measure of PTSD. It consists of 15 statements assessing the subject's feelings of denial and the occurrence within the past seven days of intrusive thoughts in regard to stressful life events. Seven items assess intrusive imagery and eight items assess avoidance tendencies. The mean and standard deviations of the IES to the PTSD scale are 39.5 and 17.2, respectively, with a range of 0-69. The mean of the intrusion subscale is 21.4 with a standard deviation of 9.6 and a range of 0-35. The mean of the avoidance subscale is 18.2 with a standard deviation of 10.8, and a range of 0-38. Zilberg, Weiss and Horowitz (1982) found that Cronbach's alphas were high and ranged from .79 to .92. Reliability across time ranged from .86 to .90.

The Sensation Seeking Scale (SSS) (Zuckerman et al., 1964, 1968) was selected since Wilson and Krauss (in press) found it was associated with PTSD among Vietnam veterans. Initially, the SSS consisted of 54 forced-choice items. Fourteen items pertained to preference for extremes of heat, cold, noise, tastes, colors, musical sounds, etc.; eight items related to preferences for novelty rather than routine and regularity; eight items pertained to preferences for new and the unfamiliar rather than the familiar; 12 items pertained to enjoyment of danger and thrill activities; six items related to social values based on the unconventionality of other people rather than predictability and reliability; four items contrasted a person's preference for security as opposed to adventure; and two items concerned a need for general excitement.

Since the construction of the original SSS, the scale has evolved to SSS Form V, consisting of 40 of the original 54 items. Four factors, thrill and adventure seeking, experience seeking, disinhibition, and boredom susceptibility, were identified and showed consistent reliability and more selective sex differences than the older forms (Zuckerman, 1979). The mean score was 21.6 (sd = 5.7) for males and 19.6(sd = 6.6) for females. Internal consistency coefficients (inter-item r's) were .84 (males) and .85 (females) (Zuckerman et al., 1968).

The VESI (Wilson & Krauss, in press) was included as a more extensive scale. It assesses the symptoms of PTSD and general psychiatric complaints on 106 items constructed in a five-point ordinal scale that defines the frequency of experiencing the problem. For example, item 7, "Feeling guilt that a buddy was killed in Vietnam and not you," can be answered at scale points 1) "Not at all—problem does not occur," 2) "A little bit—1 to 9 times a month," 3) "Moderately—10 to 14 times a month," 4) "Quite a bit—15-20 times a month," 5) "Extreme—21 to 30 times a month." Thus, across the 106 items a total score can be derived as an index of the overall severity of PTSD. The scale has been factor-analyzed and yields seven orthogonal factors:

1) depression;
2) physical symptoms, memory impairment;
3) stigmatization, alienation, and cynicism;
4) sensation seeking, authority conflict;
5) anger, rage;
6) intrusive imagery; and
7) intimacy conflict, for which total scores may be assessed and used as indices of the severity of different dimensions of the stress syndrome (Wilson & Krauss, in press).

Design

All subjects were administered the assessment questionnaires during a three-month interval (January to March, 1983). For the veterans, the questionnaires were distributed at an organizational meeting of the Northern Ohio Veterans Association and returned in stamped, self-addressed envelopes. The undergraduate subjects were administered the questionnaire in order to receive extra credit in the psychology courses in return for participation. The other subjects completed the questionnaire at the request of one of the authors (Johnson) who had previous contact with these health care agencies.

Data Analysis

First, the mean scores on each of the scales assessing PTSD were compared for each of the stressor categories. Although this analysis does not control for the time-from-event effect, it does provide a general indication of the overall severity of PTSD-related symptoms that are heuristically valuable in terms of the person × situation theoretical model presented in this chapter. Second, two stressor variables thought to be significantly associated with the onset of PTSD, i.e., degree of life-threat or loss of a significant other, were examined.

Threat

An *a priori* basis was used to group subjects together who had experienced a life-threatening, stressful event. Members of stressor categories which, by definition, involved a life-threatening event comprised the conceptual variable *Threat*. Thus, members of rape, life-threat, and combat categories define this variable. In contrast, the *No Threat* group contained the other stressor categories, except for the *No Event* category. This procedure resulted in three new stressor categories whose scores on the dimension of PTSD could be compared.

Loss

Similarly, the effects of loss of a significant other comprised the second conceptual variable and included members of the combat veteran, divorce, and death categories. The *No Loss* stressor category included the other stressor categories except for the *No Event* category. In order to avoid violating the assumptions of parametric statistics, individuals who had experienced multiple stressful life events were excluded from the *Loss* and *Threat* statistical analyses.

RESULTS

Comparison of PTSD Dimensions Across the Stressor Categories

Table 3 shows the mean scores on the VESI, SSS, BDI, and the IES for the different stressor categories. Inspection of the table indicates that the scores for Vietnam combat veterans are two to three times higher than for other stressor groups for nearly all of the dimensions of PTSD. Multivariate analyses of variance (MANOVA's) were performed to assess mean differences among the dependent variables. As suggested by Specter (1977), significant MANOVAs were followed up by separate univariate ANOVAs for each variable in the set. Since there were interactions, tests of simple effects (Winer, 1971) showed (see Table 4) that the stressor categories were significantly different from each other on all of the scales, with the exception of the SSS disinhibition subscale

Analysis of Simple Effects and Newman-Keuls Multiple Mean Comparison

PTSD DIMENSION	F-value	r^2	NEWMAN-KEULS MEAN COMPARISONS	
				Stressor Categories Significantly Different From Other Stressor Categories
VESI				
Depression	49.09††	.44	Combat veterans	All stressor categories***
Physical symptoms	24.75††	.28	Combat veterans	All stressor categories***
Stigmatization	287.76††	.82	Combat veterans	All stressor categories***
Sensation Seeking	32.41††	.34	Combat veterans	All stressor categories***
Rage/Anger	19.20††	.23	Combat veterans	All stressor categories***
Intrusive Imagery	145.94††	.70	Combat veterans	All stressor categories***
Intimacy Conflict	74.21††	.54	Combat veterans	All stressor categories***
Total PTSD	94.78††	.60	Combat veterans	All stressor categories***
Sensation Seeking Scale-SSS				
Adventure Seeking	1.88*	.03	—	—
Experience Seeking	3.90†	.06	Combat veterans/multiple trauma	No Event**
Disinhibition	.74	.01	—	—
Boredom Susceptibility	1.98*	.03	—	—
Beck Depression Inventory				
Depression	31.88††	.33	Combat veterans/multiple trauma	All stressor categories*** Life-Threat**, No Event**
Impact of Event Scale-IES				
Intrusion	27.40††	.30	Combat veterans	No Event***, Death***, Life-Threat***, Serious Illness***, Family Trauma***, Multiple Trauma***
			Rape, Divorce, Multiple Trauma, Death	No Event***, Life-Threat***
			Family Trauma, Serious Illness, Life-Threat	No Event***, Life-Threat***
Avoidance	20.60††	.24	Rape, Combat Veterans, Divorce, Multiple Trauma	No Event***, Life-Threat***
			Family Trauma, Death	No Event*, Life-Threat***
			Serious Illness, Life-Threat	No Event***
Total	36.51††	.42	Rape, Combat Veterans, Divorce, Multiple Trauma, Death	Life-Threat***, No Event***
			Family Trauma, Serious Illness	No Event***, Life-Threat
			Life-Threat	No Event***

Note: N = 409; df = 8,400

* p < .10; ** p < .05; *** p < .01; † p < .0005; †† p < .0001

Fs (8,400) > 20.60, p < .05. To test for differences in the mean scores on the PTSD dimension across stressor categories, the Newman-Keuls procedure of ranked mean comparison was used for unequal sample sizes (Winer, 1971). Table 4 indicates a summary of the significant differences found in the mean scores of the different stressor categories. By examining the mean scores shown in Table 3, it can be seen that Vietnam combat veterans have significantly higher scores on nearly all of the dimensions of PTSD being assessed with the different scales. The Newman-Keuls analysis indicated that the combat veteran scores on the VESI scales and the BDI are significantly higher than those of *all* other stressor categories.

The combat veterans and individuals who had experienced multiple trauma yielded significantly higher scores on the SSS experience seeking subscale than those in the No Event category. In addition, the Combat Veterans, Rape, Divorce, Death, and Multiple Trauma categories showed significantly higher mean scores than the Life-Threat category. Scores for the combat veterans also were significantly higher than those of the Death, Serious Illness, Family Trauma, and Multiple Trauma on the Intrusion subscale. On the Avoidance subscale, Family Trauma scores were also significantly higher than Life-Threat scores and on the IES total subscale, both Family Trauma and Serious Illness scores were higher than those of Life-Threat.

Comparison of Stressor Categories Involving a Loss of a Significant Other Versus No Loss or No Event

Table 5 shows the mean scores on the dimensions of PTSD for the stressor categories involving a loss of significant others versus those with no loss or no stressor event. Inspection of the table indicates a clear linear trend in the mean scores: Those stressor categories involving the loss of a significant other have higher scores on the PTSD scales than the No Loss stressor category which, in turn, has higher scores than the No Event group.

Table 6 indicates the results of the one-way ANOVA for the stressor groups experiencing different levels of loss. Tests of simple effects revealed that the three stressor categories were significantly different on all of the assessment scales except for the disinhibition and boredom susceptibility subscales of the SSS, Fs (2,379) > 3.74, p < .05. The results of the Newman-Keuls mean comparison test produced a large number of significant differences (p < .05) between the Loss groups which are summarized in Table 6. First, the stressor category experiencing a loss

TABLE 5
Mean Scores on PTSD Dimensions for Stressor Categories Involving a
Loss of a Significant Other Versus Those With No Loss or No Event

PTSD DIMENSION	Loss (Combat, Divorce, Death) n = 183	No Loss (Rape, Threat, Illness, Family Trauma) n = 106	No Event n = 93
VESI			
Depression	78.83	57.09	51.54
Physical Symptoms	47.73	39.48	35.85
Stigmatization	20.17	5.28	5.06
Rage/Anger	14.12	11.57	10.58
Intrusive Imagery	15.88	7.59	7.29
Intimacy Conflict	11.43	7.63	6.71
Total PTSD	203.38	140.06	127.50
Sensation Seeking Scale-SSS			
Adventure Seeking	7.01	6.98	6.12
Experience Seeking	4.94	4.58	4.13
Disinhibition	4.79	4.30	4.62
Boredom Susceptibility	3.01	2.84	2.83
Beck Depression Inventory			
Depression	14.24	7.55	5.98
Impact of Events Scale-IES			
Intrusion	17.62	13.37	7.99
Avoidance	18.55	14.69	9.12
Total	36.17	28.06	17.11

Note: Subjects who have experienced multiple trauma have been excluded.

of a loved one is significantly different from the No Event group on
every scale except the SSS subscales disinhibition and boredom susceptibility. Second, the Loss group is significantly different from the No
Loss category on all the variables except the VESI rage scale and the SSS
subscales adventure seeking and experience seeking. Additionally, the
No Loss stressor category manifests more PTSD than the No Event group
as assessed by the IES scales and the SSS adventure seeking scale. Thus,
in comparing the three stressor categories, the results indicate, as expected, that the greater the degree of loss of a significant other, the more
severe are the syndrome-specific symptoms of PTSD.

TABLE 6
Summary of Significant Differences Between Stressor Categories Involving a Loss of Significant Other Versus Those Involving No Loss or No Event
Analysis of Variance of Simple Effects and Newman-Keuls Multiple Mean Comparison Test

PTSD DIMENSION	F-Value	r^2	Newman-Keuls Mean Comparison		
			Loss vs. No Event	Loss vs. No Loss	No Loss vs. No Event
VESI					
Depression	39.52††	.17	**	**	—
Physical Symptoms	24.32††	.11	**	**	—
Stigmatization	55.99††	.23	**	**	—
Sensation Seeking	25.42††	.12	**	**	—
Rage/Anger	18.76††	.09	**	—	—
Intrusive Imagery	48.69††	.20	**	**	—
Intimacy Conflict	40.76††	.18	**	**	—
Total PTSD	45.43††	.19	**	**	—
Sensation Seeking Scale-SSS					
Adventure Seeking	3.74*	.02	*	—	*
Experience Seeking	4.73†	.02	**	—	—
Disinhibition	NS				
Boredom Susceptibility	NS				
Beck Depression Inventory-BDI					
Depression	31.67††	.14	**	**	—
Impact of Event Scale-IES					
Intrusion	93.01††	.33	**	**	**
Avoidance	81.24††	.30	**	**	**
Total	101.27††	.35	**	**	**

Note: df = 2,379

* = p < .05; ** = p < .01; † = p < .005; †† = p < .0001

Table 7 shows the results of the ANOVA for the stressor categories exposed to different degrees of Threat. As expected, the high Threat stressor category shows higher mean PTSD scores than the No Threat category which has, in turn, higher scores than the No Event category.

Table 8 indicates the results of the ANOVA simple effects and Newman-Keuls tests. As predicted, the ANOVA reveals significant differences between the stressor categories Fs $(2,379) > 4.06$, $p < .05$. Further, the Newman-Keuls comparison shows that the Threat category is significantly different from the No Threat and No Event categories on all of the VESI dimensions of PTSD. In addition, the Threat category differs significantly from the No Event category on the SSS experience seeking subscale, the BDI, and the IES. It is also significantly different from No

TABLE 7

Mean Scores on PTSD Dimensions for Stressor Categories Involving Life-Threat Versus Those Involving No Threat or No Event

	Threat (Rape, Accident/ Life-Threat, Vietnam Combat Veterans) n = 145	No Threat (Death, Divorce, Illness, Family Trauma) n = 144	No Event n = 93
VESI			
Depression	82.03	59.60	51.54
Physical Symptoms	49.68	39.70	35.85
Stigmatization	23.75	5.61	5.06
Sensation Seeking	16.13	11.47	10.58
Rage/Anger	14.66	11.71	10.47
Intrusive Imagery	17.88	7.77	7.29
Intimacy Conflict	12.14	7.91	6.71
Total PTSD	216.27	143.78	127.50
Sensation Seeking Scale			
Adventure Seeking	6.69	7.31	6.12
Experience Seeking	4.91	4.70	4.13
Disinhibition	4.70	4.52	4.62
Boredom Susceptibility	3.27	2.62	2.83
Beck Depression Inventory			
Depression	14.67	8.89	5.98
Impact of Event Scale			
Intrusion	16.56	15.56	7.99
Avoidance	17.21	17.06	9.12
Total	33.78	32.61	17.11

Note: Individuals who have experienced multiple stressful life events have been excluded.

TABLE 8

Summary of Significant Differences Between Stressor Categories Involving Life-Threat Versus Those Involving No Threat or No Event

Analysis of Variance of Simple Effects and Newman-Keuls Multiple Mean Comparison Test

PTSD DIMENSION	F-value	r^2	Threat vs. No Event	Newman-Keuls Mean Comparison Threat vs. No Threat	No Threat vs. No Event
VESI					
Depression	43.40††	.19	**	***	*
Physical Symptoms	31.68††	.14	**	***	*
Stigmatization	90.28††	.32	**	***	—
Rage/Anger	22.88††	.11	**	***	—
Intrusive Imagery	76.64††	.29	**	***	*
Intimacy Conflict	50.28††	.21	**	***	—
Total PTSD	59.65††	.24	**	***	**
Sensation Seeking Scale					
Adventure Seeking	5.71†	.03	—	*	**
Experience Seeking	4.06*	.02	*	—	*
Disinhibition	NS			—	—
Boredom Susceptibility	4.16*	.02	—	*	—
Beck Depression Inventory					
Depression	27.72††	.13	**	**	*
Impact of Event Scale					
Intrusion	68.13††	.26	**	—	***
Avoidance	61.74††	.24	**	—	***
Total	74.33††	.28	**	—	**

Note: df = 2,379
*= p < .05; **= p < .01; †= p < .005; †† = p < .0001

Threat on the SSS adventure seeking and boredom susceptibility sub-scales as well as the BDI. Finally, on the SSS adventure seeking and experience seeking subscales, the BDI, and the IES scales, the No Threat category showed significant differences from the No Event category.

DISCUSSION

The results of this preliminary study comparing stress response syndromes in different survivor groups contains a number of strengths and limitations. As an exploratory study, the present research is limited in its external validity due to the lack of a random sample, time-since-event effect, and the disparate ages of the subjects in the comparison groups. Despite these methodological problems the overall configuration of the research findings lends general support to the person × situation conceptual framework presented in this chapter and summarized in Tables 1 and 2. In particular, we explored the effects of two stressor variables, threat and loss, on the severity of symptoms which define PTSD. Overall, the results of the analyses provided strong support for the hypothesis that these variables are linked to the mechanisms which influence post-traumatic adaptive behavior.

First, it is reasonable to expect that the greater the degree of loss or life-threat, the more difficult will be the survivor's task of assimilating elements of the stressful life event into the self-structure. By way of comparison, none of the other stressor categories manifested the severity of depression or total PTSD as did the Vietnam combat veterans. Interestingly, however, the small sample of rape victims exhibited the next highest level of PTSD symptoms across the different scales, despite the lack of statistical significance due, perhaps, to the small sample size. Indeed, their level of PTSD, as assessed by the IES, is equal to that of the combat veterans, despite lower scores on the other scales. Thus, looking at the mean scores across the stressor categories there is supportive evidence to suggest that the severity of PTSD is, in part, a function of the severity of threat and loss.

Although the results summarized in Table 4 are too extensive for a detailed discussion in this chapter, it is noteworthy that there were many other significant differences found in the mean scores of the stressor categories. For example, victims of rape, multiple trauma, the death of a loved one, family trauma, and divorce showed significantly more total PTSD as assessed by the IES scale than did persons who reported no event or a life-threatening event. Clearly, the interpretation of these data illustrates the need to specify how the nature and complexity of the stressor event impacts on the unique personality of the survivor. In general, however, these results might be construed as suggesting that the more severe and complex the stressful life event, the greater is the likelihood to develop symptoms of PTSD.

The results of the analysis for the effects of a loss of a significant other through death or the termination of a love relationship provide further support to the argument made above. As Tables 5 and 6 summarize, those individuals experiencing the loss of a loved one show more severe symptoms of PTSD, as indicated by the mean scale scores on all variables except the SSS subscales disinhibition and boredom susceptibility, than do the No Loss or No Event stressor categories. Even more impressive is the finding that the No Loss category, which contains persons exposed to trauma, does show more PTSD on the IES scale than the No Event stressor category. Clearly, if the relationship between stressful life experiences and PTSD were essentially random, we would not expect to find the obtained pattern of results. Further, since depression following trauma is thought to be associated with the loss of an object of love, affection, and value (Freud, 1957; Jacobson, 1974), we would expect that the stressor categories with greater degrees of loss would have significantly higher mean scores on the VESI, BDI, and IES depression scales. As Table 5 shows, this is indeed the case inasmuch as the Loss category is significantly different from the No Event and No Loss categories on all three measures of depression or tendencies toward denial and avoidance of thoughts connected to the trauma. This same pattern of results tends to hold across the comparisons of the other stressor categories. Moreover, as Table 5 indicates, the VESI and IES scales indicate that there is a linear relationship between the degree of loss and total PTSD.

The results of the analysis for the effects of threat on adaptive functioning support the significance of this conceptual variable in the development of PTSD. Once again the data summarized in Tables 7 and 8 suggest that the greater the degree of threat, the more severe is the PTSD. In particular, the tables show that the Threat category has particularly high mean scores on depression, stigmatization, and intrusive imagery ($r^2 = .19$ to $.32$).

The impact of a life-threatening event seems to be associated with recurring images and thoughts of the trauma, feelings of helplessness and depression, and a tendency to be self-conscious as a stigmatized victim. Thus, whether one is a victim of rape, a combat veteran, or involved in a natural disaster, the survivor may feel acutely aware of a change in personal identity, social status, or sense of continuity and centeredness (Lifton, 1976). This severe stigmatization may also be an expression of the survivor's feelings that they did not "ask for what happened" and their awareness of the "just world" phenomenon (Lerner, 1974) where those who suffer "bad fate" somehow deserve it. If this is so, then the victim of a life-threatening event may be caught in a no-win cycle of events. To talk about the powerful and overwhelming trauma means risking further stigmatization; the failure to discuss the traumatic episode increases the need for defensive avoidance and thus increases the probability of depression alternating with cycles of intrusive imagery and other symptoms of PTSD.

As a summary analysis, we have presented in Table 9 the hypothesized level of stressor dimensions present in each of the nine stressor categories used in this study. This table is a useful way to integrate the theoretical considerations of PTSD discussed in Tables 1 and 2 with the results we obtained from our statistical analyses. Although Table 9 extends our discussion beyond the limits of the research data, it is especially valuable in understanding the different ways stressor events can influence the development of PTSD in different survivor groups. For example, we have hypothesized that Vietnam combat veterans have high levels of stress on eight of the 10 dimensions of stressor events, including being both an agent and victim in the trauma. Clearly, the presence of such high levels of different stressors should produce a high prevalence of PTSD in the survivor population.

To illustrate this more graphically, the table suggests that the typical Vietnam combat veteran endured a one-year trauma of a life-threatening nature in which there were frequent, rapid, recurring and unpredictable encounters with enemy troops in which the veteran was placed in an agent-victim role of high moral conflict. Further, in the combatant role he was physically immersed in death, dying, and destruction. When considered from this perspective it is not difficult to imagine that such an experience would tend to evoke significant symptoms of distress in most veterans and likely cause a high prevalence of PTSD (Figley, 1978; Figley & Leventman, 1980; Wilson & Krauss, in press). Interestingly, the results of the present study conform quite readily to the estimates theoretically derived in Table 9 for Vietnam combat veterans since the magnitude of the PTSD scores is substantially higher than that of the other stressor categories.

At the other end of the spectrum, Table 9 suggests that the prediction of PTSD may vary according to the interactive nature of dispositional (see Table 1) and stressor variables. For example, persons who have experienced multiple trauma may or may not develop PTSD depending

TABLE 9
Hypothesized Level of Stressor Dimensions Present in Different Stressful Life Events

Dimension of Stressor Event	Vietnam Combat	No Event	Death of Loved One	Rape/ Battering	Divorce	Serious Illness	Life-Threat	Family Trauma	Multiple Trauma
Degree of Life-Threat	H	L	L	H	L	L	H	L	VAR
Loss of Significant Other	H	L	H	L	H	VAR	VAR	VAR	VAR
Speed of Onset	H	L	VAR	H	L	VAR	H	L	VAR
Duration	L	L	L	VAR	VAR	VAR	L	VAR	VAR
Displacement From Home	H	L	L	H	H	L	VAR	L	VAR
Potential for Recurrence	H	L	VAR	VAR	VAR	VAR	VAR	VAR	VAR
Exposure to Death, Dying, Destruction	H	L	H	L	L	VAR	VAR	L	VAR
Degree of Moral Conflict	H	L	L	VAR	VAR	VAR	L	VAR	VAR
Role in Trauma	A,V	—	V	V	A,V	V	V	V	V
Proportion of Community Affected	L	L	L	L	L	M	VAR	VAR	VAR

Note: H, M, L, A, V, VAR are symbols for high, medium, low, agent, victim, and variable, respectively.

on the severity of the trauma and their existing psychological and economic resources to cope with it. In this situation it is necessary for the clinician or researcher to attempt to specify the nature of interactive equations that would best predict the manifestation of PTSD in an individual or survivor group which experienced the same event (e.g., flood).

In conclusion, the present study suggests that a comparative analysis of PTSD among different stressor categories yields important information on the types of events that produce syndrome-specific symptom clusters. Further, the results of this study strongly suggest that the attempt to understand and predict PTSD from a person × situation interactionist model of behavior has heuristic value. Consistent with others (Green et al., this volume), we believe that such an approach offers promise to move beyond the traditional assumptions that PTSD is caused by premorbid character pathology or is simply a reactive process to catastrophic stress. It is undoubtedly the case that some persons are more vulnerable to stress than others and that some stressors will produce stress syndromes in everyone (e.g., Hiroshima). The scientific explanation of PTSD, however, will ultimately necessitate complex theoretical predictions of how persons, situations, and stressor events jointly produce the adaptive syndromes which define post-traumatic personality processes.

REFERENCES

American Psychiatric Association. *Diagnostic and statistical manual of mental disorders* (3rd ed.). Washington, DC: American Psychiatric Association, 1980.

Beck, A. *Cognitive therapy and the emotional disorders.* New York: International Universities Press, 1976.

Beck, A.T., Ward, C.H., Mendelsohn, M., Mock, J., & Erbaugh, J. An inventory measuring depression. *Archives of General Psychiatry*, 1961, 4, 561-571.

Erikson, E. *The life-cycle completed.* New York: Norton, 1982.

Erikson, K. *Everything in its path.* New York: Simon & Schuster, 1976.

Figley, C.R. *Stress disorders among Vietnam veterans.* New York: Brunner/Mazel, 1978.

Figley, C.R. & Leventman, S. *Strangers at home: Vietnam veterans since the war.* New York: Praeger, 1980.

Figley, C.R., & McCubbin, H.I. (Eds.). *Stress in the family. Volume II: Coping with catastrophe.* New York: Brunner/Mazel, 1983.

Freud, S. (1917). Mourning and melancholia. In J. Strachey (Ed.), *Standard edition*, 14: 237-259. London: Hogarth Press, 1957.

Gleser, G.C., Green, B.L., & Winget, C.N. *Buffalo Creek revisited: Prolonged psychosocial effects of disaster.* New York: Simon & Schuster, 1981.

Green, B., Wilson, J.P., & Lindy, J. Conceptualizing post-traumatic stress disorder: A psychosocial framework (this volume, Chapter 4).

Horowitz, M.J. *Stress response syndromes.* New York: Jason Aronson, 1976.

Horowitz, M.J. Psychological response to serious life events. In V. Hamilton & D.M. Warburton (Eds.), *Human stress and cognition*. New York: Wiley, 1979.
Horowitz, M.J., Wilner, N., & Alvarez, W. Impact of event scale. A measure of subjective strength. *Psychosomatic Medicine*, 1979, *41*, 209-218.
Jacobson, E. *Depression*. New York: International Universities Press, 1974.
Krystal, H. *Massive psychic trauma*. New York: International Universities Press, 1968.
Lerner, M.J. The justice motive: Equity and parity among children. *Journal of Personality and Social Psychology*, 1974, *29*, 539-550.
Lidz, T. Psychiatric casualties from Guadal canal. *Psychiatry*, 1946, *9*, 193-215.
Lifton, R.J. *Death in life: Survivors of Hiroshima*. New York: Simon & Schuster, 1967.
Lifton, R.J. *The life of the self*. New York: Simon & Schuster, 1976.
Lifton, R.J. *The broken connection*. New York: Basic Books, 1983.
Lindy, J.D., Grace, M.C., & Green, B.L. Survivors: Outreach to a reluctant population. *American Journal of Orthopsychiatry*, 1981, *51*, 468-478.
Nace, E.P., O'Brien, C.P., Mintz, J., Ream, N., & Meyers, A.L. Adjustment among Vietnam veteran drug users two years post service. In C.R. Figley (Ed.), *Stress disorders among Vietnam veterans*. New York: Brunner/Mazel, 1978.
Niederland, W. The problem of the survivor. In Krystal, H. (Ed.), *Massive psychic trauma*. New York: International Universities Press, 1968.
Seligman, M.E. *Learned helplessness*. San Francisco: Freeman Press, 1974.
Seligman, M.E. & Garber, J. *Human helplessness*. New York: Academic Press, 1980.
Shatan, C.F. Through the membrane of reality: Impacted grief and perceptual dissonance in Vietnam combat veterans. *Psychiatric Opinion*, 1974, *11*, 6-15.
Specter, P.E. What to do with significant multivariate analysis of variance. *Journal of Applied Psychology*, 1977, *67*, 158-163.
Strober, M., Green, J., & Carlson, G. Utility of the Beck Depression Inventory with psychiatrically hospitalized adolescents. *Journal of Consulting and Clinical Psychology*, 1981, *40*, 482-483.
Wilson, J.P. *Identity, ideology and crisis: The Vietnam veteran in transition* (Vol 2). Washington, DC: Disabled American Veterans, 1978.
Wilson, J.P. Conflict, stress and growth: The effects of war on psychosocial development among Vietnam veterans. In C.R. Figley & S. Leventman (Eds.), *Strangers at home: Vietnam veterans since the war*. New York: Praeger, 1980a.
Wilson, J.P. *Towards an understanding of post-traumatic stress disorders among Vietnam veterans*. Testimony before the U.S. Senate Subcommittee on Veteran Affairs, May, 1980b.
Wilson, J.P. & Krauss, G. *The Vietnam era stress inventory*. Cleveland State University, 1980.
Wilson, J.P. & Krauss, G.E. *The Vietnam era stress inventory*. Cleveland State University, 1982.
Wilson, J.P. & Krauss, G.E. Predicting post-traumatic stress syndromes among Vietnam veterans. In W. Kelly (Ed.), *Post-traumatic stress disorder and the war veteran patient*. New York: Brunner/Mazel, in press.
Wilson, J.P. & Ziegelbaum, S.D. The Vietnam veteran on trial: The relation of post-traumatic stress disorder to criminal behavior. *Behavioral Sciences and the Law*, 1983, *4*, 69-84.
Winer, B.J. *Statistical principles in experimental research*. New York: McGraw-Hill, 1971.
Zilberg, N., Weiss, D.S., & Horowitz, M. Impact of event scale: A cross validation study and some empirical evidence supporting a conceptual model of stress response syndromes. *Journal of Consulting and Clinical Psychology*, 1982, *50*(3), 407-414.
Zuckerman, M. *Sensation seeking*. Hillsdale: L. Erlbaum, 1979.
Zuckerman, M., Kolin, E.A., Price, L., & Zoob, I. Development of a sensation seeking scale. *Journal of Consulting and Clinical Psychology*, 1964, *28*(6), 477-480.
Zuckerman, M. & Linn, K. Construct validity of the sensation seeking scale. *Journal of Consulting and Clinical Psychology*, 1968, *32*(4), 420-426.

CHAPTER

9

An Assessment of Conflicting Views on Mental Health: The Consequences of Traumatic Events

E. L. QUARANTELLI

Students of this question are sharply divided on what they see as the psychological effects of community disasters. A minority argues that mental health effects are widespread, deep, persistent, long lasting, and dysfunctional with the negative consequences similar to what can be seen in other stress situations. The majority argues that while there are immediate widespread effects, much of the reaction is surface, non-persistent, of short duration, not behaviorally dysfunctional, and that there can be significant positive psychological effects. The two positions, as well as supporting data and reasoning are evaluated, and policy implications are explored in this chapter.

INTRODUCTION

In the early 1980s, there has been much controversy in the United States in connection with the opening and reopening of nuclear power plants, and the siting of or the living next to hazardous waste sites. While many issues are involved, a central one is the question of the psychological impact on the affected population. If the Three Mile Island plant in Pennsylvania were to be started up again, would there be negative mental health consequences for the area residents? Have there been deleterious mental effects as a result of the exposure to hazardous wastes in the Times Beach, Missouri situation? Public hearings, court cases, and mass media accounts associated with these and similar events openly state and speculate about both the short- and long-term consequences of such actual or potential stressful situations on the mental well-being of the people most directly involved.

These examples highlight a very important theoretical and practical question, namely—how well or how poorly do actual and potential victims respond to extreme stress situations? The answer to this question has crucial implications for public policy in emergency planning and management and tells us much about the basic nature of human beings and societies. What is the answer to the question? What is the quality and quantity of the psychological response to extreme stress?

We should preface our answer by noting that in this chapter we are not dealing with all stress situations, individual and collective. Rather our focus is on collective stress situations, and within that category, on disasters, and within that class, on those of a community nature. Our conception of collective stress follows from Barton who sees it as a situation when "many members of a social system fail to receive expected conditions of life from the system" (1970, p. 38), and who gives as examples of such situations: pogroms, depressions, famines, civil wars, mass purges, floods, economic declines and ghost towns, reigns of terror, earthquakes, atomic wars, deaths of heads of state, hurricanes, air raids, droughts, blackouts, deteriorating slum neighborhoods, etc. We view disasters as an imbalance in the demand-capability ratio in a consensus crisis occasion, separating disasters out as this kind of social phenomena from disasters viewed as physical agents, physical impacts, assessments of physical impacts, social disruptions from physical impacts, social constructions of crises which may not involve physical impacts, and political definitions of certain crisis situations (for a discussion of the prevailing major conceptions of disaster, see Quarantelli, 1982a). In our formulation, disasters are *ad hoc,* irregular occasions which involve a crisis where there is a relative consensus that things have to be done but the wherewithal available is not enough to meet the demands of the occasion; those consensus crises which involve a community are of major interest to us.

It is important to note these matters for we shall later argue that part of the controversy which prevails stems from a failure to distinguish individual and collective stress situations. Within the latter category it is important to distinguish disasters from conflict-types of happenings such as wars, revolutions, civil disturbances, riots, terrorist and hostage-taking attacks, and other potential traumatic events (for a discussion of consensus versus dissensus or conflict-types of crises, see Quarantelli, 1970). In addition, not all disasters disrupt communities and as such there are disasters that are not community disasters (e.g., many transportation accidents). The distinctions we are making can be depicted as follows:

```
          /Extreme Stress Situations\
Individual                    /Collective\
              /Disasters __ Conflicts
        Community    Non-Community
```

What is known about the psychological responses of human beings to sudden and unexpected great stress as would occur in a community disaster? The answer is twofold: a little is known in the sense that there is no agreement about the answer in the relevant research and literature; a lot in the sense that enough has now been done and said so that a systematic assessment of the two conflicting viewpoints can be made.

Some students of the problem, seemingly the statistical minority, see the mental health effects of disasters as widespread, deep, persistent, long lasting, and dysfunctional, and that the consequences are as drastic and negative as what can be seen in other individual and collective stress situations. The apparent majority of students of the question only appear to agree that there are immediate widespread effects. Their position is that much of the reaction is surface, non-persistent, of short duration, and not behaviorally dysfunctional. They further argue that possibly unlike other kinds of individual and collective stress situations, community disasters may actually generate significant positive psychological effects. For purposes of stating the positions, we have stated them in Weberian-ideal-type terms, that is, in their purest extreme form, although in our judgment, in this particular controversy, the actual is closer to the ideal than is often the case in many scientific disputes.

We shall not only indicate the essence of the two approaches and the kinds of data they present, but we will also suggest some of the reasons for the difference in opinion. However, before zeroing in on the central issue, we think it is helpful to see the matter in a larger context, and will provide some background information on disaster studies of a social and behavioral nature. A lack of understanding of the history of disaster research can lead not only to more reinventing of the wheel, but worse, to poor and faulty scholarship including the passing on of incorrect or dubious statements, or ignoring relevant past studies and literature. Such a lack of historical knowledge and poor scholarship may be more of a problem in disaster studies than in many other areas of research. This is because, although the field is in its second generation, the great majority of those currently studying disasters come from other theoretical backgrounds and interests (Wright & Rossi, 1981). A consequence of this is much intellectual importation, which is not necessarily bad but can lead to seeing only what one brings to a study from non-indigenous sources. There are also very few scientists working in the area who have spent their professional lives researching in the area, which is not the normal career/work situation for most specialists in most research disciplines. While this more readily allows for the application of new perspectives, it is usually at the cost of not perceiving subtleties and important distinctions which any veteran worker in any area can bring to bear.

We will try to be as fair as possible in detailing the two points of view about the consequences of disasters for mental health. But we do not come to this presentation devoid of a professional judgment. Our position is that one of the existing views on the question does not fully recognize the implications of what has already been learned about behavior in community disasters, and holds partially mythological, as well as incorrect, ideas about disaster occasions.

BACKGROUND

There was almost no work done on the social and behavioral aspects of disasters until after World War II. Prior to that time, apart from historical accounts, which go as far back as the description of a plague in ancient Athens by Thucydides (1934, pp. 109-114), the corpus of the literature consisted of a handful of empirical observations (Janes, 1942; Prasad, 1935; Prince, 1920; Slade, 1932, 1933), and a few speculative essays (e.g., Carr, 1932; James, 1911; Kutak, 1938; Sorokin, 1942). Thus, it is not surprising that the post-war disaster studies could not be born out of this almost non-existent background. Rather research on disaster topics came into being indirectly because of a more primary interest in conflictive types of collective stress situations, although if earlier studies on the latter kind of phenomena had been seriously attended to, little might have happened because the expected negative effects did not surface and if implications of that had been thought through, disaster studies would have been far less likely to have been undertaken.

World War II stimulated a number of studies of civilian behavior under the extreme stress of wartime bombings. Some were very systematic and guided by social science, such as the immediate post-war, large-scale, sample surveys, of the German and the Japanese populations which had been subjected to air attacks (U.S. Strategic Bombing Survey, 1945-47). Semi-social science research was also undertaken on individual behavior and organizational problems in Britain during the war (Titmus, 1950).

The results reported in these studies were considerably at variance with pre-war expectations and prevailing views on the behavior of people under extreme stress. For example, the research showed that the civilian populations in all the countries reacted remarkably well to wartime attacks and problems. There was not the widespread personal and social disorganization that had been predicted before the war. A few of the empirical findings were that morale remained generally high, mental disorders did not significantly increase, panicky evacuations did not occur, antisocial and criminal behavior did not markedly escalate, and suicide rates went down (much of this research is summarized in Janis, 1951).

In addition, certain little known case material demonstrated a picture of impressive stability and resiliency on the part of very heavily stressed, bombed populations in certain British cities and in Hamburg, Germany, as well as among the survivors of Hiroshima. In the latter case where more than 60% of the population was either killed or injured, the less than 40% left immediately tried to reestablish the routines of life. Little overt panic, disorganized activity, or antisocial behavior occurred. The day *after* the bombing, survivors from the 12 banks got together and resumed banking services, one of the few standing steel companies resumed activities when 20% of the employees reported to work, the trolley lines were completely cleared and some electric service was restored. By the second day there was restoration of railway services and some of the phone system. The tremendous physical destruction was not matched by any comparable social disintegration (Fritz, 1965, personal communication; Janis, 1951).

Fortunately for the later development of disaster research, the results of the wartime stress studies were neither particularly nor widely noted. In the late 1940s, various federal government agencies became concerned about how the American population might react to atomic, chemical, and other newer kinds of wartime threats. Unaware of the findings about collective stress responses during World War II, they visualized the worst of scenarios, and asked what planning could be undertaken to prevent or minimize the personal and social disorganization they assumed would occur if the United States were directly subjected to attack. Afraid of widespread "panic," the agencies turned to social and behavioral science research for help (see Kreps, 1981, for some of the history of the earlier funded studies, particularly those undertaken in 1952-1957 by the National Academy of Sciences Committee on Disaster Studies). They reasoned that it might be possible to extrapolate findings from peacetime civilian disasters to potential wartime stress settings. Studies of disasters were therefore supported in roughly a half dozen universities, with the major initial research effort being at the National Opinion Research Center (NORC) at the University of Chicago during 1950-1954 (which was our own first professional involvement in the area). The NORC work involved the first interdisciplinary team effort conducting field research on a variety of disasters such as an earthquake in California, tornados in Arkansas, fires in Chicago, and a gas explosion in a Rochester, New York suburb (NORC studies are summarized in Fritz & Marks, 1954).

The starting point, the work undertaken, and the major conclusions independently reached by the half dozen centers of disaster studies around the country were very important (other early research results are reported in Chapman, 1954; Demerath & Wallace, 1957; Fritz, 1961; Logan, Killian, & Marrs, 1950; Powell, 1954). All started with the idea that the major social and behavioral problem in disasters was the personal and social breakdown and disorganization which supposedly would occur in the face of extreme stress. The researchers, it was hoped, might be able to advance some ideas on how to reestablish personal stability and social order. It was simply taken for granted that disaster behavior deviated sharply from everyday behavior; to document that, therefore, was not a research goal. Although not always successful, all the researchers attempted to do systematic field studies: They interviewed and they observed on the scene. Even as early as 1952, the NORC team conducted a month-long, random sample survey of 342 tornado-impacted households which involved a field interview instrument that took over two hours to administer (Marks, Fritz, Bucher, Earle, Endleman et al., 1954).

Most important of all, the pioneer researchers in the disaster area, from the early 1950s to the early 1960s, reached the same general conclusion—they had made a basically incorrect assumption. The personal and social disorganization in disasters that had been anticipated simply did not occur. Particularly at the individual level, behavior in the extreme stress of disasters is usually controlled rather than impulsive. Behavior generally involves the use of what is seen as appropriate means to the perceived ends; it is generally not disorganized. Behavior is mostly adaptive, that is, it is, in general, functional rather than dysfunctional for the situation. It is not that researchers found no problems. Quite the contrary, these early studies found many, especially at the group level. For example, the mobilization of all relevant organizations at times of disasters is usually problematic; certain necessary tasks such as search and rescue and allocation of casualties to hospitals are frequently poorly done; interorganizational coordination in the post-impact period may or may not occur (Fritz, 1961).

In retrospect, it can be said that the pioneer researchers accomplished two important things: They uncovered a number of myths and misconceptions about disaster behavior, and they obtained some idea of the sources of problems affecting efficiency and effectiveness of preparations for and responses to disasters. We think it is important to emphasize this because it is relevant to an understanding of the consequences of disasters for mental health. As we shall indicate later, we think some mythological views still prevail with respect to mental health problems, and the prime source of problems in disasters is not yet fully recognized.

The pioneer researchers in the disaster area established the existence of a number of myths regarding behavior in a disaster situation which are now widely accepted. The notion that panic behavior is a common phenomenon in disaster events is one example of an erroneous popular belief that was refuted by empirical research. Media accounts reporting instances of panic flight reactions at disaster sites have long been common. At times, entire communities have been described as fleeing from a potential site of disaster impact. However, the reality in the pre-impact period is that the vast majority of community residents can scarcely be induced to evacuate their homes, even when the possibility of damage and destruction is imminent (Quarantelli, 1954, 1957).

Disaster research in the mid-1950s and early 1960s not only uncovered myths, but also indicated that the roots of many disaster problems could be found in the organized effort to prepare for, respond to, and recover from major community emergencies. Often the very organizations involved in disasters play a major role in the disaster-associated problems that develop. This, of course, is not deliberate, but nonetheless agencies and groups often act in such ways that magnify or create difficulties and problems for populations threatened by or actually exposed to danger. In fact, this point is now so well-accepted by experienced disaster researchers that they draw a distinction between *agent*-generated demands and *response*-generated demands (Dynes, Quarantelli, & Kreps, 1981). Disaster agents create certain demands such as search and rescue, care of injured and dead, etc., but there are also response-generated demands. These are the needs and demands that are not created by the disaster agent itself, but by the very activities that take place when responding to the disaster occasion, and include such matters as communication, continuing assessment of the emergency situation, the mobilization of human and material resources, coordination, and control and authority. In some cases, the response-generated demands turn a minor incident into a major disaster. In other words, the response can be worse than anything the disaster agent presents.

In the 1972 Wilkes-Barre, Pennsylvania flood, about 20,000 people had to leave their homes for a lengthy period of time because of a massive flood. (We ignore the pre-impact organizational failures which did not create the disaster but almost ensured that it would have maximum destructive impact.) The displacement forced evacuees out of their homes and disrupted their lives in many major ways, but even worse, an incredible amount of bureaucratic inefficiency forced many of them to break neighborhood ties and live in trailers which were very poorly suited to the area. The Disaster Research Center found that for many households and individuals, greater social and psychological damage was occasioned by the "helpful" response of putting evacuees in unsuitable trailers in undesirable areas than was done by the disaster agent, the flood waters.

In another situation, the 1972 Buffalo Creek disaster in West Virginia, a social scientist looking at another massive relief effort said: "The end result insofar as rehousing was concerned was what might be expected if a brilliant madman set about in the most ingenious ways to maximize personal and social pathologies" (Harshbarger, 1976, p. 276). This was said of an effort in which millions of dollars were spent over several years by many well-intentioned agencies that did not know what they were doing, or perhaps worse, thought they knew what they were doing.

Our point in citing these examples is to indicate, as is said in much of the early social science disaster research, that to focus solely on the disaster agent results in the omission of a very important aspect of the situation, the organized attempt to respond to the occasion. Organizational response to a disaster or its threat is crucial since it provides the structure for possible individual responses. At one time, the National Weather Service often asked why people did not pay attention to their warnings about dangers. The problem was seen as residing in individuals, as one of perception of messages, and as a reflection of a passive or unresponsive attitude in the face of danger cues. However, social science studies of warning processes indicated that the problem was incorrectly viewed—the question to ask was not why people did not pay attention to warnings, but why alerting organizations did not issue messages that people could interpret as warnings. The deliverers of certain disaster-related services were the source of the problem, not the recipients of the services, the population at large. People did not passively perceive danger warnings; rather, the involved organizations simply were not communicating warning messages, a rather different view of the problem with drastically different implications of what could be done about it (McLuckie, 1970).

We certainly do not want to imply that all disaster problems can be solved by looking for the source of difficulties in organizations rather than in the affected individuals. However, the research of the 1950s and early 1960s did establish this approach as being a very fruitful way of looking at many disaster problems. Rather than blaming people for what is happening to them, there are many matters which can be better understood by looking at the social situation or social structure in which people must respond. The early disaster researchers also showed that if the "wrong" questions were asked, rather meaningless answers would be obtained. "Wrong" questions will be posed if mythological assumptions about disaster behavior are not uncovered and challenged.

Considerable research has been undertaken on the human and social aspects of disasters in the last 20 years. The Disaster Research Center (DRC) alone has conducted over 250 different field studies of natural and technological disasters, most of a community nature. Dozens of social scientists around the world are looking at disasters (the International Research Committee on Disasters formed in 1983 has over 250 members in 24 countries). The development of a "critical mass" of specialists in a variety of disciplines, the institutionalization of the research area through the creation of research institutes, the establishment of professional journals and newsletters, and the beginnings of collaborative cross-societal studies, and other happenings, all attest to the flourishing of the field (Kreps, 1984; Quarantelli & Dynes, 1977), and are important for this chapter in two ways.

First, all this social and behavioral research has resulted in a solid understanding of several topics. To be sure, on some matters, observations are no more than mere speculations, and with regard to a few topics, nothing is really known. But, compared to just a decade or two ago, for those who would look, much empirical knowledge exists (Barton, 1970; Drabek, in press; Dynes, 1974; Fritz, 1961; Kreps, 1984; Mileti, Drabek, & Haas, 1975; Quarantelli, 1978; Quarantelli & Dynes, 1977; Wright & Rossi, 1981).

Unfortunately, not everyone who has been examining the topic of mental health in disasters has taken advantage of the knowledge about disaster behavior in general, and the full range of specific work in the mental health area in particular. It is a little disturbing to read examinations and reviews of the literature and not find relevant references to whole bodies of research findings and theoretical formulations from the disaster area (Frederick, 1980; Hocking, 1965; Kinston & Rosser, 1974). Such lack of references attests either to poor scholarship or a deliberate avoidance of ideas that do not fit preconceptions. More importantly, it can only lead to finding what has long been known and a tendency to incorrectly generalize from limited incidents, or highly atypical events (e.g., Buffalo Creek).

Second, the work of the past decades has considerably extended our detailed knowledge about how individuals, groups, organizations, communities, and societies prepare for, respond to, and recover from both community and non-community natural and technological disasters. But certain basic themes advanced by the pioneering researchers have continued to be documented. Among the themes running through the literature are: Human beings react much better in the extreme stress of a disaster than they are usually given credit for; reasonable rather than panicky behavior is the mode; prosocial rather than antisocial behavior predominates; and activity rather than passivity emerges even at the height of the emergency periods of disasters. Organizations, on the other hand, show less adaptability and flexibility in the face of disasters than do human beings; in their efforts to mobilize resources to respond to and to recover from disasters, organizational and structural factors serve to compound communication, authority, and coordination problems, which may help to turn minor accidents into disasters, and disasters into catastrophes (Quarantelli, 1982). In much of the current literature on social problems by contemporary sociologists, disaster researchers first said and continue to say that their studies show we should "stop blaming the victims," for the source of most problems is in the social environment, especially the organizational setting within which "victims" have to act.

BELIEFS ABOUT MENTAL HEALTH CONSEQUENCES

To say that most people equate the term disaster with intense and prolonged human suffering, anguish, and loss, is to state the obvious. Even the commonsense observer would agree that the impact of a tornado, earthquake, explosion, or water surging from a crumbled dam goes far beyond the immediately recognizable loss of life and sheer physical damages and destruction associated with such events, impressive though these may be. What is even more important about a community disaster, is the disruption of life, the marked alterations of routine patterns of everyday social expectations, and day-to-day personal habits. While the physical impact of a disaster may be over in a few minutes, other consequences may extend over weeks, months, and even years. A major disaster does far more than wreck buildings and sever lifelines; it interrupts the rhythm, cycles, and very social fabric of community life.

Since disasters disrupt social life and induce psychological stress for their victims, they are part of a class of collective stress situations. But how do human beings respond in these collective stress situations? Can we assume that the social disruption occasioned by a community disaster also creates psychological disorder or malfunction among victims? The answer to this question is twofold: how people are *believed* to respond and how they *actually* respond. We will look at three belief systems. The first will be what the public at large believes—what might be called folk wisdom and mass media conceptions. Second, we will look at the theoretical notions in the mental health area relevant to consequences of disasters—what might be called the theoretical presuppositions of mental health practitioners. Third, we will briefly look at the changing models in the social sciences which have a bearing on the question.

Folk Wisdom and Mass Media Conceptions

Conventional wisdom has long held that human beings do not react well to large-scale stress. It is commonly believed that when people are faced with the threat or the actual occurrence of a major disaster, they disintegrate physically, mentally, and morally. They supposedly engage in bizarre, antisocial, irrational, and destructive acts, such as wild and disorderly panic, looting, and other forms of criminal deviance. Popular beliefs about reaction to extreme stress situations are so grim that hysterical breakdowns and psychotic episodes are thought to be common among disaster victims in the short run, and various forms of severe psychopathology are expected to be manifest among victims in the long run. In short, the image is essentially that disasters create or exacerbate severe forms of mental illness for their victims.

These common stereotypes of how persons respond to and are affected by disasters are not new. While there are undoubtedly many reasons for such stereotypes, one basic reason is that mass media and journalistic accounts often reinforce and support such beliefs. This can be seen in the images played up by news and magazine accounts of disasters dating as far back as the late 1800s and early 1900s. For example, in a *Harper's* magazine article of 1889, survivors of the Johnstown, Pennsylvania flood were described as "crazed by their sufferings." (Dieck, 1889, p. 139). A *Saturday Evening Post* account of the devastating hurricane that hit Galveston, Texas in 1900 included a report of 500 people who went "insane almost in unison" following the disaster (Perry, 1950, p. 117). Similarly, *Harpers Weekly* wrote that the 1906 San Francisco earthquake and subsequent fire brought about cases of "men gone mad" (Chard, 1906, p. 702). While the terminology used in these articles is, of course, outdated, the articles do, nevertheless, illustrate the long history of viewing disasters as leading to severe psychopathology.

Perhaps even more important, the same general stereotypes continue to be emphasized in present mass media accounts of disasters. Following a series of major floods in 1973, *Newsweek* reported that once the immediate post-impact period is over, a new reaction starts to appear among victims—this one a "kind of shared psychosis that hits just about everyone affected directly or indirectly by the events." The story goes on to assert that within a few weeks after such a catastrophe, "symptoms of emotional problems will become disturbingly obvious; the number of successful suicides rises by about a third; hospital admissions for psychiatric reasons run at double the normal rate; and the frequency of accidents skyrocket" (*Newsweek*, January 29, 1973, pp. 62-63). The more recent Mt. St. Helens volcanic eruption has generated press comments to the effect that "wife battering is up. So are suicide attempts . . . the volcano's impact on the mental health of hundreds of thousands of residents in the area will be serious and long-lasting" (Columbus Dispatch, 1980, A-7), and "Now, They're Going Crazy" (Devlin, 1980, B-1).

Do people in general share such beliefs? Three recent surveys empirically ascertained public beliefs about human behavior in disasters. The first, a survey in the state of Delaware found that large blocks of the population do, in fact, believe that disasters evoke extreme reactions in their victims. For example, these researchers report, among other things, that 74% of those surveyed agreed with the statement that "immediately following the impact of a disaster, victims are in a state of shock and unable to cope with the situation by themselves" (Wenger, Dykes, Sebok, & Neff, 1975). The second survey, conducted in a small community in Ohio not far from Xenia only months after a tornado, produced similar findings. The attribution of problems of a mental or psychological nature to victims of disasters was widespread among the population surveyed (Blanshan, 1976, personal communication). A more recent field survey in Arkansas, Wisconsin, and Mississippi also looked at the beliefs of community officials as well as the general populace about the psychological consequences of disasters. The findings are consistent with the previous studies. Officials as well as the public at large hold to the image that disasters produce extreme psychological and emotional reactions in their victims (Wenger, James, & Faupel, 1980).

The Mental Health Area

What do psychiatrists, psychologists, and other experts in the mental health field have to say about human response to disasters? (We leave aside those with direct systematic research experience in community disasters, since their views are discussed later.) Like the mass media and the majority of the general public, a large number of mental health professionals also assume that extreme emotional and psychopathological reactions are typical consequences of disasters. While the terminology used varies somewhat, psychiatric and psychoanalytically oriented writers often note that immediately after impact, victims can be expected to display what is often termed the "disaster syndrome." This condition is supposedly characterized by an unrealistic absence of emotion, inhibition of activity, docility, indecisiveness, lack of responsiveness, and automatic behavior on the part of disaster victims. An often cited numerical projection of the numbers of victims likely to display such symptoms was set forth over three decades ago by Tyhurst, one of the first professionals writing on the subject. According to Tyhurst, about 10-25% of a disaster-impacted population will show "manifestly inappropriate behavior, states of confusion, paralysing anxiety, inability to move out of bed, 'hysterical' crying and screaming, and so on" and in a post-impact stage there may be "temporary anxiety and fatigue states, psychotic episodes, recurrent catastrophic dreaming, [and] depressive reactions" (1951, pp. 766-767). Another 75% at impact will be "dazed, stunned, bewildered," show "childlike dependency," or otherwise exhibit the disaster syndrome noted above. Although an examination of Tyhurst's writings show no evidentiary research basis for such statistics, the figures are cited to this day (Boyd, 1981; Edwards, 1976; Kinston & Rosser, 1974) and sometimes are not even attributed to Tyhurst (e.g., Cohen & Ahearn, 1980).

While some recent writers in the professional area have backed off from ascribing negative and dysfunctional psychological reactions to victims in the immediate post-impact period, most still maintain the older view of the longer run. Thus, it is often claimed that during the later post-impact phases, victims are likely to exhibit reactions such as: an increase in the use of alcohol and other drugs; acute, traumatic neuroses; tormenting memories and guilt feelings over survival; and irrational hostility and scapegoating. Frederick in a recent, general listing of the effects of natural disasters names as psychological symptoms: "anxiety; insomnia; depression; anorexia; psychophysiological reactions; phobias about the event; little guilt about plight of other victims; hostility; paranoid reactions toward Governmental officials and persons with fewer losses. . . . Desire for reprisal. Aberrant characterological acts, e.g., looting, deviance, alcoholism" (1980, p. 72) and also states that

> Psychological reactions that are less frequent, but which may occur, are: disorientation, wherein confusion and memory loss develop; hysteria, wherein screaming and uncontrollable crying are apparent, or numbness develops in parts of the body not consistent with neurological structure; and psychoses, in which the individual engages in highly irrational thinking and may be temporarily out of contact with reality. Bizarre sensations may be reported, and delusions of grandeur or persecution may be apparent. (1980, p. 74)

Furthermore, the reactions are seen as long lasting. Even the absence of overt symptoms is not seen as an indication of no pathological reactions over the long run. Thus,

> disasters . . . unleash powerful behavioral reactions and emotions which often are overwhelming . . . since . . . the loss of life's familiar benchmarks induces intense stress leading to physical and

mental illness. . . . Even when there has been no loss of human life, one can expect a predictable sequence of such behaviors as shock, guilt, anger, and grief to occur among affected persons over a six- to 12-month time period. A disaster's victim's failure to display these normative reactions should not lead to the conclusion that all is well; instead, it should alert the caregiver that the victim potentially is employing maladaptive resolutions. (Schulberg, 1974, p. 85)

Furthermore, "extreme circumstances of traumatization—disasters, catastrophes and overwhelming social situations—effect marked changes in the people subjected to them and leaves them with life-long problems" (Krystal, 1968, p. 1). In fact, "there is mounting evidence that the effects of a disaster can extend over several generations. Adverse effects of significant proportions can occur in children of survivors even when born several years after a particular disaster" (Boyd, 1981, p. 748).

It is clear that mental health theorists who have written on the topic generally believe that disasters bring about immediate, widespread, persistent, serious, long lasting, and dysfunctional psychological effects.

The Social Science Perspective

The first social and behavioral researchers in the community disaster area worked with a model of behavior which they eventually found was inappropriate and inaccurate. There were four basic assumptions:

1) Disaster responses were relatively homogeneous, that is, there was a tendency to think of behavior under stress as being either/or; for instance, either people acted in an antisocial fashion or they did not;
2) Many of the responses were inappropriate or "bad," that is, they took the form of panic, looting, hysteria, shock or other forms of personal breakdown or disorganization;
3) Disaster victims primarily responded directly to the disaster agent or its immediate effects; and
4) The major explanation of disaster behavior was to be sought in the social-psychological dynamics of individual victims.

Implicitly more than explicitly, the early social and behavioral researchers thought that there were severe and widespread psychological consequences for the victims of disasters. Contrary to statement that early researchers minimized negative psychological effects (Frederick, 1980, p. 71), the first systematic disaster students assumed just the opposite. But, as noted, it was finally recognized that the initial assumptions were empirically incorrect and an invalid disaster behavior model was being used.

Eventually, a new model based on research findings has emerged (Kreps, 1984). It assumes that disaster responses are always heterogeneous and one should expect a variety of differentiated responses as hypothesized more than 40 years ago by the sociologist, Sorokin (1942). Specific behaviors can be functional or dysfunctional depending on a variety of factors, but overall disaster responses are functional and organized—even panic flight is not as impulsive, irrational, or inappropriate as was once thought (Quarantelli, 1981). The newer model recognizes that what happens after impact is as important—if not more so—than what occurs at time of impact, what we earlier noted as *response* rather than *agent* demands to which victims are exposed. Finally, in the new view the social contexts more than internal dynamics have to be understood since they provide the settings in which individual behavior occurs. This change of imagery is applied with respect to disaster behavior in general, but it clearly has major implications for approaching and explaining the consequences of disasters for mental health.

THE EMPIRICAL EVIDENCE

Let us now turn from beliefs to *actualities*. How accurate are the widespread commonsense beliefs that people react poorly to collective stress situations? How correct is the theoretical view in the mental health field that disasters are necessarily deeply traumatic events? Is there any validity to the implication of the newer social sciences model that the specific problem of psychological well-being in disasters is more complex than appears on the surface?

What is the actual evidence? What do we have beyond isolated anecdotal examples or occasional clinical impressions? Any answer obviously involves a judgment call but, in our view, there are a little over a dozen community disasters in which an effort was made to gather at least semi-systematic data on the psychological well-being and mental health-associated problems of the stressed population. We list only studies in American society (foreign studies will be noted later). These disasters and the research they generated are listed in Table 1.

The studies of these various community disasters vary in their meth-

TABLE 1
Disaster Research Citations

Big Thompson flash flood in Colorado
(Kimball, 1978; Miller, 1977; Miller, Turner, & Kimball, 1981)
Buffalo Creek dam flood
(Church, 1974; Erikson, 1976a, b, c; Gleser, Green, & Winget, 1978, 1981; Harshbarger, 1973; Lifton & Olson, 1976; Newman, 1976; Rangell, 1976; Titchener, 1975; Titchener & Kapp, 1976)
Los Angeles earthquake
(Blaufarb & Levine, 1972; Howard & Gordon, 1972; Koegler & Hicks, 1972)
Monticello, Indiana tornado
(Bowman, 1975; Zarle, 1976; Zarle, Hartsough, & Ottinger, 1974)
Mt. St. Helens volcanic eruption
(Pennebaker & Newtson, 1980; Murphy, 1981; Leik et al., 1982; Murphy, 1983)
Omaha tornado
(Bell, 1978; Bell, Kara, & Batterson, 1978; Kara, 1977; McIntire & Sadeghi, 1977; Rosenberg, Fine, & Robinson, 1980)
Rapid City flood
(Bolin, 1976; Bolin & Trainer, 1978; Hall & Landreth, 1975; Trainer & Bolin, 1976; Bolin, 1982)
Rochester, Minnesota flood
(Ollendick & Hoffmann, 1982)
St. Louis area
Tornados and floods
(Brownstone, Penick, Larson, Powell, & Nord, 1977; Penick, Larson, & Powell, 1974; Penick, Powell, & Sieck, 1976; Powell & Penick, 1980)
Teton dam collapse in Idaho
(Golec, 1980, 1983; Huerta & Horton, 1978; Huerta, Horton, & Winters, 1977)
Three Mile Island nuclear plant accident
(Bartlett, 1979; Baum, Gatchel, & Schaeffer, 1983; Bromet, 1980; Bromet & Dunn, 1981; Bromet, Schulberg, & Dunn, 1982; Dohrenwend, Dohrenwend, Houts, & Cleary, 1980; Houts & Goldhaber, 1981; Kasl, Chrisholm, & Eskenazi, 1981; Morell & Spivack, 1980)
Topeka tornado
(Drabek, Erickson, & Crowe, 1973a, 1973b, 1973c; Drabek & Key, 1975, 1983; Erickson, Drabek, Key, & Crowe, 1974; Kilijanek & Drabek, 1979; Sterling, Drabek, & Key, 1977)
Wichita Falls, Oklahoma tornado
(Bolin, 1979, 1982; Fairchild & White, 1982)
Wilkes-Barre flood
(Birnbaum, Coplon, & Scharff, 1973; Cohen & Poulshock, 1976; Heffron, 1975, 1977; Kafrisson et al., 1975; Knaus, 1975; Logue, 1978; Logue & Hansen, 1980; Logue, Hansen & Struening, 1979, 1981; Melick, 1976, 1978; Logue, Melick, & Hansen, 1981; McGee, 1973; Poulshock & Cohen, 1976, 1977; Richard, 1974; Zusman, Joss, & Newman, 1973)
Xenia, Ohio tornado
(Laubi, 1974; Taylor, 1976, 1977; Taylor, Ross, & Quarantelli, 1976)

odological rigor. We have among them, for example, a strict probability sample of 15% of the total impact population in the Xenia tornado and self-selected samples of victims who sought some kind of aid in other disasters. In some of the research, extensive data were obtained from combinations of open-ended interviews, psychological scale instruments, mental health case load documents, assessments of key informants, drug usage statistics, etc.; in other studies, only two or three questionnaire items dealt with mental health matters. However, despite the variety of data-gathering instruments used and the samples obtained, the quality and quantity of the data approach respectability. Certainly, it is substantially more defendable as acceptable data for research purposes than the anecdotes, scattered clinical and field impressions, and selective observations which passed for data just a decade ago. Since our focus is on community disasters, work done on disasters that were not somehow disruptive of ongoing community life, have not been listed. Thus, we exclude studies of psychological reactions to ship disasters (e.g., Friedman & Linn, 1957; Leopold & Dillon, 1963; Hoiberg & McCaughey, 1981). Fires which involve massive casualties (e.g., the Coconut Grove night club, see Adler, 1943, 1945; Cobb & Lindemann, 1943) are somewhat more marginal instances, but even the very well-studied Beverly Hills Supper Club fire (e.g., Lindy et al., 1981; Green et al., 1983) would be difficult to characterize as a community disaster.

In addition to this work which focused directly on victims, there has also been systematic study of the deliverers of mental health services in community disasters. For example, DRC recently examined those communities which had obtained a federal declaration of a disaster, and/or made efforts to obtain federal funds for crisis counseling and other mental health services. The study looked at how local, state, regional, and federal mental health practitioners and involved officials reach decisions on the consequences of specific disasters for mental health. Why were services provided in some disasters and not others? What did local mental health practitioners assess as disaster-related mental health needs? What consensus, if any, was there among the various agencies involved on the kinds of services that should be provided? What types of disaster-related mental health problems did practitioners actually see? These and similar questions gave us answers about the delivery of mental health services in community disasters which are counterparts to the findings and observations obtained in the research on the disaster victims (see Baisden & Quarantelli, 1981).

THE TWO POSITIONS

All the works cited in the last several pages constitute the data base we examined in making a comparison between the two major positions on the psychological effects of community disasters. We will discuss in overall terms the essence of the two positions. Rather than dealing with specific studies, we will state the relative consensus among one set of practitioners and researchers, and offer only a very few selected examples. We will use some of the research and literature from the Xenia, Ohio tornado disaster and the Buffalo Creek, West Virginia dam disaster to further examine and illustrate these two approaches, since they have been among the most intensively studied disasters insofar as the consequences for mental health are concerned.

The first position holds that since disasters are highly stressful, they are traumatic life events. These events are seen as producing among those exposed to them, very pervasive, deeply internalized, and essentially negative psychological effects. Disaster victims are viewed primarily as attempting to cope with the meaning of the trauma and disaster impact. For purposes of convenience, we will talk about this as the *individual trauma* approach.

The second approach basically holds that community disasters have differential rather than across-the-board effects. Some of the effects are positive as well as negative; many of the latter are relatively short in duration. The varying problems of victims are more closely related to the post-impact organized response than they are to the disaster impact itself. Again for want of a better term, we will talk about this as the *social sponge* approach. A sponge is an elastic porous mass of interlacing fibers; it will maintain its basic structure under all kinds of pressures and return quickly to its usual state; it can also absorb very large amounts of all kinds of liquids and other materials, and even though wet, will not lose its overall toughness. If the sponge is considered analogous to a community, and the interlacing fibers as similar to the social fabric within which all persons are embedded, the image of what is involved is also suggested in this approach.

One difference in the two approaches can be found with respect to the pervasiveness and nature of the psychological consequences. The individual trauma approach essentially argues that everyone is negatively affected. Thus, "the psychological impact of the disaster has been so extensive that no one in Buffalo Creek has been unaffected. The

overwhelming evidence is that everyone exposed to the Buffalo Creek
disaster has experienced some or all of the following manifestations of
the general constellation of the 'survivor' syndrome" (Lifton & Olson,
1975, p. 1) and goes on to note these as being death anxiety and permanent inner terror, guilt over having survived, psychic numbing and
depression, impaired human relationships, and inability to find an explanation for what had happened. "Our observations were all too consistent with a body of recent experience with 'massive psychic trauma'
of war, revolution, concentration camps, and severe disasters —
psychiatrists have regularly observed that psychological impairment can
result in virtually anyone, independently of estimates of predisposition"
(Lifton & Olson, 1976, p. 15).

Two other researchers, Titchener and Kapp, state that "disabling psychiatric symptoms such as anxiety, depression, changes in character and
lifestyle . . . were evident more than two years after the disaster in better
than 90% of our respondents." They claim that psychoanalytically oriented interviews and analyses of dreams more than two years after the
event allowed recall of almost universal instances of "nightmares" and
"obsessions and phobias about water, wind, rain, and other reminders
of the remotest possibility that the disaster could recur" (1975, pp. 1, 4).
These and other reactions "were at the traumatic level and for so long
that we must compare these syndromes, at least in structure and form,
if not in content, to psychoses" (Titchener, 1975, p. 12).

In contrast, in the social sponge approach, the differential and not
necessarily negative aftereffects of disasters are emphasized. To quote
from a report on the research carried out in Xenia for 18 months after
the disaster:

> The study found that there was an extremely low rate of severe
> mental illness, if any at all, as a consequence of the tornado. On
> the contrary, it concluded that a large percentage of the people had
> *extremely positive reactions* to the disaster. Eighty-four percent of the
> people claimed that their experiences had shown them they could
> handle crises better than they thought; and 69% reported that they
> felt they had met a great challenge and were better off for it. . . .
> Changes in the quality of social relationships are often thought to
> be related to changes in emotional well-being. Yet only 2% of the
> population admitted to worsening relationships with close friends
> and family after the tornado. Instead 27% claimed that such rela-
> tionships had improved. Similarly, a mere 3% found their marital
> relationship less satisfying since the tornado, while 28% reported
> them to be, in fact, more satisfying. (DRC, 1976)

Similar positive results have been reported elsewhere. A study of the Topeka tornado, done three years after the event, was able to match victim families and nonvictim families for which pretornado data existed. It found that victim families rated their marriages as happier than before the tornado and as happier than nonvictim families. Also, victim couples went out together more often after the tornado than before (Drabek & Key, 1983). Clearly, the individual trauma and the social sponge approaches are not reaching the same conclusions about the psychological outcomes of disasters in terms of how people feel, relate to others, or evaluate their experiences.

There is also another difference. Essentially, the individual trauma approach argues that the post-disaster, negative reactions are neither superficial nor transitory. Again, to quote from a Buffalo Creek analysis:

> We can say it [i.e., the flood] brought about an extraordinary number of psychiatric disturbances, and that even those in the very small minority without formal psychiatric diagnoses . . . tended to experience significant degrees of psychological suffering and conflict. . . . Without denying the existence of significant variation in psychological vulnerability, we have been far more impressed (as have other observers) by the degree to which the massive character of the trauma subsumed individual differences and produced strikingly consistent forms of impairment. We have also been impressed by the persistence of these expressions of psychological impairment, which in many cases increased rather than diminished over time. (Lifton & Olson, 1976, p. 15)

It is not surprising to find elsewhere the statement:

> There is, in fact, mounting evidence that the effects of disaster can extend over generations, and that adverse effects of significant proportion can occur in children of survivors, even after the children are born some years after a particular disaster . . . at Buffalo Creek one can certainly observe many families to be a "collection of severely disturbed and traumatized individuals," who could well transmit various disaster-related conflicts to subsequent generations. (Lifton & Olson, 1976, pp. 14-15)

Apart from the Buffalo Creek research, other studies, while not taking as extreme a position, also suggest long-term effects. A study of 562 women made five years after the Wilkes-Barre flood, assessed depression and anxiety states through self-rating scales and other measures. One of its conclusions was that, for all seven variables related to long-term mental health, the results consistently showed the direct flood victims had more symptoms than did non-flood victims, although differences in long run physical health problems stood out more sharply (Logue, 1978).

In contrast, another study of the Wilkes-Barre flood done three years after the event matched a flood and a non-flood control group, used the Gurin Symptom checklist, and found "both groups obtained high scores, indicative of positive mental health. The flood-group mean score was 71.0 out of a possible 80 points, while that of the non-flood group was 72.2," not a statistically significant difference (Melik, 1978, p. 338).

The social sponge approach consistently points to lack of severity, duration, and dysfunctionality in the data obtained. Again we cite a report using Xenia data:

> A year and a half later . . . only 3% of the population reported feeling at any time after the disaster that they might have a nervous breakdown. The proportion of those who did have such a fear and who reported that their symptoms actually interfered with routine social activities was insignificant. Only 1% of the population had considered suicide at any time after the tornado; only 3% reported any increase in drinking whereas 7% of Xenians claimed they consumed less alcohol. There was a slight decrease in the percentage of the population who reported using tranquilizers, falling from 20% to 16% one year later, as did the use of any kind of service from any of the local mental health agencies which fell from 10% to 5%. (DRC, 1976)

Proponents of the individual trauma approach, of course, argue that self-reports cannot be trusted. However, one analysis done in Xenia found that independent, behavioral indicators supported what victims had self-reported. Consistent with interview remarks, there was no overall change in the marriage and divorce rates after the tornado. Agencies that provided treatment and hospitalization for serious psychiatric problems actually reported a decline in demand for their services. For example, the state hospital facility most likely to be used reported a 30% drop in admissions in the year following the tornado. Similar declines in demands for services were reported in other area organizations specializing in long-run clinical treatment through the use of psychotherapy, drugs, or hospitalization. There was a significant drop in liquor sales in the two state monopoly stores in the Xenia area in the six- to 12-month period after the tornado (DRC, 1976; Taylor, 1977).

In another study conducted 18 months after the Rapid City flash flood, it was found that no significant increases occurred in the number of attempted or actual suicides or single car accidents (often considered suicide attempts); the rate of juvenile delinquency; the number of citations for driving while intoxicated; the number of automobile accidents; rates of scarlet fever, strep throat, and hepatitis; the number of prescriptions written for tranquilizers; and the utilization of community mental health center services (Hall & Landreth, 1975). Again, we see the individual trauma and the social sponge approaches reaching different conclusions about the severity, duration, and dysfunctionality of the mental health consequences of disasters.

The social sponge position does acknowledge that many disaster victims do exhibit a variety of transient emotional symptoms. In the Xenia disaster, one study over an 18-month period reported the following behavioral and psychological symptoms which might be indicators of mental health difficulties:

56% of those surveyed reported feeling depressed or low on occasion;
50% admitted being more nervous or excited some time after the tornado;
27% reported sleeping problems at times;
25% reported headaches; and
19% indicated some loss of appetite.

At a more behavioral level, 14% of those surveyed said they missed five or more days of work because of an emotional or mental health problem. There were also significant increases in the number of visits to the emergency room and outpatient clinic of the local hospital, as well as in incidents involving traffic violations and juvenile delinquency. However, in order to put this in a proper context, we should note that when the victims were asked how they felt emotionally or mentally after the tornado, 58% said they felt good or excellent, 33% said fair, and only 9% said their emotional or mental health was poor or very bad. Behaviorally, there were significant *decreases* in deaths due to heart, vascular and respiratory diseases, actual number of offenses reported to the police, and in drug- and alcohol-related case contacts by the local crisis center. There were no changes in suicide rates, overall death rates, domestic trouble calls to the police, or reports of child abuse (DRC, 1976).

Actually, the results presented above are not that different from those of the very first systematic victim population survey ever done in the disaster area—an almost ideal study, contrary to its misrepresentation in a poor survey of the literature by Kinston and Rosser (1974, p. 440). Data from a number of communities, ranging from heavily impacted to near miss by a series of tornados, found that among those surveyed:

49% reported nervousness, excitability, and hypersensitivity;
46% sleeplessness or poor sleep;
37% inability to concentrate;
29% loss of appetite;
19% headaches; and
18% anxiety dreams and nightmares (Marks et al., 1954).

What has been singled out in later studies in the social sponge approach is that the source of much such common and widespread, although relatively unimportant, behavioral difficulties is the social setting in which post-disaster relief and recovery services are obtained. Efforts to obtain services frequently generate anger, concern, worry, and anxiety, and are what some have called "secondary disasters" which are "produced by the socially organized response and in particular inequities in the distribution process" (Golec, 1983, p. 30). This is also illustrated in a Rapid City disaster study (Hall & Landreth, 1975), which concluded that while the flood did not engender a major community mental health crisis, it did result in an increase in stress for non-affluent victims. Group life in government-sponsored mobile home parks set up after the disaster was a source of stress and was probably detrimental to the psychological well-being of residents since this way of life tended to destroy their natural helping networks. It was less the impact of the disaster itself which affected victims' psychological well-being, but more the long-term impact of inefficient and ineffective federal relief efforts which accounted for the stress manifested by the victims (Hall & Landreth, 1975). In the same vein is Logue's (1980) conclusion that various stressful experiences in the recovery period following the Wilkes-Barre flood were better predictions of mental health status measured five years after the events than the actual disaster impact. Even Erikson (1976), one of the more prominent writers on the Buffalo Creek disaster, seems to accept the idea that a "second disaster" by way of the post-impact relief efforts may have contributed substantially to the negative consequences for the victims.

ACCOUNTING FOR THE TWO POSITIONS

Why are there two positions? What accounts for the differences in views? A few writers have addressed the question of inconsistencies in the findings about the psychological effects of community disasters, but the more comprehensive have emphasized the absence of methodological rigor (Green, 1982; Logue, Melick, & Hansen, 1981; Perry, 1979) in the research undertaken. This is a valid criticism of much of the work, but does not really answer why there are two approaches which report grossly different empirical findings. We think more basic factors are involved, and will discuss six possibilities:

1) First, it is possible that the different researchers and analysts are observing *actual* differences in the mental well-being of the victims they have studied. Since there has been very little overlap in the specific disasters studied by advocates of the two views, this is a hypothetical possibility. For this reason, if there were actual differences in what occurred, it is possible that different observations could be made and different conclusions reached. Until a number of the *same* disasters are systematically examined from the two different perspectives, this has to be considered a hypothetical possibility, but it seems a very unlikely explanation.

Two events, the Wilkes-Barre flood and the Three Mile Island nuclear accident, have been studied by researchers with different perspectives and inconsistent findings have been reported. Earlier we noted an inconsistency in research findings on long-term effects of the flood. A very thorough review of almost all the research undertaken on the psychological consequences of Three Mile Island also concluded that research findings were inconsistent (Warheit & Auth, 1983). However, more valid data seemed to indicate that the effects of the accident were of a subclinical type, short-lived, and self-remitting, and "there are no scientific data which support the belief that the accident produced measurable levels of gross psychopathology" (Warheit, 1984, p. 7). Leaving the qualifiers aside, just the inconsistency of research results from the same disaster would seem to be more damaging to the individual trauma than to the social sponge approach, but sets of data from but two disasters can hardly be conclusive.

2) A second possible explanation for the different results in the two approaches could be found in what is taken as acceptable data and

appropriate data-gathering designs. The individual trauma position, for example, leans in the direction of self-selected or otherwise suspect samples—the Buffalo Creek data consist mainly of material obtained in connection with some survivors pressing a lawsuit. The legal depositions gathered were not intended to be objective statements. Clinical impressions and what, to many, seem isolated anecdotal examples are also often used in the individual trauma approach. In contrast, the social sponge position, while hardly a model of ideal scientific work, leans in the direction of population surveys. It draws as close as possible to a random sample, and uses standardized scales or quantitative measures such as statistics on drug prescriptions, automobile accidents, divorce rates, agency case load figures, police and court records, etc. There are, of course, methodological questions which can be raised about these data-gathering procedures: needs assessment surveys are not epidemiological surveys, organizational records are not necessarily objective, etc., but the logic of these procedures is clear. Thus, it could be argued that the two approaches generate different results because they use different means for obtaining data.

However, even those of us who normally are very skeptical of statistics per se, cannot ignore that the quantitative kinds of data noted above are almost always at variance with what is assumed in the individual trauma approach. It is impressive to note the consistency in data such as liquor sale records, suicide rates, and family disturbance calls, which are initially amassed for reasons totally independent of attempting to measure adverse psychological effects. Nonetheless, it might be possible to explain away such data by arguing that they are not refined enough measures to capture subtle psychodynamics or that professional expertise is required for assessment (see Frederick, 1977, p. 382), so different data-gathering techniques have to remain as a hypothetical explanation for the different research findings.

3) Third and closely related to the matter just discussed is the question of the interpretation of data. Many of the theorists and researchers taking the individual trauma approach have some kind of general psychoanalytical background. There is a tendency, therefore, to look behind the overt and the manifest. In the context of the topic we are discussing, this can lead to opposite interpretations of one piece of data. For example, if disaster victims assert they have no problems or state that they are happier in the post-impact period than in the pre-impact period, the assertions can be accepted at face value if not otherwise contradicted or logically suspect. But the assertions can also be taken as evidence of just

the opposite, as evidence of the "denial" of the reality of the situation.

Researchers taking a social sponge approach are not naive; in fact, as a whole, they have considerably more field experience in a wider range of disaster occasions than do those using an individual trauma approach. But they are willing to accept data at face value only if it is consistent with other data. Furthermore, those with a social fabric approach consider overt behaviors more important than mental states. For example, in a 15% statistically random sample of the population studied six months and 18 months after a tornado in Xenia, DRC found that, in terms of scale scores on psychological well-being, those surveyed showed signs they had been affected by the tornado experience. Those who suffered the most (loss of homes, etc.) had the highest scores. Their scores were higher than a non-disaster control group, and scores generally remained as high in the 18th month as in the sixth. On the other hand, on almost all behavioral measures, whether reported by the surveyed population, the various community mental agencies, or other organizations, the post-impact figures were the same or below comparable pre-impact figures. In the unpublished analysis, DRC accepted this as evidence that the tornado had had little significant negative effect on the mental health of the affected population. What is crucial from the social fabric point of view is the lack of behavioral dysfunctionality; the individual trauma approach lays greater importance on the existence of psychological states. To the extent one approach gives greater weight to behaviors and the other to psychic states, it is very possible inconsistent research results will be reported.

4) A fourth possibility which could account for the differences in the two approaches is that different professional objectives and ideologies are often involved. Many of those using the individual trauma approach are mental health practitioners interested in giving treatment to victims. Most of those operating with the social sponge approach tend to be researchers more concerned with reaching an understanding and explanation of the phenomena they study. Frequencies of phenomena are often of some importance to researchers but if the figures are very low the observation may be of little descriptive or analytical value. Let us take a purely hypothetical case and say that only 1% of a population suffered a disease, making that phenomenon of no importance for statistical research purposes. To a mental health practitioner, the 1%, which might translate into 200 human beings, could be very important from a professional and humanitarian perspective.

Also, as a number of writers have pointed out, there is a "mental health" industry which has a vested interest in finding certain phenomena (see Margaro, Gripp, & McDowell, 1978). It is not surprising, therefore, when the psychotherapeutic establishment got involved in disaster studies about a decade ago, its professional ideology would lead to expectations of certain phenomena in such situations, which could be claimed as its province. Social science research is, of course, also an industry; some have, in fact, talked of the "disaster research" industry (Wright & Rossi, 1981) and it too has vested interests and professional ideologies. However, many of the researchers within the social sponge approach would argue that, at one level, it does not matter to their "industry" if there are or are not adverse psychological effects from disasters: Either way there are phenomena to be studied, but if there are no negative consequences there is much less justification for the psychotherapeutic establishment to be involved with the area. At a deeper level, those in the individual trauma approach, especially with an orthodox psychoanalytic background, could probably argue that the "denial" of adverse effects is itself a form of psychological defense on the part of researchers. In any case, different professional ideologies probably account for some of the differences in the two approaches.

5) A fifth possibility for the differences in the two approaches may stem from differences in conceptions of disasters. This could be true in at least three different ways: For one, the individual trauma approach tends to include within the general category of disaster the full range of individual and collective stress situations. Thus, such diverse phenomena as the Holocaust, shipwrecks, air raids, famines, mass kidnappings, plane crashes, concentration camp situations, and military combat service are all treated as the same generic phenomenon, into which are added natural and technological disasters (e.g., Kinston & Rosser, 1974). However, many researchers see the need to separate out the latter from all other stress situations. The use of a highly heterogeneous class, among other things, allows the picking of extreme and atypical cases. But since definitions and conceptions are, to a considerable extent, arbitrary matters, if the starting points are so widely divergent, the two approaches will find different phenomena.

Those who take the individual trauma approach usually do not distinguish between natural and technological disasters that disrupt community life (e.g., most transportation accidents, fires and explosions, structural collapses) and those that do not, although a few recently have started to inch toward such a distinction (Green, 1982). The importance of the community context to many is that it provides what we have called the social sponge which can absorb much of the impact. Others have talked of the "altruistic community" (Barton, 1970), and especially of the "therapeutic community" (Bates, Fogelman, Parenton, & Tracy, 1963; Fritz, 1961). The latter might be a better term to use than social sponge, except that to us it implies that some psychological damage has been done which is therapeutically repaired. In many cases, we think, the community or social fabric may actually absorb or prevent even the initial negative effects. In the first systematic disaster study, Prince (1920) hinted at this when he noted that because so many people were involved in the Halifax disaster, the blow was softened for the individual because many others shared in the suffering. The social sponge approach sees the community context as crucial, while it is at best a secondary consideration in much of the individual trauma approach.

Finally, there is a strong tendency in the individual trauma approach to see a disaster as an external agent (Berren, Beigel, & Ghertner, 1980) which necessarily negatively affects what it impacts. As Golec (1980) has astutely observed, the very term "victim" connotes an adverse consequence. What to many recent disaster researchers should be taken as a matter of empirical determination is, in the individual trauma approach, taken as given. Some of those with a social sponge orientation have in fact argued for positive consequences of disasters. As Fritz stated: "This paper will focus central attention on these beneficent results of disaster. . . . It is written in the belief that this focus is presently needed as an antidote to the overworked metaphors of pathology" (1961, p. 2). It is difficult to see anyone using the individual trauma approach even thinking of making such a statement. In fact, the focus on negative aspects is so strong that all observations of adverse psychological symptoms are taken as disaster-generated when obviously some are carried over from the pre-impact situation. In contrast, the social sponge approach argues that the psychological consequences of disasters are "a function of a variety of factors, among which disaster impact is only one" (Perry & Lindell, 1978, p. 105).

6) Sixth, some of the differences in the two approaches stem in part, we think, from different basic models being used to approach disaster phenomena. For lack of a better term, there is what we will call a "medical" view of the world which implies, among other things, that there is an objective reality responsible for pathologies of various kinds. There is also what might be called the "social problem" view of the world which assumes that difficulties are primarily the result of definitional processes having no independent existence outside the actions of in-

dividuals and groups (Mauss, 1975). In the more extreme versions, adherents of this view argue that all disasters are politically defined events and in fact have no existence outside political definitions (Brown & Goldin, 1973). It would take us too far afield to explore the very interesting implications of this view. Let it suffice to say that the medical model and the social problem model of disaster behavior, when applied to the consequence of disasters for mental health, do not lead in the same direction. The individual trauma approach tends to assume a medical model. The social sponge approach, instead, tends to assume a social problem model. How the phenomena to be studied are conceived, what is deemed important, and what should be done about it varies according to the basic model.

The basic contract in the two approaches is well set forth by a researcher who did a three-year longitudinal study on psychological aftermaths of the Teton Dam flood disaster (Golec, 1980). She writes:

> Basically, the assumptive framework on which the medical model rests leads to an interpretation which obscures the contradictions and essential features of the disaster experience and process of recovery. The medicalization of social phenomena . . . has two basic shortcomings which . . . obscure the important features of social events. The adoption of the medical metaphor to explain social conduct over-psychologizes and depoliticizes social phenomena. . . .

She further notes:

> By ignoring the social context and by focusing on the causal primary of disaster impact, the medical metaphor leads to a misunderstanding about the nature of at least some of the post-disaster problems which have important consequences for disaster victims. It also fails to recognize, therefore, that the most efficacious solution to some disaster problems may reside in changes in public policy and in intervention aimed at changing aspects of the social structure. (pp. 162-163)

This view of matters is in striking contrast to that taken in a follow-up of the Buffalo Creek disaster. It is claimed that there was overwhelming evidence of psychopathology among the victims, and that 30% of the sample continued to suffer debilitating symptoms five years after the event. The explanatory factors offered are the extent of threat to life, degree of bereavement, prolongation of physical suffering, extent of displacement or life changes, proportion of the community affected, and the human occasioning of the disaster—factors primarily associated directly with the disaster agent and with little acknowledgment of the social context involved (Gleser, Green, & Winget, 1981). To the extent that researchers such as these use primarily a variant of the medical view of the phenomena, they will see different things than do those who use a social problem model. The findings, to a considerable extent, are dictated by the implicit models, so the question becomes which is the better model, not what are the more valid research results?

We might note that, contrary to what might be implied by the medical-social problem contrast, this is not totally a division between mental health practitioners and social scientists. For example, Moore, one of the earlier disaster researchers and a sociologist, reported that "disasters lead to more long-run emotional stress than is commonly supposed" (Moore & Friedsam, 1959, p. 139; see also, Moore, 1958). On the other hand, the DRC studies of providers of mental health services in disasters which we mentioned earlier found many deliverers of mental health services, especially those imbued with a community mental health ideology, often take a social problem approach to disaster phenomena. Many take the view that there are primarily "problems in living" in the aftermaths of disasters and not much in the way of mental illness or problems. Obviously, they draw their ideas from Szasz (1961, 1970) and others who have argued about the myth of mental illness.

This reference to the myth of mental illness leads us to what we might call a sociology of knowledge explanation about the intellectual careers of the two approaches. Put very simply, the argument is that those taking the individual trauma approach are following the same incorrect path that the early disaster researchers followed in studying disaster behavior generally. There is little question that individual trauma adherents are very recent students in the area, almost all having become involved in the area within the last decade. They tend to think of mental health responses in disasters in either/or terms, failing to see that disaster responses are always heterogeneous and differentiated. There is also an assumption that disasters are necessarily bad in their consequences. They do not recognize this as an empirical matter not to be taken as a given. Actually, the range of differentiated behavior can be functional, dysfunctional, or a combination of both. The individual trauma approach still assumes that disaster victims respond primarily to the disaster agent or its immediate effects, and has not yet fully recognized that the post-impact setting created by the response demands on organizations is far more important in providing a stressful setting for victims. Finally, the individual trauma approach primarily seeks explanations in terms of the inner, psychological dynamics of victims rather than the social contexts in which they operate, and operates as if the former could be independent of the latter.

In our judgment, the individual trauma approach is still at the mythological stage that most of the social and behavioral disaster researchers were at about two decades ago. It operates with myths about homogeneity, dysfunctionality, disaster agent responses, and individual foci that have now been abandoned in most other disaster research. This lag among those taking the individual trauma approach partly results from their failing to take advantage of what is known about disaster behavior in general. That as late as 1980, one of the leading proponents of the individual trauma approach could write, "there have been numerous instances of looting, with a breakdown in community cohesiveness and cooperation after the initial stages of the disaster" (Frederick, 1980, pp. xiv-xv), is to fly in the face of all the research findings over a 30-year period on this matter. An earlier writer who imposed theoretical dogma on empirical data can be excused because she wrote at a time when most researchers still had certain mythological assumptions (Wolfenstein, 1957), but more recent theoretical statements have no such excuse.

If we were to speculate about the future, we would forecast that the individual trauma approach will become part of the developmental history of the field of disaster research. In fact, there are signs that we are entering a transition stage from mythology to reality with respect to the psychological effects of disasters. We have some studies of special populations in mind which might be thought to be more vulnerable to extreme stress than others, and some research which has been done outside the United States with respect to disaster-related mental health problems.

The elderly and children are thought by many to be especially vulnerable to extreme stress (Cohen & Ahearn, 1980). Only three systematic, direct studies of the aged in disasters have been done: in the Wilkes-Barre flood (Cohen & Poulshock, 1977); the Omaha tornado (Bell et al., 1978); and the Teton Dam disaster (Huerta & Horton, 1978) although data on the aged is sometimes part of a larger research effort (e.g., Kilijanek & Drabek, 1979; Ollendick & Hoffmann, 1982). None of the studies are very supportive of the notion that the post-impact mental health responses of the aged are likely to be worse than those of other age categories. In fact, two of the research efforts (the Wilkes-Barre and the Omaha disasters) argue that the aged coped better and made better adjustments than the similarly affected younger age group in the victim population. Very little systematic work on children has been published (Howard & Gordon, 1972), but unpublished research primarily indicates that children are more likely to reflect the reactions of their parents than anything else; not a very new idea since such speculation was advanced several decades ago (Bloch, Silber, & Perry, 1956). There is little systematic research in the literature on the reaction of special populations which supports the individual trauma approach. It is probable that we have similar misconceptions and myths about the general vulnerability of special categories of the population similar to those we have held about other aspects of disaster behavior.

Studies about mental health problems in disasters outside of the United States are also appearing and are roughly similar in content to the research on American community disasters. The most extensive studies have recently been carried on in Australia, Italy, and Nicaragua. There are some inconsistent findings from researcher to researcher. Overall, however, there is little finding of major psychopathology or psychoses in immediate post-impact periods (Bennet, 1970; Beinin, 1981), and little severe dysfunctionalities in the long run. However, many milder psychological disturbances have been reported in the short run. For instance, "there was rarity of severe psychotic reactions and panic" in the Skopje, Yugoslavia earthquake (Popovic & Petrovic, 1964, p. 1170), and a significant drop-off in numbers of new admissions for mental disorders in the hospital system after the southern Italian earthquake (Greco, Faustini, Forastiere, Galanti et al., 1981, p. 501). In a study of all admissions between 1969-1976 to Nicaragua's only psychiatric hospital, "the actual increase is not different from the trend that would have been expected had there been no earthquake" (Ahearn, 1981, p. 24), and even neurotic reactions were of short duration in a massive chemical disaster in Germany (Kroiss, 1925). In both floods in Brisbane, Australia (Abrahams et al., 1976) and in the Friuli earthquake in Italy (Cattarinussi & Pelanda, 1981), researchers found widespread but moderate psychological effects in the aftermath of the disasters. Thus, generally, there are few supportive findings for the individual trauma approach in the non-American studies.

In an Australian study of the aftermath of Cyclone Tracy which devastated the city of Darwin, an attempt was made to measure long-term effects. Perhaps the most significant finding was that victims who never left the devastated city showed a better adjustment than returning evacuees; and evacuees who had not yet returned to Darwin exhibited the most psychological problems (Milne, 1977). Continuous living in the midst of almost total destruction did not seem to have the impact that the individual trauma approach would seem to imply. On the other hand, the differences seemed to be accounted for not by what happened at the time of impact, but by the nature of the post-impact social relationships and social settings of the cyclone victims.

CONCLUSION

Let us conclude by saying the following: From our point of view, there is a basic policy question involved in all of this. Is there a disagreement here between two approaches to the consequences of disasters for mental health which has some practical significance? Is this a difference that makes a difference? Or, is this merely an academic or intellectual exercise which might be of theoretical interest and excite researchers, without having any meaningful implications in the everyday world of policy and operations?

We think there is a meaningful difference here—an important one in terms of disaster planning and response and for both deliverers and receivers of disaster-related services. If the individual trauma approach is essentially the correct one, we should be extending crisis intervention programs, preparing outreach services for victims, and generally gearing up to handle the psychic trauma of those who have to adjust to the impact of a disaster agent. If the social sponge approach is the more valid one, a different strategy and use of resources is indicated. We should be reorganizing the federal, state, and local disaster bureaucracies, giving in-service training to providers and deliverers of services, and generally gearing up to handle a social problem which is mainly the result of organizational inefficiency and ineffectiveness relatively independent of disaster agents. The individual trauma approach primarily assumes the post-disaster period as the time in which most things can be done and considers the individual, or at most the family, as the basic unit to be worked with. The social sponge approach primarily looks at the pre-disaster period as the time in which most things can be done, and considers the group or organization as the basic unit to be worked with.

In an ideal situation with unlimited resources, we suppose all approaches could conceivably be used. But in a real world with finite resources, a more specific stance should be taken. Even if practitioners and scientists want to avoid the issue, the current social climate and trends will not allow them to do so. This is an age where greater accountability is increasingly being asked of practitioners and scientists. It is a period of time when the public at large is demanding greater input into what is done for and to them as consumers, as users, or in the context in which we are talking, as disaster victims. We think that the greater accountability and the greater participation being demanded is a very healthy thing. It means, among other things, that eventually those operating as practitioners and researchers in disasters will have to take a more definite stand on the consequences of disasters for mental health.

We have presented our views on a particular controversy in the disaster research area. However, there is much that puzzles us, and we are far from certain how much any of us really understands about the nature of disasters, the nature of mental health, and the relationship between the two. The latter, particularly, becomes problematical to us when we encounter observations such as the following. In the San Fernando earthquake of 1971, the Olive View Mental Health Center in a hospital complex was very damaged, with the two-story building holding 50 patients in locked wards collapsing into a one-story structure. The 131 psychiatric patients responded "very well"; they "seemed to react during the disaster with a great deal of stability, . . . attempting to help each other." In one case:

> One patient had been hospitalized a few hours before the earthquake, and was so hyperactive and uncontrollable that he was placed in restraints—a practice used only in extreme situations. At the time of the earthquake, a nurse disengaged his restraints, and told him that an 18-year-old catatonic girl could not get out of the building without help, and it was up to him to direct her. He escorted her safely out, remained coherent for a few hours, then regressed. (Stein, 1974, pp. 40-41)

Practically none of the literature on the relationship between mental health and community disasters could provide even a hint of what might be involved in the case just cited.

REFERENCES

Abrahams, M.J., Price, J., Whitlock, F.A., & Williams, G. The Brisbane floods, January 1974: The impact on health. *The Medical Journal of Australia*, 1976, 2, 936-939.

Adler, A. Neuropsychiatric complications in victims in Boston's Coconut Grove disaster. *Journal of the American Medical Association*, 1943, *123*, 1098-1101.

Adler, A. Two different types of post-traumatic neuroses. *American Journal of Psychiatry*, 1945, *102*, 237-240.

Ahearn, F.L., Jr. A pre-earthquake and post-earthquake comparison of psychiatric admission rates. *Urban and Social Change Review*, 1981, *14*, 22-27.

Ahearn, F., & Cohen, R. (Eds.) *Disasters and mental health: An annotated bibliography*. Rockville, MD: National Institute of Mental Health, 1984.

Baisden, B. & Quarantelli, E.L. The delivery of mental health services in community disasters: An outline of research findings. *Journal of Community Psychology*, 1981, *9*, 195-203.

Barton, A.H. *Communities in disasters*. Garden City, New York: Anchor, 1970.

Bates, F.L., Fogleman, C.W., Parenton, W.J., & Tracy, G.S. *The social and psychological consequences of a natural disaster: A longitudinal study of hurricane Audrey*. Washington, D.C.: National Research Council, 1963.

Baum, A., Gatchel, J.R., & Schaeffer, M. Emotional, behavioral, and physiological effects of chronic stress at Three Mile Island. *Journal of Consulting and Clinical Psychology*, 1983, *51*, 565-572.

Beinin, L. An examination of health data following two major earthquakes in Russia. *Disasters*, 1981, *5*, 142-146.

Bell, B.D. Disaster impact and response: Overcoming the thousand natural shocks. *The Gerontologist*, 1978, *18*, 531-540.

Bell, B.D., Kara, G., & Batterson, C. Service utilization and adjustment patterns of elderly tornado victims in an American disaster. *Mass Emergencies*, 1978, *3*, 71-81.

Bennet, G. Bristol floods 1968. Controlled survey of effects on health of local community disaster. *British Medical Journal*, 1970, *3*, 454-458.

Berren, M.R., Beigel, A., & Ghertner, S.A. A typology for the classification of disasters. *Community Mental Health Journal*, 1980, *16*, 103-111.

Birnbaum, F., Coplon, J., & Scharff, I. Crisis intervention after a natural disaster. *Social Casework*, 1973, *54*, 545-551.

Blaufarb, H., & Levine, J. Crisis intervention in an earthquake. *Social Work*, 1972, *17*, 16-19.

Bloch, D.A., Silber, E., & Perry, S.E. Some factors in the emotional reaction of children to disaster. *American Journal of Psychiatry*, 1956, *113*, 416-422.

Bolin, R.C. Family recovery from natural disaster: A preliminary model. *Mass Emergencies*, 1976, *1*, 267-277.

Bolin, R.C. *Study of elderly victims of the Wichita Falls tornado*. Fargo, ND: Department of Sociology, North Dakota State University, 1979.

Bolin, R.C. *Long-term family recovery from disaster*. Boulder, CO: Institute of Behavioral Science, University of Colorado, 1982.

Bolin, R., & Trainer, P. Modes of family recovery following disaster: A cross-national study. In E.L. Quarantelli (Ed.), *Disasters: Theory and research*. Beverly Hills, CA: Sage Publications, 1978.

Bowman, S. Disaster intervention: From the inside. Paper presented at the annual meeting of the American Psychological Association, Chicago, IL, 1975.

Boyd, S.T. Psychological reactions of disaster victims. *South African Medical Journal*, 1981, *60*, 744-748.

Bromet, E. *Three Mile Island: Mental health findings*. Final Report. Rockville, MD: National Institute of Mental Health, 1980.

Bromet, E., & Dunn, L. Mental health of mothers nine months after the Three Mile Island accident. *The Urban and Social Change Review*, 1981, *14*, 12-15.

Bromet, E., Schulberg, H., & Dunn, L. Reactions of psychiatric patients to the Three Mile Island nuclear accident. *Archives of General Psychiatry*, 1982, *39*, 725-730.

Brown, M., & Goldin, A. *Collective behavior: A review and reinterpretation of the literature*. Pacific Palisades, CA: Goodyear, 1973.

Brownstone, J., Penick, E., Larson, S., Nord, A., & Powell, B. Disaster-relief training and mental health. *Hospital and Community Psychiatry*, 1977, *28*, 31-32.

Carr, L.J. Disaster and the sequence-pattern concept of social change. *American Journal of Sociology*, 1932, *38*, 207-218.

Cattarinussi, B., & Pelanda, C. (Eds.) *Disastro e azione umana* (Disaster and Human Action). Milan, Italy: Franco Angeli, 1981. (In Italian)

Chapman, D.W. Human behavior in disasters: A new field of social research. *Journal of Social Issues*, 1954, *10*, 1-72.

Chard, C. The long day: The eighteenth of April in San Francisco. *Harper's Weekly*, 1906, *50*, 700-704.

Church, J.S. The Buffalo Creek disaster: Extent and range of emotional and/or behavioral problems. *Omega*, 1974, *5*, 61-63.

Cobb, S., & Lindemann, E. Neuropsychiatric observations. *Annals of Surgery*, 1943, *117*, 814-824.

Cohen, E.S., & Poulshock, S.W. *The impact of a major natural disaster on the elderly and societal response to their needs, Wyoming Valley, Pennsylvania 1972*. Philadelphia, PA: Department of Community Medicine, University of Pennsylvania, 1976.

Cohen, R.E., & Ahearn, F.L., Jr. *Handbook for mental health care of disaster victims*. Baltimore, MD: Johns Hopkins University Press, 1980.

Cohen, S.C., & Poulshock, S.W. Societal response to mass dislocation of the elderly: Implications for area agencies on aging. *The Gerontologist*, 1977, *17*, 262-268.

Columbus Dispatch, 1980. Wife beatings, suicide attempts increase near volcano. Sunday edition, August 10: A-7.

The crisis doctors. *Newsweek*, January 29, 1973, pp. 62-63.

Demerath, N., & Wallace, A. Human adaptation to disaster: Special issue. *Human Organization*, 1957, 16: 1-40.

Devlin, S. Missoula children's lungs weathered the ash. *Missoulian*, July 27, 1980.

Dieck, H. *The Johnstown flood*. Philadelphia, PA: Weller, 1889.

Disaster Research Center. Internal memo on Xenia survey data. Columbus, OH: Disaster Research Center, The Ohio State University, 1976.

Dohrenwend, B.P., Dohrenwend, B., Warheit, G., Bartlett, G. et al. Stress in the community: A report to the President's Commission on the accident at Three Mile Island. *Annals of the New York Academy of Sciences*, 1981, *365*, 159-174.

Drabek, T.E., *Longitudinal impact of disaster on family functioning. Final report*. Denver, CO: Department of Sociology, University of Denver, 1973.

Drabek, T.E. *A review of the sociological disaster literature*. In press.

Drabek, T.E., Erickson, P., & Crowe, J. An evaluation of matched samples in quasi-experimental designs. Paper presented at the Rocky Mountain Social Science Association annual meeting, Laramie, WY, 1973.

Drabek, T.E., & Key, W.H. The impact of disaster on primary group linkages. *Mass Emergencies*, 1976, *1*, 89-105.

Drabek, T.E., & Key, W.H. *Conquering disaster: Family recovery and long-term consequences*. New York: Irvington, 1983.

Drabek, T.E., Key, W., Erickson, P., & Crowe, J. The impact of disaster on kin relationships. *Journal of Marriage and the Family*, 1975, *37*, 481-494.

Dynes, R.R. *Organized behavior in disaster*. Book and Monograph Series #3. Columbus, OH: Disaster Research Center, The Ohio State University, 1974.

Dynes, R.R., Quarantelli, E.L., & Kreps, G.A. *A perspective on disaster planning*. Report Series #11. Columbus, Ohio: Disaster Research Center, The Ohio State University, 1981.

Edwards, J.G. Psychiatric aspects of civilian disasters. *British Medical Journal*, 1976, *1*, 944-947.

Erickson, P.E., Drabek, T., Key, W., & Crowe, J. Families in disaster: Patterns of recovery. *Mass Emergencies*, 1974, *1*, 203-216.

Erikson, K.T. *Everything in its path*. New York: Simon & Schuster, 1976a.

Erikson, K.T. Loss of communality at Buffalo Creek. *American Journal of Psychiatry*, 1976b, *133*, 302-305.
Erikson, K.T. Trauma at Buffalo Creek. *Society*, 1976c, *13*, 58-65.
Fairchild, T. Mental health needs and elderly disaster victims. Unpublished paper. 1984.
Fairchild, T.J., & White, D.J. Organizational response to mental health needs of elderly disaster victims. Denton, TX: Center for Studies in Aging, North Texas State University, 1982.
Frederick, C.J. Crisis intervention and emergency mental health. In W.R. Johnson (Ed.), *Health in action*. New York: Holt, Rinehart, & Winston, 1977.
Frederick, C.J. Effects of natural vs. human-induced violence upon victims. *Evaluation and Change*, 1980, Special Issue, 71-75.
Friedman, P., & Linn, L. Some psychiatric notes on the Andrea Doria disaster. *American Journal of Psychiatry*, 1957, *114*, 426-432.
Fritz, C.E. Disaster. In R. Merton, & R. Nisbet (Eds.), *Social problems*. New York: Harcourt, Brace, & World, 1961.
Fritz, C.E., & Marks, E.S. The NORC studies of human behavior in disaster. *The Journal of Social Issues*, 1954, *10*, 26-41.
Gleser, G.C., Green, B.L., & Winget, C.N. Quantifying interview data on psychic impairment of disaster survivors. *The Journal of Nervous and Mental Disease*, 1978, *166*, 209-216. *Prolonged psychosocial effects of disaster: A study of Buffalo Creek*. New York: Academic Press, 1981.
Golec, J. *Aftermath of disaster: The Teton Dam break*. Ph.D. dissertation. Columbus, OH: Disaster Research Center, The Ohio State University, 1980.
Golec, J. A contextual approach to the social psychological study of disaster recovery. *Mass Emergencies and Disasters*, 1983, *1*, 255-276.
Greco, D., Faustini, A., Forastiere, F., Galanti, M.R. et al. Epidemiological surveillance of diseases following the earthquake of 23rd November 1980 in Southern Italy. *Disasters*, 1981, *5*, 398-406.
Green, B.L. Assessing levels of psychological impairment following disaster: Some considerations of actual and methodological dimensions. *The Journal of Nervous and Mental Diseases*, 1982, *170*, 544-552.
Green, B.L., Grace, M., Lindy, J., Titchener, J., & Lindy, J.G. Levels of functional impairment following a civilian disaster: The Beverly Hills Supper Club fire. *Journal of Consulting and Clinical Psychology*, 1983, *51*(4), 573-580.
Hall, P.S., & Landreth, P.W. Assessing some long-term consequences of a natural disaster. *Mass Emergencies*, 1975, *1*, 55-61.
Harshbarger, D. Picking up the pieces: Disaster intervention and human ecology. *Omega*, 1973, *5*, 55-59.
Harshbarger, D. An ecologic perspective on disaster intervention. In H.J. Parad, H.L.P. Resnick, & L.G. Parad (Eds.), *Emergency and disaster management: A mental health sourcebook*. Bowie, MD: The Charles Press, 1976.
Hartsough, D.M., Zarle, T.H., & Ottinger, D. Rapid response to disaster: The Monticello tornado. In H.J. Parad, H.L.P. Resnick, & L.G. Parad (Eds.), *Emergency and disaster management: A mental health sourcebook*. Bowie, MD: The Charles Press, 1976.
Heffron, E. Project outreach: Final report submitted to NIMH. Nanticoke, PA: Hazleton-Nanticoke Mental Health/Mental Retardation Center, 1975.
Heffron, E. Interagency relationships and conflict in disaster: The Wilkes-Barre experience. *Mass Emergencies*, 1977, *2*, 111-119.
Hocking, F. Human reactions to extreme environmental stress. *The Medical Journal of Australia*, 1965, *2*, 477-482.
Hoiberg, A., & McCaughey, B.G. Collision at sea: The traumatic aftereffects. Report 81-39. Naval Health Research Center, 1981.
Houts, P.S., Cleary, P. Extent and duration of psychological distress of persons in the vicinity of Three Mile Island. *Proceedings of the Pennsylvania Academy of Science*, 1980, *54*, 22-28.

Howard, S.J., & Gordon, N.S. *Final progress report: Mental health intervention in a major disaster.* Van Nuys, CA: San Fernando Valley Child Guidance Clinic, 1972.

Huerta, F., & Horton, R. Coping behavior of elderly flood victims. *The Gerontologist*, 1978, *18*, 541-546.

Huerta, F.C., Horton, R.L., & Winters, H.T. *Coping with disaster among the elderly.* Paper presented at the annual meeting of the Western Social Science Association, Denver, Colorado, 1977.

James, W. On some mental effect of the earthquake. In W. James (Ed.), *Memories and studies.* New York: Longmans, Green, & Company, 1911.

Janes, R.W. The collective action involved in the removal and relocation of Shawneetown, Illinois. Doctoral dissertation. Department of Sociology, University of Illinois, 1942.

Janis, I. *Air war and emotional stress.* New York: McGraw-Hill, 1951.

Kafrissen, S.R., et al. Mental health problems in environmental disasters. In H.L.P. Resnick, & H.L. Rubin (Eds.), *Emergency psychiatric care.* Bowie, MD: The Charles Press, 1975.

Kara, G. Adjustment to disaster impact. Master's thesis. Omaha, Nebraska: Department of Sociology, University of Nebraska at Omaha, 1977.

Kasl, S.V., Chisholm, R.F., & Eskenazi, B. The impact of the accident at Three Mile Island on the behavior and well-being of nuclear workers. *America Journal of Public Health*, 1981, *71*, 472-495.

Kilijanek, T.S., & Drabek, T.E. Assessing long-term impacts of a natural disaster: A focus on the elderly. *The Gerontologist*, 1979, *19*, 555-556.

Kimball, E.H. Recovery of the older survivors of the 1976 Big Thompson flood. Master's thesis. Fort Collins, CO: Department of Child Development and Family Relationships, Colorado State University, 1978.

Kinston, W., & Rosser, R. Disaster: Effects on mental and physical state. *Journal of Psychosomatic Research*, 1974, *18*, 437-456.

Kliman, A.S. The Corning flood project: Psychological first aid following a natural disaster. In H.J. Parad, H.L.P. Resnick, & L.G. Parad (Eds.), *Emergency and disaster management: A mental health sourcebook.* Bowie, MD: The Charles Press, 1975.

Knaus, R.L. Crisis intervention in a disaster area: The Pennsylvania flood in Wilkes-Barre. *Journal of the American Osteopathic Association*, 1975, *75*, 297-301.

Koegler, R.R., & Hicks, S.M. The destruction of a medical center by earthquake: Initial effects on patients and staff. *California Medicine: The Western Journal of Medicine*, 1972, *116*, 63-67.

Kreps, G.A. The worth of the NAS-NRC (1952-63) and DRC (1963-present) studies of individual and social response to disasters. In J.D. Wright, & P.H. Rossi (Eds.), *Social science and natural hazards.* Cambridge, MA: Abt Books, 1981.

Kreps, G.A. Sociological inquiry and disaster research. *Annual Review of Sociology*, 1984, *10*, 309-330.

Kroiss, O. Katastrophe und nervensystem. *Archiv fur Psychiatric und Nervenkrankheiten*, 1925, *74*, 39-51.

Krystal, H. (Ed.) *Massive psychic trauma.* New York: International Universities Press, 1968.

Kutak, R.I. The sociology of crises: The Louisville flood of 1937. *Social Forces*, 1938, *17*, 66-72.

Langdon, J.R., & Parker, A.H. Psychiatric aspects of the March 27, 1964 earthquake. *Alaska Medicine*, 1964, *6*, 33-35.

Laube, J.M. Psychological reactions of nurses in disaster. *Nursing Research*, 1973, *22*, 343-347.

Laube, J.M. Response of the health care work to family-community role conflict in disaster and the psychological consequences of resolution. Doctoral dissertation. Denton, Texas: College of Nursing, Texas Woman's University, 1974.

Leik, R.K., Leik, S., Ekker, K., & Gifford, G. *Under the threat of Mt. St. Helens—A study of chronic family stress.* Final Report. Minneapolis, Minnesota: Family Study Center, University of Minnesota, 1982.

Leopold, R.L., & Dillon, H. Psycho-anatomy of a disaster: A long-term study of post-traumatic neuroses in survivors of a marine explosion. *The American Journal of Psychiatry*, 1963, *19*, 913-921.

Lifton, R.J., & Olson, E. The human meaning of total disaster—the Buffalo Creek experience. *Psychiatry*, 1976, *39*, 1-18.

Lindy, J.D., Grace, M., & Green, B. Survivors: Outreach to a reluctant population. *American Journal of Orthopsychiatry*, 1981, *51*, 468-478.

Logan, L., Killian, L., & Marrs, W. *A study of the effects of catastrophe on social disorganization.* Norman, OK: University of Oklahoma Research Unit, 1950.

Logue, J.N. Long-term effects of a major natural disaster: The Hurricane Agnes flood in the Wyoming Valley of Pennsylvania, June 1972. Doctoral dissertation. New York: School of Public Health, Department of Epidemiology, Columbia University, 1978.

Logue, J.N. Mental health aspects of disasters. Paper presented at the Natural Hazards Research Application Workshop, University of Colorado, 1980.

Logue, J.N., & Hansen, H. A case-control study of hypertensive women in a post-disaster community: Wyoming Valley, Pennsylvania. *Journal of Human Stress*, 1980, *6*, 28-34.

Logue, J.N., Hansen, H., & Struening, E. Emotional and physical distress following Hurricane Agnes in Wyoming Valley of Pennsylvania. *Public Health Reports*, 1979, *94*, 495-502.

Logue, J.N., Hansen, H., & Struening, E. Some indications of the long-term health effects of a natural disaster. *Public Health Reports*, 1981, *96*, 67-79.

Logue, J.N., Melick, M., & Hansen, H. Research issues and directions in the epidemiology of health effects of disasters. *Epidemiologic Review*, 1981, *3*, 140-162.

Logue, J.N., Melick, M., & Struening, E. A study of health and mental health status following a major natural disaster. *Research in Community and Mental Health*, 1981, *2*, 217-224.

Magaro, P.A., Gripp, R., & McDowell, D. *The mental health industry. A cultural phenomenon.* New York: Wiley, 1978.

Marks, E.S., Fritz, C., Bucher, R., Earle, D., et al. *Human reactions in disaster situations.* Chicago, IL: National Opinion Research Center, University of Chicago, 1954.

Mauss, A.L. *Social problems as social movements.* Philadelphia, PA: J.B. Lippincott Company, 1975.

McGee, R.K. *The role of crisis intervention services in disaster recovery center for crisis intervention research.* Gainesville, FL: University of Florida, 1973.

McIntire, M.S., & Sadeghi, E. The pediatrician and mental health in a community-wide disaster. *Clinical Pediatrics*, 1977, *16*, 702-705.

McLuckie, B. *A study of functional response to stress in three societies.* Doctoral dissertation. Columbus, OH: Disaster Research Center, The Ohio State University, 1970.

Melick, M.E. *Social, psychological, and medical aspects of stress-related illness in the recovery period of a natural disaster.* Doctoral dissertation. Albany, NY: Department of Sociology, State University of New York at Albany, 1976.

Melick, M.E. Life changes and illness: Illness behavior of males in the recovery period of a natural disaster. *Journal of Health and Social Behavior*, 1978, *19*, 335-342.

Mileti, D.S., Drabek, T.E., & Haas, J.E. *Human systems in extreme environments: A sociological perspective.* Boulder, CO: Institute of Behavioral Science, University of Colorado, 1975.

Miller, J.A. Families in the aftermath of disaster: The Big Thompson flood of 1976. Master's thesis. Fort Collins, CO: Department of Child Development and Family Relationships, Colorado State University, 1977.

Miller, J.A., Turner, J.G., & Kimball, E. Big Thompson flood victims: One year later. *Family Relations*, 1981, *30*, 111-116.

Milne, G. Cyclone Tracy: I. Some consequences of the evacuation for adult victims. *Australian Psychologist*, 1977a, *12*, 39-54.

Milne, G. Cyclone Tracy: II. The effects on Darwin children. *Australian Psychologist*, 1977b, *12*, 55-62.

Moore, H.E. Some emotional concomitants of disaster. *Mental Hygiene*, 1958, *42*, 45-50.

Moore, H.E., & Friedsam, H.J. Reported emotional stress following a disaster. *Social Forces,* 1959, *38,* 135-139.

Murphy, S.A. Coping with stress following a natural disaster: The volcanic eruption of Mt. St. Helens. Doctoral dissertation. Portland, OR: Department of Urban Studies, Portland State University, 1981.

Murphy, S.A. Self-efficacy and social support as moderators of disaster stress. Unpublished paper, 1983.

Newman, C.J. Children of disaster: Clinical observations at Buffalo Creek. *American Journal of Psychiatry,* 1976, *133,* 306-312.

Ollendick, D.G., & Hoffman, Sister M. Assessment of psychological reactions in disaster victims. *Journal of Community Psychology,* 1982, *10,* 157-169.

Penick, E.C., Larson, S., & Powell, B. Final Report of the Lieutenant Governor's Task Force for Mental Health Delivery Systems in Time of Disaster. St. Louis, MO: Department of Psychological Services, Malcolm Bliss Mental Health Center, 1974.

Penick, E.C., Powell, B.J., & Sieck, W.A. Mental health problems and natural disaster: Tornado victims. *Journal of Community Psychology,* 1976, *4,* 64-67.

Pennebaker, J.W., & Newtson, D. *Preliminary report of the psychological impact of Mt. St. Helens.* Charlottesville, VA: Department of Psychology, University of Virginia, 1980.

Perry, G.S. Galveston. *Saturday Evening Post,* 1950, *223,* 24-25, 114, 117, 119.

Perry, R.W. Detecting psychopathological reactions to natural disaster: A methodological note. *Social Behavior and Personality,* 1979, *7*(2), 173-177.

Perry, R.W., & Lindell, M.K. The psychological consequences of natural disaster: A review of research on American communities. *Mass Emergencies,* 1978, *3,* 105-115.

Popovic, M., & Petrovic, D. After the earthquake. *Lancet,* 1964, *2,* 1169-1171.

Poulshock, S.W., & Cohen, E.S. The elderly in the aftermath of a disaster. *The Gerontologist,* 1975, *15,* 357-361.

Powell, B., & Penick, E. Psychological distress following a flood disaster. A one year follow-up of 98 victims. Unpublished paper, 1980.

Powell, J.W. Gaps and goals in disaster research. *Journal of Social Issues,* 1954, *10,* 61-65.

Prasad, J. The psychology of rumors: A study relating to the great Indian earthquake of 1934. *British Journal of Psychology,* 1935, *26,* 1-15.

President's Commission on Mental Health. Report to the President. Washington, D.C.: U.S. Government Printing Office, 1978.

Prince, S.H. *Catastrophe and social change.* New York: Columbia University Press, 1920.

Quarantelli, E.L. The nature and conditions of panic. *American Journal of Sociology,* 1954, *60,* 267-275.

Quarantelli, E.L. The behavior of panic participants. *Sociology and Social Research,* 1957, *41,* 187-194.

Quarantelli, E.L. Emergent accommodation groups: Beyond current collective behavior typologies. In T. Shibutani (Ed.), *Human nature and collective behavior.* Englewood Cliffs, NJ: Prentice-Hall, 1970.

Quarantelli, E.L. (Ed.) *Disasters: Theory and research.* Beverly Hills, CA: Sage, 1978.

Quarantelli, E.L. Panic behavior in fire situations: Findings and a model from the English language research literature. Proceedings of the 4th Joint Panel Meeting, the U.J.N.R. Panel on Fire Research and Safety. Tokyo, Japan: Building Research Institute, 1981.

Quarantelli, E.L. Human resources and organizational behaviors in community disasters and their relationship to planning. Preliminary Paper #76. Columbus, OH: Disaster Research Center, The Ohio State University, 1982a.

Quarantelli, E.L. What is a disaster? An agent specific or an all disaster spectrum approach to socio-behavioral aspects of earthquakes? In B.G. Jones, & M. Tomazevic (Eds.), *Social and economic aspects of earthquakes.* Ljubljana, Yugoslavia and Ithaca, New York: Institute for Testing and Research in Materials and Structures and Program in Urban and Regional Studies, Cornell University, 1982b.

Quarantelli, E.L., & Dynes, R.R. Response to social crisis and disaster. *Annual Review of Sociology,* 1977, *3,* 23-49.

Rangell, L. Discussion of the Buffalo Creek disaster: The course of psychic trauma. *American Journal of Psychiatry,* 1976, *133,* 313-316.

Richard, W.C. Crisis intervention services following natural disaster: The Pennsylvania recovery project. *The Journal of Community Psychology,* 1974, *2,* 211-218.

Rosenberg, S.A., Fine, P.M., & Robinson, G.L. Emotional effects of the Omaha tornado. *Nebraska Medical Journal,* 1980, *65,* 24-26.

Schulberg, H.C. Disaster, crisis theory, and intervention strategies. *Omega,* 1974, *5,* 77-87.

Shippee, G.E., Bradford, R., & Gregory, W. Community perceptions of natural disasters and post-disaster mental health services. *Journal of Community Psychology,* 1982, *10,* 23-28.

Slade, W.G. Earthquake psychology. *Australian Journal of Psychology and Philosophy,* 1932, *10,* 58-63.

Slade, W.G. Earthquake psychology II. *Australian Journal of Psychology and Philosophy,* 1933, *11,* 123-133.

Sorokin, P.A. *Man and society in calamity.* New York: E.P. Dutton, 1942.

Stein, S. An earthquake shakes up a mental health system. In A. Tulipas, C. Attneave, & E. Kingstone (Eds.), *Beyond clinic walls.* University, AL: University of Alabama Press, 1974.

Sterling, J., Drabek, T.E., & Key, W.H. The long-term impact of disaster on the health self-perceptions of victims. Paper presented at the American Sociological Association annual meeting, Chicago, IL, 1977.

Sundell, M. Problems facing a community mental health center in delivery of mental health services to a disaster area. Paper based on a presentation made at the annual meeting of the National Council of CMHCs, Washington, D.C., 1975.

Szasz, T. *The myth of mental illness.* New York: Hoelser-Harper, 1961.

Szasz, T. *The manufacture of madness.* New York: Dell, 1970.

Taylor, V.A. Delivery of mental health services in the Xenia tornado: A collective behavior analysis of an emergent system response. Doctoral dissertation. Columbus, OH: Department of Sociology, The Ohio State University, 1976.

Taylor, V.A. Good news about disaster. *Psychology Today,* 1977, *11,* 93-94, 124-126.

Taylor, V.A., Ross, G.A., & Quarantelli, E.L. *Delivery of mental health services in disasters: The Xenia tornado and some implications.* Book and Monograph Series #11. Columbus, OH: Disaster Research Center, The Ohio State University, 1976.

Thucydides. *The Peloponnesian war.* New York: Modern Library, 1934.

Titchener, J.L. Individual and family responses and recovery after disaster. Unpublished paper, 1975.

Titchener, J.L., & Kapp, F.T. Family and character change at Buffalo Creek. Paper presented at American Psychiatric Association annual meeting, 1975.

Titchener, J.L., & Kapp, F.T. Family and character change at Buffalo Creek. *American Journal of Psychiatry,* 1976, *133,* 295-299.

Titmus, R. *Problems of social policy.* London: H.M. Stationery Office, 1950.

Trainer, P., & Bolin, R. Persistent effects of disasters on daily activities: A cross-cultural comparison. *Mass Emergencies,* 1976, *1,* 279-290.

Tyhurst, J.S. Individual reactions to community disaster: The natural history of psychiatric phenomena. *American Journal of Psychiatry,* 1951, *107,* 764-769.

U.S. Strategic Bombing Survey. 1945-1947 Reports. Washington, D.C.: U.S. Government Printing Office.

Warheit, G.J. Disasters, social service disruptions, and mental health problems. Unpublished paper, 1984.

Warheit, G., & Auth, J. Disasters and mental health: A model for estimating the psychological impact of restarting the Three Mile Island unit I reactor. Unpublished manuscript, 1983.

Wenger, D.E., Dykes, J., Sebok, T., & Neff, J. It's a matter of myths: An empirical examination of individual insight into disaster response. *Mass Emergencies,* 1975, *1,* 33-46.

Wenger, D.E., James, T.F., & Faupel, C.E. *Disaster beliefs and emergency planning*. Newark, DE: Department of Sociology, University of Delaware, 1980.

Whalen, E.M. Observations on the June 1972 flood in the Wyoming Valley Area of Pennsylvania. Wilkes-Barre, PA: Luzerne-Wyoming County Mental Health Center, No. 1, 1972.

Wolfenstein, M. *Disaster*. Glencoe, IL: The Free Press, 1957.

Wright, J.D., & Rossi, P.H. (Eds.) *Social science and natural hazards*. Cambridge, MA: Abt Books, 1981.

Zarle, T.H., Hartsough, D.M., & Ottinger, D.R. Tornado recovery: The development of a professional-paraprofessional response to a disaster. *Journal of Community Psychology*, 1974, *2*, 311-320.

Zusman, J., Joss, R., & Newman, P. Project Outreach: Luzerne-Wyoming County Mental Health/Mental Retardation Joinder. Final Report. Buffalo, NY: Community Mental Health Research and Development Corporation, 1973.

RECENT TREATMENT INNOVATIONS

10

Post-trauma Stress Assessment and Treatment: Overview and Formulations

RAYMOND M. SCURFIELD

An overview and formulation of the issues, assessment and treatment of post-traumatic stress disorder (PTSD) among survivors of various traumata is provided. There is discussion of such related areas as literature findings regarding PTSD etiology, assessment, and treatment; issues and misconceptions concerning trauma survivors; problems in assessment and validation of the PTSD diagnosis; critical factors to consider in assessment; interviewing dynamics in assessment and treatment; and treatment implications regarding acute, chronic, and delayed PTSD, to include discussion of five generic PTSD treatment principles and group and family treatment.

The author wishes to acknowledge the estimated 3.7 million men and women Vietnam theater veterans and their families, and the 574 dedicated, overworked and wonderful staff of the 136 Veterans Administration Vietnam-Era Veteran Counseling Centers ("Vet Centers"); Vet Centers have provided readjustment counseling services to over 200,000 Vietnam theater veterans and their families since 1979. The author does not purport to represent the views of the V.A.

An abnormal reaction to an abnormal situation is normal behavior.
Viktor Frankl (1959)
Nazi concentration camp survivor

There are several prominent areas that must be discussed in order to provide a comprehensive overview of the assessment and treatment of post-traumatic stress. These areas include a review of the traumatic stress literature and formulation of central elements in the assessment and treatment of post-traumatic stress disorder (PTSD): 1) the critical etiological factors in the development of PTSD; 2) issues and misconceptions concerning trauma survivors; 3) problematic areas in assessment and validation of the PTSD diagnosis; 4) interviewing dynamics in the assessment process; 5) five generic PTSD treatment principles; 6) aspects of acute, and longer term PTSD treatment; and 7) peer group and family treatment.

BACKGROUND

There has been a prevalent belief that post-trauma psychological symptoms, particularly those which persist over time, are primarily due to 1) pre-morbid personality factors (e.g., factors or deficits existing prior to the trauma that "predisposed" persons to manifest psychological or somatic symptoms following the trauma), or 2) that claims for disability compensation and other forms of secondary gain were the major factors in prolonging acute stress reactions (Kalinowski, 1950). Such perspectives implied that "healthy" persons must have seemingly unlimited abilities to handle stress. Thus, as an example, a military veteran who presented significant and persistent symptoms following combat was considered to have an underlying neurotic personality (hence the terms "war neurosis" in World War I and "traumatic neurosis" in World War II [Figley, 1978; Goodwin, 1980]).

The recent publication of the *Diagnostic and Statistical Manual of Mental Disorders* (DSM-III) (American Psychiatric Association, 1980), acknowledged that almost anyone might develop psychiatric symptoms following exposure to an extremely stressful event. Particularly significant about the DSM-III classification of PTSD is the inclusion of the "chronic" (duration of symptoms at least six months or longer) and "delayed" (onset of symptoms no sooner than six months after the trauma) subtypes. PTSD criteria include: an identifiable stressor that is of such a magnitude that it would be expected to "evoke significant symptoms of distress in almost everyone," a reexperiencing of the trauma (through flashbacks, intrusive thoughts, etc.), a numbing of responsiveness to or reduced involvement with the external world, and other specific symptoms (sleep disturbances, survivor guilt, hyperalertness, memory impairment and so forth) (APA, 1980, p. 236).

PTSD ETIOLOGICAL FACTORS

One set of findings in the literature concerns the relationship between pre-morbid personality factors and post-traumatic disorders. On the one hand, several studies of Vietnam veterans indicate a primary relationship between pre-military factors and the emergence of post-trauma symptoms (Baraga, Van Kampen, Watson, Czekala, & Kuhne, 1983; Borus, 1974; Helzer, Robins, Wish, & Hesselbrock, 1979; Panzarella, Mantell & Bridenbaugh, 1978; Robins, 1978; Robins, David & Goodman, 1974; Worthington, 1978). In contrast, however, studies of mental symptoms following head injury (Ader, 1945), a 12- to 16-year follow-up of concentration camp survivors (Strom, Refsum, Eitinger, Gronvik et al., 1962), a long-term study of 36 survivors of an off-shore oil explosion (Leopold & Dillon, 1963), a follow-up study of US Air Force prisoners of war (Ursano, 1981), a study of 43 Vietnam era veterans seeking mental health services at a medical center (Foy, Sipprelle, Rueger, & Carroll, 1984), a further analysis (Ransom, 1974) of a clinical sample of World War II air crews (Grinker, Willerman, Bradley & Fastovsky, 1946), a clinical examination of 303 concentration camp survivors (Hocking, 1970), a survey of 1,500 young men before and after military service (Card, 1983), a study of Vietnam veterans being treated for substance abuse (Penk, Robinowitz, Roberts, Patterson & Dolon, 1981) and studies of natural disaster victims (Melick, Logue & Frederick, 1982), all revealed little or no correlations between pre-trauma factors, the presence or severity of post-traumatic symptoms, and the apparent primacy of exposure to trauma as one of, if not the, critical etiological factor in the emergence of PTSD.

There also is evidence to suggest that stress symptoms following exposure to severe enough trauma persist over time (Dobbs and Wilson, 1960) and may in fact increase in severity (Archibald & Tuddenham, 1965; Chodoff, 1970; Leopold & Dillon, 1963; Strom et al, 1962; Ursano, Boydstun, & Wheatley, 1981).

The Vietnam war and its aftermath have led to an explosion of published reports describing PTSD among Vietnam veterans. Most reports suggest that there is a growing incidence of PTSD and that it is related to the intensity of combat exposure (DeFazio, Rustin & Diamond, 1975; Figley, 1978, 1979; Figley & Southerly, 1980; O'Neill & Fontaine, 1972; Schnaier, 1982; Ursano, 1981; Wilson, 1980b; Wilson & Krauss, in press); to the isolation and the lack of positive social supports upon returning home (Figley & Leventman, 1980; Keane & Fairbank, 1983; Wilson & Krauss, in press) and to pre-morbid factors. Wilson and Krauss report data that provide yet a different perspective—that pre-morbid behavioral tendencies were aggravated as a consequence of combat. Finally, further analysis of a national survey of Vietnam veterans (Egendorf, Kadushin, Laufer, Rothbart & Sloan, 1981) showed that while some pre-service behavior patterns contribute to some post-war adjustment problems, so do social characteristics such as race, and most importantly, there is a continuing significant influence of war experiences (Laufer, Frey-Wouters & Gallops, this volume).

Limitations of the Literature

Unfortunately, almost none of the research to date appears to adequately incorporate all of the following: scientifically rigorous research methodology addressing the full range of pre-trauma, trauma, and post-trauma factors, examination of both clinical and non-clinical populations, and psychologically sophisticated instrumentation. For example, a number of the studies that have suggested a primary relationship between pre-military factors and PTSD have inadequately (or not at all) measured the *severity* or other more refined aspects of the trauma. There are several instruments that measure levels of exposure to trauma (Egendorf et al., 1981; Figley, 1980; Foy et al., 1984; Keane, this volume; Horowitz, Wilner, & Alvarez, 1979; Wilson & Krauss, in press). However, there has been only limited psychometric refinement or calibration of such instruments across a range of populations. Finally, only two studies are prospective in nature, e.g., they include pre-trauma data that were collected *prior* to the trauma. Both of these studies indicate a primary relationship between factors about the trauma *per se* and PTSD (Card, 1983; Ursano, 1981).

Taken in its entirety, this author concludes that the literature to date seems to support a primary role of trauma in the etiology of PTSD. However, there are sufficient other findings to suggest that assessment of the interactional and cumulative effects among all three sets of factors (pre-trauma, trauma and post-trauma) are critical to a full understanding and assessment of PTSD.

VALIDITY OF THE DIAGNOSIS OF PTSD

Reliability and validity of the DSM-III (APA, 1980) criteria for PTSD across the range of clinical and non-clinical populations is sorely lacking. One examination of stress disorder symptoms among some of the sample in the *Legacies of Vietnam* study by Egendorf et al. (1981) and a comparative analysis with the DSM-III criteria for PTSD revealed a stress disorder syndrome that essentially was quite similar to the DSM-III criteria (Boulanger, Kadushin, Rindskopf, & Juliano, 1982). Several studies, however, offer some evidence to suggest additions to, or deletions from, the DSM-III, PTSD criteria (Atkinson, Sparr, Sheff, White & Fitzsimmons, 1984; Baraga et al., 1983; Hough, Gongla, Scurfield, Corker, Carr, & Escobar, 1984; Silver & Iacono, 1984; Wilson, Smith & Johnson, this volume). In addition, the DSM-III criteria do not appear to adequately discriminate between symptoms that are part of an expected or normal process and those of a disordered process (Smith, Parson & Haley, 1983). And so, while clinicians familiar with post-traumatic stress seem to be clear in their own minds about the PTSD diagnosis, there remains a lack of a rigorously tested, empirically based validation concerning just what constitutes PTSD (Figley, 1978), DSM-III notwithstanding.

METHODS TO DIAGNOSE PTSD

Currently, there is little or no empirical basis to justify the utilization of other methods to unequivocably validate a diagnosis of PTSD that has been obtained by an expert clinical examination. The findings of two recent studies show some promise that there may be a subscale of the Minnesota Multiphasic Personality Inventory (MMPI) that correctly classifies PTSD at 82% and 83% respectively (Foy et al., 1984; Keane, Malloy & Fairbank, in press; Keane, this volume). A third study found a different set of MMPI predictors (Roberts, Penk, Gearing, Robinowitz, et al., 1982). Problem checklist items reflective of anxiety-based disorders had over a 90% correct classification rate (Foy et al., 1984).

Two recently developed instruments have been designed to obtain DSM-III diagnoses, including PTSD: 1) the Diagnostic Interview Schedule (DIS) (Robins, 1981; Robins & Helzer, 1984) and 2) the Structured Clinical Interview for DSM-III (SCID) (Spitzer & Williams, 1983). However, to date there is only one pilot study on the accuracy of the DIS PTSD section (Russel & Willenbring, 1983). Preliminary findings in another study on a DIS-based PTSD scale indicate a .83 concordance with an expert clinical examination-derived PTSD diagnosis (Hough et al., 1984).

The development of a multimethod assessment of PTSD to include physiological measures (Malloy, Fairbank & Keane, 1983) at this point in time appears to be a desirable goal, though difficult to attain so far. Two recent studies report distinctive physiological responses among PTSD patients under controlled laboratory conditions (Blanchard, Kolb, Pallmeyer & Gerardi, 1983; Malloy et al., 1983).

In conclusion, it would appear that methods, other than the expert clinical examination, to validate a diagnosis of PTSD are in the developmental and pilot test stages, and serve a useful ancillary role to the clinician-derived diagnosis (Arnold, 1985a).

DISBELIEF CONCERNING "DELAYED STRESS" AND PTSD

Most Americans have been spared exposure to severe and repeated or protracted traumatic events. Thus, the course of post-trauma symptom development, which includes a "freezing of affect" and delay in symptom onset, is difficult to appreciate among the general public. There also is a persistent disbelief that "healthy" personalities can experience prolonged psychiatric difficulties following a traumatic event, in spite of studies and clinical experiences that suggest the contrary. Indeed, typical reactions to trauma and trauma survivors seem to be laced with an aversion to even a distant or brief contact with the horrors of trauma as might be experienced through intimate interaction with trauma survivors.

Moreover, psychoanalytic theories of personality development, which are the ruling ethos in mental health, minimize or deny the importance of events and developments that occur in adolescence or adulthood—except, perhaps, as they might exacerbate preexistent personality aspects. Humanistic and existentially oriented belief systems emphasize the present, the "now" ethos. Ironically, coming from an entirely different perspective, they may also have contributed to the lack of attention paid to the impact of adult trauma.

PROBLEMATIC AREAS IN THE DIAGNOSIS OF POST-TRAUMATIC STRESS DISORDERS

There is relatively little difficulty in making an accurate PTSD diagnosis when relatively "pure" trauma-specific PTSD is present. This is particularly likely to occur when the trauma is in the patient's fairly recent past and/or when the patient and/or clinician can fairly readily perceive a link between the trauma and current symptoms. For example, a woman reports suffering violence-laden nightmares about being assaulted ever since being raped two months previously and there is no history of such nightmares prior to the rape. However, the trauma may have occurred long enough ago that it is not identified by patient or clinician as a, or the, source of current difficulties. For example, military veterans who entered Veterans Administration (or any) substance abuse programs in the 1970s routinely were *not* queried about the existence of combat-related trauma, nor was any attempt made to systematically explore the possible linkage of such trauma to the substance abuse (Figley, 1978). The veteran, in turn, was unlikely to attribute current substance abuse to military experiences *per se*.

Maladaptive Coping in Chronic and Delayed PTSD

The longer the PTSD goes untreated the more ingrained the maladaptive coping and denial patterns become. Such patterns can become entrenched to the point where they are an integral part of the presenting clinical picture. They may require specific treatment in and of themselves, along with or sequentially to treatment for PTSD. For example, paranoia, feelings of retaliation, antisocial and explosive behaviors, and rage typically may be associated with chronic or delayed PTSD, if not actually the core symptomatology. Indeed, several of these symptoms are listed in DSM-III as "associated features" of the PTSD diagnosis.

Non-exclusivity of PTSD Symptoms

Assessment is further complicated by the fact that very few PTSD symptoms are *unique* to PTSD. This non-exclusivity of PTSD symptoms requires careful examination of the sequencing and relationship of presenting symptoms to prior trauma. For example, phobic symptoms are presented (e.g., excessive fear of dark, underground places is manifested subsequent to having been raped in a poorly lit, underground parking structure). In this case, if all appropriate diagnostic criteria are met,

DSM-III would imply a primary PTSD diagnosis. One could also consider a phobic disorder as well and/or that the phobic symptoms are part of the PTSD symptom cluster—avoidance of an activity or situation that arouses recollection of the trauma.

Delayed PTSD

It is important to note both the complexity and lack of empirical data concerning "delayed" PTSD. Clinical experiences with Vietnam veterans manifesting delayed PTSD, who have been counseled at 136 Veterans Administration Vet Centers since 1979, indicate that there are several subtypes of delayed PTSD. For some veterans there is an immediate onset of symptoms, a subsequent lengthy period of apparent asymptomatic functioning and then a recurrence of symptoms; for others, there is a numbing and then acute symptom onset; for others, there is a gradual exacerbation over several years; for yet others, apparent asymptomatic functioning for lengthy periods of time (up to a decade or more) is followed by an identifiable stressful life event that triggers PTSD symptoms, and so forth. Data concerning the frequency, duration, intensity, and other parameters of patterning of the delayed or chronic PTSD are extremely limited and sorely needed.

Lack of Specificity in DSM-III

There also is a lack of clarity in DSM-III over how to evaluate the presence of psychiatric symptoms that were manifested prior to the traumatic event vis-à-vis establishing a PTSD diagnosis, e.g., does premorbidity "rule out" a PTSD diagnosis? Later this will be discussed further. There is no specification in DSM-III as to the length of time that a symptomatic episode must last to reach diagnostic criteria. Moreover, there is no specification of the course of the disorder. For example, symptoms that are irregular and occasional, versus those that are relatively constant are not differentiated. Also, there is no explication of the frequency of symptom occurrence or the duration of such an occurrence necessary to reach diagnostic criteria.

Finally, the assessing clinician may have inadequate knowledge concerning the etiology of the disorder and its diagnosis, or only assign the diagnosis in the absence of symptoms that would meet criteria for any other.

ASSESSMENT FOR DIAGNOSIS AND TREATMENT PLANNING

Comprehensive assessment for initial diagnostic and ongoing treatment planning purposes must address significant elements in pre-trauma history, the trauma itself and post-trauma functioning. There are at least four elements to consider.

Pre-trauma History

A thorough assessment of functioning prior to the traumatizing event is both appropriate and essential. This assessment should include: parent-child, peer and other authority figure relationships; behavior patterns in family, school, work and social life; and socioeconomic and other environmental factors. There may well be a pre-morbid personality that suggests an additional diagnosis or a diagnosis other than PTSD (Goodwin, 1980). One common assessment practice is that substance abuse or difficulties with authorities/institutions prior to the trauma or even after the trauma is often construed as evidence of a personality disorder *rather than* a PTSD diagnosis. However, a personality disorder diagnosis should be accompanied by a PTSD diagnosis if 1) inclusionary criteria per the DSM-III definition of PTSD are met, and 2) there is evidence to show significant difference in degree of the pre- and post-trauma symptoms, e.g., an "aggravation of condition" or a significant deterioration "beyond natural progression." Such evidence would support at least a secondary PTSD diagnosis.

The differentiation between PTSD and personality disorders, especially antisocial and borderline, can be quite problematic. It has been suggested that a diagnosis of PTSD describes in effect a change in underlying character such that an individual tends to function on a more borderline level (Parson, 1984). Wilson (1980a) provides the perspective that among Vietnam combat veterans with PTSD, for example, there has been an arrested personality development at or regression to the adolescent stage. One useful, but not necessarily sufficient, differentiating feature between PTSD and borderline personality disorder is that in the former there frequently is an aversion to social interactions, whereas in the latter there is a frequent inability to be alone (Arnold, 1985a).

There can be serious questions about typical pre-morbid assessments that are based solely on retrospective self-reports of events and dynamics that usually have occurred many years ago (Figley, 1979). There is evidence to suggest that some trauma survivors, in retrospect, idealize their pre-trauma life (Chodoff, 1970). In addition, researchers have found that a probable direction of memory bias in retrospective pre-tests is to disguise past/present differences or to distort remembrance of past attitudes into agreement with present ones (Campbell & Stanley, 1973).

Also, typical pre-morbid assessments tend to focus on individual pathology (e.g., difficulties with the law, drug usage, running away from home). Usually, there is inadequate assessment of the psychosocial context (e.g., economic, social, racial) in which the behaviors occurred, and whether the behaviors may be as explainable by environmental as by individual factors. Finally, there is usually inadequate assessment of the presence or absence of positive pre-trauma factors (demonstrated parental affection, positive task performance, self-concepts, etc.) Pre- and post-trauma differences in such positive factors may be good indicators of the possible impact of the trauma on such factors.

Immediate Pre-trauma Psychosocial Context

An area often overlooked in initial or ongoing assessment of PTSD is the immediate pre-trauma psychosocial context of the survivor and assessment of possibly long-standing or disrupted behavioral and attitudinal patterns. What is the survivor's age and psychological development at the time of the trauma? For example, has the client ever lived away from home? Perhaps the client is still struggling with adolescent issues, attempting to deal with identity versus identity confusion, and intimacy versus isolation, a process which was disrupted at the time of the traumatic event—a profile not atypical of the Vietnam combat veteran (Wilson, 1980a).

Similarly, while shame and guilt are prevalent among almost all rape victims, the intensity of these symptoms is at least partly a function of marital status, age, and life stage. These factors also appear to be differentially related to other post-rape reactions, such as (revived) concerns about separation, independence, and adequacy by the younger rape victim (Notman & Nadelson, 1976).

The Traumatic Event and Immediate (Emergency) Coping Attempts

There are important areas of assessment regarding the trauma itself and the individual's experience of the traumatic event.

Objective factors. One area concerns objective factors—the frequency, intensity, duration, and nature of the trauma. Was it a single, brief incident; was it a protracted series of clearly identified incidents or events; or was it perhaps a culmination of a number of experiences, no one of which stood out? In addition, was it a natural trauma (e.g., floods, typhoons, etc.) or human-induced—caused or perceived as caused by humans—such as rape, terrorist actions, prisoners of war, etc.

Human-induced trauma may have quite different ramifications than do natural disasters for the experiences of survivors and the onset of psychiatric symptoms (Green, Wilson, & Lindy, this volume). Natural disasters, as Figley (1979) has noted, are perceived both by the survivor and others as "acts of fate" or the result of pure chance. Therefore, the likelihood of self- or externally derived responsibility for having caused the trauma or otherwise being responsible for experiencing the trauma, is reduced. For example, Frederick (1980) states that survivors of human-induced trauma, in contrast to victims of natural disasters, typically experience guilt about the plight of other survivors. They also express 1) guilt about not preventing the trauma; 2) identification with the aggressor; 3) rejection by others; 4) humiliation; 5) suspicions by others toward the genuineness of presenting complaints; and 6) belief by others that the trauma was at least partly their fault. Finally, the gender of the survivor may play a critical role in both the stressors experienced and in the particular content and manifestations of post-trauma symptoms. For example, women Vietnam veterans have been exposed to stressors both in Vietnam and afterwards that are similar to (e.g., exposure to life-threatening stressors) and different from (e.g., sexual harrassment) those experienced by their male counterparts (Jacobs, 1983; Paul & O'Neill, 1983; Schnaier, 1982).

There also appear to be differing symptomatology among survivors of different kinds of human-induced trauma. For example, it has been reported that among rape victims, those raped by a stranger typically develop generalized fears of the unfamiliar, whereas "date rape" victims (persons raped by a date, an acquaintance, or someone previously known to the victim) typically manifest symptoms of loss of trust and integrity in friendship, and guilt (Seligman, Huck, Joseph, Namuth, et al., 1984).

Krupnick and Horowitz (1981) classified PTSD stressors into two categories—bereavement and personal injury. The symptoms most often found among trauma patients were related to bereavement (loss of significant other); they included sadness over loss, and discomfort over discovered personal vulnerability. In contrast, personal injury trauma most often included symptoms of fear of repetition of the event, and feelings of responsibility. Rage at the source of the trauma figured prominently in both bereavement and personal injury. The predominance of rage also was found in a research study of three hospital-based therapy groups with Vietnam veterans. Rage by far was the most prominent symptom dealt with in all three groups; it ranked as one of the three top symptoms discussed in 67% of the 81 total sessions. The second most prominent symptom discussed (in 44% of the sessions) was issues of impulse control, which frequently was associated with rage impulses (Scurfield, Corker, Gongla, & Hough, 1984).

Typically, a combat veteran may have experienced both bereavement and personal injury trauma, plus two other factors: repeated exposure to death, dying, and gross physical trauma; and being an agent or perpetrator of trauma. In this author's Vietnam and subsequent clinical experiences, repeated exposure to any of these four factors is typically manifested in intrusive imagery and constricted affect; in addition, repeated exposure to death and physical trauma also is manifested typically in phobic symptomatology, whereas the latter (having been an agent of trauma) typically manifests guilt, issues of personal responsibility, rage, and preoccupation with fear of loss of, or actual loss of impulse control.

Active/passive role. A second area of inquiry concerns the active/passive role of the survivor during the trauma itself, and immediately afterwards (Figley, 1983). Did the survivor act as a helpless victim, vengeful friend, calculating survivor, or out of control? What alternative roles were open to the survivor? A typical concentration camp survivor learned to be utterly passive in external behavior in order to survive. A combat veteran perhaps had a number of roles available, or only one. What impact does the role that was performed, and the actions that were pursued or not pursued, play in the person's recollection of the trauma and accompanying cognitions and feelings about self-blame and responsibility? Are the perceptions of behaviors that were taken, or not taken, accurate? Such inquiry can tell much about the specific meaning and impact of the trauma to the individual at the time, and subsequently, and identify key conflictual areas that require therapeutic interventions.

Idiosyncratic meaning of the trauma. The third area of inquiry concerns the idiosyncratic meaning of the stressor to the individual. For example, the "first kill" for one combat veteran may have been traumatic; for a second veteran it may have been a quite thrilling and not necessarily traumatic experience.

Immediate post-trauma reactions. A common misconception is that if psychiatric stress reactions do not occur during or soon after the trauma, then any subsequent psychological symptomatology is not related to the trauma per se. This is simply not true. Clinical experiences strongly suggest that there is a range of behaviors possible during or soon after the traumatic event among survivors who later manifest PTSD symptoms. Some persons collapse on the spot; others collapse once refuge is attained; some "freeze" and are literally immobilized; still others "click" into a machine-like state and efficiently carry through in their actions; others enter with emotions raging. If there is a "universal" response, it is the denial or numbing during the trauma that continues afterwards for a period of several days or weeks, an apparent latency period following the emergency period of the trauma (Figley, 1983). This pattern is typical of *acute* PTSD (Horowitz, 1981), whereas a latency period of months, years, or decades will occur in chronic or delayed cases.

Post-trauma Psychosocial Context and Reactions

Psychosocial context. Post-trauma readjustment appears to be inextricably linked with socioeconomic and other environmental factors that may impinge upon the survivor. A female rape victim, or female Vietnam veteran, for example, may find herself in a post-trauma environment that is severely sexist. Issues of self-worth, rage, feeling betrayed or abused, and other lingering reactions to the trauma may become exacerbated by similar reactions to such sexist conditions; likewise, the reactions of Vietnam veterans (and perhaps particularly ethnic minority veterans) exposed (or reexposed) after Vietnam to such stressors as racism, severe unemployment conditions, and/or discrimination because they are Vietnam veterans and/or because of their minority status. Assessment of such environmental conditions is critical to a thorough understanding of the readjustment process and possible exacerbation or prolonging of post-trauma stress symptoms.

On the other hand, some studies and readjustment counseling experiences with Vietnam veterans suggest that the presence of positive post-Vietnam social, familial, and other environmental supports can be critical to the amelioration of some of the impact of war-related trauma (Egendorf et al., 1981; Keane & Fairbank, 1983). The *Legacies of Vietnam* study also showed relationships between race and level of combat exposure, a smaller (versus urban) community setting, and the incidence of some post-Vietnam psychological symptoms (Egendorf et al., 1981). Finally, post-Vietnam symptoms and readjustment difficulties of women Vietnam veterans have been both similar to and different from those manifested by male Vietnam veterans, e.g., there are unique gender-specific as well as other types of stressors and subsequent symptomatology stemming at least in part both from experiences as women in Vietnam and as women Vietnam veterans (Jacobs, 1983; Paul & O'Neill, 1983; Schnaier, 1982). Thus, it is imperative to assess the possible impact of race, sex, social class, family support, economic and other environmental conditions on the readjustment of trauma survivors. Finally, there have been specific clinical and other deprogramming interventions soon after the trauma with survivor populations such as prisoners of war, the Iranian hostages, and rape victims (Figley, 1983). Such interventions appear to have a positive effect in preventing or lessening the severity of post-trauma symptoms.

Symptoms and reactions. Post-trauma symptoms and reactions can include one or more of a common set of symptoms. The particular configuration of symptoms is at least partly a function of the nature of the trauma itself, psychosocial conditions before and after the trauma, plus unique elements about the person. The major emotional states, or themes, that occur include various combinations of symptoms, behaviors and cognitions, any or all of which one should be alert to in assessing and treating PTSD.

Clinical experiences indicate that denial/numbing and intrusive/repetitive thoughts or memories are universal responses to trauma (Horowitz, Wilner, & Alvarez, 1979) and in and of themselves are not pathological. Probably all survivors of trauma experience at least some unpleasant aftereffects for a time-limited period, or in fairly tolerable doses: occasional sleep disturbances/terror or violence-laden nightmares, graphic and negative remembrances of the trauma, surges of painful emotions (or, conversely, blunted affect that may be in alternation with emotional surges), and/or avoidance of stimuli that arouse recollections of the event. Therefore, in order to differentiate between a "disordered" and a "normal" stress recovery process, there are at least two additional factors to consider besides the presence of PTSD symptoms. One factor is the *degree of control* over and/or preoccupation with the intrusive/repetitive thoughts. Indeed, as Horowitz (1981) states, the clinician must especially inquire about the degree of control over (or preoccupation with) such thoughts and images, as it is highly unlikely that such information will be volunteered. Related to the degree of control over intrusive imagery is a second area of inquiry—the severity of impact of post-trauma symptoms on *spheres of functioning*, e.g., social relations, occupation, leisure activities. A person may have occasional nightmares about a trauma but they remain fairly discrete experiences and do not have an appreciable or intolerable negative impact on functioning.

There also are several other important related areas of inquiry (for a

TABLE 1
Post-trauma Reactions and Symptoms

1) Fear of repetition of the original trauma, including recurrence of the actual event or intrusive thoughts concerning the trauma.
2) Fear of being hurt similar to the victim.
3) Fear of loss of control over aggressive impulses, including withdrawal or rituals to avoid aggressive expression.
4) Discomfort over vulnerability concerning both failure to prevent the trauma, and difficulties that follow the trauma.
5) Rage at the source, toward any figure who might be blamed for responsibility for the trauma, toward any persons who died, or toward any persons who are associated with the trauma.
6) Rage at those exempted from the trauma, or at those exempted from bereavement.
7) Discomfort over aggressive impulses toward anyone connected in actuality or symbolically to the personal frustrations triggered by the trauma.
8) Guilt over self-responsibility for not preventing the trauma.
9) Survivor guilt, "I survived and — didn't"; and other actions performed or not performed to survive.
10) Sadness over loss of another person, or of aspects of the self that have been lost, e.g., innocence, trust in the goodness of humanity, etc.
11) Isolation, alienation, paranoia—oftentimes directed toward authority figures.
12) Addictive disorders, including substance abuse or attempts to self-medicate or otherwise deny the impact of the trauma; thrills, risks and gambling—including gambling with fate as in chronic high-speed driving.
13) Somatic complaints—tension headaches or pains in the head, migraines, low-back syndrome, ulcers or other stomach complaints, irritable colon, hypertension, etc.
14) Significant life-style changes and/or loss of or confusion concerning values, direction and meaning in life. May be manifested through chronic (post-trauma) underachievement, "wandering" life-style, outbursts in antisocial activity, marked changes in relatedness to the country and its institutions.

Symptoms or themes 1–10 are taken mostly intact from Krupnick & Horowitz (1981). Themes 11–14 have been documented by various writers; for example, see Blank (1982).

detailed identification of specific inquiries regarding the military history of Vietnam veterans, see Scurfield and Blank, 1985).

1) *Hypernormal, excessive Type A, or obsessive/compulsive behavior* may be evident where one's self-identity and self-esteem are overly dominated by and involved in one sphere of functioning (e.g., employment) at the expense of another (e.g., meaningful, intimate relationships). This may be due in part to avoidance of coming to terms with unresolved trauma-related issues (Scurfield & Smith, 1982). This author typically has ob-

served such behavior as "white-collar PTSD" among middle- and upper middle-class veterans.

2) *Conscious attempts to cope with the trauma and its aftermath.* What were they? Did they seem to work initially, and/or were there supportive resources such as significant others available to assist the survivor? Or, were environmental factors hostile or non-supportive? How did the survivor perceive and respond to such factors then and now?

3) *The occurrence of additional trauma prior or subsequent to the identified trauma.* Have there been subsequent or additional trauma, or catastrophic events, that have occurred in the person's life? If so, what, if anything, is the interactional or cumulative impact on the course of PTSD? Does a second trauma or set of stressors exacerbate conflicts primarily related to the original trauma and/or are additional conflicts generated? For example, it is not uncommon for a subsequent trauma (such as severe illness of one's child or death of a friend) to exacerbate and apparently prolong war-related stress symptoms such as rage and grief.

A "silent rape-reaction" has been described, where a current rape reactivates the victim's reaction to a prior rape or molestation trauma (about which there has been little or no discussion with others) (Burgess & Holmstrom, 1974).

The clinical experiences of Horowitz and colleagues suggest that at some distant time from the originally identified trauma, a common pattern is for there to be a "series of tumbling relationships" (1981). For example, there is an unexpected death of a parent and the funeral occurs in January; in March a love relationship is disrupted; in May or June the person comes in presenting bereavement and other symptoms.

Finally, a pre-morbid history of traumata may become intertwined in an adult trauma. This author treated a Vietnam veteran who had a childhood of severe physical abuse by both parents, and who experienced several traumatic combat experiences. He presented with a recurring nightmare of being chased by shadowy figures clad in black, shooting at him in a forest-like setting. A Gestalt dreamwork session resulted in his completing the dream to the point where he discovered that the heretofore faceless figures clad in black had the face of his father. Subsequent therapy dealt with his PTSD both from his childhood and Vietnam.

4) *Delayed symptom onset.* Clinical experiences with Vietnam veterans strongly suggest that even in those cases where there is an apparent lengthy delay in onset or recurrence of symptoms that can be readily identified as linked to the trauma, there are usually "trouble signs" that appear within the first two or three years following the trauma. For

example, while veterans may not experience nightmares that have Vietnamese or combat scenes in them, they may experience nightmares that contain elements of death, dying, or threat to self, or that are accompanied by anxiety, fear or other feelings that *approximate the feeling states* at the time of the trauma.

Other common and not immediately apparent post-trauma symptoms may include a history of volatile work and primary relationships, social isolation that often is masked by jobs such as security guard or groundskeeping, fear of loss of control of violent urges, and other substantial alterations in life-style (in contrast to pre-combat functioning). There is one research study to date that also suggests the apparent early and continued manifestation of PTSD symptoms among Vietnam veterans. Forty-seven Hispanic Vietnam veterans, from both clinical and non-clinical populations (out of a total sample of 99), met all DSM-III inclusionary PTSD symptoms within at least one calendar year. Fully 87.5% of the PTSD-positive veterans first met such criteria during their period of Vietnam service (25.5%) or during the initial year after leaving Vietnam (61.7%). Eighty-seven percent also continued to manifest the full PTSD diagnostic inclusionary criteria each year thereafter, up until the present time (Hough, Gongla, Scurfield, Corker, & Carr, 1983). On the other hand, studies of concentration camp survivors suggest years of apparently (external) symptom-free functioning among a number of survivors who subsequently manifested PTSD symptoms (Strom et al., 1962).

5) *Significant positive outcomes may have occurred.* Are they related to the trauma? For example, Wilson's (1980b) perspective of the Vietnam stress syndrome includes heightened sensitivity to values of justice, fair play, and being treated with dignity and respect. In addition, this writer would suggest several other possible positive outcomes of exposure to trauma, particularly to the Vietnam experience (while these factors may not be crucial to an initial diagnosis of PTSD, they can be critical to ongoing assessment for treatment purposes):

(a) comradeship may have occurred at an extraordinary level of intensity and bonding including heroic, self-sacrificing behaviors that exemplified love and caring for and by one's cohorts (even though this often is overlaid by the sense of loss, and preoccupation with the negatives that occurred);

(b) a healthy questioning and/or reaffirmation of one's values and the meaning and direction in one's life;

(c) the continued ability to maintain a sense of integrity and proficiency even under very trying circumstances;

(d) heightened sensitization to the horrors that individuals, groups,

and society are capable of initiating, promoting or justifying;
(e) heightened sensitization to political behavior and dehumanization in various systems—military, governmental, health care, etc;
(f) the development of very strong convictions and the willingness to act on them; and
(g) it can be a sign of health *not* to forget the trauma experience and all of its ramifications on the difficult questions of individual responsibility versus that of the group versus that of society. Other studies affirm some of the lasting positive impacts of the Vietnam experience, at least as identified by male and female Vietnam veterans in survey research studies (Card, 1983; Schnaier, 1982).

Also, there are instances where trauma experiences have precipitated marked changes in outlook, expansiveness of world view and profound insights, perceptions, and religious or quasi-religious experiences. Viktor Frankl's experiences during and following concentration camp internment are a case in point (1959). It is important to note that *no* apparent pre- and post-trauma changes, particularly in the face of protracted or repeated trauma, or in the absence of *any* post-trauma intrusive thoughts or imagery, may well be a sign that denial or numbing is operative. Finally, assessment for forensic purposes requires yet additional areas of inquiry and consideration, to include specific exploration of the possible relationship between criminal acts and prior exposure to psychological trauma of combat (Lipkin, Scurfield, & Blank, 1983).

FACTORS THAT PRECIPITATE PTSD SYMPTOMS

Factors or stimuli may occur that in external appearance or qualities are similar to the trauma, or that are associated with the trauma, although initially, the survivor may not make a conscious connection. An example would be a person who lost both parents in an automobile crash suffers an onset of bereavement symptoms about his parents the week after he separates from his wife four months later. Or a Vietnam veteran who becomes enraged and has recurring nightmares about Vietnam after watching extensive television coverage of the hero's welcome for returning Iranian hostages (in stark contrast to that accorded most Vietnam veterans).

Events may occur that are not similar externally to the original trauma; however, they are "echoes of the original trauma" (Haley, 1978), and often are a clue to the aspects of the trauma that remain most conflictual to the person. Such factors provoke an intensity of emotion similar to that experienced during the trauma. For Vietnam veterans, as time passes after Vietnam, precipitants tend to cluster around issues of 1) self-worth, rage, betrayal, shame and/or guilt, and/or 2) intimacy, primary relationships, and child rearing. For example, a veteran goes into an almost murderous rage at the crying of his infant and this, in turn, triggers flashbacks about having been involved in the killing of children in Vietnam (Haley, 1978). Similar onsets of symptoms decades later have been reported about World War II veterans (Christenson, Walker, Ross, & Maltbie, 1981). Finally, "anniversary dates" of traumatic occurrences may be a recurring precipitant of at least some level of symptomatology (Arnold, 1985a), e.g., the date one was raped, or seriously wounded in combat.

INTERVIEWING DYNAMICS IN ASSESSMENT AND INITIAL CONTACTS WITH TRAUMA SURVIVORS

There are several important factors to consider in the actual interview sessions with survivors of trauma. First, there will almost certainly be initial ambivalence on the part of the survivor to discuss the trauma. This may be due to prior negative experiences in attempting to discuss the traumatic experience and/or a fear of losing control including 1) being unable to stop crying, 2) exploding with rage, 3) "going crazy," or 4) being engulfed again in the horror of the event. Also, there may be strong negative feelings about non-survivors, and about not being understood or accepted. Indeed, survivors frequently manifest covert and/or overt anger, bitterness, and/or distrust toward non-survivors, including clinicians. After all, why should the survivor trust or talk to you? What is your interest in or ability to understand what it was or is like?

Institutional Transference

Institutional transference often is a paramount issue, particularly when the assessment is related, or the survivor believes it may be related, to a claim for financial compensation; it is, therefore, ideal to clearly separate assessment for the purpose of financial compensation and assessment for the purpose of engagement in treatment. Also, it is important to probe the survivor's prior experiences in communicating with others about the trauma, and feelings/perceptions/projections concerning the clinician as assessor. For example, many Vietnam veterans seeking mental health services have found that clinicians typically do not systematically include a comprehensive inquiry into the veteran's military history as part of the initial diagnostic work-up or even in the ongoing treatment assessment. Such a systematic inquiry is crucial (for a comprehensive guide to the military history see Scurfield & Blank, 1985). Hence, veterans fequently feel that their military experiences have been "discounted"; and subsequent anger and resistance toward mental health professionals is a common result. Viewing or experiencing the clinician as a "typical government employee," or as a "typical shrink who wants to know about my relationship with my mother," usually will also contribute to feelings of anger toward the clinician.

Vacuums in History

A trauma survivor may not yet be ready to acknowledge the possible impact of the trauma, let alone be able or willing to discuss it in any detail. Thus, one must be alert to vacuums in history, areas that perhaps can only be adequately explored following engagement in a therapeutic trust relationship. For example, Haley states that in interviewing Vietnam combat veterans, the one thing that a clinician never believes at face value is when a veteran tells the clinician that combat had no effect on him; however, it would probably not be productive to challenge this initially, until a trust relationship begins to develop (Haley, 1974). The axiom "diagnosis follows treatment," may be more characteristic of PTSD than any other clinical diagnosis.

Open and Affective Engagement With the Client

Clinical experiences with Vietnam veterans argue against the classic detached, "blank screen" therapeutic approach, and in favor of the therapist's willingness to share affectively, to get in touch with the clinician's own destructiveness, and having some comfort in dealing with atrocity-producing and other violent or aggressive behaviors (Howard, 1976). It is this author's experience that a "detached, objective" demeanor, a routine approach to obtaining a pre-trauma history, or an authoritarian approach (Arnold, 1985b), especially during acute symptom exacerbation or early stages of therapy, are particularly likely to arouse issues of institutional transference on the part of Vietnam veterans. Such issues are likely to arise when the clinician is employed at a government facility, with or without the behaviors described above!

Clinician Countertransference

There is one other critical element—the clinician. Where does the therapist stand concerning trauma, and survivors, or concerning survivors of this particular kind of trauma? Does clinical contact stir up ambivalent, negative, or moral/judgmental feelings in the therapist, including having to deal with feelings of aggressiveness, grief, horror, rage, or loss of control, and ambivalence to look at his or her own capacity to perform similar acts under similar conditions (Haley, 1974, in press)? It is very easy to become caught up in one's own feelings and thoughts, and literally ignore the impact of the trauma on the survivor (Williams, 1980). To be able to "objectively" facilitate the survivor's search for understanding concerning the impact of the trauma and at the same time to make affective contact necessary to sustain and facilitate the assessment and treatment process, are a difficult but necessary tandem to achieve. Countertransference issues are equally critical when the clinician also is a trauma survivor. For example, the clinician who is also still dealing with unresolved trauma-related dynamics may respond by projecting anger or other feelings onto the client, or feel the need to take care of his or her own issues rather than focus on the client. On the other hand, selective sharing of the therapist's own trauma-related experiences can be very facilitative to the therapeutic process.

TREATMENT IMPLICATIONS

Several models of a post-traumatic stress recovery process have been described (Burgess & Holmstrom, 1974; Figley, 1978, 1979, 1983; Horowitz, 1979; Smith, in press). There appear to be four key factors in such a process:

1) the traumatic event and the immediate emergency coping mechanisms, e.g., denial or numbing, flight or fight;
2) the subsequent intrusion into awareness or reexperiencing of negative aspects of the trauma;
3) coping attempts to control, reduce or eliminate the disturbing

intrusions or reexperiencing, usually involving an interplay between denial and intrusion (Horowitz et al., 1979)*; and,
4) the integration or resolution of the trauma experience and its positive and negative impacts on the self and relationships with significant others, and perhaps with society as well.

In order to facilitate the stress recovery process, there are, of course, various treatment approaches (crisis intervention, psychoanalytic, behavioral, experiential, psychopharmacologic), and treatment modalities (individual, group, family) that have been described. The vast majority of such intervention approaches and modalities described in the literature are in an out-patient, clinical, or Vet Center setting. There are only a handful of descriptions of in-patient or residential treatment milieus (Adams, 1982; Arnold, 1985b; Ben-Yaker, 1982; Berman, Price & Gusman, 1982; Grinker & Spiegel, 1945; Williams & Jackson, 1972), and one description of a day-treatment setting (Brown & Huppenbauer, 1982) and of a veterans-in-prison program (Pentland & Scurfield, 1982).

It is useful to first briefly describe interventions with acute PTSD, and then to elaborate on the five principles that this author identifies as primary to the treatment of PTSD, regardless of the treatment approach or setting.

Acute PTSD Interventions

Interventions in the acute phase of post-trauma reactions with rape victims (Burgess & Holmstrom, 1974) generally follow a crisis intervention model (Caplan, 1964; Parad, 1965). There are basic assumptions that the rape is a crisis, the victim was functioning "normally" prior to the rape, the treatment is oriented to return the woman to her previous level of functioning as soon as possible, and there is active outreach to make clinical contact with the victim (Burgess & Holmstrom, 1974).

This author served as a social work officer in 1968–69 on one of the two U.S. Army psychiatric teams in Vietnam. Military psychiatry interventions with psychiatric casualties were similar to those described above for rape victims. The soldier was treated as close to his or her duty station as possible, there was a clear expectation that the soldier

---

* This author also postulates that there is another dynamic that is prevalent, if not universal, among survivors of human-induced trauma: an interplay between rage/anger and grief/sadness (this dynamic is discussed in more detail in the next section, Integration of the Trauma Experience).

would return to duty, and the soldier was returned to duty as quickly as possible following restabilization.

In acute crisis intervention, then, the objective is to restore the traumatized survivor to a pre-trauma level of functioning as quickly as possible. This is accomplished by taking advantage of the rapid therapeutic gains that can be accomplished during the time-limited period when the person's normal defenses are relatively permeable or weakened (Caplan, 1964). As the disequilibrium gradually subsides, some form of reorganization takes place. This reorganized state is either adaptive and integrative, or maladaptive and possibly destructive. Intervention *before maladaptive* reorganization is the purpose of the crisis intervention (Golan, 1974).

Longer Term PTSD Interventions and the Five Treatment Principles of PTSD Intervention

Interventions to address longer term effects of trauma are, of course, more complex than in acute treatment. Chronic, and to a lesser extent, delayed PTSD usually involve not only PTSD *per se*, but also associated symptomatology and maladaptive coping patterns that have developed over time, at least in part as a result of the survivor's struggle to cope with, or attempt to avoid, unresolved PTSD symptomatology. Such interventions can perhaps best be discussed within the context of what this author perceives to be the five key principles in the treatment of stress disorders: 1) establishment of the therapeutic trust relationship; 2) education regarding the stress recovery process; 3) stress management/reduction; 4) regression back to or a reexperiencing of the trauma; and 5) integration of the trauma experience. These principles are particularly relevant to a primarily psychodynamic treatment process, and to chronic and delayed PTSD. (The reader is encouraged to review particularly descriptive accounts of the therapeutic processes for individual psychotherapy [Parson, 1984] and rap groups [Smith, 1980a, 1980b].)

Therapeutic Trust Relationship

As indicated previously in regard to dynamics in interviewing, unusually strong authority and countertransference issues are paramount. Indeed, many clinicians feel that the core of the therapeutic effort is the establishment of a trusting and sharing relationship (Haley, 1984). It is imperative that the therapist continually monitor and confront if necessary his or her own reactions to the client's experience, including the possibility that the client will share information that the therapist will be unable or unwilling to process (Haley, 1978; Parson, 1984). Finally, projection of anger by trauma survivors onto persons who may be trying to help them is not unusual, and negative countertransference feelings may well be evoked. This appears to be particularly true for survivors of human-induced trauma such as rape (Notman & Nadelson, 1976) and Vietnam veterans.

Education Regarding the Stress Recovery Process

It is essential that the survivor be clearly and quickly educated about salient aspects of the stress recovery process, and reeducated about these same aspects at later times during the clinical interventions. Among the most important aspects to bring to the awareness of the survivor are:

1) Trauma is such a catastrophic experience that it can produce post-trauma symptomatology in almost anyone, seemingly regardless of a person's pre-trauma background;

2) It is expected and normal to have intrusive imagery, numbing, rage, grief, or other symptomatology following a trauma; this symptomatology may appear during, soon after and/or much later than the trauma. Indeed, it would be unusual *not* to have at least some "psychological aftershocks" following a trauma;

3) Many clinical experiences with trauma survivors also indicate that some survivors continue to have significant post-trauma symptomatology years or even decades following the trauma (usually when there has not been effective counseling assistance provided);

4) It is not unusual to fear that one will lose control of some emotions (crying, rage, etc.) sometime following a trauma; this does not mean that "you are going crazy," but only that you have some important things to work through about the trauma and its impact on you;

5) The symptomatology "usually gets worse before it gets better" once you start focusing on the trauma and symptoms in therapy; this appears to be a necessary step to work through what you have to work through, and it is only temporary. I will be with you throughout this process;

6) PTSD definitely *is* responsive to treatment;

7) Some symptomatology may not go away completely or forever. After all, there are a number of experiences in your life, both

negative and positive, that you literally will never completely forget. Memories or feelings about such experiences, as you know, may suddenly appear for no apparent reason, or may be triggered by something that seems to be directly connected, or to have no particular connection, to the past traumatic experience. However, upon closer scrutiny, usually it is possible to find a connection between something in your current life and the appearance of memories or feelings from the past. That will be part of what we will learn more about here, together;

8) Post-trauma symptomatology can at the very least be controlled and reduced in severity or frequency of occurrence, and possibly extinguished. In addition, you will gain understanding of what has been and is happening and might happen to you—and what you can do about it;

9) Finally, though this may be difficult to believe right now, you may even find that there will be some positive benefits to you and your life through the experiences you have had and your willingness now to face and work through what you must work through. For example, you must be very strong to have experienced what you experienced and be here, talking to me about it today.

Stress Management/Reduction

A trauma survivor with PTSD symptoms typically may present what appears to be almost uncontrollable and oftentimes multiple sources of impinging symptomatology and functional difficulties. This usually is the situation both when "pure" or PTSD-only symptoms are presented in a crisis context, or where both PTSD-specific symptoms and other ingrained maladaptive coping patterns are present. A first order of intervention is to help the survivor decide what will be worked on, and in what order and to give reassurance that there will be time set aside to work on the various concerns.

Second, it is essential that the survivor be helped to explore his or her prior coping behaviors and to sort out which ones have worked, and under what conditions. Since the survivor always has at least some coping tactics that have been effective some or most of the time, the clinician should enhance the client's utilization of these already familiar, and at least partially effective, coping techniques. In addition, the survivor can be assisted to refine and add new coping techniques as may be necessary. As more effective self-controls are instituted, the survivor then will be able to devote more attention to the longer standing issues that are directly related to the trauma and/or that have been aggravated by the trauma experience.

Clarification, control, reduction and/or stopping of distressing symptoms is, of course, crucial, particularly as it concerns intrusive thoughts and images, nightmares and other sleep disturbances, fear of loss of control over rage and grief impulses, stimuli that arouse recollections of the trauma, and paranoid-type thinking. Various behavioral techniques seem particularly effective: imaginal flooding and implosive therapy (Black & Keane, 1982; Fairbank & Keane, 1982; Keane & Kaloupek, 1982; Miniszek, 1984); systematic desensitization (Cellucci & Lawrence, 1978; Schindler, 1980); other behavioral techniques such as thought stopping, cognitive restructuring, behavioral bibliotherapy (Marafiote, 1980; Parson, 1984), and establishing "hierarchical routes of behavior" to improve impulse control (Horowitz & Solomon, 1975). There is some evidence to suggest that flooding may be most effective when used in conjunction with other treatment modalities (Miniszek, 1984).

Other authors have described success in utilizing hypnosis (Brende & Benedict, 1980; Spiegel, 1981), psychoanalysis (Haley, 1974, 1978, in press), a combination of psychoanalysis and behavioral (Parson, 1984), narcosynthesis (Kolb, 1985), abreaction (Grinker & Spiegel, 1945), and a multifaceted approach of pharmacotherapy, group or individual therapy and behavioral techniques (Friedman, 1981). Some success with psychopharmacological treatment has been described (Arnold, 1985b), especially in the treatment of sleep disorders (Friedman, 1981; Hogben & Cornfield, 1981; Ware, 1983). However, by and large, judicious restraint in the usage of medications is strongly recommended (Arnold, 1985; Van der Kolk, 1983; Yost, 1980).

It is important to note that there is only one research outcome study (Brooks & Scarano, 1982) known to this author on alternative treatment approaches with PTSD—a modest outcome evaluation study among two groups of Vietnam veterans. One group (N-8) participated in individual treatment with mental health professionals at a Vet Center, and a second group (N-10) received instruction in and practiced Transcendental Meditation (T.M.). Findings indicated that veterans in the individual treatment group showed essentially no significant change in any of the symptom outcome measures; the group who practiced T.M. regularly showed significant positive change in all of the outcome measures (e.g., depression, anxiety, insomnia, family problems) with the exception of employment. There was some evidence to suggest that a combination of T.M. and individual treatment was indicated. More definitive outcome evaluation studies of alternative treatment approaches remain a critical need in PTSD treatment research.

Regression Back to or Reexperiencing of the Trauma

Perhaps the central purpose to be achieved in the treatment of stress disorder is to facilitate the (eventual) fullest possible reexperiencing and recollecting of the trauma in the here and now; in this process, underlying feelings and conflicts that have been submerged and were heretofore unavailable to the client are uncovered (Parson, 1984). It is essential, however, that the survivor be guided through "tolerable doses of awareness," preventing the extremes of denial on the one hand and intrusive-repetitiousness on the other. In a psychodynamic treatment approach, potentially overwhelming affective responses require active interventions to allow interpretations and clarrification of specific fantasies, remembrances and impulse configurations, and to reduce feelings of powerlessness (Horowitz, 1974; Horowitz & Solomon, 1975). Behavioral treatment (such as was identified in the previous section) focuses on techniques to reduce, desensitize or extinguish unwanted or adversive symptoms.

Several of the treatment techniques and approaches identified in the previous section are also relevant to a facilitation of reexperiencing of the trauma, e.g., hypnosis, abreaction, narcosynthesis, "in vivo" techniques (Parson, 1984), and so forth. This author has found Gestalt experiential techniques to be particularly helpful both for resolving recurring nightmares and for promoting a full reexperiencing of the trauma.

Finally, this author postulates that primary to the treatment and recovery process of survivors of human-induced trauma is the interplay that occurs and should be facilitated, between rage or anger and grief or sadness (and/or other strong emotions, especially fear) (Ott & Mc-Greevy, 1984). In this author's experience, an initial treatment focus on rage/anger almost always will uncover grief/sadness as well, and vice versa. For example, Vietnam veterans who are preoccupied with grief and guilt over the loss of close friends in Vietnam will, in the course of the grief work, usually manifest anger at the friend who died, at oneself for one's own possible responsibility for the death, and perhaps at others exempted from the trauma or who the survivor sees as having had any association with the trauma (such as the government or society).

On the other hand, a rape victim who may initially focus on her rage at what occurred will usually also uncover substantial grief over the violation that occurred to her body, her possible (at least temporary) loss of trust in establishing a female/male relationship, etc. The emergence of fear also is not uncommon, e.g., rage reactions as a defense against or avoidance of fear impulses. In conclusion, this author would encourage clinicians to be sensitive to the exploration of what seem to be inextricably linked trauma-related symptoms—grief and rage (and, to a lesser extent, fear)—in the course of facilitating a full reexperiencing of the trauma.

Integration of the Trauma Experience

The "final step" in the stress recovery process is the integration of all aspects of the trauma experience, both positive and negative, with the survivor's notions of who he or she was before, during, and after the trauma experience. This involves accepting full personal responsibility for one's own actions (Smith, 1980a, in press) and understanding what was beyond one's own control. In this regard, clarification and atonement or penance may be crucial in dealing with guilt (Horowitz & Solomon, 1975), particularly among survivors of human-induced trauma, and among Vietnam combat veterans in particular (Smith, 1980a, in press). The guilt issue is critical and complicated when the survivor has been an agent or perpetrator of trauma as well as a victim, e.g., combat veterans who have killed civilians or engaged in "unnecessary" or abusive violence (Laufer et al., this volume; Scurfield, Corker, Gongla, & Hough, 1984). Indeed, frequently some behaviors are inexcusable to the survivor, and "trying to help explain them away" or attempting to justify them can be quite counterproductive to the stress recovery process. Working through such "moral pain" (Marin, 1981) can be an essential part of the treatment.

Finally, the reader is reminded of the potential positive aspects of trauma experiences (identified in an earlier section, Post-Trauma Symptoms and Reactions). As tragic as catastrophic events are, they almost always have some positive aspects as well. For example, one Vietnam veteran client had been preoccupied for years over his sense of personal responsibility for the death of his buddy (he had been temporarily out of Vietnam on an "R&R" trip when his buddy was killed). Through the treatment process and one particularly poignant role play scene where he talked to his dead buddy, he came to acknowledge his previously unspoken love for his lost comrade, the intense bonding that had occurred in their relationship, his capacity for a peer love relationship (something that he had denied to himself ever since Vietnam), at the same time fully acknowledging his grief over the loss. Helping the client to fully experience both the negative and positive aspects of the trauma experience is critical to a full integration of the trauma experience.

Finally, the impact of chronic and delayed PTSD, and perhaps to a somewhat lesser extent, acute PTSD (depending on the nature and circumstances concerning the traumatic experience), on one's social support system (Kadushin, Boulanger & Martin, 1981) is usually significant. Thus, there is a need for the clinician and survivor to address these associated areas of difficulty. Group treatment and family treatment are two modalities that appear particularly suited to this task.

Group Treatment

Group treatment with other survivors is considered by a number of clinicians to be the treatment of choice for PTSD. This modality offers several advantages:

1) reduction of isolation and provision of a sense of community, comfort, and support (network therapy);
2) reduction of feelings of stigma and restoration of self-pride;
3) confrontation by peers that seems more acceptable and reality-oriented because it comes from those with similar extraordinary experiences;
4) the opportunity to process "unfinished business" from the trauma and post-trauma experiences in a supportive and understanding environment; and
5) help to express emotions freely.

Combat Vietnam veteran rap groups also provide a forum to clarify one's values and ideology, obtain a historical/political perspective of the war and one's role in it, and the opportunity to engage in social/political action at the grass roots level (Brende, 1981; Lifton, 1978; Scurfield et al., 1984; Shatan, 1973; Smith, 1980a, 1980b; Walker & Nash, 1981; Williams, 1980; Wilson, 1980b). There also has been at least one report on the special role that an all-women Vietnam veterans group can provide (Jacobs, 1983).

It is crucial for mental health professionals who are leading Vietnam combat veteran rap/therapy groups to be willing to "lay back" and facilitate a flow of peer-initiated interactions. Initially, subtle rather than directive leadership will promote the group's development of trust toward the facilitators. Subsequently, facilitators can gradually introduce "therapy techniques" into the group process (Scurfield et al., 1984). Finally, while discussion of trauma experiences is essential, dwelling on them or ignoring other possible critical factors can allow participants to avoid dealing with current and longer standing life issues (apart from tauma-related issues) and can be used as "excuses" for current behaviors and situations.

It is important to emphasize that the research to date on PTSD treatment, including group therapy, is almost entirely of a clinical narrative or retrospective/descriptive nature (the several previously referenced case studies on behavioral therapy being the exception). The only empirical study on group treatment of PTSD known to the author is an exploratory/descriptive study of the process and content of three Vietnam veteran therapy groups at a VA medical center (Scurfield et al., 1984). This study is important for its documentation of the consistency of findings across three independently run therapy groups in terms of the issues and symptoms dealt with in the groups, the interplay that occurred between current life issues and Vietnam experiences, the therapeutic themes that were the foci of the groups, and specific interventions utilized by the facilitators that suggest incorporation of elements from both traditional "therapy" groups and from "rap" groups to optimize a "rap/therapy" group process.

Family Treatment

It is generally recognized by clinicians experienced in working with trauma survivors that there usually is a substantial impact on the family as well. In spite of this obvious dynamic within the family system, there are relatively few literature references on this matter. There are several reports regarding the impact on the families of concentration camp survivors (Barocas, 1971; Freyberg, 1980; Rustin & Lipsig, 1972; Trossman, 1968) and on the families of rape victims (Notman & Nadelson, 1976). For example, there are rape victims whose spouses became psychologically unable to provide them support following a rape. Such victims have been described as particularly vulnerable to adverse post-rape reactions (Notman & Nadelson, 1976).

There is a small body of mostly theoretical and clinically descriptive literature on the general impact of PTSD on the families of Vietnam veterans (Figley, 1978; Harrington & Jay, 1982; Hogancamp & Figley, 1983; Stanton & Figley, 1978). There are also some descriptions of the specific impact of PTSD on the spouse or partner dyad (Brown, 1984; Carroll, Rueger & Foy, 1983; Palmer & Harris, 1983; Scarano, 1982; Williams, 1980), and on the children of Vietnam veterans (Haley, 1984, in press; Scarano, 1982). Few studies have focused on the impact on and relationship between PTSD and the family (Danieli, this volume; Davis & Friedman, this volume; Silver & Iacono, in press). These studies confirm the descriptive accounts by others of the significant impact of PTSD on the family system, both on the partner and, to a lesser extent, on the child subsystems. Clearly, it should be a routine part of the assessment and treatment planning process to give full consideration to the possible impact of PTSD on the family and appropriate inclusion of one or more other family members as part of the treatment, either concurrently, conjointly, or sequentially to PTSD treatment with the survivor. For example, significant other groups have been quite successful as part of the therapy interventions with Vietnam veterans at Vet Centers (Brown, 1984).

SUMMARY

In summary, assessment and treatment of survivors of trauma are quite challenging tasks. Disagreements, lack of understanding or consensus, and issues abound regarding what are the prominent etiological factors in the development of the disorder; the validity and reliability of the PTSD diagnosis per DSM-III criteria; the validity of a number of findings reported in the literature from a research methodology standpoint; the differentiation between a "normal" and a "disordered" stress recovery process; the course and patterning of various PTSD subtypes; and the relative efficacy of differential treatment approaches.

On the other hand, there is a general consensus that the trauma itself is one of, if not the most important factor to assess, and that a full consideration of pre-trauma, trauma, and post-trauma factors is ideal. In addition, it appears that there are both similarities and differences regarding the nature and course of post-trauma symptomatology in response to various kinds of trauma. Also, very intense and complex transference and countertransference dynamics are present in the assessment and treatment of PTSD. Finally, it is recognized that a clear set of crisis intervention strategies has evolved in the treatment of acute PTSD; for treatment of delayed and chronic PTSD, there appears to be a wide range of treatment strategies, techniques, modalities, and settings that have been reported to have success, by themselves and in various combinations.

If there is any consensus regarding the various treatment approaches

250 · Trauma and Its Wake

that have been utilized, it may be that multimethod approaches to treatment are most widely practiced. The special function that peer group treatment can provide is generally recognized. Finally, while the potential impact of trauma on the family members of trauma survivors has been acknowledged, there is relatively little description of that impact in the literature.

In conclusion, assessment and treatment of PTSD involve a challenging set of factors, including the apparent need for special professional and personal qualities on the part of the clinician. These include the willingness and sensitivity to probe quite directly into various aspects of trauma experiences, the ability to honestly face one's own reactions and those of the survivor to such probes, and the sensitivity to navigate the murky boundaries between uncovering that which the survivor has been trying, oftentimes so desperately, to avoid contact with, and the full integration of the trauma experience into one's current existence. "There are things that cause you to lose your reason or you have none to lose" (Frankl, 1959, p. 18). Indeed, extraordinary events and reactions to them require extraordinary efforts, both by the client and the clinician.

REFERENCES

Adams, M. PTSD: An inpatient treatment unit. *American Journal of Nursing*, 1982, *82*, 1704-1705.

Ader, A. Mental symptoms following head injury. *Archives of Neurology and Psychiatry*, 1945, *53*, 34-44.

American Psychiatric Association. *Diagnostic and statistical manual of mental disorders* (3rd ed.). Washington, D.C.: American Psychiatric Association, 1980.

Archibald H., & Tuddenham, R. Persistent stress reactions after combat. *Archives of General Psychiatry*, 1965, *12*, 475-481.

Arnold, A. Diagnosis and principles of treatment. In S. Sonnenberg, A. Blank, & J. Talbot, (Eds.), *The trauma of war: Stress and recovery in Vietnam veterans*. Washington, D.C.: American Psychiatric Press, 1985a.

Arnold, A. Inpatient treatment of Vietnam veterans with post-traumatic stress disorder. In S. Sonnenberg, A. Blank, & J. Talbot, (Eds.), *The trauma of war: Stress and recovery in Vietnam veterans*. Washington, D.C.: American Psychiatric Press, 1985b.

Atkinson, R., Sparr, L., Sheff, A., White, R., & Fitzsimmons, J. Diagnosis of post-traumatic stress disorder in Vietnam veterans: Preliminary findings. *American Journal of Psychiatry*, 1984, *141*(5), 694-696.

Baraga, E., Van Kampen, M., Watson, C., Czekala, J., & Kuhne, A. Defining post-traumatic stress disorder: Are the DSM-III criteria necessary and sufficient? Unpublished manuscript that provides preliminary data concerning DSM-III PTSD criteria for an in-patient substance abusing population. Veterans Administration Medical Center, St. Cloud, MN, 1983.

Barocas, H. Manifestations of concentration camp effects on the second generation. *American Journal of Psychiatry*, 1971, *130*, 820-821.

Ben-Yaker, M. The influence of various therapeutic milieus on the course of group treatments in two groups of soldiers with combat reaction. *Series in Clinical and Community Psychology*, 1982, *8*, 151-155.

Berman, S., Price, S., & Gusman, F. An inpatient program for Vietnam combat veterans in a Veterans Administration hospital. *Hospital and Community Psychiatry*, 1982, *3*, 919-922.

Black, J., & Keane, T. Implosive therapy in the treatment of combat related fears in a World War II veteran. *Journal of Behaviorial Therapy & Experimental Psychiatry*, 1982, *13*(2), 163-65.

Blanchard, E., Kolb, L., Pall Meyer, T., & Gerardi, R. A psychophysiological study of post-traumatic stress disorder in Vietnam veterans. *Psychiatric Quarterly*, 1983, *54*, 220-229.

Blank, A., Stresses of war: The example of Vietnam. In L. Goldberger, & S. Breznitz, (Eds.), *Handbook of stress.* New York: The Free Press, 1982, 631-644.

Borus, J. Incidence of maladjustment in Vietnam returnees. *Archives of General Psychiatry*, 1974, *30*, 554-557.

Boulanger, G., Kadushin, C., Rinoskopf, D., Juliano, M. et al. Post-traumatic stress disorder: A valid diagnosis? Paper presented at the American Psychological Association meeting, Washington, D.C., 1982.

Brende, J. Combined individual and group therapy for Vietnam veterans. *International Journal of Group Psychotherapy*, 1981, *31*, 367-378.

Brende, J., & Benedict, B. The Vietnam combat delayed stress syndrome: Hypnotherapy of "dissociative" symptoms. *American Journal of Clinical Hypnosis*, 1980, *23*, 34-40.

Brooks, J., & Scarano, T. Transcendental meditation in treatment of post-Vietnam veteran adjustment. Paper presented at the National Conference on the Treatment of Post-Vietnam Stress Disorder, Cincinnati, OH, Oct. 19, 1982.

Brown, P. Legacies of a War: Treatment considerations with Vietnam veterans and their families. *Social Work*, July-August, 1984, *29*, 372-379.

Brown, S., & Huppenbauer, S. Treatment of post-traumatic stress disorder of Vietnam veterans in a partial hospitalization center. Proceedings of the Annual Conference on Partial Hospitalization. American Association for Partial Hospitalization, Louisville, KY, 1982.

Burgess, A., & Holmstrom, L. Rape trauma syndrome. *American Journal of Psychiatry*, 1974, *131*, 981-986.

Campbell, D., & Stanley, J. *Experiemental and quasi-experimental designs for research.* Chicago, IL: Rand McNally, 1973.

Caplan, G. *Principles of preventive psychiatry.* New York: Basic Books, 1964.

Card, J. *Lives after Vietnam: The personal impact of military service.* Lexington, MA: Lexington Books, 1983.

Carroll, E., Rueger, D., & Foy, D. The marital problems of Vietnam combat veterans. Paper presented at the Annual Meeting of the American Psychiatric Association. New York, May, 1983.

Cellucci, A., & Lawrence, P. The efficacy of systematic desensitization in reducing nightmares. *Journal of Behavioral Therapy and Experimental Psychiatry*, 1978, *9*, 109-114.

Chodoff, P. Late effects of the concentration camp syndrome. *Archives of General Psychiatry*, April 1963, *8*, 323-333.

Chodoff, P. The German concentration camp as a psychological stress. *Archives of General Psychiatry*, January 1970, *22*, 78-87.

Christenson, R., Walker, J., Ross, D., Maltbie, A. Reactivation of traumatic conflicts. *American Journal of Psychiatry*, July 1981, *138*, 984-985.

Danieli, Y. The treatment and prevention of long-term effects and intergenerational transmission of victimization: A lesson from Holocaust survivors and their children (this volume, Chapter 12).

Davis, R.C., & Friedman, L.N. The emotional aftermath of crime and violence (this volume, Chapter 6).

DeFazio, V., Rustin, S., & Diamond, A. Symptom development in Vietnam veterans. *American Journal of Orthopsychiatry*, 1975, *43*, 640-653.

Dobbs, D., & Wilson, W. Observations on persistence of war neurosis. *Diseases of the Nervous System*, December 1960, *21*, 686-691.

Egendorf, A., Kadushin, C., Laufer, R., Rothbart, G., & Sloan, L. Legacies of Vietnam: Comparative adjustment of veterans and their peers. A study prepared by the Center for Policy Research for the Veterans Administration. Superintendent of Documents, Government Printing Office, Washington, D.C., 1981.

Fairbank, J., & Keane, T. Flooding for combat-related stress disorders: Assessment of anxiety reduction across traumatic memories. *Behavior Therapy*, 1982, *13*, 499-510.

Figley, C. (Ed.). *Stress disorders among Vietnam veterans*. New York: Brunner/Mazel, 1978.

Figley, C. Combat as disaster: Treating combat veterans as survivors. Paper presented at the Annual Meeting of the American Psychiatric Association. Chicago, IL, May 14, 1979.

Figley, C. Catastrophes: An overview of family reactions. In C.R. Figley & H.I. McCubbin (Eds.), *Stress and the family Vol. II: Coping with catastrophe*. New York: Brunner/Mazel, 1983.

Figley, C. & Leventman, S. *Strangers at home: Vietnam veterans since the war*. New York: Praeger Publishers, 1980.

Figley, C., & Southerly, W. Psychosocial adjustment of recently returned veterans. In C. Figley, & S. Leventman (Eds.), *Strangers at home*. New York: Praeger Publishers, 1980.

Foy, D., Sipprelle, R., Rueger, D., & Carroll, E. Etiology of post-traumatic stress disorder in Vietnam veterans: Analysis of pre-military, military and combat exposure influences. *Journal of Consulting and Clinical Psychology*, 1984, *52*, 79-87.

Frankl, V. *Man's search for meaning: An introduction to logotherapy*. Boston: Beacon Press, 1959.

Frederick, C. Effects of natural vs. human-induced violence upon victims. *Evaluation and Change*. Minneapolis Medical Research Foundation, Inc./NIMH, Mental Health Services Development Branch. Special Issue: Services for Survivor (is as titled in original issue), 1980, 71-75.

Freyberg, J. Difficulties in separation-individuation as experienced by offspring of Nazi Holocaust survivors. *American Journal of Orthopsychiatry*, 1980, *50*(1), 87-95.

Friedman, J. Post-Vietnam syndrome: Recognition and management. *Psychosomatics*, 1981, *22*, 931-943.

Golan, N. Crisis theory. In F. Turner (Ed.), *Social work treatment*. New York: Free Press, 1974.

Goodwin, J. The etiology of combat-related post-traumatic stress disorders. In T. Williams (Ed.), *Post-traumatic stress disorders of the Vietnam veteran*. Cincinnati: Disabled American Veterans, 1980, 1-23.

Grinker, R., & Spiegel, J. *Men under stress*. Philadelphia: Blakiston, 1945.

Grinker, R., Willerman, B., Bradley, A., & Fastovsky, A. A study of psychological predispostion to the development of operational fatigue. In A. Glass (Ed.), *Neuropsychiatry in WWII, Vol. II*. Washington, D.C.: Medical Department, U.S. Army, 1946, 191-214.

Haley, S. When the patient reports atrocities. *Archives of General Psychiatry*, Feb. 1974, *30*, 191-196.

Haley, S. Treatment implications of post-combat stress response syndromes for mental health professionals. In C. Figley (Ed.), *Stress disorders among Vietnam veterans*. New York: Brunner/Mazel, 1978, 254-267.

Haley, S. The Vietnam veterans and his pre-school child: Child rearing as a delayed stress in combat veterans. *Journal of Comprehensive Psychotherapy*, 1984, *14*(1), 114-121.

Haley, S. Some of my best friends are dead: The Vietnam veteran and his family. In W. Kelly (Ed.), *Post-traumatic stress disorder and the war veteran patient*. New York: Brunner/Mazel, in press.

Harrington, D., & Jay, J. 1982. Beyond the family: Value issues in the treatment of Vietnam veterans. *Family Therapy Networker*. May-June 1982, 13-15, 44-45.

Helzer, J., Robins, L., Wish, E., & Hesselbrock, M. Depression in Vietnam veterans and civilian controls. *American Journal of Psychiatry*, 1979, *136*, 526-529.

Hocking, F. Extreme environmental stress and its significance for psychopathology. *American Journal of Psychotherapy*, 1970, *24*, 4-26.

Hogancamp, V.E., & Figley, C.R. War: Bringing the battle home. In C.R. Figley, and H.I. McCubbin (Eds.), *Stress in the family. Volume II: Coping with catastrophe*. New York: Brunner/Mazel, 1983.

Hogben, G., & Cornfield, R. Treatment of traumatic war neurosis with phenelzine. *Archives of General Psychiatry*, 1981, *38*, 440-445.

Horowitz, M. Stress response syndromes. Character style and brief psychotherapy. *Archives of General Psychiatry*, 1974, *31*, 768-781.

Horowitz, M. Presentation at the Veteran's Administration Training Conference on post-traumatic stress disorders. San Francisco: September 9, 1981.

Horowitz, M. & Solomon, G. A prediction of delayed stress response syndromes in Vietnam veterans. *Journal of Social Issues*, 1975, *31*, 67-80.

Horowitz, M., Wilner, N., & Alvarez, W. Impact of event scale: A measure of subjective stress. *Psychosomatic Medicine*, 1979, *41*(3), 209-218.

Hough, R., Gongla, P., Scurfield, R., Corker, T., & Carr, C. et al. Natural history of post-traumatic stress disorder. Paper presented at the Annual Meeting of the American Psychological Association, Anaheim, CA., August, 1983.

Hough, R., Gongla, P., Scurfield, R., Corker, T., Carr, C. & Escobar, J. Post-traumatic stress disorder among Hispanic Vietnam veterans. Research project on clinical and non-clinical population of Hispanic Vietnam veterans. Veterans Administration, Brentwood VA Medical Center, Los Angeles, 1984.

Howard, S. The Vietnam warrior: His experience and implications for psychotherapy. *American Journal of Psychotherapy*, 1976, *30*, 121-135.

Jacobs, M. Culture and illness: An analysis of post-traumatic stress disorder among women veterans of Vietnam. Department of Anthropology, University of Washington, Seattle, WA. Unpublished manuscript, 1983.

Kadushin, C., Boulanger, C., & Martin, J. Long-term stress reactions: Some causes, consequences and naturally occurring support systems. *Legacies of Vietnam: Comparative adjustment of veterans and their peers*, (Vol. 4). Washington, D.C.: U.S. Government Printing Office, 1981.

Kalinowski, L. Problems of war neuroses in light of experience in other countries. *American Journal of Psychiatry*, 1950, *107*, 340-346.

Keane, T., & Fairbank, J. Survey analysis of combat-related stress disorders in Vietnam veterans. *American Journal of Psychiatry*, 1983, *140*(3), 348-350.

Keane, T., Fairbank, J., Caddell, J., Zimering, R., & Bender, M. A behavioral approach to assessing and treating post-traumatic stress disorder in Vietnam veterans (this volume, Chapter 11).

Keane, T., & Kaloupek, D. Imaginal flooding in the treatment of post-traumatic stress disorder. *Journal of Consulting and Clinical Psychology*, 1982, *50*, 138-140.

Keane, T., Malloy, P., & Fairbank, J. The empirical development of an MMPI subscale for the assessment of combat-related post-traumatic stress disorder. *Journal of Consulting and Clinical Psychology*, in press.

Kolb, L. The place of narcosynthesis in treatment of chronic and delayed stress reactions of war. In S. Sonnenberg, A. Blank, & J. Talbot (Eds.), *The trauma of war: Stress and recovery in Vietnam veterans*. Washington, D.C.: American Psychiatric Press, 1985.

Krupnick, J., & Horowitz, M. Stress response syndromes. *Archives of General Psychiatry*, 1981, (April), *38*, 428-435.

Laufer, R., Frey-Wouters, E., & Gallops, M. Traumatic stressors in the Vietnam war and post-traumatic stress disorder (this volume, Chapter 5).

Leopold, R., & Dillon, H. Psycho-anatomy of a disaster: A long-term study of post-traumatic neuroses in survivors of a marine explosion. *The American Journal of Psychiatry*, 1963, (April), *119*, 913-921.

Lifton, R. Advocacy and corruption in the healing profession. In C. Figley (Ed.), *Stress disorders among Vietnam veterans*. New York: Brunner/Mazel, 1978.

Lipkin, J., Scurfield, R., & Blank, A. Post-traumatic stress disorder in Vietnam veterans: Assessment in a forensic setting. *Behavioral Sciences and the Law*, Vol. 1(3), 1983, 51-67.

Malloy, P., Fairbank, J., & Keane, T. Validation of a multimethod assessment of post-traumatic stress disorders in Vietnam veterans. *Journal of Consulting and Clinical Psychology*, 1983, *51*, 488-494.

Marafiote, R. Behavioral strategies in group treatment of Vietnam veterans. In T. Williams (Ed.), *Post-traumatic stress disorders of the Vietnam veteran*. Cincinnati: Disabled American Veterans, 1980, 49-70.

Marin, R. Living in moral pain. *Psychology Today*, 1981, Nov., 68-80.

Melick, M., Logue, J., & Frederick, C. Stress and disaster. In L. Goldberger, & S. Breznitz (Eds.), *Handbook on stress: Theoretical and clinical aspects*. New York: Free Press, 1982, 613-630.

Miniszek, N. Flooding as a supplemental treatment for Vietnam veterans. Paper presented at the 3rd National Conference on Post-traumatic Stress Disorders, Baltimore, MD. September 24, 1984.

Notman, M., & Nadelson, C. The rape victim: Psychodynamic considerations. *American Journal of Psychiatry*, 1976, *133*(4), April: 408-412.

O'Neill, D., & Fontaine, G. Counseling for the Vietnam veteran. *Journal of College Student Personnel*, 1973, *14*, 153-155.

Palmer, S., & Harris, M. Supportive group therapy for women partners of Vietnam veterans. *The Family Therapist*, 1983, *4*(2), 3-11.

Panzarella, R., Mantell, D., & Bridenbaugh, R. Psychiatric syndromes, self-concepts, and Vietnam veterans. In C. Figley (Ed.), *Stress disorders among Vietnam veterans*. Brunner/Mazel, New York, 1978, 148-172.

Parad, H. (Ed.). *Crisis intervention: Selected readings*. New York: Family Service Association of America, 1965.

Parson, E. The reparation of the self. Clinical and theoretical dimensions in the treatment of Vietnam combat veterans. *Journal of Contemporary Psychotherapy*, 1984, *14*(1), 4-56.

Paul, E., & O'Neill, J. The psychosocial milieu of nursing in Vietnam and its effect on Vietnam nurse veterans. Vietnam Nurse Project, Northwestern State University of Louisiana, Shreveport, LA. Unpublished manuscript, 1983.

Penk, W., Robinowitz, R., Roberts, W., Patterson, E., Dolon, M., & Atkins, H. Adjustment of differences among male substance abusers varying in degree of combat experience in Vietnam. *Journal of Consulting and Clinical Psychology*, 1981, *40*, 426-437.

Pentland, B., & Scurfield, R. Inreach counseling and advocacy with veterans in prison. *Federal Probation*, 1982, *46*(1), 21-28.

Ransom, S. A study of neurotic traits. In *Neuropsychiatry in World War II, Vol. II*. Washington, D.C.: Medical Department, U.S. Army, 1974, 365-373.

Roberts, W., Penk, W., Gearing, M., Robinowitz, R., Dolon, M., & Patterson, E. Interpersonal problems of Vietnam combat veterans with symptoms of post-traumatic stress disorder. *Journal of Abnormal Psychology*, 1982, *91*, 444-450.

Robins, L. Interaction of setting and predisposition in explaining novel behavior: Drug initiations before, in and after Vietnam. In D. Kandel (Ed.), *Longitudinal research in drug use: Empirical findings and methodological issues*. Washington, D.C.: Hemisphere, 1978.

Robins, L. National Institute of Mental Health Diagnostic Interview Schedule. *Archives of General Psychiatry*, 1981, *38*, 381-389.

Robins, L., David, D., & Goodman, D. Drug use by U.S. army enlisted men in Vietnam: A follow-up on their return home. *American Journal of Epidemiology*, 1974, *99*, 235-249.

Robins, L., & Helzer, J. PTSD section for the Diagnostic Interview Schedule. St. Louis, MO: Washington University (unpublished scale), 1984.

Russel, H. & Willenbring, M. Pilot study utilizing the PTSD section of the Diagnostic

Interview Schedule. Unpublished manuscript. Psychology Service, Minneapolis VA Medical Center, Minneapolis, MN, 1983.

Rustin, S., & Lipsig, F. Psychotherapy with the adolescent children of concentration camp survivors. *Journal of Comtemporary Psychotherapy*, 1972, *4*, 87-94.

Scarano, T. Family therapy: A viable approach for treating women partners of Vietnam veterans. *The Family Therapist*, 1982, *3*(3), Dec., 9-16.

Schnaier, J. Women Vietnam veterans and mental health adjustment. A study of their experiences and post-traumatic stress. Master's thesis, University of Maryland, 1982.

Scurfield, R., & Blank, A. A guide to the Vietnam veteran military history. In S. Sonnenberg, A. Blank, & J. Talbot (Eds.), *The trauma of war: Stress and recovery in Vietnam veterans*. Washington, D.C.: American Psychiatric Press, 1985.

Scurfield, R., Corker, T., Gongla, P., & Hough, R. Three post-Vietnam "rap/therapy" groups: An analysis. *Group*, 1984, *8*(4), 3-21.

Scurfield, R., & Smith, J. Discussion at Veterans Administration Readjustment Counseling Region I Training, White Haven, PA. May 5, 1982.

Seligman, J., Huck, J., Joseph, N., Namuth, T. et al. The date who rapes. *Newsweek*, 1984, April 9, 91-92.

Shatan, C. The grief of soldiers: Vietnam combat veterans' self-help movement. *American Journal of Orthopsychiatry*, 1973, *43*, 640-653.

Silver, S., & Iacono, C. Factor-analytic support for DSM-III's post-traumatic stress disorder for Vietnam veterans. *Journal of Clinical Psychology*, 1984, *40*, 5-14.

Silver, S., & Iacono, C. Symptom groups and family patterns of Vietnam veterans with post-traumatic stress disorder. In C.R. Figley (Ed.), *Trauma and its wake. Vol. II: Theory, research and treatment of PTSD*. New York: Brunner/Mazel, in press.

Smith, J. The roles, stages and structure of rap groups in the treatment of post-traumatic stress reaction. Paper presented at the Symposium on Post-Combat Stress Disorder. Department of Psychiatry, Dartmouth Medical School, New Hampshire, Nov. 21, 1980a.

Smith, J. Vietnam veterans: Rap groups and the stress recovery process. Unpublished manuscript. Reprints from: Dr. J. Smith, Stress Disorder Program, Brecksville VA Medical Center, Brecksville, Ohio, 1980b.

Smith, J. Sealing over and integration: Modes of resolution in the post-traumatic stress recovery process. In C.R. Figley (Ed.), *Trauma and its wake. Vol. II: Theory, research and treatment of PTSD*. New York: Brunner/Mazel, in press.

Smith, J., Parson, E., & Haley, S. On health and disorder in Vietnam veterans: An invited commentary. *American Journal of Orthopsychiatry*, 1983, *53*(1), January, 27-33.

Spiegel, D. Vietnam grief work using hypnosis. *American Journal of Clinical Hypnosis*, 1981, *24*, 330-340.

Spitzer, R., & Williams, J. Instruction manual for the structured clinical interview for DSM-III (SCID). Unpublished manuscript, 1983.

Stanton, M., & Figley, C. Treating the Vietnam veteran within the family system. In C. Figley (Ed.), *Stress disorder among Vietnam veterans: Theory, research and treatment*. New York: Brunner/Mazel, 1978, 281-289.

Strom, A., Refsum, S., Eitinger, L., Gronvik, O. et al. Examination of Norwegian ex-concentration camp prisoners. *Journal of Neuropsychiatry*, 1962, (Sept-Oct) *4*, 43-62.

Trossman, B. Adolescent children of concentration camp survivors. *Canadian Psychiatric Association Journal*, 1968, *13*, 121-123.

Ursano, R. The Vietnam era prisoner of war: Pre-captivity personality and the development of psychiatric illness. *American Journal of Psychiatry*, 1981, *138*, 315-318.

Ursano, R., Boydstun, J., & Wheatley, R. Psychiatric illness in U.S. air force Vietnam prisoners of war: A five-year follow-up. *American Journal of Psychiatry*, 1981, (March) *138*, 310-314.

Van der Kolk, B. Psychopharmacological issues in post-traumatic stress disorder. *Hospital and Community Psychiatry*, 1983, *34*, 683-691.

Walker, J., & Nash, J. Group therapy in the treatment of Vietnam combat veterans. *International Journal of Group Psychotherapy*, 1981, *31*, 376-389.

Ware, J. Tricyclic antidepressants in the treatment of insomnia. *Journal of Clinical Psychiatry*, 1983, *44*, 25-28.

Williams, C. The veteran system with a focus on women partners: Theoretical considerations, problems and treatment strategies. In T. Williams (Ed.), *Post-traumatic stress disorders of the Vietnam veteran*. Cincinnati, OH: Disabled American Veterans, 1980, 73-124.

Williams, M., & Jackson, R. A small group living program for Vietnam era veterans. *Hospital and Community Psychiatry*, 1972, *23*, 141-144.

Williams, T. (Ed.). *Post-traumatic stress disorders of the Vietnam veteran*. Cincinnati, OH: Disabled American Veterans, 1980.

Wilson, J. Conflict, stress and growth: Effects of war on psycho-social development among Vietnam veterans. In C. Figley & S. Leventman (Eds.), *Strangers at home: Vietnam veterans since the war*. New York: Praeger Publishers, 1980, 123-165.

Wilson, J., & Krauss, G. Predicting post-traumatic stress syndromes among Vietnam veterans. In W. Kelly (Ed.), *Post-traumatic stress disorder and the war veteran patient*. New York: Brunner/Mazel, in press.

Wilson, J.P., Smith, W.K., & Johnson, S.K. A comparative analysis of PTSD among various survivor groups (this volume, Chapter 8).

Worthington, E. Demographic and pre-service variables as predictors of post-military service adjustment. In C. Figley (Ed.), *Stress disorders among Vietnam veterans*. New York: Brunner/Mazel, 1978, 173-187.

Yost, J. The psychopharmacologic treatment of the delayed stress syndrome in Vietnam veterans. In T. Williams (Ed.), *Post-traumatic stress disorders of the Vietnam veteran*. Cincinnati, OH: DAV, 1980.

11

A Behavioral Approach to Assessing and Treating Post-traumatic Stress Disorder in Vietnam Veterans

TERENCE M. KEANE, JOHN A. FAIRBANK,

JUESTA M. CADDELL, ROSE T. ZIMERING,

and MARY E. BENDER

Behavioral approaches to the assessment and treatment of psychological problems have received much attention in recent years. The present chapter is among the first to extend the principles of behavioral learning to our understanding of combat-related PTSD. Specifically, this chapter proposes a conditioning model to help explain the severe symptomatology that accompanies the PTSD diagnosis. From this conceptual model, both assessment and treatment procedures have been developed and are presented in the chapter. The section on assessment includes a description of the multimethod, psychophysiological assessment currently in use in our program. The section on treatment describes the use of both stress management training and imaginal flooding (implosive) therapy.

INTRODUCTION

A 33-year-old white male Vietnam combat veteran presented at our Veterans Administration Medical Center for evaluation of psychological distress. The client reported that he was married with two adolescent children and employed on a full-time basis. He served in Vietnam from 1967 to 1968 with the United States Marine Corps. As a machine gunner with the infantry, he was exposed to heavy and direct combat on a routine basis. He reported that his primary duty involved participating in combat patrols or other major military combat operations. During one of these combat operations, the veteran was stranded in the jungle (classified as missing in action) for approximately two-and-a-half months with a five-man combat patrol squad, three of whom were severely injured and totally dependent on him and one other comrade for survival. During this time, their food supplies were depleted; in order to survive, the veteran and the other healthy squad member were forced to kill North Vietnamese soldiers to obtain food supplies for their wounded comrades. They themselves survived on insects, lizards, and any other available source of nourishment.

Events that occurred during this time, as well as during other combat experiences, led this individual to present with two primary complaints of disturbed sleep (including nightmares of Vietnam combat experiences) and dissociative-like flashback episodes which he had labeled as "blackouts." The intake interview revealed additional psychological symptoms presenting a clinical picture consistent with post-traumatic stress disorder. Although this veteran had extensive combat experience, and was exposed to many highly stressful situations during the course of his combat duty, he identified four distinct combat events that were distinguishable from other experiences by their particularly traumatic content. Examples of these events include: 1) during a three-day battle (which only three men survived) an already severely wounded comrade was killed as he stood up behind this veteran to protect him from enemy fire from the rear of his position; and 2) while MIA, the client killed an enemy combatant in hand-to-hand combat to obtain food for his wounded comrades. He subsequently discovered that the soldier was a young woman.

The client reported that he had nightmares of these specific combat events from one to seven nights per week. He indicated that he often fought in his sleep while dreaming or awoke "in a cold sweat." He *estimated that he was getting approximately three to five hours of sleep per night, that he often had difficulty falling asleep, and was also awakening throughout the night. Additionally, this veteran reported that in the presence of certain environmental stimuli which resembled Vietnam (e.g., smelling odors similar to gun powder), he reacted violently with subsequent amnesia to the episode. For example, he reported that he had physically attacked a man who almost injured his daughter by shooting fireworks at her on the streets of a large city. He had no memory of the attack after it was over.*

This individual stated that he felt extremely anxious, tense, and depressed during much of the waking day and was easily startled. He indicated that he had begun to worry about his job performance stating that he found it difficult to concentrate on his work and that he often found memories of combat traumas intruding in his thoughts. Although these memories were very disturbing to him, the veteran indicated that he had never talked with anyone about these events or their effect on him. He was especially concerned about the dissociative-like flashback episodes and feared that he might injure his family during one of these episodes. He requested help in understanding and controlling these episodes, as well as assistance in coping with memories of traumatic combat events.

This clinical case presents a picture of the typical Vietnam veteran seeking help at one of the 172 VA Medical Centers, over 130 Readjustment Counseling (Vet) Centers, and many Community Mental Health Centers and private practitioners' offices across the country. Vietnam veterans, perhaps because of the more liberal attitude toward mental health problems now prevalent in our country, are requesting and receiving psychological services to help them learn to cope more effectively with their memories of combat.

As a result, the psychological problems of Vietnam veterans pose a major challenge to the health care delivery system of our country. A significant proportion of the 2.5 million Vietnam veterans are having problems in readjustment to civilian life (Egendorf, Kadushin, Laufer, Rothbart & Sloan, 1981). The specific behavioral problems and diagnoses of Vietnam veterans are undoubtedly diverse, but chief among the many problems is combat-related post-traumatic stress disorder (PTSD), either alone or in conjunction with other major psychological disorders. The exact incidence of PTSD in the Vietnam veteran population is currently unknown, but estimates generally range from 15% to 35% of those who served in Vietnam (Egendorf et al., 1981; Wilson, 1980). Accordingly, a great need exists for conceptual models, assessment instruments, and treatment approaches developed for and validated on Vietnam veterans.

The purpose of the present chapter is to offer a learning theory conceptualization of PTSD and to describe an evaluation and treatment program designed specifically for Vietnam veterans with combat-related PTSD. We will describe in some detail the methods used to arrive at a PTSD diagnosis, including our structured interview, standardized psychometric instruments, and a laboratory-based psychophysiological procedure. Moreover, the major treatment components used in our program will be presented. Specifically the use of implosive (flooding) therapy and stress management will be described as they apply to the treatment of PTSD.

PTSD IN THE VIETNAM VETERAN POPULATION

Few would dispute that the nature of combat is stressful, terrifying, and conceivably traumatic. This issue becomes somewhat more complex, however, when the long-term or chronic effects of combat are addressed. Some researchers have found that pre-military factors have precipitated the development of chronic PTSD (Worthington, 1978), while others have found no significant pre-military differences in the development of PTSD (Foy, Sipprelle, Rueger, & Carroll, 1984). In a recent survey, Keane and Fairbank (1983) asked mental health professionals (psychologists, psychiatrists, and psychiatric social workers) in Veterans Administration Medical Centers to rate the degree to which combat is traumatic and the extent to which the psychological effects of combat are enduring. These experienced professionals generally agreed that specific events in combat can be classified as traumatic and that the psychological effects of combat can be long lasting. In addition, those surveyed minimized the role of physiological abnormalities and pre-existing psychological or personality disorders in the development of combat-related stress disorders. The details of the specific traumatic event and social support variables at the time of the trauma and at time periods subsequent to the trauma were factors considered critical to the development, maintenance and exacerbation of traumatic stress disorder among those most experienced in working with combat disorders.

This survey also found that mental health professionals rated Vietnam combatants as more seriously disturbed than combatants of other wars.

One can speculate that the absence of social support on returning home, the ideological conflict surrounding our country's participation in the war, the one year tour of duty, or any of the other factors that distinguish Vietnam from other wars (Figley, 1978) might be responsible for this surprising, yet convincing finding.

Although there is considerable agreement that Vietnam veterans seeking help at VA Medical Centers are more disturbed than combatants of other wars seeking help at these same centers (Keane & Fairbank, 1983), there is very little empirical information currently available on the specific psychological disorders prevalent in this group of veterans. Egendorf et al. (1981), evaluated the psychological and social functioning of Vietnam veterans. This study found extraordinarily high rates of psychological and social dysfunction among Vietnam veterans, and due to sampling problems these findings were probably conservative estimates. In assessing overall psychological adjustment, these authors used primarily a locally developed stress disorder scale. Unfortunately, the scores on this scale obtained in the Center for Policy Research study cannot be readily translated into diagnostic categories. Accordingly, the incidence of PTSD in the Vietnam veteran population has not yet been determined, although the psychological problems of Vietnam veterans have been well-documented (Fairbank, Langley, Jarvie, & Keane, 1981; Foy et al., 1984; Penk, Robinowitz, Roberts, Patterson et al., 1981; Roberts, Penk, Gearing, Robinowitz et al., 1982).

In summary, the psychological problems of a significant segment of the Vietnam veteran population appear to be diverse and severe. Combat-related PTSD is one of the major disorders for which Vietnam veterans seek treatment. Yet very little empirical information is available to guide the clinician in conceptualizing, assessing or treating PTSD. The present chapter will address this void from a behavioral perspective.

THE BASIC BEHAVIORAL THEORY FOR CONCEPTUALIZING PTSD

Conditioning and Learning

Mowrer's (1947, 1960) two-factor learning theory offers the basic framework for our conceptualization of PTSD. Essentially, Mowrer's theory claims the importance of both classical Pavlovian conditioning and instrumental learning in the development of psychopathology. *Classical conditioning* involves learning by association and is most easily and simply explained by Pavlov's original experiments with dogs. Presentation of food to a hungry dog invariably elicits a salivary response. In this case, the food is considered the unconditioned stimulus (UCS). When a bell is repeatedly paired sequentially with food (i.e., bell-food), this eventually leads to a salivary response even when the food is not forthcoming. The organism has learned to respond physiologically to a previously neutral stimulus, now the conditioned stimulus (CS). If the important stimulus (UCS—the food) in the pairing is aversive or negative (e.g., shock), then the organism learns to associate a negative physiological response (e.g., the increased heart rate associated with fear) with the formerly neutral stimulus. This is called *aversive conditioning*.

The second factor in Mowrer's two-factor theory is that an organism will behave in whatever way necessary to avoid an aversive stimulus. This is the *instrumental learning* component of the theory. When aversive conditioning occurs (bell-shock), the organism is motivated to avoid both the neutral stimulus (CS) as well as the actual aversive stimulus (UCS) in order to reduce the likelihood of being exposed to the UCS. In shuttlebox performance studies, organisms will literally avoid a single CS (e.g., a bell) dozens of times, so as not to be exposed to the aversive stimulus (UCS). Responding remains strong even during extinction trials when presentations of the conditioned stimulus (the bell) are no longer paired with the aversive UCS.

In an effort to parallel human trauma, Solomon and his associates (Solomon, Kamin & Wynne, 1953; Solomon & Wynne, 1954) employed a high intensity (they called it traumatic) shock as the aversive UCS*. The organisms exposed to this conditioning paradigm continued avoidance in the shuttlebox for even greater numbers of extinction trials. These researchers compared this persistent avoidance behavior to that of the most severe phobics.

Levis and his associates (Levis & Boyd, 1979; Levis & Hare, 1977; Stampfl & Levis, 1967) developed a model of psychopathology that circumvented some of the criticisms of Solomon's studies. They offered a serial conditioning paradigm that involved the sequential presentation of several neutral stimuli (e.g., buzzer-tone-light) prior to the presentation of a moderately aversive stimulus (shock). This model of human learning led to durable conditioning. With the serial presentation of CS's, organisms avoided the CS complex for hundreds of trials in shut-

---

* Although Solomon's studies provided a framework for studying fear and avoidance in laboratory settings, these studies were criticized for the shock intensity used and for specific methodological problems (Brush, 1957).

tlebox performance. These findings have been replicated numerous times in independent laboratories (Levis & Hare, 1977; Mineka, 1979). Accordingly, the two-factor learning theory of psychopathology has generated much experimental evidence and clearly yields a reliable analogue to human fears, phobias, and stress disorders—human problems that are characterized by persistent avoidant behavior.

Extinction to the Cues of Trauma

There is a wealth of scientific data supporting the notion that prolonged exposure to conditioned stimuli in the absence of the UCS leads to a decrement in anxiety (Mineka, 1979; Wilson & Davison, 1971). This exposure is called extinction. Extinction in the animal model described above would involve the presentation of the bell alone without the presentation of shock. If an organism is unable to avoid exposure to the CS, then the organism will experience an immediate increase in anxiety. This increase in anxiety will subside with prolonged or repeated presentations of the CS. It is this reduction in arousal to the cues of the traumatic conditioning experience that forms one of the major goals of a behavior therapy approach to the treatment of PTSD. The therapeutic techniques of implosive therapy and systematic desensitization have as their basic tenet extinction of anxiety through exposure to the conditioned stimuli (Rimm & Masters, 1979). Implosive therapy, for example, relies upon the notion that anxiety reduction is most efficient when anxiety to the CS is intentionally elicited. Alternatively, systematic desensitization involves the presentation of the CS while the individual remains in a state of deep muscle relaxation. Both of these techniques have been widely used with a variety of stress disorders, function through similar mechanisms (extinction), and are well-accepted therapeutic approaches to anxiety reduction (Kazdin & Wilcoxin, 1976; Levis & Hare, 1977).

APPLICATION OF THE THEORY TO PTSD

Conditioning and Avoidance of Aversive Cues

Individuals who have experienced a life-threatening trauma become conditioned to the wide assortment of stimuli present during the event. Other people present, the place, the time of day, and even cognitions become associated with the anxiety from the event and are capable of evoking extremely high levels of arousal.

For Vietnam veterans with PTSD psychological stress is clearly not limited to the specific cues associated with traumatic events. Other cues associated with the events seem to elicit unusually high levels of arousal.* Cues that were associated with the trauma include other people accompanying the survivor (e.g., fellow combatants), perpetrators of the trauma (e.g., enemy attacks), the location of the trauma (i.e., environmental cues), the time of the traumatic event, the date of the traumatic event, and any other salient dimensions or stimuli present during the experience. In the absence of extinction, any or all of these elements may begin to evoke emotional and physiological responses comparable to those experienced during the traumatic event. Moreover, these cues may further condition other similar or associated cues to evoke the same physiological response. This process is called *higher order conditioning* (Brown, 1961).

A second and related principle, *stimulus generalization*, also helps to explain the number of stimuli that can evoke recollection of the trauma and its associated physiological arousal. Essentially, the more similar a novel stimulus (e.g. the smell of diesel fuel at a filling station cueing the trauma of a chopper crash) is to the stimulus present during the original trauma, the stronger will be the response to the novel stimulus. With both higher order conditioning and stimulus generalization operational, the quantity and quality of cues capable of evoking the aversive memory or its physiological component may greatly increase. In other words, a host of cues in the combatant's environment can begin to evoke the feelings associated with the traumatic event.

With the increase in stimuli conditioned to the trauma, an individual with PTSD finds it increasingly difficult to avoid cues that evoke the memory of the trauma. Moreover, other aversive interpersonal interactions (e.g., marital disputes, vocational problems), or any stressful circumstances that evoke physiological arousal can elicit the memory of the traumatic event, due to stimulus generalization. This unfortunately impedes or even precludes rational problem-solving and successful resolution of the present-day life stressor, since the veteran may be overwhelmed at the time by the memories of the traumatic event. This inability to deal with current stressors contributes to the many maladaptive associated features of PTSD (e.g., divorce, unemployment).

---

* This arousal to diverse cues can be explained by several widely accepted psychological principles. Additionally, the factors surrounding the Vietnam war also interact with an individual's combat experiences to provide the complex behavioral disorder presently seen in Vietnam veterans with PTSD.

Why Doesn't Extinction Occur Over Time?

Perhaps the hallmark symptom of PTSD is the reliving or recollection of the traumatic event in the form of intrusive thoughts or nightmares (Figley, 1978; Horowitz, 1976). Yet, despite frequent reliving of the event, extinction does not occur. Indeed, individuals with chronic PTSD (beyond six months) seem to become increasingly disturbed over time. Extinction would occur, we believe, when there is exposure to all elements (CS's) of the memory, so that those components of the memory that are extinguished are not reconditioned by the unexposed components of the traumatic memory. Exposure to the entire memory of the trauma would in fact promote extinction and foster adaptive recovery from the trauma. We would like to propose several reasons why this exposure does not always occur naturally.

Subsequent to a traumatic experience, the survivor attempts to review the event for specific details and cues that will enhance learning, memory, and adaptation (coping). This process of review for memory consolidation would be considered normal for any significant event that an individual experiences. In the case of a traumatic event wherein one's life is threatened, this process of memory review involves recollection of stimulus cues, many of which have acquired negative emotional valence through conditioning, much like the conditioning discussed in the Solomon and Levis models of psychopathology. The memories themselves are so aversive and anxiety-provoking that the motivation to enhance consolidation of the memory is compromised by the extreme aversion associated with the memory. Accordingly, the combatant attempts to avoid recollection.

Other factors also limit exposure to the entire memory. In the case of trauma experienced in combat, the likelihood for immediate review of the aversive memory is reduced by opportunities for continued expression of anger and hostility (emotions that compete with the anxiety of trauma) in the form of further combat experiences. Moreover, the competing emotions of aggression and hostility are socially reinforced by the military environment, while experiences that allow exposure to traumatic memories with their attendant feelings are either ignored or punished. These consequences are provided either implicitly through indoctrination of the feelings a soldier *should have*, or explicitly through the overt reactions of peers and superiors to emotional displays. Thus, little exposure to these memories occurs during the time immediately following combat-related trauma.

An additional factor in reducing exposure to the elements of traumatic memories is a process known as *affective state dependent retention* (Bower, 1981). Since the traumatic event was assuredly accompanied by sustained, extreme levels of psychological and psychophysiological arousal, the memory storage was completed in a physiological state markedly different from that in which the memory review will occur. This pronounced change in physiological and psychological states directly interferes with recollection of the specific cues of the event. Thus, important elements of the memory that need exposure in order to promote anxiety reduction are not accessible in the unaroused state. According to the data regarding state dependent retention, memories stored in one affective state can best be recollected only when that state is simulated (Keane, 1976; Weingartner, Miller, & Murphy, 1977). Consequently, access to the traumatic memory is limited by the change in state and as a result the individual has few opportunities for exposure. However, when physiological arousal is induced by any source, the individual's behavior can be influenced by the memory of the trauma since the physiological arousal is similar to that present during the traumatic memory.

In conclusion, little exposure or extinction to the cues of the traumatic memory can occur as a function of 1) avoidance of aversive memories (efforts to "just forget" the horror of the event), 2) negative reinforcement for competing emotions and behavior (anger, a more acceptable alternative, inhibits anxiety to the memories), 3) positive reinforcement for competing emotions and behaviors (peer pressure to adopt a survivor mode of behavior), and 4) affective state dependent storage of memories (elements of the memory are inaccessible due to change in physiological state). Consequently, a significant life event can have continued psychological and behavioral effects, often without the individual attributing his or her behavior change to the specific traumatic event.

Other Factors Involved in the Clinical Manifestation of PTSD in Vietnam Veterans

Negative Reinforcement. Behavioral disturbances often associated with PTSD such as anger and aggression are viewed as emotions that are incompatible with anxiety and become well-learned behaviors through the principle of negative reinforcement. Negative reinforcement postulates that behavior leading to a reduction in an aversive state (e.g., anxiety) is reinforced and thus likely to be repeated. Some of the multidimensional problems that are encountered clinically with PTSD veterans, alcohol or drug abuse, anger, and social alienation, for example, are conceptualized as behavioral patterns that are functionally reinforced by their capacity to reduce aversive feelings.

Behavioral Contrast. A symptom often reported by Vietnam veterans is a lack of interest in activities, whether they be familial, vocational, or avocational. Although this lack of interest in activities can be attributable to depression, another factor, *behavioral contrast*, appears to play an important role for some. The reinforcement value of current-day activities is overshadowed by the reinforcement from activities in Vietnam. For example, activities and experiences in Vietnam were thrilling and often involved life and death decisions and actions. The individual's role was critical to the outcome of missions. Thrill-seeking behavior was commonplace (Wilson et al., this volume). In contrast, non-combat activities and the life-style found in America after the return home seems trivial in comparison. This results in growing discontent, boredom, and apathy, complicating the clinical picture for PTSD veterans.

Multiple Traumatic Events and Low Social Support. Possibly the most relevant distinction between combat-related PTSD and other types of PTSD is the number of separate and distinct traumatic events that a combatant might experience (Figley, 1978). Moreover, for the Vietnam veteran these multiple traumas were often experienced in an environment with low levels of social support, a variable frequently mentioned as influencing the impact of significant life stressors (Rabkin & Struening, 1976). In addition, their return to the United States was also marked by low levels of social support, further exacerbating their psychological problems (Figley, 1978; Figley & Leventman, 1980; Keane & Fairbank, 1983). While causality may not be logically concluded in interpretations of these studies, it is reasonable to speculate that the extremely low levels of social support experienced by Vietnam veterans subsequent to their military service contributed to the complex psychological problems these individuals have had since Vietnam.

Assessment of Combat-related PTSD

The relative success of any treatment program for combat-related PTSD will depend upon the accuracy of the assessment procedures used to detect the disorder. Two important and treatment-relevant functions of assessment for PTSD are 1) to determine if the veteran seeking evaluation meets acceptable criteria for a diagnosis of combat-related PTSD, and 2) to determine if other diagnosable psychological disorders, especially those that directly influence formulation of treatment strategies (e.g., psychosis), exist concurrently with the PTSD diagnosis. Hence,

assessment procedures for PTSD are needed that are at once comprehensive, reliable, valid, and discriminating.

Prior to formal psychological assessment for PTSD, it is useful to obtain
archival data from the veteran's VA and/or military service records, such
as the VA administrative record, VA C-file, or service medical record
(SMR)*. Although these archival data do not provide information on the
existence of traumatic events per se, they do provide objective evidence
that the veteran served in Vietnam in a combat-related capacity, an
important consideration in pursuing further assessment (Atkinson, Henderson, Sparr & Deale, 1982).

The Structured Clinical Interview

Evaluation of PTSD in Vietnam combat veterans requires a thorough
assessment of the veteran's current functioning, pre- and post-military
history, and Vietnam experiences. The interview portion of our assessment demands at least three to four hours of contact with the veteran,
typically divided into at least two separate sessions. This aspect of the
assessment usually has two purposes: first, to determine the degree to
which the veteran meets the DSM-III criteria for PTSD, and second, the
functional analysis of the patient's current problems in preparation for
designing a treatment program for the amelioration of symptoms. To
promote good rapport, familiarity with the general information about
the Vietnam war, and an awareness of the social and political climate
to which the veterans returned are critical for conducting the clinical
interview and to understanding the veteran's current level of functioning.

Throughout the assessment, careful observation is made of the veteran's behavior and affect, particularly when discussing his or her Vietnam experiences. Some veterans display a somewhat constricted affect,
showing virtually no response even to discussion of traumatic events,

---

* The goal of this procedure is to verify that the veteran actually served in the United
States military in Southeast Asia during the Vietnam era (i.e., August 5, 1964 through
May 7, 1975). Perhaps the most cost-efficient means of verification is to examine a copy
of the veteran's military separation papers, i.e., his or her DD-Form-214. Pertinent information listed on the DD-214 includes 1) the veteran's military occupational specialty (MOS),
2) major overseas duty assignments, and 3) campaign ribbons, decorations, medals,
badges, and commendations received. For example, examination of the DD-214 of the
veteran presented in the introduction to this chapter revealed that 1) this veteran's MOS
was combat infantry (11B20; LT WPNS INF), 2) he served with the United States Army
4th Infantry Division in the Republic of Vietnam (4th INFDIV, USARV), and 3) he was
awarded the Vietnam Service Medal (VSM) and Vietnam Campaign Medal (VCM).

while more frequently individuals show obvious increases in arousal (e.g., shifting in the chair, increased smoking), depression (facial grimaces, loss of eye contact, dysphoric mood), anger and hostility (emotions that compete with the anxiety of trauma), or avoidance (e.g., asking to take a break, introducing irrelevant topics). In the face of such avoidance, an expression of appreciation by the therapist of how difficult it must be to discuss these painful experiences is followed by a reminder of their importance in understanding the veteran's problems and helping to find a solution. The information gathered during the structured clinical interview falls under three broad categories: current status (see Appendix A), psychological and social history, and military experience. The structured interview forms that we employ to assess for presence of combat-related PTSD in Vietnam veterans appear in Appendix B.

Current Status. Current functioning is usually discussed first. After obtaining standard demographic data (age, marital status, number of marriages, number of children and ages, current living situation, education, employment status, medical history) the veteran is asked to describe the factors that led him to seek help. These symptoms are carefully assessed in terms of frequency, duration, intensity, and pervasiveness in the patient's life, while information regarding antecedent events and consequences is obtained with an eye towards establishing functional relationships. Information regarding the onset of symptoms or their exacerbation is also obtained.

1) *Anxiety and depression.* Virtually all patients with PTSD report chronic anxiety, which they may describe as an inability to relax, difficulty concentrating on anything, or "bad nerves." Precise and complete information about the stimuli or events that seem to be related to increased anxiety can contribute to an understanding of the patient's psychopathology and aid in treatment formulation. Features of depression may not be reported immediately, but are often elicited by asking the veteran to describe his mood in general. Depressive symptomatology frequently found among veterans with PTSD includes sleep and appetite disturbance, anhedonia, guilt, hopelessness, and suicidal ideation. Previous suicidal attempts are not uncommon, and sometimes precipitate referral. Suicidal or homicidal ideation and plans are assessed during every interview.

2) *Reexperiencing the trauma.* Discussion of sleep problems provides an opportunity to assess a primary feature of PTSD: reexperiencing of traumatic events through intrusive recollections or recurrent dreams. Ques-

tioning about what keeps the patient from falling asleep, or what wakes him or her up, often lead to reports of intrusive thoughts or nightmares about Vietnam experiences. Some veterans report hypnogogic experiences in which they behave violently, destroying furniture or aggressing against their spouses as if in combat.

While nightmares are very frequently reported by veterans with PTSD, some reexperience their trauma during waking hours as well as, or instead of, during sleep. They report that they are unable to stop thinking about certain events, and become anxious, depressed, or begin to self-medicate when they think about them. Occasionally, clients experience brief flashback episodes that may range from fleeting sensations to extended periods in which the patient actually behaves as if he or she were in combat. Evaluation of the extent to which intrusive thoughts of combat experiences interfere with daily activities or lead to avoidance of normal interactions can aid in distinguishing a symptom of PTSD from simple waking memories or normal sadness triggered by a situational event reminiscent of tragic events.

3) *Numbing of responsiveness.* This cardinal feature of PTSD can be assessed by having the veteran elaborate on symptoms of anxiety or depression. For example, clients who report persistent anxiety may note that their tension increases when they are around people, and that they therefore avoid social contact. Traumatized veterans may report that they do not enjoy any activities that they once found pleasant. More specific information about this symptom is obtained through questions about the patient's marital relationship (and/or friendships), including satisfaction with the relationship, openness of communication (including information about current problems and about Vietnam experiences), sexual satisfaction and problems, and relationships with children, if any. Veterans with PTSD typically report that they have few close friends, rarely discuss their combat experiences with anyone, and prefer to be alone most of the time.

4) *Startle response.* Investigation of anxiety-producing events may lead to reports of an exaggerated startle response. Many veterans with PTSD report such extreme responses as taking cover or "hitting the deck" following sudden loud noises (e.g., car backfiring, door slamming, or thunder), particularly if the noises resemble gunfire or artillery. Unexpected contact with another person, such as a slap on the back or being bumped accidentally, may produce an automatic protective or aggressive response.

5) *Other symptoms.* Additional features of PTSD may be revealed by elaboration of the patient's presenting problems, or through more direct

questioning. An employment history, including current employment satisfaction and success, number of jobs and percentage of time employed since military discharge, specific skills in which the veteran is trained, and any injuries or disabilities that may preclude or interfere with employability, provides data relevant to general stability or adjustment.

Information about the veteran's use of alcohol, currently and historically, is important in identifying not only a very common feature of the disorder, but also a typical strategy for coping with other symptoms. Details about the quantity and frequency of alcohol consumption and "binges," situational events that often lead to drinking, and the effect of alcohol on other symptoms (i.e., alleviation or exacerbation) are gathered for assessment as well as treatment planning purposes (cf. Keane, Caddell, Martin, Zimering, & Fairbank, 1983).

Violence and aggressive behavior are not uncommon among veterans with PTSD. Details about aggression and destructiveness, number of arrests (and charges) for misdemeanors and/or felonies, convictions, and prison or jail terms provide additional data related to the diagnosis of PTSD, specifically regarding the symptoms of impulsivity, irritability, and emotional lability. Questioning regarding possession and use of a weapon may provide a wide range of responses. Some veterans report that they carry a weapon with them at all times, sleep with it within reach at night, and would not hesitate to use it if provoked, while others claim that they would not have a weapon in their house for fear of unknowingly using it during a flashback or dissociative episode. Both patterns of behavior are encountered among patients with PTSD.

6) *The mental status exam.* While some symptoms suggesting disorders of content or form of thought may be evident throughout the interview, specific questions are required to assess such features as paranoid ideation, auditory or visual hallucinations, delusions, or magical thinking. Hallucinations limited to combat-related events are occasionally reported by veterans with PTSD and do not necessarily warrant a concurrent diagnosis of psychosis. Rather, these can be considered as reliving specific events that actually occurred. However, non-combat related hallucinations, delusions, or other evidence of psychotic thought processes may indeed indicate psychosis. Importantly, a diagnosis of psychosis does not preclude a concurrent diagnosis of PTSD, if the patient meets the diagnostic criteria for both disorders (e.g., Sierles, Chen, McFarland, & Taylor, 1983).

Psychological and Social History. Following the assessment of current symptoms, additional information is obtained regarding the veteran's pre-military psychological and social functioning in order to obtain more compelling data regarding the impact of the Vietnam experience on the veteran's life. Questions are asked regarding the patient's family structure, school performance (academic and behavioral), any legal problems he or she may have had, and alcohol and drug use *prior to Vietnam.* While some patients have a tendency to recall their pre-Vietnam records as unblemished, pointed questioning usually produces more precise recollections. Family history of mental illness, as well as previous diagnoses or psychological treatment of the patient are recorded. It is important to note, however, that the presence of preexisting behavior problems or personality disorders does not rule out the possibility that the patient's current problems are at least in part a function of traumatic combat experiences.

Military Experience.

1) *Combat exposure.* Following establishment of rapport and the gathering of information regarding current problems, a transition is made to a discussion of military experiences (cf. Appendix A). This portion of the interview begins with general information regarding branch of service, date of enlistment and date and type of discharge. Date of arrival in Vietnam, number and length of tours, primary and secondary military occupation, and areas or sectors in which the veteran was stationed can all provide some indication of the amount of exposure to combat that the veteran experienced. The individual is asked to estimate frequencies of exposure to specific events in Vietnam. Responses to quantifiable questions such as, "How often, if ever, did you go on combat patrols or similar dangerous duties?" or "How often did you actually see someone hit by incoming or outgoing rounds, or see them immediately after they had been shot?" provide an overall estimate of the amount of combat to which the veteran was exposed. Appendix A includes the combat index used in our program to describe the experiences of the veteran. Combat exposure scales such as this also can be useful in comparing the veteran with other veterans in systematic research (see Figley, 1977 and Wilson & Krauss, 1980 for additional examples of combat indices).

2) *Traumatic events.* During the course of the initial assessment of symptoms, or during the questions regarding the Vietnam experience, the veteran may reveal some combat experiences that were particularly traumatic. However, it is important for the development of individual-

ized treatment plans that the veteran be asked to identify the specific events that remain particularly disturbing today. An introduction to this question may be made, acknowledging that many of the events that happened in Vietnam were distressing, but emphasizing that everyone had different experiences and the importance of describing the specific events that continue to be most troubling. For example, the interviewer may ask the veteran questions such as, "Which events are you not able to prevent from coming to mind?" or "What comes back to haunt you over and over?" The therapist might offer as an example something that the patient had mentioned dreaming about, or some of the combat experiences reported, asking if there is one in particular that he or she thinks about a lot. Most combat veterans with PTSD recall at least one event that fits this description. Events frequently mentioned during this portion of the interview include the death of a buddy, being overrun or ambushed, or incidents in which civilians, particularly women and children, were killed. Occasionally, patients are reluctant to discuss these events, fearing either their own response to talking about the events, or the therapist's response to a particularly gruesome event (e.g., judgment of the patient's behavior). Such reluctance seems to be best handled with genuine empathy and reassurance that the therapist understands that being in a stressful situation such as combat can lead people to do things that they might never do under normal circumstances.

Discussion of traumatic events often produces an exacerbation of symptomatology such as anxiety or depression; the patient may cry, or express guilt about his or her behavior or survival. Feelings of anger are often elicited by recollection of these events as well. As mentioned previously, the therapist should take note of the particular response the veteran has to this portion of the interview. Afterwards, the therapist may express recognition and appreciation of the emotional distress experienced while discussing the events.

3) *The use of standardized psychological inventories.* The information that has been gathered from the structured clinical interview is combined with the results of psychometric and laboratory assessments in an effort to determine the presence or absence of PTSD and the relative severity of the veteran's symptoms. Several recent studies (Fairbank, Keane, & Malloy, 1983; Foy et al., 1984) have investigated the clinical utility of a variety of standardized psychological inventories for evaluating the problems of Vietnam veterans. These inventories included measures of overall adjustment, such as the Minnesota Multiphasic Personality Inventory (MMPI; Hathaway & McKinley, 1967), measures of depression such as the Beck Depression Inventory (BDI; Beck, Ward, Mendelson,

274

Trauma and Its Wake

Mock & Erbaugh, 1961), and measures of generalized anxiety, such as the State-Trait Anxiety Inventory (STAI; Spielberger, Gorsuch & Lushene, 1970). In one study, Fairbank et al. (1983) administered the MMPI, BDI, Zung Depression Scale (Zung, 1965), STAI, and Fear Survey Schedule-II (Geer, 1965), to three groups of Vietnam veterans; 12 combat veterans with a reliable diagnosis of PTSD, 12 combat veterans who were well-adjusted (Normal), and 12 non-combat Vietnam era veterans with other diagnosed, nonpsychotic psychological disorders (Psych). We found that the PTSD group obtained the highest mean levels of psychological distress on each of these standardized, commonly used psychological inventories. In addition, our finding of consistency among the measures of depression (e.g., mean BDI, Zung, and MMPI Scale 2 scores) for the PTSD group indicated that unusually high levels of depression were associated with PTSD. Thus, evaluation of depressive symptomatology in veterans with PTSD would appear to be especially critical since this information may directly influence the formulation of individual treatment plans.

Findings from the Fairbank et al. (1983) study also suggest that the MMPI in particular may be helpful in discriminating veterans with PTSD from other groups of veterans. As shown in Figure 1, veterans with PTSD showed overall higher mean clinical scale and F-scale elevations than appropriate veteran control groups. Many of the comparisons between the PTSD group and the two control groups were statistically significant. In addition, analyses of the 2-point profile codes revealed that the highest mean clinical scale elevations were on Scales 8 and 2 for the PTSD group. Standard interpretations of the 8–2 MMPI profile contain descriptions of the symptoms necessary for a diagnosis of PTSD (e.g., Graham, 1977). Findings consistent with these results have also been reported by Foy et al. (1984). However, the sample size in each of these two studies was relatively small and additional research is required before any definitive conclusions are drawn about the effectiveness of standardized psychometric inventories for improving diagnostic hit rates for individual veterans with combat-related PTSD (cf. Penk et al., 1981; Roberts et al., 1982).

4) *Multimethod behavioral assessment.* The principles of behavior theory presented in the introduction to this chapter predict that individuals with PTSD should show evidence of increased arousal/anxiety during even relatively *brief* exposure to stimuli associated with traumatic conditioning events. Thus, Vietnam veterans with PTSD are likely to show measurable levels of distress across multiple-response systems, e.g., behavioral, cognitive, and psychophysiological, when exposed to stimuli

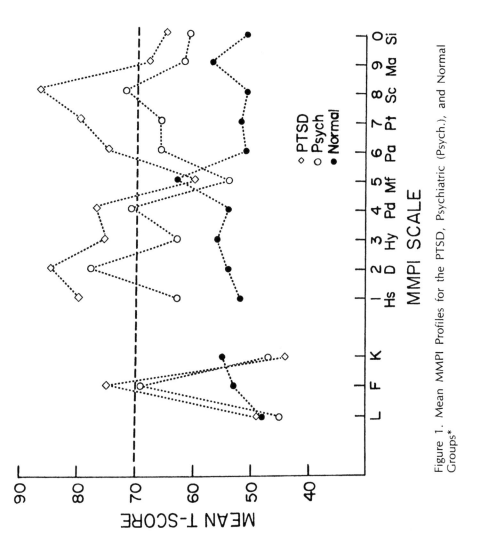

Figure 1. Mean MMPI Profiles for the PTSD, Psychiatric (Psych.), and Normal Groups*

*Reprinted by permission from Fairbank, Keane, & Malloy, 1983. Copyright 1983 by the American Psychological Association, Inc.

associated with combat experiences. Conversely, most individuals with PTSD should demonstrate relatively little arousal to stimuli not associated with combat events. In a study that represents a direct clinical application of principles of behavior theory, Malloy, Fairbank, and Keane (1983) designed and validated a tripartite (psychophysiological, behavioral, cognitive) assessment procedure for combat-related PTSD.* The results of this study indicated that PTSD veterans responded with increased arousal to combat stimuli across all three response systems, while their response to the neutral stimuli was comparable to two other comparison groups. For example, heart rate data revealed that only veterans with a diagnosis of PTSD responded differentially to the combat-relevant stimuli. Malloy et al.'s (1983) data on diagnostic hit rates (100% of PTSD patients were correctly classified, no controls were classified as PTSD) strongly suggest that multimethod behavioral assessment provides the clinician with important information that increases the validity of PTSD diagnoses. Similar findings of higher levels of physiological arousal during exposure to combat stimuli in Vietnam veterans with PTSD have been reported by other investigators (Blanchard, Kolb, Pallmeyer & Gerardi, 1982).

For the veteran described at the beginning of this chapter, the results of his multimethod assessment revealed increased arousal to the combat stimuli as compared to the control stimuli across all three response systems (behavioral, psychophysiological, cognitive). With regard to the psychophysiological component of this assessment, this veteran's heart rate averaged 85 beats per minute (bpm) during control slides and 94 bpm during combat slides. The behavioral component revealed that the veteran viewed all nine control (neutral) slides, but terminated the combat slide sequence at the seventh slide. The cognitive component indi-

---

* Specifically, we measured the behavioral, cognitive, and psychophysiological responses of three groups of veterans during controlled laboratory presentations of Vietnam combat-relevant visual and auditory stimuli and combat-irrelevant (neutral) visual and auditory stimuli. The three experimental groups were: (1) Vietnam combat veterans with a reliable diagnosis of PTSD (Stress); (2) Vietnam combat veterans who were well-adjusted (Normal); and (3) Vietnam era veterans with nonpsychotic psychological disorders other than PTSD (Psych), Veterans in each group viewed two videotapes that were presented in the following order: first, a videotaped sequence of nine neutral slides (i.e., trip to a shopping mall with appropriate sound effects), and second, a videotaped sequence of nine combat-relevant slides (combat assault in Vietnam with appropriate sound track). Measures of arousal from three response systems were continuously monitored during both the combat and neutral stimuli conditions, and included (1) a behavioral avoidance measure, i.e., number of stimuli voluntarily viewed by the veteran, (2) psychophysiological measures such as tonic heart rate and number and magnitude of electrodermal responses, and (3) a cognitive measure, i.e., patient ratings of subjective units of distress (SUDS).

cated higher levels of subjective anxiety (as measured by an 11-point Subjective Units of Distress Scale - SUDS) for the combat slides as compared to the control slides. Average SUDS rating was 5.8 (range 4-9) during the combat slides and 2.7 (range 0–6) during the control slides. Thus, although continued research on the reliability and validity of multimethod behavioral assessment procedures for PTSD is needed, initial findings on the utility of this procedure for assessing combat-related stress disorders are encouraging.

Behavioral Treatment of Combat-related PTSD

The Vietnam Stress Management Program (VSMP) is a behaviorally oriented clinical research program that incorporates two major approaches in its treatment of Vietnam veterans with PTSD—implosive therapy (flooding) and stress management. Although our purpose is to empirically compare treatment outcome of implosive therapy and stress management therapy individually, both techniques could readily be combined to provide a more comprehensive treatment program for combat-related PTSD. A description of each approach will be presented with emphasis on relevant issues for the treatment of Vietnam veterans.

The Technique of Implosive Therapy (Flooding). The implosive therapy technique used in the treatment program for Vietnam veterans is an adaptation of the technique developed by Stampfl and Levis (1967). As previously stated, we assume that the Vietnam veteran's response to memories of specific traumatic events is the primary factor in the manifestation of PTSD symptoms (i.e., intrusive thoughts, nightmares, avoidance of activities). It is also assumed that the traumatic memories may be motivating other maladaptive behaviors such as alcohol consumption and aggression. Thus, the memory of these traumatic events is the target of the implosive therapy technique.

Implosive therapy consists of the repeated imaginal presentation of the veteran's traumatic event until the scene no longer evokes high levels of anxiety (extinction through exposure). Thus, the goal of implosive therapy is to eliminate avoidance of the memory and, through exposure, reduce anxiety to the traumatic combat events. The purpose of this treatment is not to change the nature of the trauma, but to decrease the individual's anxiety response to memories of the trauma. Following successful treatment, these events remain traumatic in nature, and are likely to be recalled with sorrow; however, avoidance of the memories and associated levels of anxiety are markedly reduced. In our program, the two principle phases of treatment include relaxation training followed by repeated presentation of the scenes.

1) *Relaxation training.* Relaxation training is used for two purposes: a) to facilitate the patient's ability to imagine a scene, and b) to decrease residual anxiety following the presentation of traumatic scenes.

Training the patient in progressive muscle relaxation techniques may involve four sessions. An adaptation of Bernstein and Borkovec's (1973) progressive muscle relaxation training is used in the following way: a) the patient learns 16 muscle group relaxation using a tension-relaxation sequence for each muscle group; b) muscular tension is dropped from the sequence and the patient is trained in relaxation alone of the 16 muscle groups; c) the patient is given cue-controlled training in which he or she is instructed to repeat cue words (e.g., "heavy, loose and warm") as he or she relaxes the muscles. These cue words become associated with relaxation and can be used to accelerate the response within the therapy session and in situations that warrant the use of an adaptive coping response. During this time, the patient is encouraged to practice relaxation at home with an audiotaped instruction in order to facilitate learning of the response.

2) *Pleasant imagery training.* At the end of the fourth relaxation training session, the client is instructed in pleasant imagery based on the work of Lang (1977). The client is asked to imagine a pleasant scene that evokes relaxation (e.g., lying on a beach, fishing in a quiet pond, etc.) while the therapist presents details of the setting to be visualized. The patient is instructed to attend to both the stimulus (external cues) and response elements (internal cues) of the imagined scene.

The purpose of the pleasant imagery training is to both increase the state of relaxation and determine the patient's ability to imagine a pleasant or non-aversive scene with therapist guidance. If the patient is able to form clear visual images and can imagine other sensory cues such as sound, smell and touch, then therapy can proceed. If the veteran finds this task difficult, additional training in imagery is required.

3) *Implosive therapy.* Prior to initiating implosive therapy, the client is asked to list his traumatic memories in ascending order according to their anxiety-inducing properties. He then assigns a subjective rating to each of the events that are to be treated using a 0–10 (0 = not at all anxious, 10 = most anxious), self-report anxiety scale. The least anxiety-provoking scene is presented first in order to maximize the likelihood that the client will imagine the cues of the scene, despite their apparent aversiveness.

There are four basic components to conducting implosive therapy with the patients: a) setting the scene, b) presentation of symptom-contingent traumatic cues, c) the use of additional cue categories, and d) session parameters.

a) *Setting the scene.* At the onset of each implosive therapy session the patient is asked to practice relaxation exercises in order to decrease competing thoughts and enhance imagery. The therapist then begins to develop the scene in which the traumatic event occurred. To do so, visual, auditory, tactile and olfactory imaginal cues are presented to facilitate the subject's realistic imagination of the scene. The therapist relies heavily throughout the entire session on patient feedback for detailed scene descriptions. For example, the therapist may begin a scene for the client described in the case study as follows:

> I want you to see yourself back in Vietnam now. Allow yourself
> to go back. See yourself in the jungle . . . you are missing in ac-
> tion . . . look around, what do you see (hear, smell, feel)?

In this way the therapist guides the patient to imagine the time, place, and persons involved in the traumatic event with intermittent and regular feedback from the patient. Both stimulus (what do you see, hear, smell) and response (what are you feeling) cues are critical when introducing the scene.

b) *Presentation of symptom-contingent traumatic cues.* After the general setting of the traumatic event is established and it is evident from patient feedback that the veteran can visualize the scene, the therapist supportively guides the patient through imagination of the traumatic event. This phase may be initiated by a simple question, "Then what did he/you do?" The patient is slowly and gradually presented with cues of the specific event, emphasizing and prolonging in imagination the elements of the memory that are most anxiety-provoking.

Presentation of the traumatic event focuses heavily on the specific details of the event. Any environmental cues that are associated with and/or precede the traumatic event, as well as those cues which depict the actual event, are called symptom-contingent. Upon presentation, these cues elicit the manifest symptoms of the disorder (heightened arousal), hence the name symptom-contingent. The following is an example of the symptom-contingent cues that could be presented for the traumatic event described in the case study in which the client attacks an enemy soldier to secure food for his wounded comrades:

It is nighttime. You are crouched in the brush on the edge of the NVA encampment. You are positioned close to the perimeter guard. What do you hear? . . . What do you see? . . . You study the pattern of the guard's steps. Feel your heart racing as you prepare to attack him. You wait until he is close to you. You can hear his breathing. What do you feel? . . . The guard turns away from you now. You leap up and grab him from behind forcing your hand hard into his throat, as you drive your knife into his kidney. Feel the knife sinking into the flesh, as warm blood gushes out. You can feel it on your hands and body. . . . Smell it. The guard crumples to the ground, lying face up. Look at the body. The guard's shirt is torn open. You see the outline of a breast. Look at her face . . . this guard is not a man . . . it's a woman . . . you've killed a woman!

Every patient will have specific details from the trauma that are idiosyncratically important and anxiety-producing. These details are identified in assessment and are emphasized and presented several times within a session. Critical details may also be identified during the course of scene presentation through nonverbal indicators of anxiety (grimacing, moaning, fidgeting, etc.) that are observed during specific cue presentation.

c) *The use of additional cue categories.* In addition to symptom-contingent cues, which are directly correlated with environmental components of the traumatic event, Levis (1980) outlines two additional stimulus cue categories that are incorporated into our implosive therapy treatment: reportable, internally elicited cues and unreportable cues hypothesized to relate to reportable, internally elicited cues (hypothesized cues).

Reportable, internally elicited cues are the patient's aversive thoughts, feelings, or images which are associated with the traumatic event. These cues represent the patient's cognitive reaction to the event and may include such feelings as guilt, anger, and grief. Reportable, internally elicited cues could be presented in the implosive scene that was described above, in the following way:

You check the guard's pulse. Dead. She's dead. You're stunned. You can't believe you've killed a woman. Feel the anger well up inside of you. You came to Vietnam to serve your country, not to kill women. You feel dirty and ashamed. Think now, how you were brought up to protect women. Feel the guilt, the shame, as you look down on the woman's body.

These cues are based on those feelings which have previously been reported by the veteran.

The cues that are not reported, yet hypothesized to relate to reportable, internally elicited cues, represent guesses or hypotheses as to the emotional and/or cognitive consequences of the traumatic event. These cues are suspected to represent additional components of the total CS complex. Levis and Hare (1977) suggest the general use of the following hypothetical cues: fear of bodily injury, fear of dying, fear of aggressive behavior, punishment for wrongdoing, and fear of rejection. After the veteran has been flooded to both symptom-contingent and reportable internally elicited cues the unreportable, hypothesized cues discussed above can be presented.

The following is a continuation of the previously described scene incorporating the hypothetical cues suggested by Levis (1980). Examples of specific cue types will be noted in parentheses.

As you hover over her lifeless body, you imagine the pain and terror she felt as you drove the knife into her back. The horror is still in her eyes as she stares upward. As you look at her, you can feel the pain, the terror. Suddenly she looks different to you. Her eyes, her nose, her mouth, they are all changing. They begin to look like your face—it's you lying there now, in a pool of blood. Now it's you, not the guard. Feel your back ripped apart where the knife tore into you, feel that burning pain (fear of bodily injury). You think of the life that you had ahead of you as you feel your breath slow down and weaken. You know you are dying and you feel terrified, alone. Feel that hopeless, empty feeling (fear of dying).

In addition, we propose that hypothesized cues may remain active in the patient's current life following higher order conditioning to the original traumatic event. In other words, the veteran's present-day cognitions (e.g., guilty thoughts, etc.) may come to elicit fear responses by virtue of their association with, or similarity to, other cues (cognitive and environmental) present during the traumatic event. For example, the veteran will often report that he fears rejection by significant others should they learn of his actions in Vietnam. He may also express concern that he might lose control and severely injure someone (because he once behaved in a violent manner in combat). Such fears contribute significantly to interpersonal difficulties. The veteran is unable to have meaningful or close, interpersonal relationships given that he anticipates these consequences. Therefore, in order for extinction to be complete these hypothetical cues could be incorporated in additional flooding scenes. The following are examples of the presentation of such cues based on the traumatic event previously outlined:

1) As you walk into your house you are greeted by the cold stares of your family. Instantly, you realize that they know what you did in Vietnam. They know that you killed a woman. You feel the panic building inside you . . . your thoughts are racing . . . you scream out trying to explain what happened—explain why you killed her. Your family won't listen to you. Your wife says, "How could I love a man who could kill a woman?" She gathers your children close to her. You can see the fear in their eyes. Your own children are terrified of you. They turn away from you and leave you alone and empty (fear of rejection and punishment for wrongdoing).

2) You are at home with your family. It has been a hard day for you at work. You already feel tense and nervous. Vietnam has been on your mind many times today and as you sit down to rest it forces into your thoughts again. Your wife approaches you and begins to complain about a household chore you had promised to do but have not done. Feel your body tense up. You just want her to leave you alone. Your wife continues to question when you will get to the job. You begin to feel more and more angry. You want her to shut up . . . You want to shut her up. And you know how to do it. You've done it before; you've killed a woman. You are both angry and terrified now. As you look at your wife you can see the face of the VC woman you killed. You just want to get rid of the nagging. "Shut up," you scream, but she just keeps on. You jump up and grab her and begin hitting her harder and harder. You've lost control . . . you can't stop yourself. You are attacking your wife whom you love and want to protect (fear of aggressive behavior and loss of control).

For many veterans, the sole use of symptom-contingent cues is sufficient to result in significant clinical change for the patient. When indicated, the use of the additional cue categories can help patients whose fears and anxieties are even more complex. The combination of cue categories has been useful in several reported case studies (Fairbank et al., 1983; Fairbank & Keane, 1982; Keane & Kaloupek, 1982) described above and has resulted in a marked reduction of both trauma-related anxiety and PTSD symptoms in our patients.

d) *Session parameters.* Termination of scene presentation is based on the therapist's evaluation of anxiety reduction to that scene. Throughout each flooding session the therapist can monitor patient anxiety levels by requesting subjective ratings on the 0–10 anxiety scale. Typically, the patient's anxiety will be at a moderate level (5–6) at the outset of the session, increase to maximum levels (9–10) during traumatic and hypothetical cue presentation, and then decrease from the maximum level following repeated or prolonged presentation of the scene.

A decrease of subjective ratings of anxiety to a low level across successive sessions is one indicator that the anxiety associated with the traumatic memory has been reduced. If repeated scene presentation within a single session does not reduce anxiety within that session, the same scene will be treated again in the next treatment session. In addition to the use of subjective ratings to determine when to proceed to the next traumatic event, the therapist can also expect a decrease in motoric arousal, an effect that has been reliably associated with anxiety reduction (Fairbank et al., 1983).

To close each session in a positive manner, the therapist guides the patient through deep muscle relaxation. This is followed by a general discussion of the event, the individual's response to the scene, the possible triggering of related features of the memory, and the provision of considerable emotional support by the therapist to the veteran.

In summary, the use of the implosive therapy technique with PTSD Vietnam veterans is intended to reduce anxiety to traumatic combat events, related stimuli, and disturbing cognitions via an extinction procedure. Through the imaginal presentation of both stimulus-contingent cues and hypothetical cues, the therapist attempts to expose the veteran to all elements of the stimulus complex and thereby achieve symptom reduction and improved psychological functioning.

Stress Management Package. Our clinical research program is designed to compare the use of implosive therapy alone to the use of stress management techniques alone. Unlike implosive therapy, which focuses on the trauma, stress management techniques are applied to the client's current symptomatology. That is, the client is taught specific skills that can help him more effectively cope with the social, behavioral, and cognitive deficits typically found in PTSD. Our stress management package incorporates adaptations of several techniques including progressive relaxation (Bernstein & Borkovec, 1973), cognitive restructuring (Ellis, 1962), problem-solving (D'Zurilla & Goldfried, 1971) and anger control (Novaco, 1975).

The stress management treatment techniques for PTSD are applied in an educational format. The patient is informed that therapy does not achieve symptom reduction by removing the everyday stressors from his life. Instead, the staff intends to instruct the patient in how to better control his emotional reactions to stressors and to choose more appropriate behavioral responses to stressful situations.

The focus of the initial sessions includes the rationale for treatment, introduction to relaxation training, and problem identification. Since the specific symptoms of PTSD vary across patients, therapist and patient must first identify the symptoms to be targeted in treatment. The patient is asked to rank-order the symptoms according to the amount of dysfunction the symptoms cause in his life. Techniques that apply to those symptoms ranked highest are then presented. Additional symptoms are covered gradually throughout the course of treatment. Homework assignments allow the patient to practice techniques presented in the therapy sessions and monitor symptom changes.

1) *Relaxation training.* The progressive muscle relaxation technique described in the implosive therapy section is also used for stress management treatment. Although the technique is the same, its application varies.

Relaxation training is seen as a more central component of the stress management treatment package. For example, following the initial four sessions, relaxation training is conducted regularly throughout treatment with emphasis on the reduction of muscle groups relaxed during a given session. In addition, homework assignments are utilized to facilitate patient practice of the relaxation technique. The patient is given an audiotaped relaxation script for this purpose and may eventually be able to relax himself without use of the tape.

Relaxation has specific applicability to the following symptoms of PTSD: a) sleep disturbance/nightmares, b) intrusive thoughts, and c) increased irritability and anger.

a) *Sleep disturbance/nightmares* (Figley & Southerly, 1977). The patient is encouraged to use relaxation as an aid to sleep onset at both the beginning of the evening and following awakenings. Often veterans will depend on alcohol or other nonprescription drugs to decrease their fear of sleep and nightmares, and the relaxation technique is offered as an adaptive alternative to substance abuse.

b) *Intrusive thoughts* (Zimering, Caddell, Fairbank, & Keane, 1984). Following an intrusive thought of Vietnam, veterans may experience high levels of anxiety. This may disrupt the patient's functioning in major life areas such as vocational performance and interpersonal/marital relationships. The veteran is advised to use relaxation training to reduce this anxiety instead of other maladaptive habits (e.g., leaving home, substance abuse).

c) *Increased irritability and anger* (McDermott, 1981). Veterans with PTSD often experience difficulty in control of aggression which may be due in part to chronic levels of high anxiety. Relaxation is used here to help the patient maintain lower levels of anxiety, thereby reducing the probability of an anger episode.

2) *Cognitive restructuring.* The second component of the stress management package utilizes cognitive restructuring techniques. Essentially, a Rational-Emotive Therapy—RET (Ellis, 1962) approach is applied to specific symptoms of PTSD. The patient is taught the ABC model (Activating Event-Beliefs-Consequence) to assist in analyzing problem situations. Particular emphasis is placed on identifying irrational beliefs and negative self-statements that appear to have originated following the patient's traumatic experiences in Vietnam. The patient is instructed to dispute negative self-statements and irrational beliefs and to replace them with rational, realistic beliefs and positive self-statements. The therapist coaches the patient on recognizing unreasonable cognitions and on generating alternative, rational beliefs. Rational beliefs may be rehearsed both in the session and outside the session for those situations that are particularly troublesome and occur with high frequency.

The following symptoms are particularly amenable to the use of cognitive restructuring: a) increased irritability and anger, b) interpersonal difficulties—feelings of detachment and withdrawal from others, and c) guilt.

a) *Increased irritability and anger.* The patient is taught to recognize his unreasonable expectations about his environment and those around him. Priority is given to helping the patient recognize those irrational beliefs having to do with Vietnam that could lead to anger episodes. These irrational beliefs may include: beliefs about how others, particularly non-Vietnam veterans, should view the war (e.g., You can't talk about Vietnam or have an opinion unless you've been there. Anyone who opposed the war has no right to their opinion and deserves anything I might choose to do to them. Conscientious objectors are anti-American and should never have been allowed back into this country); irrational beliefs about the rights of Oriental people (e.g., Gooks shouldn't be allowed in this country after what they did to us); and irrational beliefs about how Vietnam veterans should be treated (e.g., People should just leave me alone. I don't have to take anything from anyone now. I have done my time and no one can tell me what to do).

The link between these beliefs and anger is drawn for the patient (via the ABC model) and alternate rational beliefs are generated, e.g., People are individuals and I cannot realistically judge an Oriental person I might see today in the U.S. by what happened to my buddies in Vietnam. I cannot expect everyone to treat me fairly, and I am going to have hassles in my life. These problems have nothing to do with my having served in Vietnam. I will just have to work on solutions to those hassles.

b) *Interpersonal difficulties—feelings of detachment and withdrawal from others* (DeFazio, Rustin & Diamond, 1975). Veterans often express irrational beliefs which interfere with their interpersonal functioning. Combat veterans routinely report a unique and powerful emotional bond that develops among men who serve together in combat. Veterans with PTSD often indicate that, following the loss of such a comrade, they avoid forming other close emotional attachments. The veterans relate that they had such irrational beliefs as: "If I get close to someone they will die and I can't stand that again" and, "Every time I care about someone, something bad happens to them." Again, the patient's irrational beliefs are identified and rational self-statements are substituted (e.g., Of course, anyone I care about will eventually die, but it is relatively unlikely that they will be snatched away from me as were my buddies in Vietnam. I would be unfair to both myself and my friend [lover, spouse] to enter this relationship intending to keep them at a distance. I won't experience the rewarding parts of the relationship with such an attitude).

Patients also express a great deal of concern about the impression others have formed of Vietnam veterans. This concern is often manifested in interpersonal interactions as the veteran maintains an emotional distance from significant others to avoid possible evaluation of his participation in the Vietnam war. While it is true that Vietnam veterans have received "bad press" in some instances and public opinion is sometimes unfavorable toward the veterans, it is non-functional for a Vietnam veteran to remain estranged from others in response to these circumstances. Therefore, the veteran is given feedback regarding the nature of his interactions with significant others and the role his cognitions play in that estrangement. The patient is encouraged to disclose appropriately to significant others, with the understanding that another's reactions cannot always be predicted. The therapist may choose to use modeling and role-playing to first counterattack irrational cognitions regarding the outcome of the veteran's self-disclosure, and then demonstrate possible alternative methods of self-disclosure.

c) *Guilt* (Egendorf, Remez, & Farley, 1981). Almost invariably, Vietnam veterans with PTSD express guilt about their actions in Vietnam. As delineated in the DSM-III diagnostic criteria for PTSD, the guilt may take the form of survival guilt or guilt about behavior required to survive. In combat, these veterans were often in situations which led to behaviors that conflicted with well-learned cultural mores and beliefs. Accordingly, guilt has proved to be one of the most difficult symptoms to effectively reduce as a function of cognitive restructuring. However, it does appear to be useful to change the veteran's self-damning cognitions. Our patients typically express feelings of worthlessness (e.g., I've killed innocent people. I shouldn't be alive now; I should have been killed in Vietnam like my buddies; I'd be better off than I am now. I don't deserve to live). To dispute such negative self-statements, the therapist focuses on the environmental contingencies and the situational specificity of behavior required in combat as opposed to the behaviors one would demonstrate under less stressful circumstances. Through this approach we do not attempt to excuse the acts committed, but rather offer a rational explanation for the veteran's behavior in combat. The intent is to prevent the patient from overgeneralizing about his behavioral patterns based on actions committed during the life-threatening stress of combat. The veteran is coached to make more positive self-statements: "I performed this behavior while in combat; my life and the lives of my buddies were at stake. I would not do such a thing now. I hate what I have done but I must carry on with my life. The best I can do is to live now in such a way that I can benefit others and myself. It serves no purpose for me to continually punish myself."

3) *Problem-solving*. The problem-solving procedure used in the stress management package utilizes the following four basic steps: identifying the problem, generating alternatives, evaluating alternatives, and choosing the alternative action. Only the first two steps of the procedure differ significantly from standard problem-solving as it would be used with any other patient population. Therefore, specifics of identifying the problem and generating alternatives will be addressed.

The focus of problem identification is to target the *specific* situation or environmental antecedents that may trigger the PTSD symptomatology. A wide variety of stimuli across all sensory modalities may act as antecedents to symptom onset including hot or rainy weather, helicopters, Oriental people, war movies, the smell of fish, etc. The therapist guides the patient in identifying particularly troublesome situations by giving homework assignments. The patient is instructed to monitor symptom frequency (e.g., nightmares, anger episodes) and environmental antecedents (e.g., time, place, setting).

Few of the reported symptoms of the disorder are present consistently day after day (e.g., a veteran may have combat nightmares only a few nights a week). Therefore, self-monitoring of symptoms by the patient is particularly important not only to isolate those situations in which a particular symptom is likely to occur, but also to determine the frequency of symptom occurrence prior to and during intervention.

We have found the problem-solving technique to be effective in the treatment of the following symptoms: 1) reexperiencing of the trauma through intrusive thoughts, nightmares and flashbacks; 2) interpersonal difficulties (treatment of interpersonal difficulties related to anger control will be discussed more fully in a separate section); and 3) exaggerated startle response. In this section we will discuss generating alternative behaviors for symptoms of PTSD.

a) *Escape situation.* When confronted with a stimulus associated with Vietnam, the veteran may have the option of escaping the stimulus, thereby breaking the stimulus-response chain that may elicit PTSD symptoms. For example, a veteran who sees and hears a helicopter overhead may escape the stimulus by going indoors away from the sight and sound of the helicopter. Of course, it may not always be feasible for the veteran to escape from the stimulus (as when the stimulus is encountered while on the job), and in those instances he may choose an alternate solution from the list below.

b) *Avoid situation.* In specific situations, presence of Vietnam-related stimuli may be predicted by the veteran's self-monitoring of symptoms. Once identified, the veteran may be able to avoid those situations. As in escaping a situation with a Vietnam-related stimulus, avoiding such a situation is also an attempt to break the stimulus-response chain leading to the disorder's symptoms.

For example, some veterans report that contents of many news broadcasts (e.g., political unrest, military conflicts, heavy loss of life in accidents or natural disasters, etc.) can precede the occurrence of nightmares and intrusive thoughts. We would, therefore, hypothesize that these news stories have served as CS's for the veteran's own traumatic events. With recognition of this hypothesized causal relationship the veteran can choose to avoid viewing the news broadcast.

c) *Deep muscle relaxation/pleasant imagery.* Veterans are also encouraged to use relaxation training and/or pleasant imagery as previously described as an anxiety-reduction technique when confronted with Vietnam-related stimuli. As the veteran becomes more skilled in using relaxation, he may be able to achieve relaxation relatively quickly, making this technique adaptable to a wide variety of settings. While it may be impractical for a veteran to escape or avoid Vietnam stimuli while on the job, it is likely that he could implement the relaxation technique and effectively reduce his Vietnam-related anxiety in a few minutes time.

d) *Cognitive restructuring.* Use of cognitive strategies previously described may be beneficial in the reduction of anxiety. Based on veteran self-reports, it appears that following exposure to a combat-related CS, the veteran's cognitions may exacerbate his anxiety level. That is, his self-statements are likely to reinforce the stimulus-response chain by pairing the Vietnam stimuli with an increased anxiety response (e.g., seeing a helicopter may lead the veteran to think, "That looks like the medevac that lifted my buddy out the day he died"). The veteran is encouraged to substitute statements which would inhibit associations between current environmental stimuli and traumatic combat memories (e.g., "I am not in a combat zone, I am at home. That helicopter is probably on a routine drill and has nothing to do with Vietnam").

e) *Anger control techniques.* Although difficulty in anger control is not a primary symptom of PTSD, the treatment of this problem will be highlighted in this section due to the high frequency with which veterans report these difficulties.

There are essentially three elements to the technique utilized with veterans in our program—the basic problem-solving format, training in assertiveness, and discrimination training. A problem-solving approach to anger control difficulties would first involve identifying those situations which are likely to lead to an anger episode. Next, as in other problem-solving approaches, the goal is to interrupt the stimulus-response chain with an alternate behavior. This end may be achieved by the veteran's implementing any of the techniques presented in the problem-solving section.

Additionally, the therapist will teach the patient alternative positive behaviors. Using an assertion training framework, emphasis is placed on differentiating aggressive versus assertive responses, with skill training including therapist modeling of appropriate behavior, patient rehearsal, and therapist performance feedback.

Finally, it is important to communicate to the patient that anger is not inherently a *bad* emotion. Rather, extreme anger or anger in response to trivial matters is undesirable. Discrimination of those situations which warrant anger, as opposed to those situations which do not, is stressed.

Additionally, the patient is coached to maintain a "goal-oriented" mind set. He or she is instructed that extreme anger or overreacting often interferes with accomplishing a goal and the patient is encouraged to maintain a low level of anger in response to only those situations that warrant anger.

To summarize, the stress management package is a skills training approach designed to target specific PTSD symptomatology impairing the veteran's current level of functioning. The focus of stress management therapy is not the memories of traumatic combat events (as in implosive therapy), but rather the veteran's presenting symptomatology (e.g., anger episodes, sleep disturbance, interpersonal difficulties, etc.), and the presentation of techniques that are designed to reduce those symptoms.

While there is empirical evidence of the therapeutic value of implosive therapy with Vietnam veterans (Fairbank & Keane, 1982; Keane & Kaloupek, 1982), it has not yet been empirically demonstrated which treatment approach yields superior clinical outcome. The purpose of our present research is to compare the efficacy of implosive therapy versus a stress management approach. As a result, each type of treatment is administered independently. However, clinical intuition would indicate that a combination of both treatment approaches would add incremental value to either treatment alone. Indeed, a combination of the two treatment approaches would address psychological symptoms related to the actual trauma as well as the veteran's current distress.

SUMMARY

This chapter presented the behavioral conceptualization of PTSD that we currently employ in the Vietnam Stress Management Program at the Jackson, Mississippi Veterans Administration Medical Center. This conceptualization is derived in part from Mowrer's two-factor learning theory and Stampfl and Levis's serial conditioning paradigm. Additional elements of our theory are derived from standard behavioral principles as they apply to PTSD in Vietnam veterans. From this conceptualization, we have developed both assessment and treatment methods that are effective in identifying Vietnam veterans with PTSD (Fairbank et al., 1983; Malloy et al., 1983), and treating the often severe and debilitating symptoms of PTSD (Fairbank & Keane, 1982; Keane & Kaloupek, 1982).

Since the symptoms of PTSD can be quite diverse and some symptoms are preeminent for one person and not another, we have attempted to bring together in this chapter the many techniques from our treatment program that have been applied to the patients treated in Jackson. While it was not our intention to fully explain each of the techniques employed, we did attempt to provide sufficient information regarding how we apply the techniques, to what symptoms we apply these techniques, and the rationale for such applications. Further detailed presentations of the techniques discussed can be found in other readily available sources in the psychological literature.

One final issue deserves mentioning. The relationship that develops between traumatized veterans and the therapist is a strong and typically positive one. The interpersonal communication during therapy is often greater than any experienced by the patient since the time of the trauma. Clearly, this rapport is a direct result of the support given to the patient as therapy proceeds to help him cope with the emotionally charged memories of the trauma. The development of this close interpersonal relationship with the therapist can serve as a model to the patient for the development of future satisfactory interpersonal relationships. Therapy can conclude by having the patient identify the factors associated with positive feelings toward another person, discussing the active role the patient had in developing the relationship with the therapist, and by having the patient rehearse behaviors typically associated with initiating positive and supportive interpersonal relationships.

Although we have learned much about assessing and treating PTSD since the inception of this diagnostic category in 1980, there remains a tremendous amount of research to be done.

1) Controlled clinical trials are needed to document which techniques, with which patients and in what order will be most effective in reducing the symptoms of PTSD.
2) Comparative outcome studies with and without medication are needed to provide guidance to clinicians in the field.
3) Studies on women with PTSD from Vietnam need to be conducted.
4) Refinement in assessment and treatment techniques is also needed.
5) Research on the effect that PTSD has on the psychological adjustment of the spouses and children of PTSD veterans would also be an extremely valuable contribution.
6) The methods of assessment and treatment developed here need to be extended to the survivors of other traumatic events.

Not surprisingly, the cost and the toll of our participation in Vietnam has gone well beyond the Vietnam era. At present, it is wholly unclear

292   *Trauma and Its Wake*

how long the psychologically devastating consequences of combat will
pervade our society.

REFERENCES

Atkinson, R.M., Henderson, R.G., Sparr, L.F., & Deale, S. Assessment of Vietnam vet-
    erans for posttraumatic stress disorder in Veterans Administration disability claims.
    American Journal of Psychiatry, 1982, *139*(9), 1118-1121.
Beck, A.T., Ward, C.H., Mendelson, M., Mock, J., & Erbaugh, J. An inventory for mea-
    suring depression. *Archives of General Psychiatry*, 1961, *4*, 561-571.
Bernstein, D.A., & Borkovec, T.D. *Progressive relaxation training*. Champaign, IL: Research
    Press, 1973.
Blanchard, E.B., Kolb, L.C., Pallmeyer, T.P., & Gerardi, R.J. The development of a psy-
    chophysiological assessment procedure for post-traumatic stress disorder in Vietnam
    veterans. *Psychiatric Quarterly*, 1982, *4*, 220-229.
Bower, G.H. Mood and memory. *American Psychologist*, 1981, *36*, 129-148.
Brown, J.S. *The motivation of behavior*. New York: McGraw-Hill, 1961.
Brush, F.R. The effects of shock intensity on the acquisition and extinction of an avoidance
    response in dogs. *Journal of Comparative and Physiological Psychology*, 1957, *50*, 547-552.
DeFazio, V.J., Rustin, J., & Diamond, A. Symptom development in Vietnam era veterans.
    American Journal of Orthopsychiatry, 1975, *45*, 158-163.
D'Zurilla, T.J., & Goldfried, M.R. Problem solving and behavior modification. *Journal of
    Abnormal Psychology*, 1971, *78*, 107-126.
Egendorf, A., Kadushin, C., Laufer, R.S., Rothbart, G., & Sloan, L. (Eds.). *Legacies of
    Vietnam: Comparative adjustment of veterans and their peers*. New York: Center for Policy
    Research, 1981.
Egendorf, A., Remez, A., & Farley, J. Dealing with the war: A view based on the individual
    lives of Vietnam veterans. In A. Egendorf, C. Kadushin, R. Laufer, G. Rothbart & L.
    Sloan (Eds.), *Legacies of Vietnam: Comparative adjustment of veterans and their peers*, Vol.
    V. New York: Center for Policy Research, 1981.
Ellis, A. *Reason and emotion in psychotherapy*. New York: Lyle Stuart, 1962.
Fairbank, J.A., Gross, R.T., & Keane, T.M. Treatment of posttraumatic stress disorder:
    Evaluating outcome with a behavioral code. *Behavior Modification*, 1983, *7*, 557-568.
Fairbank, J.A., & Keane, T.M. Flooding for combat-related stress disorders: Assessment
    of anxiety reduction across traumatic memories. *Behavior Therapy*, 1982, *13*, 499-510.
Fairbank, J.A., Keane, T.M., & Malloy, P.F. Some preliminary data on the psychological
    characteristics of Vietnam veterans with posttraumatic stress disorders. *Journal of
    Consulting and Clinical Psychology*, 1983, *51*, 912-919.
Fairbank, J.A., Langley, K., Jarvie, G.J., & Keane, T.M. A selected bibliography on post-
    traumatic stress disorders in Vietnam veterans. *Professional Psychology*, 1981, *12*(5),
    578-586.
Figley, C.R. *The American Legion Study and psychological adjustment among Vietnam veterans*.
    Lafayette, IN: Purdue University, 1977.
Figley, C.R. (Ed.). *Stress disorders among Vietnam veterans*. New York: Brunner/Mazel, 1978a.
Figley, C.R. Symptoms of delayed combat-stress among a college sample of Vietnam
    veterans. *Military Medicine*, 1978b, *143*. 107-110.
Figley, C.R., & Leventman, S. (Eds.). *Strangers at home: Vietnam veterans since the war*. New
    York: Praeger, 1980.
Figley, C.R., & Southerly, W.T. *Residue of war: The Vietnam veteran in mainstream America*.
    Paper presented at the Annual Meeting of the American Psychological Association,
    San Francisco, August 1977.

Foy, D.W., Sipprelle, R.C., Rueger, D.B., & Carroll, E.M. Etiology of post-traumatic stress disorder in Vietnam veterans: Analysis of premilitary, military and combat exposure influences. *Journal of Consulting and Clinical Psychology*, 1984, *52*, 79-87.

Geer, J.H. The development of a scale to measure fear. *Behavioral Research and Therapy*, 1965, *3*, 45-53.

Graham, J.R. *The MMPI: A practical guide*. New York: Oxford University Press, 1977.

Hathaway, S.R., & McKinley, J.C. *Minnesota Multiphasic Personality Inventory: Manual for administration and scoring*. New York: Psychological Corporation, 1967.

Horowitz, M. *Stress response syndromes*. New York: Jason Aronson, 1976.

Kazdin, A.E., & Wilcoxin, L.A. Systematic desensitization and nonspecific treatment effects: A methodological evaluation. *Psychological Bulletin*, 1976, *83*, 729-758.

Keane, T.M. *State-dependent retention and its relationship to psychopathology*. Unpublished manuscript, State University of New York at Binghamton, 1976.

Keane, T.M., Caddell, J.M., Martin, B., Zimering, R.T., & Fairbank, J.A. Substance abuse among Vietnam veterans with posttraumatic stress disorders. *Bulletin of the Society of Psychologists in Addictive Behaviors*, 1983, *2*(2), 117-122.

Keane, T.M., & Fairbank, J.A. Survey analysis of combat-related stress disorders in Vietnam veterans. *American Journal of Psychiatry*, 1983, *140*(3), 348-350.

Keane, T.M., & Kaloupek, D.G. Imaginal flooding in the treatment of a posttraumatic stress disorder. *Journal of Consulting and Clinical Psychology*, 1982, *50*, 138-140.

Lang, P.J. The psychophysiology of anxiety. In H. Akiskal (Ed.), *Psychiatric diagnosis: Exploration of biological criteria*. New York: Spectrum, 1977.

Levis, D.J. Implementing the technique of implosive therapy. In A. Goldstein, & E.B. Foa (Eds.), *Handbook of behavioral interventions: A clinical guide*. New York: Wiley, 1980.

Levis, D.J., & Boyd, T.L. Symptom maintenance: An infrahuman analysis and extension of the conservation of anxiety principle. *Journal of Abnormal Psychology*, 1979, *88*(2), 107-120.

Levis, D.J., & Hare, N.A. A review of the theoretical rationale and empirical support for the extinction approach of implosive (flooding) therapy. In M. Hersen, R.M. Eisler, & P.M. Miller (Eds.), *Progress in behavior modification*, Vol. 4. New York: Academic Press, 1977.

Malloy, P.F., Fairbank, J.A., & Keane, T.M. Validation of a multimethod assessment of posttraumatic stress disorders in Vietnam veterans. *Journal of Consulting and Clinical Psychology*, 1983, *51*(4), 488-494.

McDermott, W.F. *The influence of Vietnam combat on subsequent psychopathology*. Paper presented at the Annual Meeting of the American Psychological Association, Los Angeles, 1981.

Mineka, S. The role of fear in theories of avoidance learning, flooding and extinction. *Psychological Bulletin*, 1979, *86*, 985-1010.

Mowrer, O.H. On the dual nature of learning: A reinterpretation of "conditioning" and "problem solving." *Harvard Educational Review*, 1947, *17*, 102-148.

Mowrer, O.H. *Learning theory and behavior*. New York: Wiley, 1960.

Novaco, R.W. *Anger control: The development and evaluation of an experimental treatment*. Lexington, MA: D.C. Heath, 1975.

Penk, W.E., Robinowitz, R., Roberts, W.R., Paterson, E.T. et al. Adjustment differences among male substance abusers varying in degrees of combat experience in Vietnam. *Journal of Consulting and Clinical Psychology*, 1981, *49*(3), 426-437.

Rabkin, J.G., & Struening, G.S. Life events, stress, and illness. *Science*, 1976, *194*, 1013-1020.

Rimm, D.C., & Masters, J.C. *Behavior therapy: Techniques and empirical findings* (2nd ed.). New York: Academic Press, 1979.

Roberts, W.R., Penk, W.E., Gearing, M.L., Robinowitz, R. et al. Interpersonal problems of Vietnam combat veterans with posttraumatic stress disorder. *Journal of Abnormal Psychology*, 1982, *91*(6), 444-450.

Sierles, F.S., Chen, J., McFarland, R.E., & Taylor, M.A. Post-traumatic stress disorder and concurrent psychiatric illness. *American Journal of Psychiatry*, 1983, *140*, 1177-1179.

Solomon, R.L., Kamin, L.F., & Wynne, L.C. Traumatic avoidance learning: The outcomes of several extinction procedures with dogs. *Journal of Abnormal and Social Psychology*, 1953, *48*, 219-302.

Solomon, R.L., & Wyne, L.C. Traumatic avoidance learning: The principles of anxiety conservation and partial irreversibility. *Psychological Review*, 1954, *61*, 353-385.

Spielberger, C.D., Gorsuch, R.L., & Lushene, R.E. *Manual for the state-trait anxiety inventory (Self-evaluation questionnaire)*. Palo Alto, CA: Consultant Psychologist Press, 1970.

Stampfl, T.G., & Levis, D.J. Essentials of implosive therapy: A learning-theory-based psychodynamic behavioral therapy. *Journal of Abnormal Psychology*, 1967, *72*, 157-163.

Weingartner, H., Miller, H., & Murphy, D.L. Mood-state-dependent retrieval of verbal associations. *Journal of Abnormal Psychology*, 1977, *86*, 276-284.

Wilson, G.T., & Davison, G.C. Processes of fear reduction in systematic desensitization: Animal studies. *Psychological Bulletin*, 1971, *76*, 1-14.

Wilson, J.P. Conflict, stress, and growth: The effects of war on psychosocial development among Vietnam veterans. In C.R. Figley & S. Leventman (Eds.), *Strangers at home*. New York: Praeger, 1980.

Wilson, J. P. & Krauss, G. E. *Vietnam era stress inventory*. Unpublished inventory, 1980.

Worthington, E.R. Demographic and preservice variables as predictors of post-military service adjustment. In C.R. Figley (Ed.), *Stress disorders among Vietnam Veterans*. New York: Brunner/Mazel, 1978.

Zimering, R.T., Caddell, J.M., Fairbank, J.A., & Keane, T.M. Post-traumatic stress disorder in Vietnam veterans: An empirical evaluation of the diagnostic criteria. Paper presented at the Association for Advancement of Behavior Therapy, Philadelphia, November, 1984.

Zung, W. A self-rating depression scale. *Archives of General Psychiatry*, 1965, *12*, 63-70.

CHAPTER

12

The Treatment and Prevention of Long-term Effects and Intergenerational Transmission of Victimization: A Lesson From Holocaust Survivors and Their Children

YAEL DANIELI

The heterogeneity of responses of families of survivors to their Holocaust and post-Holocaust life experiences, described within and beyond the current notions of post-traumatic stress disorder, emphasizes the need to guard against expecting all victim-survivors to behave in a uniform fashion and to match appropriate therapeutic interventions to particular forms of reaction. The discussion delineates the meanings

An earlier version of this chapter was funded by the National Institute of Mental Health Contract # 092424762, 1982.

295

of the victimization rupture, preventive and reparative goals, and principles and modalities of treatment (professional and self-help) of the long-term effects and intergenerational transmission of the traumata. Highly needed training, which is traditionally absent, should include working through therapists' "countertransference" difficulties.

Once upon a time there were gas
chambers and crematoria; and no
one lived happily ever after.

(Langer, 1975, p. 124)

Having heard this "modern fairy tale," Langer states "one is compelled to acknowledge the new reality rushing into the void and to rewrite the Little Red Riding Hoods of our youth and past, granting to an amorphous wolf the triumphant role that fairy tales may deny but the history of the Holocaust confirms" (1975, p. 165). In his book, *The Destruction of the European Jews*, Hilberg (1961) too states that "only a generation ago, the incidents described in this book would have been considered improbable, infeasible, or even inconceivable. Now they have happened" (p. v). A country considered the most civilized and cultured in the western world committed the greatest evils that humans have inflicted on humans, and thereby challenged the structure of morality, human dignity, and human rights, as well as the values that define civilization. The Nazi Holocaust massively and mercilessly exposed the potential boundlessness of human evil and ugliness, in a silently acquiescing world.

Of the 8,861,000 Jews living in Europe prior to World War II, it is estimated that 400,000–500,000 survived the Nazi Holocaust in the underground, by hiding or escaping, in ghettos, or in slave labor camps, and no more than 75,000 outlived the Nazi death camps (Epstein, 1977, 1979; see also Dawidowicz, 1975).

Common sense dictates that it is inevitable for the massive traumata experienced by the remains of European Jewry to have had immediate and possibly long-term effects on these victim-survivors and even their offspring. Nevertheless, the vast literature on these consequences reveals an arduous struggle in law (Kestenberg, 1982), but particularly in psychiatry, to prove the existence of these effects. Some excellent reviews of the psychiatric literature can be found in articles in Krystal (1968), Krystal & Niederland (1971), Chodoff (1975), Israel-Netherlands Symposium (1979), Dimsdale (1980), and others. Only in 1980 did the evolving descriptions and definitions of the "survivor syndrome" in that literature win their way into the *Diagnostic and Statistical Manual of Mental Disorders* (APA, 1980) as a separate, valid catergory of "mental disorder"—309.81 Post-traumatic Stress Disorder.

Literature on the intergenerational transmission of the psychological effects of the Holocaust on survivors' offspring (children born after the war) began with Rakoff's article (1966). A review of this literature and an up-to-date bibliography can be found in Wanderman (1979), Danieli (1981c, 1982a) and Bergman and Jucovy (1982). The most recent literature voices concern about the transmission of pathological intergenerational processes to the third and succeeding generations.

In this chapter I will first present a brief summary of the differing post-war adaptational styles in survivors' families, which I have identified and described in detail elsewhere (Danieli, 1981a, 1981c). This typology and the observations in it have been supported in a study by Rich (1982). The heterogeneity of responses to the Holocaust and to the post-Holocaust life experiences in families of survivors—implied herein in the proposed taxonomy—is, in part, intended to guard mental health professionals against the grouping of individuals as "survivors," all of whom are expected to exhibit a single "survivor syndrome" (Krystal & Niederland, 1968), and the expectation that children of survivors will similarly manifest a single "child of survivor syndrome" (cf. Phillips, 1978). I will then present a preliminary theoretical model of victimization trauma and some implications for treatment considerations and goals, modalities, and modes.

While my discussion is based primarily on work with Jewish survivors of the Holocaust and their offspring, I believe that it also applies to other victim-survivor populations.

DIFFERING ADAPTATIONAL STYLES AMONG HOLOCAUST SURVIVOR FAMILIES

Background

One way that survivors coped with the prolonged horrors of the Holocaust was to sustain the hope of reuniting with their families. While some did find a few surviving relatives, most learned where and how their family members and friends had perished. Unable to fully comprehend their tragedy or to express their grief or rage, they were confronted with the task of rebuilding their lives. "Marriages of despair," formed on short acquaintance, which disregarded differences in pre-war socioeconomic and educational status, life-style, age, or other ordinary criteria for marriage, were frequent between adult survivors. Recreating a family was a concrete act to compensate for the losses, counter the massive disruption in the order and continuity of the survivors' lives, and undo the dehumanization and loneliness they had experienced.

The most tangible fulfillment of hope for the continuity and renewal of life was to bring a child into the world. Many survivors gave birth in displaced persons (DP) camps as soon as it was physically possible. Almost without exception, the newborn children were named after those who had perished. Often viewed as a blessing, miracle, gift, or symbol of victory, the children were to be the future in a world free of oppression and equal to or even better than the idealized pre-war world of their parents.

In addition to the difficulties shared by most immigrants to the United States, the majority of Holocaust survivors encountered a unique cluster of pervasive negative societal reactions and attitudes comprised of indifference, avoidance, repression, and denial of their Holocaust experiences.

The "Conspiracy of Silence"

Survivors' war accounts were too horrifying for most people to listen to or believe. Additionally, bystanders' guilt led many to regard the survivors as pointing accusing fingers at them. Survivors were also faced with the pervasively held myth that they had actively or passively participated in their own destiny by "going like sheep to the slaughter" and with the suspicion that they had performed immoral acts in order to survive. Reactions such as these ensured the survivors' silence about their Holocaust experiences.

The resulting "conspiracy of silence," which has existed both between the Holocaust survivors and society, and between survivors and the mental health professionals for over 30 years, had a significant negative impact on the survivors' post-war familial and sociocultural adaptation and, consequently, on their long-term capacity for intrapsychic integration and healing.

Survivors were forced to conclude that nobody cared to listen, and that no one who had not undergone the same experience "could really understand" them. Their profound isolation, loneliness, and mistrust of society intensified, and the task of mourning their massive losses became impossible. The silence imposed by a world that did not want to hear them proved particularly painful to those who had survived the war determined to bear witness.

The only option left to survivors, other than sharing their Holocaust experiences with each other, was to withdraw completely into their newly established families. Children of such families, although remembering their parents' and lost families' war histories "only in bits and pieces," attested to the constant psychological presence of the Holocaust at home, verbally and nonverbally, or in some cases, reported having absorbed the omnipresent experience of the Holocaust through "osmosis."

From data obtained in clinical and semi-clinical work with survivors and offspring participating in the Group Project for Holocaust Survivors and Their Children, begun in the New York City area in 1975, I have formulated four major categories of survivor families: victim families, fighter families, numb families, and families of "those who made it." These categories are of special significance in establishing the resulting identity and self-image of the children.

These findings were derived from work with 75 survivors, ages 37-74, and approximately 300 children of survivors, ages 17-33, some of whom are married and parents themselves. All families had at least one member who survived the Holocaust, and at least one child born after the war. Since many of these people were well-adjusted by most external criteria, this sample consisted of a wider range of adjustment than is traditionally reported in clinical literature on the sequelae of the Holocaust in the families of its survivors, which usually focuses on what I call "victim families" (see, for example, Barocas, 1975; Rakoff, et al, 1966; Sigal, Silver, Rakoff, & Ellin, 1973; Trossman, 1968).

Below is a brief summary of the four family classifications which I have described in detail elsewhere (Danieli, 1981a, 1981c, 1981d). It should be noted that, although the survivor parent's post-war posture may or may not be identical with his or her war experiences, most survivors who headed victim or numb families were former concentration camp inmates; most of those in the fighter category were partisans and resistance fighters during the war.

Victim families. The post-war home atmosphere of survivors whose dominant identity was that of victim was characterized by pervasive depression, worry, mistrust and fear of the outside world, and by symbiotic clinging within the family. Catastrophic overreactions to everyday changes were common. Somatization, while serving as an unconscious expression of survivors' chronic grief and rage, was also used to control and manipulate other family members.

Physical problems were far more acceptable in victim families than psychological problems, which the parents viewed as evidence of Hitler's posthumous victory. Psychological help was also seen as a threatening intrusion into the symbiotic network of the family.

Yet another means of keeping the family a totally closed system was teaching mistrust to the children. Taking orders or instructions from outside authorities was experienced, at best, as passive humiliation. Children in such families were often trained to be survivors of future Holocausts and frequently reported panic and guardedness when Holocaust imagery intruded into their daily experiences. The long-term result of such experiences was often keen political liberalism.

Victim families insisted that the inside doors of their homes remain open at all times. Any assertion of healthy independence and privacy needs by their children threatened parents, who felt they were reliving their war experiences, when being separated meant total and permanent loss. The demands for symbiotic devotion and for fulfilling family goals were most heavily visited upon first-born children.

Security based on physical, nutritional, and material survival was of paramount concern in these homes. For most parents, joy, self-fulfillment, and existential questions were "frivolous" luxuries.

Survivor parents appeared to be both very certain and "disaster smart" to their children in protecting them against any negative eventuality in life. Being "right" and in control in their families, even if arbitrarily so, seems to have compensated for the survivors' prevailing sense of passive helplessness and demoralization during the Holocaust. Because wrong decisions during the war invariably meant death, many children also behaved as though every decision were a matter of life and death. Survivor parents were frequently lost and disoriented, however, in dealing with the American reality and it then became the children's task to become the family's mediators with the outside world. Thus, roles in these families were reversed and overprotection became mutual.

The children were also called upon to be the mediators inside the homes, as parents' marriages of despair frequently turned into interminable complaining about their mutual disappointments. For the male survivor, at a disadvantage compared to the female in achieving psychological recovery and in reestablishing his traditional role as head of the family (Danieli, 1981a), making a new life often became merely "making a living." Typically, the husband became a compulsive worker and took a subsidiary position in the emotional and interpersonal life of the family. The wife would frequently berate her husband in front of her children. The offspring were called upon to take sides, to serve as confidants, to compensate for a parent's disappointment in marriage, and to parent their parents.

For reasons related to the war, the management of rage and aggression was an enormous problem for survivors. Moreover, life after the war did not afford the survivors adequate opportunity for expression of their bottomless rage, leaving them only indirect, mostly intrafamilial, means to express and experience it. The immense conflict and the meaning of aggression in their lives and their roles as parents severely inhibited the victim survivors' ability to serve as authority figures for their off-spring—to set limits and to provide them with reasonable discipline and constructive channels for their normal aggression. The children's fear of being wrong, and their inhibition of anger and assertiveness, tended to block creative self-initiated tasks of these often disproportionately bright, ambitious, and talented offspring.

Guilt was one of the most potent means of control in these victim families, keeping many adult children from questioning parents about their war experience, expressing anger toward them, or "burdening" them with their own pain.

Being totally passive and helpless in the face of the Holocaust was perhaps the most devastating experience for victim survivors, one that was existentially intolerable. Because guilt presupposes the presence of choice and the power to exercise it, much of what has been termed "survivor's guilt" (Niederland, 1964) may be an unconscious attempt to deny or undo this helplessness. Guilt as a defense against utter help-lessness links both generations to the Holocaust. The children, in their turn, are helpless in their mission to undo the Holocaust both for their parents and for themselves.

Guilt also operates as a vehicle of loyalty to the dead, keeping both generations engaged in relationships with those who perished, and maintaining a semblance of familial continuity.*

Overprotectiveness and overinvolvement in all aspects of their par-ents' lives diminished the offspring's ability to establish outside rela-tionships in general, and marital and sexual relationships in particular.

---

*For additional functions of guilt, see Danieli, 1984.

Many dreaded being on their own and becoming adults. Most feared having children, to whom they might transmit their Holocaust legacy and upon whom they would inflict a world that might suffer another Holocaust. Despite their conscious wish to make the family whole and large once again, this fear usually prevailed.

Although many children of survivors were extraordinarily driven to achieve academic or professional success, the offspring of victims often felt that surpassing their parents meant leaving them behind, and as a result often unconsciously destroyed their success and accomplishments. Overly concerned not to hurt, and keenly sensitive to another's pain, the children of victim survivors frequently entered the helping professions.

Fighter families. The term fighter was chosen to convey either the way such survivors described their physical or spiritual role during the Holocaust or the posture they adopted after the war to counteract the image of the victimized Jew. However, many who were fighters during the war lived as victims after liberation and this incongruous transformation bewildered their offspring, impairing their development of cohesive self-images.

It is important to emphasize that using the word fighter to connote the dominant identity of these survivors does not imply that active fighting, rather than sheer luck, saved all who escaped the fate of the six million Jews who died in the Holocaust.

The home atmosphere of fighter survivors was permeated by an intense drive to build and achieve, and the home was filled with compulsive activity. Any behavior that might signify victimization, weakness, or self-pity was not permitted. Illness was faced only when it became a crisis. Although physical illness was more acceptable than psychological disturbance, both were experienced as narcissistic insults. Pride was fiercely held as a virtue; relaxation and pleasure were superfluous.

Families of fighters, like those of victims, did not trust outside authorities. Unlike victims, however, they permitted and encouraged aggression against and defiance of outsiders, thus escaping the victim families' double bind.

Intergenerational overinvolvement and overprotectiveness were found in fighter families, but without the burden of distress and worry characteristic of victim families. Some fighter marriages were formed during the war, after a longer acquaintance period than the marriages of despair mentioned earlier.

Children of fighters had difficulty in sharing and delegating responsibility to others, both interpersonally and professionally. Their contempt and intolerance of any dependency in themselves and others acted as a deterrent to forming peer and marital relationships.

In these families, the offspring had to establish a fighter/hero identity in order both to belong to the family and to separate from it. In their search for validation and esteem, children frequently sought out or created dangerous situations.

Numb families. In numb families, both parents were frequently the sole survivors of their individual families which before the war had included a spouse and children. The post-war home atmosphere was characterized by pervasive silence and depletion of all emotions, the parents capable of tolerating only a minimal amount of stimulation, either pleasurable or painful. Some children were too frightened to imagine what could have led to such constriction and lifelessness in their parents. As a result, their own inner spontaneity and fantasy life were severely restricted.

In numb families, the parents protected each other and the children protected the parents. Children were expected to somehow grow up on their own and to take care of themselves. Despite the infrequency of physical and verbal contact with their parents, they were also expected to understand that they were loved because of their parents' pained efforts to support them financially.

Offspring often adapted by numbing themselves, which resulted in their appearing less intelligent and capable of achieving than they were, or by being perpetually angry in an apparent effort to evoke negative attention instead of none at all.

The children frequently adopted outside authorities and peers as family in an attempt to seek identification models and to learn how to live. In desperate attempts to please their parents, they tried to achieve generally accepted social standards, but often felt out of place, forlorn, and not genuinely involved in their pursuits.

Since they rarely felt central or important at home, the children did not believe that others would consider them worthy of attention. In their unconscious fantasies, their (future) spouses served as the parental figures they were deprived of. Their powerful need to be babied often curbed a desire for children of their own.

"Families of those who made it". This fourth group is less homogeneous than the other three. Many of these survivors were motivated by a wartime fantasy and desire to "make it big," if they were liberated, in

order to defeat the Nazis. Persistently and single-mindedly, they sought higher education, social and political status, fame and/or wealth. As with other survivor families, they used their money primarily for the benefit of their children.

Outwardly, this group was more completely assimilated into American society than other survivors. Some achieved a "normal" posture by completely denying and avoiding their past and any reminders of it. Children of this group reported feeling cheated and bitter at finding out, usually indirectly, about their heritage. The denial in these families often resulted in inner numbing, isolation and somatization, and in this respect they resembled the numb families (see also Krystal, 1975, 1978; Oswald & Bittner, 1968).

This is the only survivor group of the four discussed to have a high rate of divorce. Some who, right after the war, married other survivors, eventually divorced. While most of "those who made it" were too young at liberation to rush into marriage, they also tended to marry non-survivors.

The survivor's role in these families was the dominant one. His or her ambitions became those of the family members. Although proud of their parents' achievements, the children reported feeling emotionally neglected by them, except in those areas leading to their own demonstrable success. In contrast to their emphasis on good appearances, the parents unconsciously encouraged semi-delinquent behavior in their adolescent children, using their money or position to rescue them from the consequences.

Some survivors in this group devoted much of their careers, money, and political status to demand commemoration of and attention to the Jewish experience during the Holocaust, and dignity for its victims. They used their Holocaust experiences as a means to understand the roots of genocide, to find ways to prevent its recurrence, and to aid victimized populations in general. The Holocaust was also a central theme in the works of members of this group who were involved in the arts.

Despite some willingness to undertake psychotherapy as a culturally acceptable pursuit, "those who made it" tended to deny the long-term effects of the Holocaust upon themselves and their children and would rarely discuss the Holocaust as a factor in their psychological lives.

SOME IMPLICATIONS FOR TREATMENT

My focus on the relationship between Holocaust experiences and post-war adaptational styles among survivors' families precludes discussion of pre-Holocaust background considerations that are critical to understanding post-war adjustment. These may include the characteristics and dynamics of the survivor's family of origin in pre-World War II European Jewish life, as well as such demographic factors as the nationality, age, education, occupation, and marital and social status of the survivor at the onset of the Holocaust. These background considerations should be explored in psychotherapy with survivors and their children in order to (re)establish the sense of integration, rootedness and continuity so damaged by their traumata. Furthermore, since children of survivors seem to unconsciously repeat their parents' Holocaust experiences in their own lives, those experiences should be explored in detail with the children as well.

The individual survivor's war history is crucial to the understanding of survivors' offspring. They seem to have consciously and unconsciously absorbed their parents' Holocaust experiences into their lives almost *in toto*. Holocaust parents, in the attempt to give their best, taught their children how to survive and, in the process, transmitted to them the life conditions under which they had survived the war.

Many children of survivors, like their parents, manifest Holocaust-derived behaviors, particularly on the anniversaries of their parents' traumata. Moreover, some have internalized as parts of their identity the images of those who perished and, hence, simultaneously live in different places (Europe and America) and different time periods (1942 and the present.)

Very close to most, if not all, families of survivors is the concern about the meaning of being a Jew after the Holocaust (Danieli, 1981b). Most of these families are extremely small. The Holocaust deprived them of the normal cycle of the generations and ages, and of natural death (Eitinger, 1980). Each family tree is laden with death and losses. Indeed, the most painful and intolerable struggle underlying all attempts at coping with and integrating the impact of the Holocaust into the lives of these families is the genuine impossibility of mourning. As one 74-year-old fighter, recently rewidowed and the sole survivor of a family of 72 people, put it, "Even if it takes one year to mourn each loss, and even if I live to be 107 [and mourn all members of my family], what do I do about the rest of the six million?"

The taxonomy that I have proposed for categorizing the families of Holocaust survivors is not intended to represent or imply pure and mutually exclusive types, nor to blur the commonality of core issues confronting Holocaust survivors and their offspring. It is intended to alert mental health professionals to the heterogeneity within and *beyond* the post-traumatic stress syndrome, and its (potentially) differential effect on victim/survivor family members. Indeed, the heterogeneity of responses to the Holocaust and to post-Holocaust life experiences in families of survivors emphasizes the need to match appropriate therapeutic interventions to particular forms of reaction, and to respect the unique individuality of each victim/survivor. This need similarly exists in working with other victim/survivor populations.

SOME THEORETICAL CONSIDERATIONS

Before discussing my approach to treatment I will discuss a set of reflections which is the basis of my approach.

The goals of the Group Project for Holocaust Survivors and Their Children, which are preventive as well as reparative, are predicated on two major assumptions: 1) that awareness of the meaning of post-Holocaust adaptational styles and the integration of Holocaust experiences into the totality of the survivors' and their offspring's lives will be liberating and potentially self-actualizing for both; and 2) that awareness of transmitted, intergenerational processes will inhibit the transmission of pathology to succeeding generations.

While psychological/internal liberation from the trauma of victimization is the ultimate goal of treatment for survivors, the central and guiding dynamic principle is integration. That is, integration of the trauma into one's life span in such a way that it will become a meaningful part of the survivor's and the survivor's offspring's identity, hierarchy of values, and orientation of living. It is a longitudinal integration along the time dimension which gains a full perspective of the victimization experiences and their impact upon one's life space at any point in time. An essential aspect of the establishment of such perspective is that when we speak of integration in the case of victimization, we speak of integrating the *extraordinary* into one's life—that is, confronting and incorporating aspects of human existence that are not normally encountered in ordinary everyday life. In the case of victimization in the Holocaust, we often speak of reconstituting the (inner) world of one's shattered life.

In Figure 1, the concentric circles on the horizontal plane represent the individual within his or her complex physical/intrapsychic/identity, familial, social/communal, religious/cultural, national, and international spheres or systems. If one envisions this plane as moving along the vertical vector (like an elevator shaft), which represents the continuous life-time dimension in one's conception of life from past to present through one's future, an individual ideally should simultaneously be able to move freely along both the horizontal and vertical dimensions.

Victimization causes a rupture, a possible regression, and a state of being "stuck" in this free flow, which I will call *fixity*. The time, duration, extent, and meaning of the victimization for the individual, as well as post-victimization traumata and the conspiracy of silence or second wound (Symonds, 1980), will determine the elements and degree of

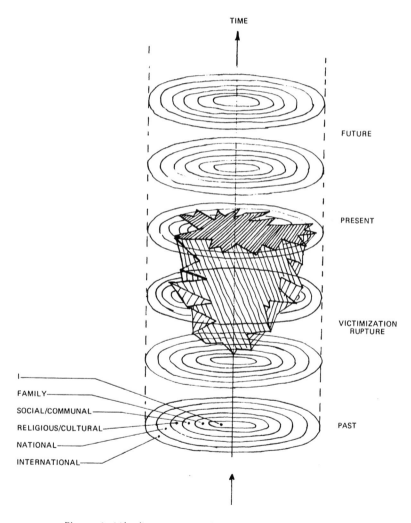

Figure 1. Life dimensions and the victimization rupture

rupture, the disruption, disorganization and disorientation, and the severity of the fixity. The massive catastrophe of the Holocaust not only ruptured continuity but also destroyed all the individual's existing supports and was, as previously described, pervasively exacerbated by the conspiracy of silence that followed it.

Elsewhere (Danieli, 1981e) I questioned, in principle, the possibility of full integration of the Holocaust by its survivors and their offspring alone, while humanity, Western culture, and society in general have not yet done so. However, the Group Project for Holocaust Survivors and Their Children still maintains that the attempt to reestablish the sense of continuity, belongingness and rootedness, and to effect perspective and integration through awareness, are our optimal vehicles in possibly achieving our reparative and preventive goals of liberation from the traumata (see Lifton, 1973, 1979).

Especially with these individuals, repairing the rupture and thereby freeing the flow rarely has the meaning of "going *back* to normal." This is true both in terms of (re)adapting to "normal society" or returning to pre-victimization ways of being and functioning, as if one could resurrect one's previous (destroyed) fabric of life. In fact, the latter hope in particular is not only unrealizable, but clinging to it possibly attests to attempted denial of the survivor's Holocaust experiences and thereby to fixity.

Cognitive recovery involves the ability to develop a realistic perspective of what happened, by whom and to whom, and accepting the reality that it happened the way it did. For example, what was and was not under the victim's control, what could not be, and why. Accepting the impersonality of the events also removes the need to attribute personal causality, and consequently, guilt and false responsibility. An educated and contained image of the events of victimization is potentially freeing from constructing one's view of oneself and of humanity solely on the basis of those events. For example, having been helpless does not mean that one is a helpless person; having witnessed or experienced evil does not mean that the world as a whole is evil; having been betrayed does not mean that betrayal is an overriding human behavior; having been victimized does not necessarily mean that one has to live one's life in constant readiness for its reenactment; having been treated as dispensable does not mean that one is worthless; and, taking the painful risk of bearing witness does not mean that the world will listen, learn, change, or become a better place.

The task of therapy within the theoretical framework presented above is to help survivors and children of survivors achieve integration of an experience which produced the state of fixity that has halted the normal flow of life in at least the four styles described earlier. Indeed, when psychotherapy dwells on certain periods in the survivors' lives and neglects others, it hinders survivors and their offspring from meaningfully recreating the flow within the totality of their lives, and may perpetuate their sense of disruption and discontinuity (see also, de Wind, 1972).

The long-term treatment modalities especially aim at the individual's "getting better" rather than merely "feeling better." "Getting better" involves a continuous and consistent unraveling and working through of the individual's or the family's particular (unconscious) rigidified and self-perpetuated victim-survivor context or stance, in the direction of liberation and (full) self-actualization. In this process, we harness and ally ourselves with the individual's or family's present as well as past strengths and pro-life forces, such as general cognitive abilities, the elements of one's active control and mastery in the act of survival, and the rebuilding of life, hope, determination, courage, loyalty, humor, and source of goodness, support, and love in one's memories and in one's current life. The latter potentially engender one's ability for self-soothing, giving, trusting, experiencing and accepting love, asking for and accepting another's help, attaining a sense of wholeness, healing, and recovery. These abilities must develop for the individual to be able to gain perspective, integrate and contain elements of his or her Holocaust or other victimization experiences, such as evil, hate, (helpless) rage, murder, violence, brutality, destruction, chaos, injustice, shame, degradation and humiliation, indifference, loss and mourning.

The Project provides individual, family, group, and community assistance in a variety of non-institutional settings. The meaning of institutions for survivors and their offspring, and their particular sensitivity to being stigmatized or labeled crazy (stemming in part from the Nazi practice of gassing the sick and mentally ill), specifically precluded making the Project part of a mental health institution.

Therapeutic methods and foci used by the professionals who staff the Project—all dictated by our goals and the needs of this population—are the dynamic/psychoanalytic, Gestalt, Transactional Analysis and Psychodrama, desensitization and Cognitive Behavior. These may be applied to all the treatment modalities provided by the Project.

The Group Project offers opportunities to participate in six types of groups (for a schematic presentation of these groups, see Danieli, 1981f). Each prospective participant is interviewed in order to determine the appropriate therapeutic modality. Many of the participants choose to combine a variety of modalities (e.g., individual and group therapy).

The central therapeutic goal of integrating disruption and discontinuity in part informed the diagnostic and therapeutic decision to construct a three-generation family tree (Danieli, in press) during the initial interviews with newcomers to the Project. Although it triggers an acute sense of pain and loss, it reaffirms the importance of continuity. One invaluable yield of exploring the three-generation family tree is that it opens communication within families and between generations. Breaking the silence about the Holocaust and pre-Holocaust experiences within the family is generally helpful in family therapy, but it is particularly crucial for aging survivors and their children (Danieli, 1981e). For issues and concerns particular to aging survivors, see Blau and Kahana (1981).

THE CENTRAL ROLE OF THE GROUP MODALITY

From its inception in 1975, the Project has recognized the vital importance of self-help and has capitalized on group and community therapeutic modalities to counteract the sense of isolation and alienation suffered by Holocaust survivors and their children. By participating in groups, survivors and offspring who are plagued by mistrust and the feeling that nobody who had not undergone the same experiences would "really understand" them, can discuss and share their current concerns and past experiences (Hays & Danieli, 1976).

Group modalities have been particularly helpful in compensating for countertransference reactions. Whereas a therapist alone may feel unable to contain or provide a "holding environment" (Winnicott, 1965) for his or her patients' feelings, the group as a unit is able to. While any particularly intense interaction invoked by Holocaust memories may prove too overwhelming to some people present, others invariably come forth with a variety of helpful holding reactions.

The group offers a place for abreaction and catharsis as well as a multiplicity of options for expressing feelings, and naming, verbalizing and modulating them. It also encourages mutual caring which ultimately enhances self-care in these individuals.

Identification with "their group," initially based on common background alone, facilitates positive change. As Foulkes (1948) suggested:

> The deepest reason why these patients . . . can reinforce each other's normal reactions and wear down and correct each other's

(pathological) reactions, is that *collectively they constitute the very norm, from which, individually, they deviate.* (p.29, author's italics)

In addition, the groups and community established by the Project serve to rebuild a sense of extended family and community lost to these individuals during the Holocaust.

Finally, these modalities acknowledge the central role of "we-ness" in the identity of the survivors, as manifested in their common use of "we" rather than "I," particularly when describing their Holocaust experiences. The Holocaust was a group phenomenon, and perhaps only collectively can its survivors find a meaningful response to it. This seems true particularly with regard to mourning, issues of Jewish identity after the Holocaust, and the relationship of the survivors and their children with the non-Jewish world.

TRAINING AND COUNTERTRANSFERENCE

Traditional training does not usually prepare professionals to deal with *massive, real, adult traumata* and their long-term effects (see also Wallerstein, 1973). I therefore cannot overemphasize the paramount importance of the training/peer supervision seminars and workshops held by the professionals staffing the Project for the survivors and their offspring. While the eagerness to read and research all available and relevant materials has produced much knowledge and understanding, and the genuine caring and desire to help have been unquestionable, the commitment that made the task of integration a fulfillable one was the professionals' struggle and openness to work through their countertransference reactions—their contribution to the conspiracy of silence, the obstacles they had erected on the road to awareness and integration of their patients' Holocaust experiences, and their long-term and intergenerational effects. Attention to their own reactions and mutual support have also helped reduce the incidence of burnout among these professionals.

I hope that increased awareness of the countertransference reactions, which I have identified and elaborated upon elsewhere (Danieli, 1980, 1984), will liberate professionals to optimally serve this and other victim-survivor populations. My research (Danieli, 1982a) strongly suggests that the source of these reactions is the Holocaust, rather than the actual encounter with its survivors and their offspring. I believe that therapists' difficulties in treating other victim-survivors may similarly have their roots in the nature of the victimization.

REFERENCES

American Psychiatric Association. *Diagnostic and statistical manual of mental disorders* (3rd ed.). Washington, D.C.: American Psychiatric Association, 1980.

Barocas, H.A. Children of purgatory: Reflection on the concentration camp survival syndrome. *International Journal of Social Psychiatry*, 1975, 21, 87-92.

Bergman, M.S., & Jucovy, M.C. (Eds.). *Generation of the Holocaust.* New York: Basic Books, 1982.

Blau, D., & Kahan, J. The aging survivor of the Holocaust. *Journal of Geriatric Psychiatry*, 1981, 14(2),

Chodoff, P. Psychiatric aspects of the Nazi persecution. In S. Arieti (Ed.), *American handbook of psychiatry* (Vol. 6, 2nd ed.). New York: Basic Books, 1975.

Danieli, Y. Countertransference in the treatment and study of Nazi Holocaust survivors and their children. *Victimology: An International Journal*, 1980, 5(2-4), 355-367.

Danieli, Y. Differing adaptational styles in families of survivors of the Nazi Holocaust: Some implications for treatment. *Children Today*, 1981a, 10(5), 6-10, 34-35.

Danieli, Y. Exploring the factors in Jewish identity formation (in children of survivors). In G. Rosen (Ed.), *Consultation on the psychodynamics of Jewish identity: Summary of proceedings.* American Jewish Committee and the Central Conference of American Rabbis, March 15-16, 1981b.

Danieli, Y. Families of survivors of the Nazi Holocaust: Some short- and long-term effects. In C.D. Spielberger, I.G. Sarason & N. Milgram (Eds.), *Stress and anxiety* (Vol. 8). New York: McGraw-Hill, 1981c.

Danieli, Y. Matching interventions to different adaptational styles of survivors. In S. Meiri (Ed.), *Massuah: A yearbook on the Holocaust and heroism* (Vol. 9) Tel-Aviv: M. Stern Press, 1981d.

Danieli, Y. On the achievement of integration in aging survivors of the Nazi Holocaust. *Journal of Geriatric Psychiatry*, 1981e, 14(2), 191-210.

Danieli, Y. The group project for Holocaust survivors and their children. *Children Today*, 1981f, 10(5), 11,33.

Danieli, Y. Group project for Holocaust survivors and their children. Prepared for National Institute of Mental Health, Mental Health Services Branch. Contract # 092424762. Washington, D.C.: 1982a.

Danieli, Y. Therapists' difficulties in treating survivors of the Nazi Holocaust and their children. Doctoral dissertation, New York University, 1981. *University Microfilms International*, 1982b, 949-904.

Danieli, Y. Psychotherapists' participation in the conspiracy of silence about the Holocaust. *Psychoanalytic Psychology*, 1984, 1(1), 23-42.

Danieli, Y. The diagnostic and therapeutic use of a three-generational family tree in working with survivors and children of survivors of the Nazi Holocaust. In A. Wilson (Ed.), *The Holocaust survivor and the family.* New York: Praeger, in press.

Dawidowicz, L.S. *The war against the Jews 1933-1945.* New York: Holt, Rinehart & Winston, 1975.

de Wind, E. Persecution, aggression and therapy. *International Journal of Psychoanalysis*, 1972, 53, 173-177.

Dimsdale, J.E. (Ed.), *Survivors, victims and perpetrators.* New York: Hemisphere Publishing Corp, 1980.

Eitinger, L. The concentration camp syndrome and its late sequelae. In J.E. Dimsdale (Ed.), *Survivors, victims, and perpetrators: Essays on the Nazi Holocaust.* New York: Hemisphere, 1980.

Epstein, H. Heirs of the Holocaust. *New York Times Magazine.* June 19, 1977, 12-15; 74-77.

Epstein, H. *Children of the Holocaust; Conversations with sons and daughters of survivors.* New York: Putnam and Sons, 1979.

Foulkes, S.H. *Introduction to group analytic psychotherapy.* London: Heineman, 1948.

Hays, D., & Danieli, Y. Intentional groups with a specific problem orientation focus. In M. Rosenbaum & A. Snadowsky (Eds.), *The intensive group experience*. New York; Free Press, 1976.

Hilberg, R. *The destruction of the European Jews.* London: Allen, 1961.

Israel-Netherlands Symposium on the Impact of Persecution (Jerusalem, October 1977). The Netherlands: Ministry of Cultural Affairs, Recreation and Social Welfare, 1979.

Kestenberg, M. Discriminatory aspects of the German Indemnification Policy: A continuation of persecution. In M.S. Bergman & M. Jucovy (Eds.), *Generations of the Holocaust.* New York: Basic Books, 1982.

Krystal, H. (Ed.). *Massive psychic trauma.* New York: International Universities Press, 1968.

Krystal, H. Affect tolerance. *The Annual of Psychoanalysis*, 1975, *3*, 179-219.

Krystal, H. Trauma and affect. *The Psychoanalytic Study of the Child*, 1978, *33*, 81-116.

Krystal, H., & Niederland, W.G. Clinical observations on the survivor syndrome. In H. Krystal (Ed.), *Massive psychic trauma*. New York: International Universities Press, 1968.

Krystal, H., & Niederland, W.G. (Eds.). *Psychic traumatization: Aftereffects in individuals and communities.* Boston: Little Brown, 1971.

Langer, L.L. *The Holocaust and the literary imagination.* New Haven: Yale University Press, 1975.

Lifton, R.J. The sense of immortality: On death and the continuity of life. *American Journal of Psychoanalysis.* 1973, *33*, 3-15.

Lifton, R.J. *The broken connection.* New York: Simon & Schuster, 1979.

Niederland, W.G. Psychiatric disorders among persecution victims: A contribution to the understanding of concentration camp pathology and its aftereffects. *Journal of Nervous and Mental Diseases*, 1964, *139*, 458-474.

Oswald, P., & Bittner, E. Life Adjustment after severe persecution. *American Journal of Psychiatry*, 1968,

Phillips, R.E. Impact of Nazi Holocaust on children of survivors. *American Journal of Psychotherapy*, 1978, *32*, 370-378.

Rakoff, V.A. A long-term effect of the concentration camp experience. *Viewpoints*, 1966, *1*, 17-22.

Rakoff, V., Sigal, J., & Epstein, N.B. Children and families of concentration camp survivors. *Canada's Mental Health*, 1966, *14*, 24-26.

Rich, M.S. Children of Holocaust survivors: A concurrent validity study of a survivor family typology. Unpublished doctoral dissertation, California School of Professional Psychology, Berkeley, 1982.

Sigal, J.J., Silver, D., Rakoff, V., & Ellin, E. Some second generation effects of survival of the Nazi persecution. *American Journal of Orthopsychiatry*, 1973, *43*, 320-327.

Symonds, M. The "second injury" to victims. *Evaluation and Change* (Special issue), 1980, 36-38.

Trossman, B. Adolescent children of concentration camp survivors. *Journal of the Canadian Psychiatric Association*, 1968, *13*, 121-123.

Wallerstein, R.S. Psychoanalytic perspectives on the problem of reality. *Journal of the American Psychoanalytic Association*, 1973, *31*(1), 5-33.

Wanderman, E. *Separation problems, depressive experiences and conception of parents in children of concentration camp survivors.* Unpublished doctoral dissertation, New York University, 1979.

13

Ethnicity and Traumatic Stress: The Intersecting Point in Psychotherapy

ERWIN RANDOLPH PARSON

This chapter discusses a number of critical variables focusing on the psychological, social, and interpersonal readjustment problems and needs of persons with strong ethnocultural identifications who suffer from traumatic stress following a catastrophic episode or episode pattern. The author believes that the intersecting point of ethnicity and traumatic stress needs to be understood in its synergistic impact upon the patient, as well as on the therapeutic process. Ethnicity shapes how the patient perceives, understands, accepts, and adapts to his or her traumatic stress pathology. Transethnic competency is thus essential, and there is the need for therapist awareness of the patient's "cultural-behavioral norms," as well as for overcoming ethnocentric views in their trans-cultural or transethnic interventions.

People from various ethnic groups who seek relief for their mental, interpersonal, and social symptoms often present a complex array of problems, especially if they have survived a traumatic episode. Ethnicity factors and their interaction with traumatic responses are the focus of this chapter.

Divergent ethnocultural groups have coexisted in America for over 200 years. These groups, however, have tended toward what this author has called *ethnic adhesion* (1980) rather than *ethnic liquescence* as implied by the "melting-pot" hypothesis. Elsewhere (1980) I have noted that the "melting-pot" hypothesis is an unworkable one, since it assumes a priori that ethnic differences are unimportant. Psychotherapists, counselors, and other helping professionals need to thus disengage from the "blanket perspective" to the "quilt perspective," in which each patch is different but essential to the final product and pattern configuration.

All ethnically focused clinical, sociological, anthropological, and experimental studies converge to one central conclusion regarding ethnic America: Ethnic identification is an irreducible entity, central to how persons organize experience, and to an understanding of the unique "cultural prism" they use in perception and evaluation of reality. Ethnicity is thus central to how the patient or client seeks assistance (help-seeking behavior), what he or she defines as a "problem," what he or she understands as the causes of psychological difficulties, and the unique, subjective experience of traumatic stress symptoms. Ethnicity also shapes how the client views his or her symptoms, and the degree of hopefulness or pessimism toward recovery. Ethnic identification, additionally, determines the patient's attitudes about sharing troublesome emotional problems with therapists, attitudes toward his or her pain, expectations of the treatment, and what the client perceives as the best method of addressing the presenting difficulties.

Unless ethnic variables are taken into account, interventions are bound to fail (Acosta, Yamamoto, & Evans, 1982; Marsella & Pederson, 1979; Parson, 1984b; Sue, 1981), though degree of assimilation and socioeconomic status are important qualifiers. Actually, ethnic differences and identification have been observed to be "far more important than differences in . . . economic system. Men who would not die for a . . . dogma would . . . cheerfully die for a difference rooted in ethnic origins" (Greeley, 1969, p. 5). Thus, the client's ideas, feelings, beliefs, values, gestures, intonations, perceptions, and evaluations, can only be understood within the patient's ethnocultural context.*

This chapter focuses on the dynamic interaction between ethnicity

---

*A recent conference on ethnicity and treatment asserts that providers may run the risk of engaging in unethical or at least ineffective practice when they fail to consider these relevant ethnocultural variables in psychotherapy (Korman, 1973).

variables and traumatic stress in the treatment process. Additionally, it provides an overview of the various challenges that confront the cross-ethnic therapist or counselor in any useful psychotherapeutic venture with traumatized individuals. The chapter is divided into four general areas that pertain to ethnicity and the treatment of post-traumatic stress responses or disorders: 1) Human Catastrophic Episodes and Traumatic Stress; 2) Ethnicity and Ego Identity; 3) Diagnostic Considerations in the Context of Ethnicity and Traumatic Stress; and 4) Transethnic Psychotherapy with Traumatized Persons.

The reader should keep in mind that no generalization is perfect, and that this chapter is written with the intention of raising therapist awareness from ethnocentrism to an awareness of multiple ethnocultural belief systems, as well as to develop an appreciation for the *relative* nature of our own cultural values. Thus, ethnic characterizations used to describe the clients in the case studies do not intend to contribute to existing stereotypes which are insulting to members of various ethnic groups. However, some generalizations are obviously necessary if useful ethnic value analysis is to occur.

HUMAN CATASTROPHIC EPISODES AND TRAUMATIC STRESS

Clinical, experimental, and field studies have revealed that severe traumatic life events induce a peculiar set of symptoms and reactions (Figley, 1978). Though specific reactions and symptoms may differ from person to person, there are a few that are common to most survivors of traumatic episodes: quasi-hallucinatory waking experiences reminiscent of the original trauma (or "flashbacks"); terrorizing recollections during sleep ("traumatic dreams"); nervousness; irritability; explosiveness; somatic complaints; emotional numbing (to ward off intrusion); withdrawal; and problems in intimacy. Survivors of traumatic events are persons whose "protective psychic shield" was overrun by traumatic intensities, too overwhelming to have been mastered and regulated by the ego. Any human being, irrespective of ethnic origins or predisposition, is likely to succumb to a stressor of sufficient intensity. Many traumatic symptoms and reactions ranging from mild to severe, from normal to pathological, and from acute to chronic states, can be found in those who have experienced the horrors of the Holocaust (Furst, 1967; Krystal, 1968); the Hiroshima Blast (Lifton, 1968); severe head injuries (Ader, 1945); rape trauma (McDonald, 1979); industrial accidents (Bloch

& Bloch, 1976); and other personal injuries (Horowitz, Wilner, Kaltreider, & Alvarez, 1980). Additionally, stress symptomatology is observed in women with miscarriages (Friedman & Cohen, 1980); in hostages taken in prison (Wolk, 1981); in repatriated prisoners of war (Corcoran, 1982; Ursano, 1981; Ursano, Boydstun, & Wheatley, 1981); in survivors of combat in the Yom Kippur War (Moses, Bargel, Falk, HaLevi et al., 1976); in veterans of World War II and Korea (Archibald & Tuddenham, 1965); and in veterans of the Vietnam War (Figley, 1978; Parson, 1984b).

In terms of the black combat veteran, in 1978 the Washington Urban League reported that a "mental disorder" was the most problematic disability interfering with the readjustment process after combat trauma (Washington Urban League, 1978). A late study mandated by the United States Congress and reported in 1981, substantiates this observation. As reported by Egendorf (1982), this latter investigation concluded that those who served in Vietnam have more problems than their peers in education and employment, and have higher incidences of arrests, drug use, and more medical and psychological complaints. This study, called "Legacies of Vietnam," also reported that blacks and Chicanos suffered significantly more readjustment problems than white veteran survivors in psychic, social, vocational, and academic functioning. The following research findings are pertinent here:

1) Blacks and Chicanos have suffered more stress disturbances than their white counterparts (the Comparative Factor);
2) Though being in heavy combat was the most crucial factor in severe forms of post-trauma stress reactions and symptoms, for the black veteran merely being in the theatre of war was sufficient to produce stress-related problems (the Theatre-Presence Factor);
3) Almost 70% of black veterans in heavy combat suffer stress reactions;
4) In general, 40% of black veterans, as compared with 20% of white veterans, are traumatically stressed today (Kadusha, Boulanger, & Martin, 1981);
5) Black veterans who suffered stress reactions immediately following the war are more likely to be stressed today than whites (the Residual Stress Factor).

The Comparative Factor indicates that blacks and Chicanos suffered more post-combat stress reactions and disorders compared to whites and, that for black veterans, a longer period of time (Residual Stress

Trauma and Its Wake

Factor), regardless of the degree of combat exposure (Theatre-Presence Factor). Thus, whereas white combat veterans' stress-related problems were related primarily to *heavy* combat, for blacks merely being in the theatre of war (in-country) was sufficient to induce traumatic stress. There are at least two explanatory avenues for this vulnerability phenomenon: 1) blacks' strong affective identification with the Vietnamese civilian (or the "gook"-identification); and 2) the "stress-primed" orientation to life.

Clinical experience reveals that some soldiers, especially those of ethnic minority backgrounds, established a strong emotional affinity with the Vietnamese nationals, referred to as the "gook"-identification, and defined as the conscious and unconscious emotional identification with the devalued, maligned, abused, and helpless aspects of the Vietnamese people (Parson, 1982; 1984b). Such empathic involvement with these people would tend to induce psychic stress, anguish, and guilt, especially in those who actually killed Vietnamese civilians (or even the VC). As one ethnic minority veteran put it, "How could you kill them and not be affected by it on a deep level? They're just like you (the minority veteran) in so many ways." The latter factor (that is, the "stress-primed" orientation) relates to the hypothesis that many veterans of ethnic minority heritages had lived a life of *cumulative "trauma"* stemming from racism and the generalized climate of institutional neglect, discrimination, and systematic exclusion. It is now widely known that the ethnic minorities were overrepresented in the Project 100,000 induction program of the 1960's (Phillips, 1980). The case studies below illustrate the diversity of factors associated with transethnic treatment.

Case Studies

> *E.S., a 28-year-old Puerto Rican woman, had been raped three blocks from her home. She had no previous psychiatric problems, and had grown up in a middle- to upper middle-class family. Her presenting problems or symptoms were: headaches, nausea, recollection of the traumatic (rape) event, withdrawal, irritability, anger, "crying spells," and seeming disinterest in her family and surroundings. E.S. was referred by a non-Puerto Rican family physician to a psychologist for treatment because of a peculiar dissociative episode reported to the physician by the client's mother a few days before.*

> *A.K. is a 44-year-old Jewish man who sought help for his*

emotional problems related to a severe car accident that had left him comatose for over an hour, two years ago. Since the accident he has been unable to work. He had held a variety of prominent positions in the corporate world, and now describes himself as "a vegetable, a brainless vegetable, with no hope." A.K. complained of helplessness, intrusive recollections, nervousness, irritability, rage reactions, lack of memory and concentration, and attending impairment. His wife asked him for a divorce after the accident, and his children (three sons and two daughters) were described as nonsupportive and lacking in understanding.

T.L. is a verbally talented 66-year-old Irish-American veteran of World War II, whose chief complaints were related to his combat experience. Though he has no recollection of killing during the war, he nevertheless has suffered during the last 25 years frightening traumatic dreams of being chased and almost caught by the enemy who would then torture him to death. These dreams often disrupted his sleep and caused strain in his marriage. He expressed strong feelings of guilt and pessimism, and appeared "one-tracked" in his mind that he was being punished for his "war crimes." The client felt his suffering was a "just due," and showed great hopelessness that things would ever improve for him.

A.G. is a 48-year-old Italian man whose traumatic injury to his spine left him severely physically disabled. As a building contractor he had worked most of his adolescent and adult years in construction and had prided himself on his physical fitness and strength. He presented a clinical picture marked by depression, irritability, anger, tremulousness, recurrent traumatic memories and dreams. He felt that his family could not understand him, and that, as the last resort, he sought assistance for his depression. He lost his sense of humor (commedia dell'arte) with which he had amused himself and others for years. A.G. has four sons and three daughters, all of whom are perplexed at his recent withdrawal, anger, and irritability.

These four cases portray a common set of traumatic symptoms. From the clinical therapeutic position, however, perhaps the most critical factor in each case is the ethnic identity of the survivor. Any clinician who desires to be truly helpful to any of these four patients will have to develop *cultural expertise* (Sue, 1981) in each of the ethnic groups represented by these patients. Acquisition of transcultural competence with all ethnic groups may not be possible for most therapists; however, the capacity to be sensitive to cultural differences and open to the ethnically different patient, will promote efficacy in the treatment process with members of these groups.

ETHNICITY AND EGO IDENTITY

The patient's perceptions, evaluations, and conclusions about nature, people, things, and institutions relate to his or her attitudes, values, opinions, convictions, beliefs, and concepts. Through these, the individual's mode and method in thinking, loving, feeling, making decisions, and defining events are organized in a culturally coherent manner. Quite often this coherence is misunderstood, devalued, or unrecognized by nontransethnic therapists. The culturocentric therapist is one whose world view is closed and narrow, and whose biases create a closed system that blocks out new vital information on cultural diversity. The ethnocentric therapist can be very "damaging to many culturally different clients" (Sue, 1981, p. 73).

It is quite apparent that the melting pot ideology still persists in our culture, and that therapists still maintain a rigidity in view, expectation, and evaluation when it comes to the ethnic group clients. Though white middle-class criteria for intervention remain useful and have wide applicability, preparatory and concurrent study in conducting psychotherapy with members of ethnic groups is essential. Devereaux (1969) studied the Plains Indians assiduously, and used his acquired knowledge base to enhance his ordinary technique typically used with most American patients. Like many other successful transethnic therapists, Devereaux knew that only by understanding the nature of ethnocultural identity in these individuals could he hope to effect any meaningful change.

Westernized assumptions about mental health and illness often disregard the importance of a well-integrated cultural identity in persons of varying ethnic heritages. Research and clinical evidence is clear on the special attributes of a coherent ethnic identity in terms of personality flexibility, inner freedom, and emotional security (Cobbs, 1972; Klein, 1980). In this writer's many years as a professional psychodiagnostician and director of an institute for psychological diagnostic testing, only a few psychological reports that integrate clinical diagnostic findings with ethnicity factors have been taken seriously. For example, an eight-year-old Puerto Rican girl was referred for psychological testing because she was "hearing things" (the collision of drinking glasses in a closed refrigerator) and "seeing things" (a woman sitting on her bed at night). Further exploration suggested that this young child may have had special faculties (facultades), a highly valued possession in the Puerto Rican culture where strong belief in spiritism as a way of life is held in high esteem. This girl revealed no evidence of psychopathology; in fact, her Rorschach revealed a well-integrated and cohesive identity and general psychological functioning. It is probably no surprise that most research on diagnoses of ethnic group patients show higher prevalences of more severe diagnoses, compared to white middle-class patients (Adebimpe, 1981; Carter, 1974; Marsella & Pedersen, 1981; Sue, 1981).

Since it is now well-known that the melting pot hypothesis has not, and probably will not, become a reality for most ethnic group people, it is time for psychometricians to become *ethnopsychometricians* when dealing with persons whose realities are strongly influenced by their patrimonial predilections. Ethnoculturally sensitive and informed diagnosticians have had the experience of testing a child or adult, or assessing a family and discovering that the presenting symptoms and problems could be best understood within the ethnocultural matrix with which the patient identifies. When this approach and sensitivity are present, diagnoses are often less severe, and appropriate treatment planning and/or referral action are effected.

Naturally, the degree of acculturation or assimilation into the dominant culture must always be considered with patients who are identified as "ethnic minorities" (such as Afro-Americans, Puerto Ricans, Cuban Americans, Mexican Americans, and Asian Americans , including Koreans, Japanese, Chinese and American Indians), and those identified as "ethnic majorities" (such as Italian Americans, Irish Americans, German Americans, Polish Americans, Jewish Americans, Greek Americans, and French Americans).

Central to increased diagnostic accuracy and therapeutic effectiveness with the ethnic group client is the concept of *ego identity*, a composite of childhood and later experiences during the individual's development. This forms a consistent and coherent intrapsychic structure that organizes current perceptions, values, belief systems, and establishes an *internal standard* against which all experiences are evaluated. In the context of assessment and treatment of the traumatized patient of an ethnic group, it becomes imperative that the professional develop an openness to cultural diversity and think in terms of a *patrimonial ego identity* (or "cultural ego identity"). Erikson (1950), in this regard, states that ". . . only an identity safely anchored in the 'patrimony' of a cultural identity can produce a workable psychosocial equilibrium" (p. 412). Erikson's statement has tremendous and far-reaching implications for health and mental health professionals, as it provides an added criteria for good psychosocial functioning. The client's cultural identity is very important and should be integrated in any assessment or treatment experience with the ethnically different patient, since mental health may include culturally determined, non-Western criteria as well.

DIAGNOSTIC CONSIDERATIONS IN THE
CONTEXT OF ETHNICITY AND TRAUMATIC
STRESS

In the *Diagnostic and Statistical Manual,* (first edition; DSM-I), published in 1952, persons suffering from catastrophic events and manifesting symptomatology of stress reactions or disorders were given the diagnosis of "gross stress reaction," while the diagnosis of "transient situational disturbances" appeared in DMS-II in 1968. Both editions placed emphasis on predisposition, which stemmed from the influence of psychoanalysis. In DSM-III, the term "post-traumatic stress disorder" created a new and useful nosological entity that could be applied to any clinical situation in which the client had been subjected to "a psychologically traumatic event that is generally outside the range of usual human experience" (APA, 1980). Utilizing the provision of an atheoretical and adynamic, criterion-referenced system of diagnosis, the DSM-III outlines specific criteria:

1) a recognizable stressor-event;
2) the reexperiencing of the original traumatic event through dreams or flashback phenomena;
3) numbing of emotions; and
4) specific symptoms and reactions.

Though DSM-III aims toward a reduction in clinician variability by its criterion-referenced system of diagnosis, its implicit assumption that these criteria can be used with equal validity across cultures is probably erroneous (Parson, 1984a). For example, it may be difficult to determine the degree of psychological impairment with traumatized black clients, because of their culturally determined *trained capacity for interior-exterior incongruity* (Parson, 1984b). Additionally, what may be "a healthy cultural suspiciousness and adaptive response to the experience of racism" may be misdiagnosed as paranoia (Adebimpe, 1981), with the manifestation of cultural hypervigilance toward non-minority clinicians. Likewise, in working with the Irish American, the degree of subjective ailment may be difficult to assess due to the cultural inclination to disavow illness and pain. In contrast, Italian Americans tend to exaggerate their ailments dramatically, while WASP patients, like the Irish, prefer to "play down" pain and discomfort to clinicians. As Zborowski's (1969) study pointed out, the accuracy of patients' self-reports about their symptoms and pain may differ according to each patient's ethnic background. For example, while Jewish and WASP patients were accurate in describing their symptoms, Irish and Italians were not as accurate (Zborowski, 1969).

In American-dominant culture the expression of emotions is discouraged; however, from a transcultural viewpoint, many ethnic group persons express emotions freely, including the Italians and Jews. Italians are often misdiagnosed as having "psychiatric problems" (Zola, 1966), while western medical professionals were distrustful of Jewish Americans' manner of free, direct expression of suffering (Zborowski, 1969).

In reference to the case studies, E.S., the Puerto Rican woman survivor of a rape episode, was referred for treatment by her physician after she had a "physically violent" dissociative episode. Upon assessment this author became aware that the patient had undergone a culturally accepted manner of expressing stress and conflict called *ataques*. This cultural phenomenon resembles hysterical convulsions, and often leads to misdiagnoses in Puerto Rican women.

A.K., the Jewish client who sought assistance for his emotional problems following an automobile accident two years before, expressed subjective ailment, pessimism, and helplessness that were more related to the dissolution of his family than to the painful effects of his post-traumatic stress disorder. This is because many Jewish individuals depend upon their families for a sense of well-being and personality integrity (Sanua, 1978). For A.K. family life was everything, and he felt there could be no life without his family. This centrality of family in the life of the individual is called "familism" (Bardis, 1961), and is indispensable to acquiring an adequate prediagnostic understanding of the nature and degree of the patient's psychopathology. A.K. felt that his suffering was not being shared with his wife and children, and was a profound burden of isolation and loneliness for him. Like the Irish, the Jewish individual often is unable to see through present pain to the future when things might become better. Instead, they often assume the posture of "This is just the way it is!" (McGoldrick, Pearce, & Giordano, 1982). Additionally, A.K.'s emphasis on "doing something," on helping beginning entrepreneurs get started in their businesses, was an aspect of the culturally derived need to "accomplish something."

From a very young age, Jewish children from traditional family systems are strongly encouraged to develop their intellectual faculties, and the family climate, managed by the mother, fosters the fruition of the children's intellectual achievements (McGoldrick, Pearce, & Giordano, 1982). Thus, A.K.'s complaint and characterization of himself as "a vegetable, a brainless vegetable, with no hope" is no idle chatter. This self-assessment, in conjunction with a scattered and dysfunctional family support system, is the equivalent of his stating that his life is over. A.K.'s life situation was unbearable and he unconsciously sought refuge in the memory of his deceased mother and had great longings for the "good old family days" when his family of origin was so supportive and he was so happy. Naturally, the clinical assessor or diagnostician would need to make a determination of possible suicidal ideation and behavior in such cases.

Diagnostic confusion over the appropriateness of emotional expression results in an overabundance of affective disorders in Italians (Robert & Myers, 1954).

Wylan and Mintz (1976) found that while Irish Americans were intolerant of emotionality in other people, Jewish persons found this acceptable. However, Jewish Americans had no tolerance for thought disorders. Thus, in the case of A.K., his obsession about being a "vegetable" takes on greater significance in the diagnostic encounter. T.L., the 66-year-old World War II veteran of Irish heritage, also revealed his intolerance of emotional expression in himself as well as in his wife, who is Italian. This cultural predilection was responsible for some of the difficulty the clinician had in determining the degree of subjective ailment and the nature of T.L.'s psychopathology. The patient typically seems to "adjust" to his pain, apparently preferring his discomfort to attaining relief. T.L. viewed his pain as "just due" for some sin he had committed. Though he did not kill in the war, he *felt* that he must have killed someone. "After all," he reasoned, "war is about killing people, isn't it?"

The clinician must also assess the degree of ethnicity in the patient. Thus, he or she should seek to determine

1) the language spoken in the home;
2) how well English is spoken;
3) the stresses of migration and length of time in the United States;
4) the community of residence and opportunities for linking with fellow countrymen;

5) the educational attainment and socioeconomic status;
6) the degree of religious faith;
7) the nature of political affiliation; and
8) the presence of intermarriage.

The clinician is to note that factors such as race, gender, socioeconomic status, personal and familial variables, and experiences are also very important in diagnosis of mental, social, and interpersonal difficulties in ethnic group clients.

The generalizations outlined so far are meant to provide guidelines for the clinician; their presentation and discussion in no way intends to subvert the more *individual* and creative aspects of the patient. It is recognized, however, that generalizations are inevitable in such discussions of multiethnic realities in the diagnostic and therapeutic processes.

Sue (1978) has outlined a general theory that he believes would eliminate or significantly reduce the incidences of "oppression in counseling" the culturally different. Though he emphasized primarily the ethnic minorities, this author has found his schema to be useful with the "ethnic majorities" as well. Sue uses the term "world views" to connote the cultural relativity and uniqueness of perception, beliefs, and behavior in general. His schema utilizes Rotter's (1966) concept of locus of control along the lines of internal/external control or the internal/external dimension. Persons who believe that they are in control of their own fate, that they can exert activity on their world, thereby effecting changes, are regarded as having "inner control" (IC). Conversely, those who believe that they are pawns at the hand of fate are governed by "external control"(EC). To Rotter's concept, Sue added another dimension, namely, "locus of responsibility." Combining both dimensions, "locus of control" and "locus of responsibility," he forms four quadrants as shown below in Figure 1—internal locus of control-internal locus of responsibility (IC-IR), external locus of control-internal locus of responsibility (ER-IR), external locus of control-external locus of responsiblity (EC-ER), and internal locus of control-external locus of responsibility (IC-ER).

This writer's experience with ethnic Americans, in conjunction with extensive reviews of pertinent literature over the years, locates the American middle-class and Anglo-American individuals (WASP) in Quadrant I, since this group of people take full responsibility for their fate, and believe they can improve their lot in life through their own efforts. Diagnosticians and therapists who belong to this quadrant may find it difficult to understand most members of the ethnic minorities

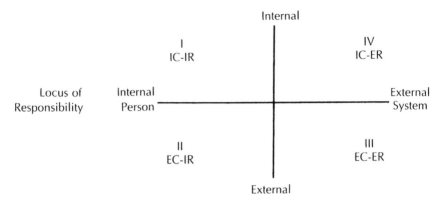

Figure 1. Adaptation of Rotter and Sue's Schema of Perception and Experience of Control (Adapted from Sue, 1978)

who, for the most part, fall in Quadrant III, in response to discrimination, racism, and exclusion.

In the context of traumatic stress reactions and disorders, this writer has observed that even the most acculturated, middle-class person had a tendency to revert to his or her ethnic past in organizing coping strategies after a traumatic event. Additionally, many patients who are ordinarily ICs may use a more EC orientation during stress. The Anglo-American may thus choose a more EC-ER style in coming to terms with the traumatic event and its psychological and emotional aftermath. Quadrant II (EC-IR) patients tend to blame themselves for their trauma, and manifest self-loathing with intense superego strictures and persecutory anxieties.

Many Vietnam veterans, after over a decade of silent suffering, self-blaming, and self-hatred in relation to the war and its ills, have become more proactively involved in life and its processes, as they seek better ego identities and positive self-feelings. Many of these combatants have converted their EC-IR into an IC-ER orientation. This phenomenon has also been observed for many years in survivors of the Holocaust (DesPres, 1980) and Hiroshima (Lifton, 1968) in their human struggle to reassert control over their lives and to find meaning and happiness out of a past of unspeakable horror and suffering.

This writer has found Horowitz et al.'s (1980) recent event stress scale a useful aid in the diagnostic process. The scale evaluates "serious life events such as bodily damages resulting from accident, assault, illness or surgery, or object loss, such as the death of a loved one" (p. 85).

TRANSETHNIC PSYCHOTHERAPY WITH TRAUMATIZED PERSONS

Professionals need to reevaluate their exclusive reliance on white middle-class criteria for health and illness in ethnic group populations. As indicated earlier, such criteria may be deemed *unethical* when applied to ethnic minority patients (Korman, 1974), as well as to indigent white Americans. Since "different cultures tend to shape different kinds of psychopathology, and may respond to and define mental health and mental illness in divergent ways" (Parson, 1980, p. 19), it becomes essential that helping professionals prepare themselves fully for *transethnic psychotherapy.** There are a number of useful initiatives the would-be transethnic therapist could take to accomplish this work. The following recommendations are offered:

1) Awareness of the "acculturation strain" and the tripartite nature of the patient's struggle to reassert control over psychological reactions to traumatic stress, his or her biculturality and, with the ethnic minority group patient, his or her experience of having been viewed as inferior by the larger society.
2) Awareness that the patient's "assumptive world" (Frank, 1961) may differ importantly from white American dominant standards, and that though class differences are viewed as chiefly responsible for "world view" differences, socioeconomic status is an insufficient explanatory concept. Middle-class–oriented ethnic group members are still tied emotionally to their culture and to their ethnic identities, especially in catastrophe.
3) Develop a flexible and broad theoretical and technical approach, tempered by an adequate knowledge base in ethnicity and mental health (for example, the works of: Hsu and Tseng (1972); Marsella and Pedersen (1981); Sue (1981); and others.
4) Develop self-awareness and understanding of clinician's own

---

*Transethnic psychotherapy refers to a bi-ethnic treatment situation characterized by ethnic identity differences in the treatment dyad between therapist and patient, and by transethnic interpersonal transactional processes occurring with the full awareness of intrinsic differences and similarities between the treatment pair.

ethnocentrism and "ethnic narcissism," and move beyond personal biases that damages a therapist's capacity for effective work with other ethnic group patients.

5) Systematic study of the psychohistorical/ethnohistorical roots of the ethnic groups the therapist intends to treat is highly recommended. For as Sue pointed out, referring to the black patient, "Black history should not be taken for granted or ignored in counseling. . . ." (1981, p. 142).

6) Engage in specialized training programs to achieve a multiethnic perspective, combining both didactic and experiential self-reflective aspects (for example, the specialized training programs that appear in Brislin and Pedersen's book, *Cross-Cultural Orientation Programs*).

7) If needed, seek professional supervision from a mental health professional or peer-oriented supervision on clinical dimensions in assessing and treating traumatized patients of ethnic backgrounds.

The Tri-Dimensional Treatment Plan

Psychotherapy with ethnic group patients presents a host of challenges. The complexities of this work call for a multifaceted, multilevel approach to comprehensive care. A generic treatment approach this author has found very useful in working with survivors of ethnic group membership is called the *Tri-Dimensional Treatment Plan*, and features three phases: 1) The Orientation Phase; 2) The Psychoecological Therapy Phase; and 3) The Ethnicity-Focused Psychotherapy Phase.

The Orientation Phase

Referring to the four case studies (E.S., A.K., T.L., and A.G.), the orientation phase is especially critical to successful treatment. E.S. came to realize that her symptoms were normal and predictable, and that most women would manifest her reactions following a rape ordeal. Like the other patients, E.S. was introduced to brief educational information on rape, the victims or survivors, their feelings, and fears, and the impact of rape upon the woman's family. The therapist's expectations were shared, after E.S. had been given ample opportunity to discuss her expectations of treatment. Like A.K., T.L., and A.G., E.S. felt relieved and understood by the therapist.

During this phase the therapist discusses some of the inherent difficulies in working with an ethnically different client (if this is the case), and expresses his or her willingness to help and to learn about the patient's culture. Clinical vignettes, slides, and films may be used, often with great success. One of the basic reasons for failure in the treatment of the culturally different patient is the therapist's inability to *make contact* with the patient during the first interviews. It is this writer's belief that perhaps the only way to make contact in a traumatic stress/ethnic group context is to allay anxiety, offer hope, and communicate some appreciation and respect for the patient's culture. A genogram is often developed, and vital explorations into the patient's ethnic background are begun during the orientation phase.

Basically the Orientation Phase aims to:

1) reduce anxiety by providing useful and meaningful information and conveying the therapist's interest in the client, not only in his or her symptoms (as a "sick" person), but in the patient as a human being whose culture is respectable and important;
2) lay the foundation for a solid working relationship;
3) reduce the drop-out rate from treatment;
4) allow the client to make an informed decision to continue in treatment; and
5) increase trust.

The Psychoecological Therapy Phase

This aspect of the treatment focuses on the immediate and pressing environmentally generated problems that the patient is unable to handle by himself. Interventions at this phase intend to alleviate internal stress by removing or mitigating the adverse impingements from the environment; secure vital services in the community; assist in healing broken links with the cultural community; and initiate the patient's family involvement in the treatment process. In A.K.'s case, it was very important to his treatment that his family become an integral aspect of the beginning phase of his treatment, since the Jewish family acts as a sacred, irreducible entity whose integrated support contributes immensely to well-being, and its disintegration to illness and despair (Sanua, 1978). His persistent need to "achieve something" was met by the therapist's securing an invitation from a local agency that assists new entrepreneurs in keeping their businesses afloat. Likewise, E.S.'s family became sympathetic and more supportive of her, and the silent "accusations" of her around her ordeal (rape) came to an end. Experience has shown that in most cases the first two phases may be implemented concurrently.

The Ethnicity-Focused Psychotherapy Phase

This phase of the proposed tri-dimensional treatment plan addresses the emotional problems and reactions to traumatic events more directly than the first two phases, with the goal of altering dysfunctional mechanisms, and restoring confidence and morale in the ethnic group client. This is often accomplished by inviting the patient to reconnect with his or her emotional life, which, for the most part in traumatic states, is "neglected" by the survivor, due to inherent pain in the emotional reliving of the traumatic episode. Thus, during this phase inquiries, entreaties, and explorations are to be conducted with utmost cultural sensitivity. The therapist must understand the meaning of suffering and pain to the specific ethnic group to which the client belongs, and creatively organize the treatment around this understanding.

For example, T.L.'s self-presentation in the initial interview was characterized by a profoundly self-effacing, affectless, confessional style, which was understood by the therapist as a basic characteristic of Irish Americans in stress. Irish people frequently utilize therapy as an opportunity to confess their "sins," rather than to reflect upon their emotional experiences for insight. Bleak pessimism and selflessness are integral to the clinical presentation of some Irish Americans (Greeley, 1981). T.L.'s reluctance to discuss his war experiences was related to his culture-based fear of condemnation by the therapist after discovering T.L.'s "sinfulness," though the client was not himself aware of what this might be. In exploring his traumatic dreams and other traumatic symptoms, he told the therapist that Irish people "prefer dreaming to reality." When asked to describe what he meant by this, he proceeded with an "emotion-denying," intellectualizing explanation, somewhat unaware that his comment might have something to do with his unwillingness to face up to his inner world of fear and terror. T.L. was also unable to give specifics of the contents of his traumatic dream. His typical "detour around" verbalizations are somewhat related to his culture (Greeley, 1981), as is his penchant to use innuendo and metaphor to avoid emotionally threatening situations.

Commenting on this basic ethnic-intensive tendency, Scheper-Hughes (1979) states that conversations among modern, rural, Irish people are marked by "double talk, obfuscation, interruptions, and nonsequiturs" (p. 82). This characterization was clearly observed in treatment, and served as a formidable culture-based "resistance." T.L. was extremely mystifying in discussing his life experiences and his traumatic dreams. Such "word-engineering" and avoidance date from years of English oppression of the Irish. Like Afro-Americans, who, during slavery and oppression, developed sophisticated forms of "uncommunicating communications," and hid their true feelings from their oppressors (Andrews & Owens, 1973), many Irish Americans are very difficult to engage in straightforward communication about personal issues they do not want to share with therapists and strangers (McGoldrick et al., 1982).

Again, like Afro-Americans, the Irish are inclined to make good appearances as a culturally adaptive practice. As pointed out by McGoldrick et al. (1982), though Irish individuals can express their emotions, there seems to be a cultural basis for their emotional inhibitions. Success is also suspect, and many Irish people believe that tragedy comes to the successful. This belief was noticed quite frequently during T.L.'s treatment. With this patient, it was important for the therapist to offer reassurance and support, and make selected short-term achievable goals. Additionally, the therapist articulated his understanding of T.L.'s cultural style of "resistance" and oblique communication.

These and other cultural traits are not negative, and should be respected for their deep, cultural value to the patient. Therapists' attempts to uncover significant, emotional responses in patients like T.L. will be very disappointing, but worse, these actions can induce severe regressions in the patient. Thus, the therapist found that his attempts to explore T.L.'s feelings and traumatic dreams were a technical error, and that particular countertherapeutic behaviors in the patient seemed related to the therapist's unwitting "insults" to the patient's "ethnic narcissism." The therapist disclosed to the patient that he believed he had said a number of things that the therapist now realized might have offended him, and proceeded to catalog these events. The patient sighed with relief, and felt understood and respected. Systematic self-relaxation and other behaviorally oriented techniques proved very useful to T.L., enabling him to feel a sense of accomplishment.

The therapist then turned to a specific technique he believed would be culturally useful with T.L.—the *oblique experience technique*. This approach involves the therapist's relating an experience of another person who struggled with a similar emotional issue and reached some resolution. Together, the therapist and patient arrive at conclusions based on the oblique experience, and formulate solutions, while working toward the "oblique resolution." Only much later did the treatment move toward a "frontal" exploration of T.L.'s pain and traumatic stress reactions. Through the oblique method, T.L. allowed himself to identify with the oblique character, his distress and emotional turmoil, thereby attaining some relief vicariously. This approach seemed consistent or congruent with the Irish oblique mystique in both communication and affective reactive style.

A.K. and A.G., unlike T.L., were very expressive of their feelings, and were bent upon disclosing their pain and dispair. A.G., an Italian, pressed for immediate resolutions of his mental upset and traumatic psychic reactions, unlike A.K., who seemed willing to take as long as possible to achieve relief from his problems and understand their nature and source. In the Italian family, the father is the undisputed family authority, and takes much pride in providing for his family. A.G.'s paralysis eroded his power base within the family system. Having always been the strong head of the family, Italian fathers, as a group, endure great stress. McGoldrick et al.'s (1982) overview on ethnicity reports that Italians had the lowest rates of hospitalization compared to most other ethnic groups; and that as a group these Americans under-utilize mental health services, chiefly due to their strong reliance on the healing properties of a supportive family organization. It is thus imperative to include the patient's family and extended family members in the treatment with some Italian patients. This involvement was especially critical since the family system had become virtually dysfunctional in its attempt to accommodate to A.G.'s disability. It needs to be stressed that treatment of this patient would be impossible without significant familial involvement. Therapy focused on A.G.'s deep sense of humiliation, helplessness, "loss of face" with his family, depression, and devastated self-esteem. When he was robbed of his physical mobility, cherished physical strength, and control over family life, his depression highlighted his profound sense of loss. Aside from offering emotional release, opportunity for catharsis, grief work, and integration of his losses, perhaps the most important and ultimately the most therapeutic accomplishment of the process was to repair the broken family boundaries and heal the fragmented, dysfunctional family system.

Acquiring pertinent knowledge and understanding of the nuances of ethnic differences will enhance therapist effectiveness, and offer the patient useful alternatives to his or her pain and traumatic states. The therapeutic intersecting point in *cross-ethnic traumatic states* involves recognition of the unique technical requirements of working effectively with survivors' psychological and interpersonal infirmities (Figley, 1978; Parson, in press) in the therapeutic dyad or family ethnocultural context. Thus, E.S.'s traumatic stress had a specific, culturally determined impact on her family, which created intense guilt feelings for her for having subjected her family to this ordeal. A.K.'s traumatic stress and hypochondriasis could not have been optimally treated in its cultural context unless the therapist was aware of the Jewish cultural dictum, *Shver zu zein a yid* or "It's tough being a Jew." A.K.'s dramatic expressions of pain and anguish were consistent with his cultural orientation and emphasis on suffering, resignation, and pessimism. In general, Jewish Americans in distress approach assistance rather pessimistically (Zborowski, 1969). For them, traumatic suffering is to be shared with the family; and, essentially, every family member experiences (empathically) the suffering. It thus became imperative that the treatment aim at restoring the family's integrity in order to offer A.K. an effective support system.

Treatment with ethnic Americans requires a complicated, trust-building period, which begins during the orientation phase, and depending on the patient's needs, the family may also be part of the treatment. The more transethnically competent the therapist, the less likely the therapist will misunderstand and inadvertently hurt the patient's "ethnic narcissistic" position.

CONCLUSION

The therapeutic work toward mastery of traumatic stress reactions and disorders with ethnic group persons is a painstaking process for both therapist and patient. This chapter emphasizes the importance of therapists becoming transethnically competent before attempting to treat patients who strongly identify with their ethnic customs and heritage. Therapists are encouraged to study, seek supervision, reexamine their own ethnocentrism, and maintain an openness to learn from their clients. These kinds of actions, when taken by therapists, reflect humility and an acknowledgment that their formal training and experience may need to be modified by incorporation of ethnically relevant information, training, and experience. This awareness often frees the therapist to relax his or her own ethnocultural defensiveness around racial and cultural issues. Therapist ethnocentric "blind spots" account for most of the reported underutilization of mental health services by ethnic minorities. This writer believes that it is virtually impossible to make patients feel understood and empathically confirmed if the therapist does not comprehend the patient's cultural-behavioral norms. This is especially true when the patient has been traumatized by a catastrophic event, such as a flood (like the "Black Water" catastrophe), car accident (such as patient A.K.), war (like patient T.L.), rape (patient E.S.), and physical traumata (as in the case of A.G.). Unempathic slights and gestures, improperly worded statements, as well as a lack of awareness about the patient's ethnic experience, only lead to additional narcissistic injury to persons who have already been narcissistically mortified by their trauma.

Cross-cultural psychotherapy with traumatized individuals consistently reinforces the fact that symptoms differ among ethnic groups, as do definitions of a "problem," of mental health and disability, of physical illness, and of psychic pain. Therefore, the clinician needs to comprehend the various cultural accommodations to mental illness characteristic of the ethnic groups in question, and ethnic group members' help-seeking behavior and expectations. Ethnic group members thus also differ in regard to mental health care utilization.

In this chapter, "ethnicity" is defined as a constellation of patterns of ideas, behaviors, and emotional styles based upon a common ancestry shared by a group of people. By all evidence, the dominant culture has been unsuccessful in bringing about "cultural neutralization" (as implied in the melting pot hypothesis). For, despite some modulation of strong ethnocultural values in some Americans, ethnicity still remains a powerful force in the lives of most individuals. It determines the nature of love, work, recreation, values, success, and failure. Since ethnic identity incorporates individual and familial continuity, it is not difficult to understand why survivors tend to seek "resolution" of their traumatic stress reactions in the cultural roots of their identity. This is to say that post-traumatic stress, which fosters internal disorganization, may result in a "cultural regression" in the survivor. In actuality, trauma and its aftermath can cause survivors to lose their sense of who they are.

In making clinical-cultural assessments, the degree of cultural assimilation, as well as a number of other variables (such as time since migration of the family, nature of the cultural community where patient lives, age, gender, personal psychiatric history, etc.) are essential in determining the degree of mental health and illness, and in charting a course for the treatment. For the most part, in working clinically with ethnic group patients, it is usually necessary to develop a comprehensive, individualized, cultural treatment plan, with specific immediate goals (a day to a week), short-term goals (one to four weeks), extended short-term goals (one to three months), and long-range goals (four to six months), based upon mutual agreement between therapist and patient.

In the long run, any psychotherapeutic encounter will have to address the patient's helplessness, dislocation, pessimism, depressive affect, psychic pain, and horrifying memories. Aside from the content of the psychotherapy, the treatment process must address a number of critical therapeutic *functions:* reducing *isolation and existential aloneness* while providing opportunity for emotional "exercise"; opportunity to *learn and experience* self and others in a different way; and to *develop control, increased self-esteem and self-regulation* over traumatic emotional arousal and problematic memories.

In conclusion, the transcultural therapist must master a variety of cognitive, behavioral, experiential, and dynamic methods, along with social and community therapies, in conjunction with a solid, coherent transcultural sophistication and broadened world view.

REFERENCES

Acosta, F.X., Yamamato, J., & Evans, L. *Effective psychotherapy for low-income and minority patients.* New York: Plenum, 1982.

Adebimpe, V. Overview: White norms and psychiatric diagnosis of black patients, *American Journal of Psychiatry,* 1981, *138,* 279-285.

Ader, A. Mental symptoms following head injury. *Archives of Neurology and Psychiatry,* 1945, *53,* 34-43.

American Psychiatric Association. *Diagnostic and statistical manual* (1st ed.). Washington, D.C.: American Psychiatric Association, 1952.

American Psychiatric Association. *Diagnostic and statistical manual* (2nd ed.). Washington, D.C.: American Psychiatric Association, 1968.

American Psychiatric Association. *Diagnostic and statistical manual* (3rd ed.). Washington, D.C.: American Psychiatric Association, 1980.

Andrews, M., & Owens, P.T. *Black language.* Los Angeles: Seymour-Smith, 1973.

Archibald, H., & Tuddenham, R. Persistent stress reactions after combat. *Archives of General Psychiatry,* 1965, *12,* 480.

Bardis, P.D. Familism among Jews in suburbia. *Social Science,* 1961, *36,* 190-196.

Bloch, B., & Bloch, N., Analytic group psychotherapy of post-traumatic psychoses. *International Journal of Group Psychotherapy,* 1976, *26,* 47-57.

Brislin, R., & Pedersen, P. (Eds.). *Cross-cultural orientation programs.* New York: Gardner Press, 1976.

Carter, J. Recognizing psychiatric symptoms in black Americans. *Geriatrics,* 1974, *29,.97-99.*

Cobbs, P. Ethnotherapy in groups. In L. Doloman & B. Berzon (Eds.), *New pespectives on encounter groups.* San Francisco: Jossey-Bass, 1972.

Cochrane, R. Mental illness in immigrants in England and Wales: Analysis of mental hospital admissions—1971. *Social Psychiatry,* 1961, *12,* 25-35.

Corcoran, J. The concentration camp syndrome and USAF Vietnam prisoners of war. *Psychiatric Annals,* 1982, *12,* 991-994.

DesPres, T. *The survivor: An anatomy of life in the death camps.* New York: Oxford University Press, 1980.

Devereaux, G. *Reality and the dream: Psychotherapy with a Plains Indian.* Garden City, NY: Doubleday, 1969.

Egendorf, A. The postwar healing of Vietnam veterans. *Journal on Hospital and Community Psychiatry.* 1982, *33*, 901-912.

Erikson, E.H. Growth and crisis of the healthy personality. In E.H. Erikson (Ed.), *Identity and the life cycle.* New York: International Universities Press, 1950.

Figley, C.R. (Ed.). *Stress disorders among Vietnam veterans.* New York: Brunner/Mazel, 1978.

Figley, C.R., & Leventman, S. (Eds.). *Strangers at home.* New York: Praeger, 1980.

Frank, J.D., *Persuasion and healing.* Baltimore: Johns Hopkins Press, 1961.

Friedman, R., & Cohen, K. The peer-support group: A model for dealing with the emotional aspects of miscarriage, *Group*, 1980, *4*, 42-48.

Furst, S. (Ed.). *Psychic trauma.* New York: Basic Books, 1967.

Greeley, A.M. *Why can't they be like us?* New York: Institute of Human Relations Press, 1969.

Greeley, A.M. *The Irish Americans.* New York: Harper & Row, 1981.

Horowitz, M., Wilner, N., Kaltreider, N., & Alvarez, W. Signs and symptoms of post-traumatic stress disorder. *Archives of General Psychiatry*, 1980, *35*, 85-92.

Hsu, J., & Tseng, W.S. Intercultural psychotherapy. *Archives of General Psychiatry*, 1972, *27*, 702.

Kadushin, C., Boulanger, G., & Martin, J. Long-term stress reactions: Some causes, consequences, and naturally occurring support systems. In *Legacies of Vietnam: Comparative adjustment of veterans and their peers.* Washington, D.C.: U.S. Government Printing Office, 1981.

Klein, J. *Jewish identity and self-esteem: Healing wounds through ethnotherapy.* New York: Institute on Pluralism and Group Identity, 1980.

Korman, N. National Conference on levels and patterns of professional training in psychology. *American Psychologist*, 1973, *29*, 441-449.

Krystal, H. *Massive psychic trauma.* New York: International Universities Press, 1968.

Lifton, R.J. *Death in life: Survivors of Hiroshima.* New York: Random House, 1968.

Marsella, A., & Pedersen, P. (Eds.). *Cross-cultural counseling and psychotherapy.* New York: Pergamon Press, 1981.

McDonald, J. *Rape: Offenders and their victims.* Springfield, IL: Charles C Thomas, 1979 (third printing).

McGoldrick, M., Pearce, J., & Giordano,J. *Ethnicity and family therapy.* New York: Guilford, 1982.

Moses, R., Bargal, D., Falk, A., HaLevi, H. et al. A rear unit for the treatment of reactions in the wake of the Yom Kippur War. *Psychiatry*, 1976, *39*,(2), 153-168.

Parson, E.R. NYSCP's commitment to minority psychologists and patients. *The New York Society of Clinical Psychologists Newsletter*, Summer, 1980, 14-19.

Parson, E.R. The "gook"-identification: Its role in stress pathology in minority Vietnam veterans. Presented at the National Conference on Post-Vietnam Stress Syndrome, Cincinnati, Ohio, October 18, 1982.

Parson, E.R. The "gook"-identification and posttraumatic stress disorders in black Viet Nam veterans. *Black Psychiatrists of America Quarterly*, 1984a, *13*(2), 14-18.

Parson, E.R. The reparation of the self: Clinical and theoretical dimensions in the treatment of Viet Nam combat veterans, *Journal of Contemporary Psychotherapy*, 1984b, *14*(1), 4-52.

Parson, E.R. The intercultural setting: Encountering the psychological readjustment needs of black Americans who served in Vietnam. In S. Sonnenberg, A.S. Blank, & J. Talbot (Eds.), *The psychiatric effects of the Vietnam war.* Washington, D.C.: The Psychiatric Press, in press.

Robert, B. & Myers, J. Religion, natural origins, immigration and mental illness. *American Journal of Psychiatry*, 1954, *110*, 759-764.

Rotter, J. Generalized experiences for external versus internal control reinforcement. *Psychological Monographs*, 1966, *80*, 1-28.

Sanua, V. The contemporary Jewish family: A review of the social science literature. In G. Babis, (Ed.), *Serving the Jewish family.* New York: KTAV, 1978.

Scheper-Hughes, N. *Saints, scholars, and schizophrenics*. Berkeley: University of California Press, 1979.

Sue, D.W. Eliminating cultural oppression in counseling: Toward a general theory. *Journal of Counseling Psychology*, 1978, 25, 422.

Sue, D.W. *Counseling the culturally different*. New York: Wiley, 1981.

Ursano, R. The Vietnam era prisoner of war: Precaptivity personality and the development of psychiatric illness. *American Journal of Psychiatry*, 1981, 38, 315-318.

Ursano, R., Boydstun, J., & Wheatley, R. Psychiatric illness in U.S. Air Force Vietnam prisoners of war: A five-year follow-up. *American Journal of Psychiatry*, 1981, 138, 310-314.

Washington Urban League Pamphlet. Washington D.C.: The Urban League, 1978.

Wolk, R. Group psychotherapy process in the treatment of hostages taken in prison, *Group*, 1981, 5, 31-36.

Wylan, L., & Mintz, N. Ethnic differences in family attitudes toward psychotic manifestations with implications for treatment programmes. *International Journal of Social Psychiatry*, 1976, 22, 86-95.

Zborowski, M. *People in pain*. San Francisco: Jossey-Bass, 1969.

Zola, I.K. Culture and symptoms: An analysis of patients' presenting complaints. *American Sociological Review*, 1966, 5, 141-155.

14

Illness-related Post-traumatic Stress Disorder: A Cognitive-Behavioral Model of Intervention with Heart Attack Victims

CAROL R. HARTMAN and

ANN WOLBERT BURGESS

The purpose of this chapter is to present a model which adopts principles of cognitive and behavioral strategies as a means of intervention with the post-traumatic stress disorder manifested after a heart attack. This model is used during phases of recovery and rehabilitation with the victim, the victim's key family members and co-workers. Presently,

The research for this paper was supported by the Robert Wood Johnson Foundation Grant #6244, "Demonstrations to Increase the Rate of Return to Work of Heart Attack Victims."

the efficacy of this intervention effort, which is being carried out by nurses, is being evaluated as part of an overall return-to-work project sponsored by the Robert Wood Johnson Foundation.

Mr. Roberts, age 54, was sitting tensely on the edge of the sofa of his living room looking intently at the nurse-clinician who was making a follow-up visit. It was 15 days since his heart attack. His eyes were in a fixed gaze on her face as she talked. The nurse noticed that if she smiled ever so slightly, Mr. Roberts smiled also. She asked him how he relaxed. With something of an outburst of breath behind his words and his arms moving toward the ceiling, he said, "I don't know how to relax." The nurse, after a brief pause, looked up toward the ceiling. Mr. Roberts followed suit, the nurse said, "Have you ever watched clouds?" Mr. Roberts, with his eyes now fixed on the ceiling said, "Yes." The nurse, watching Mr. Roberts, asked, "When you see those clouds, can you feel the warm sun?" He again said yes as he leaned back against the sofa. His body began to relax. The nurse asked, "Where are the clouds?" Mr. Roberts said, "On the farm." When his work was done, he remembered he would lie in the haystack, relax and watch the clouds. His visibly relaxed position changed to one of increased tension as he told the nurse how hard he worked on the farm and of his strict and demanding father. The nurse chose to ignore the latter statements and simply said, "Oh, then it's that you've forgotten how to relax." Mr. Roberts blinked and with puzzlement on his face said yes.

The nurse used the above experience to help Mr. Roberts relax more deeply and rehearse his use of visualization of the relaxing clouds to help him in stressful situations, such as leaving his office and walking to the bus.

A month after the visit, a phone call revealed that Mr. Roberts had joined a cardiac rehabilitation program near his home. He reported that he no longer had the chest pain or irritation while waiting for the elevator when leaving work and that there was no pain while walking to the bus. He frequently used the visions of clouds to calm himself. He reported feeling tense over the selection of a rehabilitation program. It was not the one suggested by the physicians at the hospital. The hospital staff did not like or trust the rehabilitation program in Mr. Robert's community. The nurse asked Mr. Roberts if he was getting what he wanted from the program, and he said he was. The hospital program was traditional and Mr. Robert's community program was based on holistic health practices. The nurse then asked who had the conflict. Mr. Roberts laughed and said, "The doctors." The nurse utilized Mr. Roberts' need to make his own decisions by underscoring that by paying attention to his body, if he is not feeling right, he can ask for consultation and/or change.

INTRODUCTION

The case of Mr. Roberts represents what we believe to be an important cornerstone for treating post-myocardial infarct patients. It is acknowledged that serious illness is a traumatic stressor with sequelae that can impede full recovery.

The purpose of this chapter is to present a model for cognitive and behavioral interventions being used with heart attack victims such as Mr. Roberts. The concept of post-traumatic stress disorder (PTSD) has been extended to apply to victims of severe illness, in this case those who have had a myocardial infarction (heart attack). Interventions take place within relevant phases of the post-heart attack experience. The model serves as a guide to rehabilitative care being used in conjunction with existing acute and rehabilitative services in a number of hospitals in the Greater Boston area. The treatment population is a group of heart attack subjects who are diagnosed as having had moderate to moderately severe attacks without complications, and are undergoing a medical regime, rather than heart surgery. There is an intervention group and a non-intervention group. A critical outcome criterion is return to work.

In designing the program, it was assumed that failure to return to work was a maladaptive response to the crisis event. Indeed, it was a demonstration of the impairment associated with PTSD. Moreover, it was assumed that from the time of the heart attack until total recovery, certain reactions could be viewed as functional coping. The victim, the victim's family and co-workers need to adjust their emotions, thinking patterns, and social interactions to the information associated with the heart attack and the subsequent recovery. For the victim, this includes the heightened awareness of his or her body and its functioning, as well as focused attention to life-style habits. The implications are that the individual's stress response to severe illness and the interventions to reduce negative aspects of responses must take into consideration the family and co-workers.

PHASES OF RECOVERY AND THE COGNITIVE-
BEHAVIORAL APPROACH

The four phases of recovery from a heart attack are defined by time, activity, and the critical social structure emergent within each phase. The phases are defined as: the crisis phase; the immediate post-crisis phase; the transition to optimum level of functioning; and total integration. The nursing task is to diagnose the phases of recovery in terms of functional coping capacity and to provide the matching level of cognitive-behavioral intervention.

The Crisis Phase

This period starts with the heart attack, the emergency lifesaving measures taken, admission to a cardiac unit, and the people involved. Activities are aimed at cardiac stabilization and discharge; achieving a survival level is the dominating goal of victim, staff and critical family members.

Immediate Post-Crisis Phase

The second phase involves the transition from hospital to home and the immediate return to family activities. An expanded maintenance level of functioning and coping is the objective during this phase. This brings into question life-style activities and needed changes within the home and work setting.

Transition to Optimum Level of Functioning

This third phase includes maximization of functional coping levels within the home and a preliminary return to work. The victim moves further from the sick role. This requires shifts for the family. The work setting now begins a direct assimilation of the scope and limits of the returning workers.

Total Integration

The fourth phase is integration within the home and at the work setting. The aim is obtaining and maintaining an optimum level of health functioning.

COGNITIVE-BEHAVIORAL APPROACH

The notion of cognitions forming a mediating basis for behaviors has ancient roots. Attitudes associated with the success or failure of individuals to surmount serious illness have been part of the earliest concepts of healing. In recent years, the investigation of cognitions and their relationship to both voluntary and involuntary behavioral responses has demonstrated a strong correlation between emotional arousal, physiological responses, and thinking patterns (see Keane et al., this volume). The evolution of these models and theoretical positions into systematized therapeutic approaches to people with mental disorders, as well as individuals at risk for physical illness, or those who have known physical diseases and injuries, has been increasing (Beck, 1976; Beck & Emery, 1979; Ellis 1977; Ellis & Harper, 1975; Grieger 1982).

Biofeedback programs instituted with people suffering from migraine headaches, hypertension and pain demonstrate the efficiency of relaxation strategies in reducing the autonomic responses in these disorders. (Adrasik, Coleman, & Epstein, 1982; Adrasik & Holroyd, 1980; Beck & Emery, 1979; Holroyd, Adrasik & Noble, 1980; Janis 1980). Biofeedback not only increases the individual awareness of the physiological cues associated with the distressing states, but also allows the individual to experience the power of cognition in interrupting the processes. Increasing the awareness of one's own response patterns and the awareness of one's self-control over cognitions provides a potentially powerful basis for behavioral change (Bandura, Adams & Beyer, 1977; Rush & Beck, 1977; Teasdale & Rezin, 1978).

These concepts are particularly relevant to heart attack victims, since their life-styles most often must be altered in an attempt to lessen the potential for further heart attacks. Investigations into the belief systems of people subject to chronic heart disease have uncovered patterns which, while often linked with a successful life activity such as work, are also associated with severe stress (Jenkins, 1971).

A historical review of pathological responses to heart attack does underscore that disease is contributory to maladaptive behavior and psychopathology (Meyendorf, 1979). A cognitive-behavioral model of treatment develops strategies which utilize belief patterns in such a manner that new ways of viewing old propositions are introduced and eventually adopted, as illustrated in the Roberts case.

Research indicates that when individuals are forced or coerced by a strong, external stimulus to change, adherence to changed behaviors, such as dieting or not smoking, diminishes over time. However, when these changes are experienced as desired and controlled activities by the person, there is a greater possibility of adherence to changed behavior patterns (Jenkins, 1971; Roskies & Avard; 1983; Roskies, Spevack, Surkis, Cohen, & Gilman, 1978).

It is clear from the research on heart attack victims that emotional impact of sudden illness sometimes exceeds the physical impact. Investigations of people who have survived successful heart surgery, for example, indicate that there can be as high as 50% "no return to work" occurrence, regardless of improved physiological status (Mitchell, 1975; Stern, Pascale, & Ackerman, 1977). Studies examining prior personality characteristics do not predict who will successfully comply with rehabilitative regimes. The linking of the rehabilitative response to the type of intervention is beginning to emerge in the literature. Romirowsky (1980) identified differences in anxiety level, freedom to express aggression, and restricted level of leisure time activity between coronary bypass surgery clients and those who had pacemakers. The bypass group appeared most concerned about surviving the actual surgery, believing that post-operative survival was tantamount to having been fully cured. The pacemaker group appeared more concerned about the problems of continued living after surgery.

Soloff's (1978) comparative study of medically and surgically treated coronary patients in a cardiovascular rehabilitation program indicated that surgically treated patients reported less mood disturbances prior to training and demonstrated greater gains in exercise tolerance than the medically treated group. The medical group had more mood disturbance prior to training and greater mood improvement in the six-week rehabilitation program. Improvements in mood were independent of improvement in exercise tolerance. Group differences in mood state as determined by the investigation's method of measurement and analysis could not be attributed to the use of defensive denial, time from discharge, severity of coronary disease, or age of patient. The author concluded that the psychological and physical impact of the bypass surgery contributes to the mood and physical performance of post-operative patients.

These studies not only support the premise that heart attack is a stressor of profound significance, but also the conclusion that the intervention sets in motion certain psychological patterns which either support rehabilitation or interfere with it.

The investigations detail differential recuperation patterns to different medical management regimes. In addition, they suggest that the beliefs and internal psychic constructions developed by the victim with regard to how the specific intervention works play an important role in how life-style behavior is changed. Further, it might be speculated that not only does this process go on in the victim, but that it also affects those close to him. This includes family and those in the work setting (Stern, 1977).

The establishment of the heart attack as a unique stressor which sets into effect immediate-impacting cognitions and the need to have early intervention in the alteration of cognitions which are deleterious to the health of the individual is critical. To develop a method of intervening which can be used by those most in contact with the victim is also important, given the fact that, despite the rehabilitation programs effecting good physiological responses, there is indication that psychological responses militate *against* maximum recovery (Roskies, 1978, 1983).

Theoretical Basis of Cognitive-Behavioral Approach

Our model relies on the theories of Beck, Ellis and Harper, Rehm, and Seligman, (Beck, 1976; Ellis & Harper, 1975; Rehm, 1977; Seligman, 1975), as well as the recent advancements in Neuro-Linguistic Programming (Bandler & Grinder, 1976; Cameron-Bandler, 1980; Dilts, Grinder, Bandler, R., Bandler, L., & DeLozier, 1980). All of these authors emphasize a type of personal control over internal thought processes as an aim for therapeutic interventions.

Neuro-Linguistic Programming (NLP) provides a technology for assessing behavior and designing therapeutic strategies specific to individuals as well as to the social network. The major theoretical propositions of cognitive therapies and major propositions of NLP are briefly reviewed.

Cognitive Theories of Intervention

Ellis advanced the ABC theory of Rational-Emotive Therapy (Ellis, 1977). The theory states that it is not the event we experience (at A) that determines how we react (at C), but rather our thoughts or ideas (at B) that do so. This theory places cognition in the position of mediator of behavior. Grieger and Grieger (1982) expanded the original model by emphasizing the mediating principles of cognition with particular relationship to cognitive schemata operant in racial prejudice. Basically, their principles try to operationalize how learned cognitive schemes are manifested as dispositional traits and how cognitions mediate aversive events or how we keep negative events from repeating themselves.

Cognitions as dispositional traits are the learned, enduring, personal values of life and have various influences on emotional arousal. These belief schemes dispose the individual to certain emotional reactions by:

1) leading people to search (sort) out and selectively attend to situational stimuli of a certain type;

2) influencing the situational event and the experiences through a process of evaluation (e.g., "I am good if I do the work, terrible if I do not");

3) keeping emotionally loaded (past negative) events alive and anticipated future happenings vivid (e.g., "My wife never does what I like, and she is going to say no when I ask her to go to the movies tonight"); and

4) indirectly creating events that prompt behavior consistent with perception (e.g., the faculty member drops by the Dean's office to ask about an important grant application. The Dean is taking off his boots from the snow, states that he just got back to the office, and requests that the faculty member make an appointment. The faculty member leaves, mumbling to himself, "Just proves he really doesn't like me.").

Moreover, cognitions mediate aversive events and maintain a negative perception of them. People appraise an experience by giving attributions (e.g., can't be done; it's crazy, good, deplorable) to the event itself. The outcome of various attributions to the event are emotional states which are viewed, for example, as awful or unbearable. These cognitions thus "hold the event" in a negative state for the individual (e.g., "I will feel stressed, pressured, bad, if the work is not done," or "The boss should not ask me to do extra work after being ill, it's terrible that he does this to me"). The attributes themselves reflect certain basic beliefs, such as this event "should not have happened," which reveals a presupposition about unfortunate events. These presuppositions often reveal logical errors in terms of reality, though the behavior emanating from these beliefs has a logical relationship and reinforcement consequence to the belief itself. "It's wrong for me to have a heart attack, I'm too young; I have a family," as an example leads to depressed emotional states and frustration. An occurrence of an event such as a heart attack, with its high stress state and disruption, holds the potential for the solidification of cognitions which can have positive or negative consequences for the individual, both in the present and the future.

Beck (1976) has developed a specific approach to challenge the irrational cognitions of individuals suffering from depressive disorders. He has demonstrated rapid and effective reduction of depressive symptoms, supporting the assumption of the occurrence change during stressful times. He postulates three dominant ideations in depression: a negative view of oneself, a negative view of the world, and a negative view of the future. Rush and Beck (1977) have identified patterns associated with cognitive errors. They include:

1) sorting for negative: "I know they won't accept me back at work when they find out I've had a heart attack";
2) demanding perfection: "How can I remain a manager of the company when I have to stay out of work";
3) polarization of thoughts: "Once you've had a heart attack, you're no longer a man";
4) maxlmizing or minimizing: "It was just a little heart attack. People are making too much of a fuss";
5) arbitrary interpretation of events: "I'm having a pain in my arm; I wonder if I'm having a heart attack"; and
6) distortion of time: "I don't have enough time to do those exercises."

Rehm (1977) has focused on cognitions associated with self-control. (Examples include problems of self-acceptance where individuals attach a sense of worthwhileness to the behaviors and appraisal of others but not to themselves. People engage in self-downing, self-berating, and demandingness of self, in relation to their performance: "I'm stupid, terrible for thinking these thoughts, not knowing, etc." Low frustration tolerance has been explored in terms of cognitive errors (e.g., "I want what I want when I want it; it's terrible that I'm thwarted; I can't stand it when things go wrong"). The logical errors in the presuppositions are: that one should or must not be thwarted; you are not valued unless you get what you want right away; bad things happen only to me; I'm being ignored; I'm not liked, that's unfair, etc., and result in the evolution of emotions of anger, pain, and disappointment.

Similarly, Seligman (1975) has proposed a cognitive theory of depression, the central tenet of which concerns the effect of the independence of behavior from outcome. Learned helplessness, which is his definition of depression, is marked by passivity, retarded learning, lack of aggressive competitiveness, weight loss and undereating. These responses, it is believed, are not related to trauma, but to the existential experience of having no control over the trauma. The aim of therapeutic intervention from this model is for the individual to regain a sense of personal control. Interventions are directed toward altering the individual's basic premise of helplessness.

All of the cognitive models presented thus far have revealed that, in the application of clinical interventions, the cognitive patterns are sustained, in part, by an unconscious internal dialogue carried on by the client. Many of the intervention strategies attempt to address aspects of this subjective process, altering the structure of beliefs. The intervention strategies emphasize attending to these internal thought patterns and noting the individual's capacity for emotional arousal. Clients are encouraged to utilize a variety of activities which, under their control, interrupt the negative processes, such as saying to themselves, "My premise is not true," or, "I can change the subject." This aspect of intervention allows for a natural link with NLP tenets.

NEURO-LINGUISTIC PROGRAMMING (NLP)

Unlike the cognitive theories presented thus far, Neuro-Linguistic Programming alters the usual focus of therapeutic intervention from the content of communication to a focus on the structure of communication and its consequences. Structure is addressed by engaging clients in different behaviors, and experiential states can be encouraged that disrupt patterns that limit choice (Dilts et al., 1980). A basic premise of NLP is that patterned behavior represents a cybernetic interaction between responses, mind, and body, and that, regardless of etiology (the initial event), the structure of the process can be considered causal in the maintenance of a patterned response (symptoms). Change in symptoms occurs when the pattern is disrupted by altering its structure. Patterns can be challenged verbally and through non-verbal activity with the aim of the challenge being increased behavioral flexibility for the client. The specifics of the increased choices are unique to the individual. The outcome of the therapeutic intervention, therefore, is pattern interruption and, for the client, a corresponding increased flexibility in choosing ways of attaining positive life goals. The details of an individual's life provide the context for the person's behavior. That context may be addressed through altering or adapting the structure of behavioral patterns associated with internal states, external behavior, beliefs and values, and which are expressed in linguistic patterns.

In the NLP scheme a person is represented by three major systems: Sensory System, Program System (Meta Programs), and Operations System (Patterned Operations). Since a cybernetic relationship is assumed to exist among these three major systems, there is high probability that change in one system will produce change in all three systems.

Sensory System

The sensory system is basically defined by the central nervous system which mediates the peripheral nervous system and major sense organ functions such as sight, hearing, touch, taste and smell.

Program System (Meta Programs)

Of particular importance to our intervention efforts are the systems of Meta Programs and Patterned Operations. The conceptual scheme used to map Meta Programs is based on time, activity, person, and criteria for closely held beliefs (Cameron-Bandler, 1980, 1981, 1982).

Some important questions to be considered in evaluating what a person says and does and their importance in shaping his behaviors and internal and external responses are: Does the individual show a preference for sorting his or her experiential world by person, place, information, or thing? Does the individual focus primarily on the past, present, or future? Does the individual primarily compare self/self, self/other, or other/other? Is the individual's behavior initiated by what another does, feels, thinks, or by what the individual does, feels and thinks. How does the person distinguish between self and others? Do the person's patterns change in different social contexts? Are the patterns of time, activity, person, and criteria altered? If so, in what ways? Does the individual locate criteria for right and wrong within others or within himself?

These questions do not cover all the principles involved in assessing Meta Programs, but it is a brief guide to how the parameters of time, activity, person, sorting habits and criteria can be abstracted from linguistic patterns. These parameters can be used to help focus attention on what is most valued and familiar to the individual. Information about the structure of a unique personal value and belief system allows interventions to be designed in a manner which "fits" for the client. The client may then detail his or her own desired changes. This respect for and sensitivity to the client's beliefs and values enhance rapport and motivation for change.

In designing intervention strategies, a question to be asked is how the structures of Meta Programs work for the client. If the structures limit behavioral flexibility, strategies for change aim at opening up choices. It has been found that, whatever the theoretical orientation, interventions result in behavior change by the client's participation in one or more of the following activities: combining (verbal and non-verbal information); sorting (verbal and non-verbal information); separating (verbal and non-verbal information); adjusting criteria; and rehearsing new behavior. The skill of the therapist can be realized in the ability to select interventions which engage one or more of the five activities in such a manner that the client's negative pattern of behavior can be disrupted.

Operations System (Patterned Operations)

The third major system to be addressed in the designing of interventions is that of Patterned Operations. Bandler and Grinder (1976) have utilized an association between neurological responses and linguistic structures to link the use of predicates (verbs, adverbs, and adjectives) to eye movement patterns. While it has been recognized that we store experiences auditorially, visually, and kinesthetically, the theory that an individual may have a distinct preference for one system over another, and that the preference is discernible in language and eye movement patterns is new. Strategies for remembering, making decisions, learning, etc., can reflect these preferences and either enhance or detract from the efficiency of these tasks, as well as influence how receptive one is to the communication patterns of another.

These operations are in part identified by eye movements. Eye movements above a median line (i.e., looking upward to the left or right) and straight ahead while defocusing indicates that the person is drawing primarily on visual representations of an experience he is verbally describing. Similarly, lateral eye movements indicate an internal auditory experience; looking down to the right indicates a kinesthetic experience; and looking down to the left indicates that the person is attending to an internal dialogue. (The latter is generally the eye movement pattern for those who are right-handed; it is reversed for lefties.) Combining with the non-verbal responses are corresponding language patterns emphasizing a preferential use of auditory, visual, and kinesthetic predicates. Examples of auditory predicates are: hear, sounds, ringing; examples of visual predicates are: see, clear, bright, focus; examples of kinesthetic (olfactory, gustatory) predicates are: feels, touching, smells, bitter. Rather than learning this scheme and expecting everyone to fit into it, NLP training insists that the therapist calibrate the verbal and non-verbal patterns of a client to his or her predicates. This procedure respects the unique characteristics of the client and allows the therapist to gain rapport with the client by using the preferred sensory language of the client.

When the tenets of cognitive behavioral therapy are combined with the NLP model and applied to the phases of PTSD post-myocardial infarct as outlined for the post-heart attack victims, a comprehensive method is provided for assessing and intervening in relevant and specific ways. Outcome can then be assessed not only in terms of the broad parameters of recovery but to unique aspects of the client, spouse, employer, and work setting.

The following clinical example is used to highlight applications of NLP strategies. The example demonstrates how a client's rigid concept of who is right and who is wrong leads to the belief that there is only one way to behave. This, in turn, leads to confusion on how to relate to bodily responses following a myocardial infarction.

Mrs. Smith, a 38-year-old single mother and factory worker, insisted on leaving the hospital to return home to her demanding children, boyfriend, and dependent in-laws. This is an excerpt from the nurse clinician's initial home visit upon discharge:

Mrs. Smith: I'm going to write the American Heart Association because I didn't have specific symptoms. (Looks directly at the nurse)
Nurse: What are "specific symptoms"?
Mrs. Smith: I don't know but I had burning in my chest (looks away, down to right) I didn't think anything was wrong, you know, that serious (looks up at nurse, lateral left down) even when I got home the next morning, I went to the doctor and he sent me to the hospital. (Silence, looking down to right) I get burning twinges. I guess that's to be expected. (Looks up, focus on nurse)

Important characteristics manifested in Mrs. Smith's comments are as follows: she relates to the past, she has a hyperawareness of bodily sensations, she is unclear as to their significance in part because they do not match her ideas of what the experts say regarding a heart attack.

She requests that the nurse match her confusion as to the seriousness of her symptoms ("you know"). She moves to the present and projects into the future her attempts to interpret twinges in the future and indirectly asks if her guess is correct. Her eyes diverting down to the right plus her language underscores strong internal kinesthetic responses.

Nurse: Why do you guess that?

[The nurse had a variety of alternatives—asking why focuses the client on her beliefs as to why she is guessing. However, the client responds with a presupposition regarding cause.]

Mrs. Smith: I overdid it. (Eyes move laterally to the left) I'm scared and confused. (Looking at nurse)
Nurse: Scared?
Mrs. Smith: Scared of dying and I don't know what to do. (Reaches for a cigarette on coffee table)
Nurse: Smoking?
Mrs. Smith: Gives me something to do. I have to find something to replace it. (Lights cigarette)
Nurse: Does doing something like work help?
Mrs. Smith: Don't think I will return to the job—too much dust. Think I'll be a nurse's aide. (Eyes to left, lateral, then right lateral, right up)

Separating out Mrs. Smith's questions of right and wrong results in extreme tension. The tension is so great she takes a cigarette to relieve the tension and states she needs to find something to take its place. The nurse purposely moves the client from the present state to the future and links action with tension reduction; that is, testing the response to combining two behaviors. Mrs. Smith reveals concerns she has about her job and her lack of control over the environment. She suggests for herself a change in jobs. The statement about her present work situation reveals an underlying belief that the cause of her illness comes from outside factors. Her belief pattern is polarized between the outside and the fear that movement and action on her part now can precipitate an attack. She does reveal that her future concerns will be focused on some changes. She pictures herself as a nurse's aide. The question is how is it possible that she does not attend to changes needed in the present? A hypothesis is that Mrs. Smith can make a change in the present only when she is sure it is absolutely right for her.

Nurse: Let's see if I'm following you. You have lots of feelings. In the future you believe a job change is necessary, but right now you're scared and confused. You are feeling things in your body and you don't know how they fit in with what you are doing. You don't want to do anything which puts you in jeopardy but you aren't sure the experts know what is right for you.

Mrs. Smith: Yeah, I don't want to do the wrong thing. I can't be sure. (Looks at nurse)

An important point is that the nurse assumes that the behaviors Mrs. Smith evokes are not engaged in with the purpose of hurting herself. Rather, Mrs. Smith does not consider alternatives because she cannot be absolutely sure of the outcome. Taking the cigarette in front of the nurse indicates how strongly linked the smoking habit is with tension reduction for Mrs. Smith. The nurse does not focus on the smoking behavior but does begin to focus more directly on the cognitions of right and wrong and the need for security before something (new behavior) is engaged. The rigidity of this belief pattern comes from the restrictions it places on possible options but, more importantly, the preoccupation with, "Is this right or wrong for the future?" curtails adequate attention to present experiences which give information regarding states of relaxation and behavioral changes which either increase or reduce tension.

Nurse: How can you be sure something is right or wrong for you?

Mrs. Smith: (Puzzled) I don't know. (Pause, eyes down left) I guess try to find out how it feels. (Looks up at nurse)

[The nurse challenges Mrs. Smith's criteria for right and wrong by asking her how she can be sure. Mrs. Smith searches for her own criteria and concludes that she has to do something and then check on how it feels.]

Nurse: (Takes a deep breath, changes position in her chair, relaxes her shoulders. As the nurse does this, Mrs. Smith, who is now paying attention, follows suit, changing her position, and relaxing in her chair.) Do you think the experts have the right answer?

Mrs. Smith: No, there are answers in general, but they don't fit my symptoms. (Looks off to right, back to the nurse)

Mrs. Smith is more relaxed at this point. There has been a modification in the rigid concepts of right and wrong and Mrs. Smith has introduced the framework of trial and error as a means of testing and finding out information in the present. This helps her move away from experiencing a present state of confusion as negative, thus reducing tension and fear associated with doing the wrong thing.

Nurse: Well, since you have brought them (symptoms) up, (Smiles) maybe you and I can focus on how you feel in the here-and-now, and what you do and think that is associated with how you feel.

Mrs. Smith: Well, when I look around the house, I see all the things that need to be done and I see . . . nobody helps out . . . and I think I'll do it because I can't stand it, and . . . and it's my job. . . . (Eyes move around the room, body becomes tense, she leans forward, her fist becomes clenched)

Nurse: How do you feel now?

Mrs. Smith: (Glance drops down, looks at her hands) I'm tense.

Focusing on the present state reveals many external and internal sources of pressure for the client with concomitant physical reactions. Many internal patterns of beliefs about herself with regard to others play a strong part in increasing her state of tension. However, before these are challenged, it is important to help Mrs. Smith recognize how her thoughts play a role in states of tension and relaxation, thus providing her an immediate experience of self-control.

The case example illustrates the impact of nursing intervention on relevant patterns of belief and their association with physical tension and psychic confusion. Mrs. Smith's eye movements and sensory-based language guide aspects of the nurse's responses. The example aims at demonstrating how identifying immediate belief patterns and concomitant non-verbal responses (e.g., eye movement, body posture) become the primary source of data for structuring both verbal and non-verbal nursing behaviors, which direct the client to experiences designed to offset negative patterns. The client's ongoing responses can be used to evaluate the immediate effects of the intervention.

CONCLUSION

This chapter has aimed at describing a model for structuring intervention efforts with PTSD emerging from serious illness. The concept of PTSD assumes an overwhelming life event which not only impacts on the victim, but also impacts on those people surrounding the victim. This sets up a social nexus which can either enhance adaptation to the stressful event or impede a positive adjustment. Consequently, the model suggests that intervention efforts must address the social context of the victim as well as the victim. This is particularly true in the early, post-traumatic period. However, clinical practice has indicated that PTSD can continue to be activated at a much later period of time from the actual event.

Clearly, our cognitive-behavioral approach focuses on how information is being stored and utilized. This is in contrast to other intervention approaches which focus on linking maladaptive responses to earlier, pre-traumatic events and personality structure, regardless of the traumatic event. The cognitive-behavioral principles direct intervention efforts toward reshaping beliefs about what has happened, so that noxious physiological states and their psychological responses are addressed in a more flexible and useful cognitive framework. The same process is used in altering interpretations regarding social interaction.

Early pioneering studies of victims, such as those surviving the Coconut Grove fire, led to a number of important outcomes: the concept of delayed grief reaction, and emphasis on crisis intervention as an effort to curb serious psychiatric illness. What we are learning now is that crisis intervention, while most useful, needs to be structured around more specific outcomes than were previously understood (Lindemann 1944). The later effects of traumatic life events suggest that PTSD is the result of far more complex aspects of the integration process of trauma. Cognitive-behavioral principles help direct detailed attention to the structure of the integration efforts during the post-recovery period.

By looking at the kinds of adjustments people make to specific stressful life events, we gain insights into the structure of cognitive coping necessary for recovery. This is a promising area for a more focused intervention. When limiting structures are identified, methods to impact on these structures can be evaluated directly in terms of behaviorally identifiable outcomes for clients.

REFERENCES

Adrasik, F., Coleman, D., & Epstein, L.H. Biofeedback: Clinical and research considerations. In D.M. Doleys, R.L. Meredith, & A.R. Ciminero (Eds.), *Behavioral psychology in medicine: Assessment and treatment strategies.* New York: Plenum Press, 1982.

Adrasik, F., & Holroyd, K.A. A test for specific and non-specific effects in the biofeedback treatment of tension headache. *Journal of Consulting and Clinical Psychology*, 1980, *48*, 575-586.

Bandler, R., & Grinder, J. *The structure of magic*, Vol. I. Palo Alto, CA: Science and Behavior Books, 1976.

Bandura, A., Adams, N.E., & Beyer, J. Cognitive processes mediating behavioral change. *Journal of Personality and Social Psychology*, March 1977, *35*(3), 125-139.

Beck, A.T. *Cognitive therapy and the emotional disorders*. New York: International University Press, 1976.

Beck, A.T., & Emery G. *Cognitive therapy of anxiety and phobic disorders*. Philadelphia: Center for Cognitive Therapy, 1979.

Cameron-Bandler, L. *They lived happily ever after*. Cupertino, CA: Meta Publications, 1980.

Cameron-Bandler, L. Master practitioner program in NLP. Cambridge, MA, 1981.

Cameron-Bandler. L. Advanced practitioner program in NLP. Cambridge, MA, 1982.

Dilts, R., Grinder, J., Bandler, R., Bandler, L., & DeLozier, J. *Neuro-linguistic programming. Vol. I. The study of the structure of subjective experience*. Cupertino, CA: Meta Publications, 1980.

Ellis, A. *Reason and emotion in psychotherapy*. New York: Lyle Stuart, 1962; Paperback ed., Citadel Press, 1977.

Ellis, A., & Harper, R.A., *A new guide to rational living*. Englewood Cliffs, NJ: Prentice-Hall, 1975.

Grieger, R., & Grieger, I.Z. *Cognitive and emotional disturbance*, New York: Human Sciences Press, 1982.

Holroyd, K.A., Andrasik, F., & Noble, J.A. A comparison of EMG biofeedback: A credible pseudotherapy in treating tension headache. *Journal of Behavioral Medicine*, 1980, *3*, 29-39.

Janis, I. Preventing pathogenic denial by means of stress inoculation. In S. Breznitz (Ed.), *The denial of stress*. New York: International Press, 1983.

Jenkins, C.D. Psychologic and social precursors of coronary disease, *New England Journal of Medicine*, 1971, *284*, 244-245.

Lindemann, E. Symptomatology and management of acute grief. *American Journal of Psychiatry*, 1944, *101*, 141-146.

Meyendorf, R. Psychopathology in heart disease aside from cardiac surgery: A historical perspective of cardiac psychosis. *Comprehensive Psychiatry*, 1979, *20*(4), 326-331.

Mitchell, K. *Motivational factors of a successful return to work after myocardial infarction*. Unpublished doctoral dissertation, Pennsylvania State University, 1975.

Rehm, L.P. A self-control model of depression. *Behavior Therapy*, 1977, *8*, 787-804.

Romirowsky, A. Psychological adaptation patterns in response to cardiac surgery. *Journal of Rehabilitation*, 1980, *3*, 50-52.

Roskies, E., & Avard, J. Teaching health managers to control their coronary-prone (Type A) behavior. In K. Blankenstein, & J. Polivy (Eds.), *Self-control and self-modification of emotional behavior*, New York: Plenum Press, 1983.

Roskies, E., Spevack, M., Surkis, A., Cohen, C., & Gilman, S. Changing the coronary-prone (Type A) behavior pattern in a non-clinical population. *Journal of Behavioral Medicine*, 1978, *1*, 201-216.

Rush, A.J., & Beck, A.T. Cognitive therapy of depression and suicide. *American Journal of Psychotherapy*, 1977, *1*, 201-219.

Seligman, M. *Helplessness: On depression, development, and death*, San Francisco, CA: W.H. Freeman, 1975.

Soloff, P. Medically and surgically treated coronary patients in cardiovascular rehabilitation: A comparative study. *International Journal of Psychiatry in Medicine*, 1978, *9*(1), 93-106.

Stern, M., Pascale, L., & Ackerman, A. Life adjustment post-myocardial infarction. *Archives of Internal Medicine*, 1977, *137*, 1680-1685.

Teasdale, J.D., & Rezin, V. The effects of reducing frequency of negative thoughts on the mood of depressed patients—Test of cognitive model of depression. *British Journal of Sociology and Clinical Psychology*, 1978, *17*, 65-75.

15

Diagnosis and Treatment of Traumatic Stress Among Women After Childhood Incest

MARY ANN DONALDSON and RUSSELL GARDNER, JR.

This chapter describes a treatment program derived from experience with 26 adult women seen clinically who had experienced incest as children. Twenty-five met diagnostic criteria for delayed or chronic post-traumatic stress disorder (PTSD) as operationally defined in the third edition of the Diagnostic and Statistical Manual of Mental Disorders *or DSM-III (APA, 1980). Horowitz's concept of stress response syndrome (SRS) enhanced their individual and group psychotherapy. A questionnaire designed and administered to register SRS components experienced introspectively served usefully as a self-assessment tool early in therapy. Group therapy proved useful in later or consolidation phases.*

INTRODUCTION

Childhood incest apparently affects the daily lives of numerous families. Only recently, however, has this family interaction seemed to require examination. What thoughts, feelings and memories occur acutely and which persist? How does the experience become transformed into psychopathology and into what kinds? Such questions have been answered more by conjecture or ad hoc observations than from systematic data collection. From a sample of women who presented in the clinical practice of a social worker (M.D.) at a family social service agency we conclude that many are afflicted severely and such childhood experience has haunting effects in adult life.

How frequent is such incest? Herman-Lewis and Hirschmann (1981) in their book *Father-Daughter Incest* compiled survey estimates of incest frequency. From these data one-fifth to one-third of all women reported a childhood sexual encounter with an adult male. As many as one million American women may have been involved in father-daughter incest (Herman-Lewis & Hirschmann, 1981). If one includes other types of incest such as brother-sister, grandfather-granddaughter, or uncle-niece, the numbers of those involved become very large. Forward and Buck (1978) estimate that 10 million people may have experienced incest. Risk does not divide along demographic or class lines but cuts across all socioeconomic and cultural characteristics. Most known victims are female and perpetrators male. Most reported cases involve father-daughter incest, although there is some conjecture that brother-sister incest may in fact be more common. Although females usually first become victims in late childhood, victimization can begin as early as infancy. The incestuous experience is rarely an isolated incident but often occurs over weeks, months, or years. However, ongoing molestation often remains undetected owing to the secrecy of the behavior, and the clinician may learn of such childhood events only when the adult presents a symptom picture or sometimes after treatment had been long under way.

Although the problem of incest is often discussed in the literature, treatment approaches for victims are sparsely reported (Herman, 1981; Meiselman, 1978; Mrazek & Kempe, 1981; Tsai & Wagner, 1978). In this chapter, however, we discuss this sample of adult women who were victims of childhood incest primarily from this viewpoint. As the DSM-III category of PTSD accurately described the symptom picture of the women who appeared with this history, we formulated a treatment approach from Horowitz's conceptualization of stress response syndrome (SRS) (Horowitz, 1976; Krupnick & Horowitz, 1981).

REVIEW OF LITERATURE

Traditionally, incest seemed extremely rare with an estimated prevalence of perhaps one in a million children truly afflicted (Rosenfeld, 1979b). Incest as a scientific issue was initiated by Breuer and Freud (1895) in relationship to the pathogenesis of hysteria, but later Freud (1925) focused on fantasies of incest and disavowed his earlier impression of the role of actual incest. This refocus on indisputable mental functions (including his own) instead of more conjectural historical events was a key development in the history of psychoanalysis and the concept of the Oedipus concept with its assumption of universal tendencies to incestuous action. Controversy rages still about whether the early cases of Freud were, in fact, incest rather than fantasy (Malcolm, 1983).

We comment on such historical controversy only to note the power of incest (and invariable secrecy about it) to elicit powerful feelings which in turn may have contributed to a general underreporting of incestuous events. However, considering recent reports of higher incidence and a heightened awareness of women's issues in general, authorities now strongly encourage that reports be considered reality unless very clearly demonstrated to be fantasy (Rosenfeld, Nadelson, & Krieger, 1979). An error in this direction is far less serious for victims than problems which ensue when they encounter disbelief in the face of reality.

INCEST IN CHILDREN: IS IT STRESSFUL?

Herman-Lewis and Hirschmann (1981) reviewed professional literature which suggests that sexual encounters between child and adult family members may have no harmful effect, especially if the child chose to become involved in the encounter. On the other side of the debate, more recently evolving studies indicate unpleasant to severely negative and long-term effects of such actions (Cohen, J.A., 1981; Forward & Buck, 1978; Gross, 1979; Gross, Doerr, Caldirola, Guzinsk, & Ripley, 1981; Herman-Lewis & Hirschmann, 1981; Meiselman, 1978; Rosenfeld, 1979b; Selby, Calhoun, Jones, & Matthews, 1980; Summitt & Kryso, 1978; Tsai, Feldman-Summers, & Edgar, 1979). DSM-III's Axis IV uses repeated physical or sexual abuse as an example of an extreme psychosocial stressor (6 on a 7-point scale). The DSM-III discussion of Axis IV concisely summarizes the stress literature and lists three augmenting or ameliorating factors which need to be considered when evaluating the stress in a person's life. These three criteria are listed here as they provide a framework for understanding better the literature on child incest:

1) the amount of change caused by the stressor compared to an average person's life;
2) the degree to which the event is desired and under the individual's control; and
3) the number of stressors. (APA, 1980, p. 26)

Change in Life

Many behavioral and emotional changes have been reported in child victims. Difficulty with friends, school failure, isolation from peers, teenage pregnancy, drug abuse, suicide attempts, sexual acting out, hysterical seizures, intense guilt, and low self-worth have all been associated with child and adolescent victimization (Gross, 1979; Herman-Lewis & Hirschmann, 1981; Krieger, Rosenfeld, Gordon & Bennett, 1980; Rosenfeld, 1979b; Selby et al., 1980; Summit & Kryso, 1978). These apparently strong reactions exemplify drastic changes in the child's life. Home is no longer a place of safety and refuge but a site of high stress. Victims never know when the abuse will occur again, what the abuse will entail, or what will happen if others find out. The life-changing circumstances become even more pronounced if the incest becomes publicly known since the child is then often removed from the home and must endure legal proceedings.

Control of Stressful Events

In their 1980 study, Krieger et al. reviewed a debate concerning a child's voluntary versus involuntary participation, and use of the terms "participant" versus "accidental victim." Participant victims in therapy were often found to be "seductive" or "flirtatious" whereas accidental victims were "shy" and "withdrawn." The assumption is that the participant victims willingly comply with the incest so that less pathology results.

But other researchers strongly disagree with this differentiation. Herman-Lewis and Hirschmann (1981) state that "consent and choice are concepts that apply to relationships of peers." The relationship between child and adult involves a power differential, because the child is dependent on the adult for basic needs. Others feel that the child's being seductive implies learned behavior (Rosenfeld, 1979a), or identification with the adult aggressor (Krieger et al., 1980), more than truly willing participation. In any event, the child's coping devices or defensive reactions may obscure an easy understanding of these behaviors, and the power differential between child and parent on the one hand, and the evidence for negative effects in "willing participants" on the other, makes a case for free participation a difficult one.

Number of Stressors

DSM-III's discussion of family factors found to be stressors for children and adolescents includes distant relationships between parents, cold or distant parental behavior between parent and child, parental intrusiveness, inconsistent parental control, or loss of family members. The literature strongly supports the idea that incestuous families are dysfunctional families and often include a number of the stressors listed above. Breakdown in family roles including depressed-dependent mothers, parent-child role reversals between mother and daughter, poor family communication, poor sibling relationships, dysfunctional marital relationships, poor ego boundaries between family members, and alcoholic fathers are reported dynamics in incestuous families (Anderson & Shafer, 1979; Browning & Boatman, 1977; Giaretto, 1976; Meiselman, 1978; Rosenfeld, 1979c; Selby et al., 1980; Summit & Kryso, 1978; Wells, 1981). In summary, the children in many incestuous families experience a number of stressors beyond the incest itself.

THE PROCESSING OF A STRESSFUL EVENT

Horowitz (1976) outlines an ideal course for processing a stressful event. The stressed person is less deleteriously affected if he or she:

1) perceives the event correctly;
2) translates the perceptions into a clear meaning;
3) relates the meaning to one's enduring attitude;
4) decides on appropriate action; and
5) revises memories, attitudes and belief systems to fit a new developmental line made necessary by the experience.

If the child's incestuous experience is discovered and reported and treatment becomes mandatory, many of the above steps do ensue. However, most children keep the incest a secret out of covert or overt threat and deep shame and guilt so that for such children all of the above steps may be prevented.

Returning to Horowitz's model, he notes that if ideal processing cannot take place, the thoughts, feelings and memories associated with the event occupy active memory storage, the contents of which always push toward release (Horowitz, 1976). This push is experienced as intrusive-repetitious thoughts. Since these thoughts and memories are so overwhelming, they are actively put away or denied. Hence, a cycle occurs in which intrusive-repetitious thoughts alternate with denial and reports of numbing.

Along with this cycle, various other themes of thoughts and feeling can be expected as elaborated in a subsequent publication by Krupnick and Horowitz (1981). These SRS themes include fear and anxiety, anger and frustration, guilt and remorse, shame and self-disgust, and sadness. In reviewing long-term effects of incest many of these themes are revealed along with other symptoms. Anxiety, guilt, low self-esteem, depression, social isolation, difficulty with intimate relationships, tendency to sexualize relationships, identity problems, sexual dysfunctions, sexual promiscuity, and substance abuse have been reported (Brooks, 1982; Carozza, 1981; Cohen, T., 1981; Forward & Buck, 1978; Herman, 1981; Herman-Lewis & Hirschmann, 1981; Meiselman, 1978; Rist, 1979; Rosenfeld, 1979a; Tsai et al., 1979).

Does Childhood Incest Cause Post-traumatic Stress Disorder in Adults?

Post-traumatic stress disorder (PTSD) has been discussed in the literature, especially regarding Vietnam War veterans and other war veterans (Horowitz & Solomon, 1975). Horowitz's original work (1976) discusses PTSD with adults who have experienced various life crises. In general, the phenomenon of delayed stress has not been widely studied regarding children, although Terr (1981a, 1981b, 1983) has documented profound stress syndrome effects in children as a result of the Chowchilla incident wherein the children were temporarily buried inside a bus. There is no reported inquiry discussing incest in terms of the stress response syndromes, either from the perspective of current child victims or past adult victims. When the present authors (Donaldson & Gardner, 1982) reviewed our experiences with an initial sample of 26 consecutively encountered incest victims, we found that all but one met diagnositic criteria for DSM-III PTSD regarding the incest trauma.

All women in the senior author's caseload at an outpatient family service agency in a rural midwest area who presented incest as a problem in the course of their workup or treatment were included in this study. Incest is defined here as a definite sexual approach resulting in physical contact between a child and that child's family member(s). Nineteen women had been referred to the senior author specifically regarding incest, two additional discussed incest as their presenting problem, and the remaining five revealed incest as a problem as therapy progressed (three of those five revealed incest within the first three sessions, one after approximately twelve sessions and another after approximately one year of therapy). In 23 of the 26 cases information on incest was volunteered independently of clinician inquiry. Presenting symptoms included lack of sexual response, depressed feelings, anxiety attacks, and relationship difficulties. Characteristics of their adult psychiatric and psychosocial histories are tabulated in Tables 1 and 2. Of the women in the sample, 13 were single, 5 married, and 8 divorced. Of the 26 women, 25 were Caucasian and one Native American (Indian). Twenty-three lived at a middle-income status, while three lived in unstable and low-income life-styles. At treatment onset, 17 were employed outside of the home, three were full-time homemakers, four were students, and two were unemployed. Half of the women came from families of origin that had exhibited chemical dependency, and over half from families that exhibited spouse abuse (15), and child abuse (14). Ten families of origin possessed multiple incest victims among siblings.

We used DSM-III diagnostic criteria for delayed (or chronic) post-traumatic stress disorder in evaluating their case histories and symptom profiles. With respect to Part A of the diagnostic criteria, which requires the existence of a stressor, these clients by definition met this criterion from Axis IV considerations. Parts B and C of the diagnostic criteria each requires at least one of three criteria and part D requires at least two of six listed specific symptoms. Based on overall data analysis we found that 25 of the 26 women met these criteria. For Part B, reexperience of

TABLE 1
History of Psychiatric Difficulties

	No.*	%
Hx of antidepressant use	3	11
Hx of quasi-physical medical complaints	6	23
Suicidal behavior	12	46
Alcohol abuse	8	31
Psychiatric hospitalization	3	11

* Overlapping categories

TABLE 2
Adult Relationship Experiences

	No.*	%
Physical abuse	9	34
Sexual abuse (non-family)	12	46
Isolation from men	9	34
Emotional isolation	16	61
Promiscuity	13	50
Sexual unresponsiveness	16	61
Lesbian activity	3	11

* Categories may overlap

the trauma, the mean criteria were 2.2 (S.D. = 0.8), and for C, numbing of responsiveness, the mean was 1.8 (S.D. = 0.8). In category D, 2.9 symptoms (S.D. = 1.0) were present. One symptom in category D, survivor guilt, was never noted. Summarizing the data differently, each of the 12 criteria and listed symptoms in Parts B, C, and D, with this one exception, was noted at least twice and of these, 6.9 were tabulated on average (S.D. = 2.0). The person in the sample who fell short of the diagnosis of post-traumatic stress disorder met criteria from only two parts, A (stressor) and B (recurrent and intrusive recollections of the event).

Methodologic Comment: Is There a Sampling Problem with a Clinical Population?

Women who seek treatment may have suffered as a result of their incestuous experience more than other women with similar trauma who do not seek treatment. Might there be a dosage effect? Might less extensive stimuli or a more supportive environment lessen pathologic responses? Tsai et al. (1979) compared a clinical sample with a non-clinical sample (women responding to a newspaper ad) and found (see Table 3) that the former had had more exposure to the sexual abuse with the abuse lasting into adolescence. The Donaldson and Gardner group (1982) demonstrated these characteristics even more strikingly. The mean age of our patient population's last molestation was 15.6 years, greater than Tsai et al.'s clinical sample which in turn was greater than the non-clinical sample. Thus, the emotional characteristics of our treatment sample may not be generalizable to many incest victims since their "dosage" of sexual abuse was so high.

TABLE 3

Comparison of Control Sample with Two Clinical Groups

	Tsai et al. "nonclinical"		Tsai et al. "clinical"		Donaldson & Gardner	
	M	s.d.	M	s.d.	M	s.d.
Present age	29.2	9.3	31.5	8.6	28.2	6.8
Age of last molestation	9.23	3.91	12.37	3.67	15.6	7.1
Duration of molestation (years)	2.5	3.3	4.7	4.1	8.1	7.0

A CLINICAL INTERVENTION WITH INCEST VICTIMS

The collaboration between the authors on this project began when the senior author attended a Psychiatry Grand Rounds in which a patient with delayed PTSD secondary to war trauma was presented and Horowitz's SRS used as a guide to the treatment. Adult women who had been incest victims and were in treatment with the author seemed well-characterized by the diagnosis and the conceptual scheme allowed a firmer course of therapeutic action.

Assessment of Patients

Attempts to assess the clients diagnostically with PTSD ensued (see above). We asked all 26 women to fill out a questionnaire* aimed at registering their introspectively experienced SRS characteristics with the idea that this might become a self-assessment tool for those potentially engaging in treatment. Fifty-two questions adopted from the Horowitz group required a rating on a 6-point scale ranging from 0 ("never") to 3 ("half the time") to 5 ("always").

In addition, a series of 11 essay questions on a separate form made open-ended inquiry about their experiences and later life events. The patients at the time of questionnaire response had been seen individually for 17.1 (S.D. = 19.3) sessions and in the group format 14.1 (S.D. = 15.8) sessions. Twenty of the 26 women provided ratings on the formal questionnaires. Sixteen women wrote out responses to the essay questions.

Table 4 represents a simple analysis of the questionnaire responses

*For further information contact Mary Ann Donaldson, The Village Family Service Center, 1721 South University Drive, Fargo, ND 58103.

TABLE 4
SRS Categories and Questionnaire Responses

Category	Responses	Question	% Answering
Fear and Anxiety	being alone or abandoned	I get frightened and anxious when alone.	55
	recurrence of the event	I still get frightened and anxious when I'm alone with the man who sexually abused me.	62
		I get frightened that someone will hurt me sexually.	43
	losing control	I get frightened that I will become so angry I won't be able to control what I do.	65
		I get frightened that I will lose control over my thoughts.	54
	physical assault	I get frightened that someone will hurt me physically.	49
Anger and Frustration	need to blame	When I feel angry about the incest I blame my victimizer.	56
		When I feel angry about the incest I blame my mother.	45

TABLE 4 (cont'd)

Category	Responses	Question	% Answering
	anger at fate	When I think about the incest I feel very angry.	70
		When I feel angry about the incest I blame fate.	35
	anger at those spared	I feel angry at those people who were not victims of incest.	25
		I feel angry at other family members who were not victimized.	10
Guilt and Remorse	guilt over responsibility	I blame myself for the incest—I made it happen somehow by what I said or how I acted.	45
		When I feel angry about the incest I blame myself.	45
	guilt over hostility	I feel guilty that I am so angry about the incest.	45
Shame and Self-disgust	helplessness	I feel helpless in many areas of my life.	57
	lacking control	I do not feel a sense of control in regard to personal relationships.	62

	I do not feel a sense of control in regard to my job (school).	46
loss of self-confidence	I feel that I cannot trust myself.	45
	I do not feel confidence in myself.	84
	I do not like being a woman.	45
personal vulnerability	I feel vulnerable in personal relationships with women (girls).	45
	I feel vulnerable in personal relationships with men (boys).	77
disrupted basic sense of trust	I have difficulty in trusting women (girls).	45
	I have difficulty in trusting men (boys).	83
Sadness		
grief over loss	I feel I really lost something because of the incest.	75
emptiness	I feel that my life is empty.	60
	I feel empty inside.	54

in terms of the SRS categories listed. Table 5 provides data on the frequency of flashbacks, nightmares, and shaking prior to therapy.

In this sample all incestuous contacts had been between a female child and an older male family member. All of the women in this sample population had experienced a sense of relatedness with the perpetrator over time either through close physical proximity or emotional connectedness. The perpetrators included the father in 17 cases; stepfather in four; brother(s) in four; grandfather, four; uncle, four; and multiple perpetrators, five. As seen in Table 6, the content of the incestuous behavior varied from inappropriate physical touching to intercourse. Table 7 indicates the interaction of incest with other family pathology.

Treatment Model and Procedure

Conceptualizing the SRS as an adaptation mechanism as formulated by Horowitz (1976) provides not only a model through which to interpret the complex symptom picture but a contract for treatment as well. This view of the problem and its solution seems to provide the patient with a sense of power, an expectation for the course of treatment, a way to conceptualize her thoughts and feelings, and a general sense of hope. Applicable components of the Horowitz model include:

1) After a traumatic event, the afflicted person is less bothered in later life if he or she undergoes an ideal psychological processing.
2) This ideal course is interfered with by overly powerful memories persisting in "active memory storage" when "processing" does not occur.
3) Therapeutic actions of treatment break the cyclical alternation of denial and numbing and intrusive-repetitious thoughts by providing a safe environment in which one can experience the emotional response without automatic denial and numbing of the emotions.
4) Simple conscious recollection of memories, emotional catharsis, or review of thoughts and beliefs are not enough by themselves, but must proceed simultaneously and repeatedly for the best working-through process.

We found that most women come to therapy after experiencing the typical alternation between denial and numbing with intrusive-repetitious thoughts for many years. Some written statements from their essay

TABLE 5
Frequency of Flashbacks, Nightmares, and Shaking

Experience	Not applicable	Never	Occasionally	Half or more of the time	Total
Flashbacks					
at work (school)	0	4	6	10	20
when alone	0	4	6	10	20
when with a man (boy)	0	5	2	13	20
during sexual closeness	1	4	1	14	20
Nightmares	1	5	7	7	20
Shaking	2	6	10	2	20

TABLE 6
Type of Incest Experience

	No.*	%*
Intercourse	12	46
Oral contact	9	34
Genital fondling	21	80
Breast fondling	23	88
Attempted fondling	3	11
Physical abuse in addition to sexual abuse	11	42

* Categories may overlap

TABLE 7
Family Pathology

	No.*	%*
Chemical dependency	13	50
Domestic violence	15	58
Child abuse	14	56
Multiple incest victims in sibship	11	44

* Categories may overlap

answers exemplify their adaptive reactions prior to therapy: "Prior to the therapy I blocked it [incest] out of my mind. Tried not to think of it. Lived in a world of make believe and avoidance. Locked it up and threw away the key."

The therapy should provide a safe environment through which the victim can experience the emotional response to the traumatic event(s) without automatic denial and numbing of the emotions. To break through the powerful denial, a process of memory recollections is a starting point. While the memories are vivid the women are encouraged to experience the emotional responses that they felt at the time of the event, as well as how they tried to make sense of it. As the denial becomes a less effective defense, the women begin experiencing various emotions as clarified by the following client statements.

I thought I had dealt with it quite well and was very open about what had happened. But discussing it caused me to get very tense, cold, and shaky. I was very afraid of the process of getting in touch with my feelings and resisted the idea that I wasn't aware of my true feelings. I was afraid to continue and needed encouragement to do so. I especially needed to have somebody say that I would be OK on the other side of this process. There was a feeling of great fear for my sanity and a deep dread of what I may discover.

Very, very intense—the day that it first surfaced in the office I felt that it was happening to me right then. I felt like I was in labor panting and pushing to get it out. I felt immense pressure from inside. I thought I was going to blow apart. I felt my body reacting the way it did when the incest occurred. I felt immense pain and fear. I thought I was going to die.

As incest became part of their awareness, all the women experienced intrusive-repetitious thoughts. Examples included visual imagery of the events, guilt and remorse that somehow they should have prevented the interaction, fantasies of torturing or killing the victimizer, frighteningly imagining the molestation occurring again, and feeling shamefully that others "knew" of the incest. These thoughts occur at various times; for example, 70% experience this during sexual intimacy. One patient wrote, "I think about it when I have sex with my boyfriend—except if I'm drunk." Family interactions or even thinking about them may cause thoughts or memories to intrude. Twelve of the 19 who still have some contact with the family member who had abused them indicated they still feel frightened and anxious when alone with him, 20% "often," and 42% "always."

After the initial breaking through of the massive denial, therapy proceeds in a step-by-step manner. The memories, perceptions about the memories, and feeling reactions must be experienced in doses. It is important for the therapist to allow the woman to maintain a balance between her denial and her emotional reactions. The therapist moves beyond the defensive capacity in steps without the woman being overwhelmed by the strong content contained within active memory. As the woman is more and more able to recall the event and experiences less intense emotional reactions, cognitive reprocessing is extremely important. Table 8 provides a possible pattern to this reprocessing with examples of reconceptualizations.

It is important that the reprocessing or reconceptualizations occur in a way that the woman is able to experience increased self-esteem, increased trust and confidence within herself, and an alleviation of the strong emotions associated with the incest. This process of working through is done in both individual and group therapy.

TABLE 8
Reconceptualizations of Stress Responses

Category	Stress Response	Reconceptualization
Fear and Anxiety	I'm afraid I will always be alone.	I can have close relationships. I need not be alone.
	I'm afraid of losing my mind.	I can control my emotional behavior, I won't go crazy.
	Other people will hurt me.	I can protect myself now.
Anger and Frustration	I hate myself—I let this happen.	I am not a bad person, I no longer blame myself.
	I hate my mother—she didn't protect me.	My mother disappointed me, but I no longer hate her.
	I hate my father—I want to hurt him.	My father is responsible for the sexual abuse, but I can stop hating him.
Guilt and Remorse	I am responsible for the incest—I caused it.	I am not responsible for the incest—I was a victim.
	I am being punished for being a bad person.	I do not understand fully why the incest happened, but I was not being punished for being bad.
Shame and Self-disgust	I shouldn't feel so angry and hateful.	I have a right to feel angry.
	I will always be helpless.	I can exert control in many areas of my life,
	I cannot control my life.	I need not be a victim in all areas.
	I am not confident in myself, I don't trust myself.	I feel confident in some areas of my life, I trust myself.
Sadness	I cannot trust anyone.	I can trust some people.
	I lost my childhood.	I lost a lot, but not everything. I can salvage some relationships.
	I cannot feel, I am empty.	I can feel, I'm not empty.

As the women work through some of the initial blocking and are able to think and feel about the incest without being overwhelmed, they are referred to group therapy with other incest victims. The use of group therapy has been proposed by others (Meiselman, 1978; Tsai & Wagner, 1978) and has been very helpful in this setting as well. A surprising feature of such a group is the quickly developing intensity of the group process relating perhaps, on one hand, to previous therapeutic work and on the other, to a perceived sense of relief in coming together with other incest victims: All are women, all have been victimized often, with long periods of guilty secrecy before divulging the incest. A comment that women in these groups have made consistently is that "no one understands." Only within the group context can these women seem to find what they consider real support and understanding. Coming to the group seems to be "coming out of the closet" or a public acknowledgment of victimization. Women participating seem constrained to accept the incest as a part of their life and also acknowledge that they have reacted as victims. Some client quotations summarize the group's helpfulness. "Having a place where people understood how I felt because they feel the same. Not feeling so isolated and alone with all the feelings." "The group has kind of replaced the loss of the security of a family. I don't have to work hard to be accepted. I don't have to explain what it (incest) was like and how I felt—they all know and understand."

Follow-up Summary of the Initial 26 Patients

At this writing, two years after the initial workup, only one of the original 26 patients still requires regular therapy (her continued work is not for the trauma alone but for the additional trauma of a more recent rape). Of the remaining 25, 16 completed the long-term course of individual and group therapy that has become standard at the family service agency. These 16 women stayed in group treatment through their groups's ending phase (the timing of this was a mutual decision of the group members according to the standard procedure used here). All of the 16 women communicated their feeling that their incest experience was no longer a live issue in terms of continued symptoms of PTSD. Eight of these 16 women have gone on to public education and volunteer work in order to help other incest victims.

Besides the 16 who completed the prescribed course of therapy, five completed individual therapy to a point where they left therapy after considerable discussion of their status had occurred. All of these five women felt relief from the stress associated with the incest. Four of the original 26 women left therapy in the early phase of treatment. In our judgment these women left prematurely.

To summarize, we gained a distinct clinical impression that 21 of the original 26 women demonstrated marked relief by working through their SRS.

CLINICAL ISSUES

The diagnosis of PTSD and the concept of SRS have proved extremely helpful, we feel, because the afflicted women have been able to attain personal control of the disorder, first conceptually and then via active participation in the corrective process. For example, the use of the SRS questionnaire as a self-assessment tool in conjunction with didactic information conveyed a recognition of the client's own strength and of the faith others possessed about her own recuperative processes. The women readily understood the concept of unworked-through stress and seemed then to accept the symptoms of PTSD as by-products of these unresolved, still-alive issues. Vivid nightmares, bothersome intrusive thoughts, and numbing-denial become more controllable if they clearly fit into some kind of a psychobiological process experienced by anyone encountering severe trauma. The theory becomes a practical aid as we have used it, helping to change an external locus of control to internal, with the therapist's role emphatically that of someone who explains, and then aids the patient's own processes.

The theory turns out to be applicable to other patients as well, such as past victims of rape, childhood molestation, and domestic violence. Further, this approach provides an anchor for particularly difficult cases. Since the working-through process of PTSD can go on for a long period of time, knowing and understanding the theory helps the therapist "go with the process" of the patient. A woman who was kidnapped and raped over a period of weeks provides an illustrative case. Initially she remembered only part of the event but then nightmares and flashbacks of other parts of the trauma began "breaking through." These alternated with intense denial at times to the point of a dissociative reaction. The diagnosis of PTSD and the theory of SRS allowed the therapist to make sense of this process and help to reassure the patient that even trauma of this severe extent can be worked through.

With respect to current-day families, we feel husbands are secondary victims for whom consideration is warranted. They often have difficulty understanding "why she's making such a big deal about it." As they are affected also, should they be included in experimental variations of the treatment approach?

RESEARCH ISSUES

This study is a report of ongoing clinical work which has been considerably facilitated by a research-derived theory. We recognize readily, of course, the necessity of doing prospective research in which therapists using contrasting theoretical formulations (to which each is equally committed) deploy different treatments to equivalent groups. Measurements should be made before and after, using standardized measures. Other dependent measures may include total duration of treatment, therapist time and treatment cost. Follow-ups to assure stability of effect would be necessary. Such research was impractical for our setting but the results reported here may provide pilot data justification for others better equipped to make further inquiry.

This population contained severely traumatized and severely impaired women. Future research should measure the dosage of trauma necessary to cause PTSD, or the degree to which this factor operates in association with other contributing factors. In the DSM-III discussion of delayed PTSD, the text states that the disorder is more severe and long-lasting when the stressor is of human design. We suggest that this may be even more true when the designer is of the family—when the perpetrator is not an anonymous rapist but someone presumed to be trustworthy and whose presence persists. Many women continue to see the perpetrator on a regular basis—which serves as a frequent reminder of the sexual abuse. Indeed, for this sample of patients, the question of whether he and/or other family members should be confronted after "all those years" was a crucial issue in group therapy.

This raises a potential subject for future investigation bearing on the normal family function of providing trust. An unclear issue at this time is to what degree the pathological effects seen in the SRS are the result of the incest stimulus itself versus the absence of sources of social support, which indeed may be an important remedial, mediating factor (Antonovsky, 1979), usually helping the child minimize strains resulting from stressful stimuli. This came particularly to our attention as we pondered the striking loneliness evident in the experiences of group members. We conjectured that this feeling may have arisen from deficient family trust at a critical developmental period.

Do younger patients exhibit PTSD or variations similar to those documented by Terr (1981a, 1981b, 1983) seen in survivors of the Chowchilla incident? Another possibility could entail augmentation of stress syndrome features if the syndrome is not dealt with more immediately: Might the PTSD worsen with time?

In summary, we have a clinical impression of a treatment for incest-related PTSD which derives from the research formulation of SRS. This will hopefully stimulate research to investigate how the pathogenesis of this striking disorder can be understood, as well as to determine what the factors are that have contributed to these positive treatment results.

REFERENCES

American Psychiatric Association. *Diagnostic and statistical manual of mental disorders* (3rd ed.). Washington, DC: American Psychiatric Association, 1980.

Anderson, L.M., & Shafer, G. The character-disordered family: A community treatment model for family sexual abuse. *American Journal of Orthopsychiatry*, 1979, *49*, 436-445.

Antonovsky, A. *Health, stress, and coping.* San Francisco: Jossey-Bass, 1979.

Breuer, J., & Freud, S. (1895). Studies on hysteria. In J. Strachey (Ed.), *Standard Edition 2:* 1-10. London: Hogarth Press, 1955.

Brooks, B. Familial influences in father-daughter incest. *Journal of Psychiatric Treatment and Evaluation,* 1982, *4*, 117-124.

Browning, D.H., & Boatman, B. Incest: Children at risk. *American Journal of Psychiatry,* 1977, *134*, 69-72.

Carozza, P.M. Young female incest victims in treatment. *Clinical Social Work Journal,* 1981, *9*, 165-174.

Cohen, J.A., Theories of narcissism and trauma. *American Journal of Psychotherapy,* 1981, *35*, 93-100.

Cohen, T. The incestuous family. *Social Casework: The Journal of Contemporary Social Work,* 1981, *62*, 494-497.

Donaldson, M.A., & Gardner, R., Jr. *Stress responses in women after childhood incest.* Paper presented at the Annual Meeting of the American Psychiatric Association, Toronto, Ontario, Canada, May 15-21, 1982.

Forward, S., & Buck, C. *Betrayal of innocence: Incest and its devastation.* New York: Penguin, 1978.

Freud, S. (1925). An autobiographical study. *Standard Edition 20:* 1-71. London: Hogarth Press, 1959.

Giaretto, H. The treatment of father-daughter incest: A psychosocial approach. *Children Today,* 1976, *5*, 2-35.

Gross, M. Incestuous rape: A cause for hysterical seizures in four adolescent girls. *American Journal of Orthopsychiatry,* 1979, *49*, 704-708.

Gross, R.J., Doerr, H., Caldirola, D., Guzinsk, G.M., & Ripley, H.S. Borderline syndrome and incest in chronic pelvic pain patients. *International Psychiatry in Medicine,* 1981, *10*, 79-96.

Herman, J. Father-daughter incest. *Professional Psychology,* 1981, *12*, 76-79.

Herman-Lewis, J., & Hirschmann, L. *Father-daughter incest.* Cambridge, MA: Harvard University Press, 1981.

Horowitz, M.J. *Stress response syndromes.* New York: Jason Aronson, 1976.

Horowitz, M.J., & Solomon, G.F. Delayed stress response in Vietnam veterans. *Journal of Social Issues,* 1975, *31*, 67-80.

Krieger, M.J., Rosenfeld, A.A., Gordon, A., & Bennett, M. Problems in the psychotherapy of children with histories of incest. *American Journal of Psychotherapy*, 1980, *34*, 81-87.

Krupnick, J.L., & Horowitz, M.J. Stress response syndromes. *Archives of General Psychiatry*, 1981, *38*, 428-435.

Malcolm, J. Annals of scholarship: Trouble in the archives. Part 1. *The New Yorker*, December, 5, 1983a, 59-152.

Malcolm, J. Annals of scholarship: Trouble in the archives. Part 2. *The New Yorker*, December 12, 1983b, 60-118.

Meiselman, K.C. *Incest—A psychological study of cause and effects with treatment recommendations*. San Francisco: Jossey-Bass, 1978.

Mrazek, P.B., & Kempe, C.H. (Eds.). *Sexually abused children and their families*. New York: Pergamon Press, 1981.

Rist, K. Incest: Theoretical and clinical views. *American Journal of Orthopsychiatry*, 1979, *49*, 680-691.

Rosenfeld, A.A. Endogamic incest and the victim-perpetrator model. *American Journal of Diseases of Children*, 1979a, *133*, 406-410.

Rosenfeld, A.A. Incidence of a history of incest among 18 female psychiatric patients. *American Journal of Psychiatry*, 1979b, *136*, 791-795.

Rosenfeld, A.A. The clinical management of incest and sexual abuse of children. *Journal of the American Medical Associates*, 1979c, *245*, 1761-1764.

Rosenfeld, A., Nadelson, C.C., & Krieger, M. Fantasy and reality in patients reports of incest. *Journal of Clinical Psychiatry*, 1979, *40*, 159-164.

Selby, J.W., Calhoun, L.G., Jones, J.N., & Matthews, L. Families of incest: A collation of clinical impressions. *International Journal of Social Psychiatry*, 1980, *26*, 7-16.

Summit, R., & Kryso, J. Sexual abuse of children: A clinical spectrum. *American Journal of Orthopsychiatry*, 1978, *48*, 237-252.

Terr, L.C. "Forbidden games": Post-traumatic child's play. *Journal of the American Academy of Child Psychiatry*, 1981a, *20*, 741-760.

Terr, L.C. Psychic trauma in children: Observations following the Chowchilla school-bus kidnapping. *American Journal of Psychiatry*, 1981b, *138*, 14-19.

Terr, L.C. Chowchilla revisited: The effects of psychic trauma four years after a school-bus kidnapping. *American Journal of Psychiatry*, 1983, *140*, 1543-1550.

Tsai, M., Feldman-Summers, S., & Edgar, M. Childhood molestation: Variables related to differential impacts on psychosexual functioning in adult women. *Journal of Abnormal Psychology*, 1979, *88*, 407-417.

Tsai, M., & Wagner, N.N. Therapy groups for women sexually molested as children. *Archives of Sexual Behavior*, 1978, *7*, 417-427.

Wells, L.A. Family pathology and father-daughter incest: Restricted psychopathy. *Journal of Clinical Psychiatry*, 1981, *42*, 97-202.

16

Use of the Environment and the Legal Impact of Resulting Emotional Harm

JEFFREY C. SAVITSKY and DONALD M. HARTSOUGH

The courts have traditionally been hesitant to compensate victims for emotional injury when no physical injuries occur. However, there are a number of exceptions to this policy. The present chapter reviews these policies and exceptions within the context of injuries that result from land use projects. In particular, this chapter contains a description of the legal and psychological aftermath of the nuclear accident at Three Mile Island. Efforts to block the restart of this nuclear power plant resulted in legal actions which ultimately involved the U.S. Supreme Court. In addition, this legal controversy served to demonstrate the reaction of the courts to the emotional impact of land use projects.

Use of the environment, as through construction or mining, will inevitably affect people who live and work in the vicinity of the project. The construction of a new building in a downtown area, for instance, may cause both temporary and long-term crowding, traffic delays, noise and much inconvenience. These types of environmental changes can create stress for many people. Even land use projects which take place in rural areas can have an impact on people. Those who have either owned or used land which is changed for a project may find their routines altered, their familiar patterns disrupted and their comfort lessened. It is even possible that the stresses which result from a project will not be the direct product of physical changes to the environment but instead will reflect dissatisfaction and fear over the nature of the project's goals.

The impact of land use projects can, therefore, range from specific changes in the quality of the physical environment to less easily observed but nonetheless real emotional stresses. This chapter will focus on these latter, less easily defined effects—emotional stresses which result from land use projects. We will also explore the legal impact of negative emotions when these result from environmental use projects. When an environmental use project causes others to experience stress or even emotional damage, are these less easily defined, less observable outcomes of any real legal significance? How have the courts balanced our needs for progress through use of the environment with our wishes to remain secure, comfortable, and free of stress?

This chapter will first explore the potential emotional impact of land use projects. The research literature on disaster, the extreme form of negative environmental change, will be briefly presented. Then traditional legal notions about emotional damages will be described. After reviewing the legal theories which are used by the courts to evaluate claims for emotional damages, we will outline a series of recent legal-environmental events which surrounded a nuclear accident at Three Mile Island, Pennsylvania. This latter series of events will be used as a case study, an example of the current status of emotional factors in one area of federal environmental use law.

EMOTIONAL EFFECTS RESULTING FROM ENVIRONMENTAL USE AND DISASTER

Our efforts to make progress and to amass wealth require use of the environment. Digging mines, erecting buildings, and damming rivers are some of the ways that we may use resources such as space, air, and water. Each time someone uses the natural resources, there will be an intrusion on the privacy and freedom of others to some extent, but when the use of the environment yields castastrophic mistakes or injury to others then we are likely to term it a disaster. When an event actually comes to bear the label of disaster may be a matter of subjective opinion, but it appears that disasters can have negative emotional effects on the people who suffer the resulting environmental conditions.

The short-term psychological effects of disaster have been outlined in several reviews (Green, 1980; Kinsten & Rosser, 1974; Melick, Logue, & Frederick, 1982; Perry & Lindell, 1978). These short-term emotional reactions include sleep disturbances, fear, anxiety, tension, psychosomatic symptoms, exaggerated startle reactions, phobias and other avoidance behaviors, depression and fatigue. For most victims, the psychological effects of disaster are transient and situational (Chamberlin, 1980; Melick, et al., 1982; Perry & Lindell, 1978). However, if the victim experiences profound loss in addition to the disaster, acute grief is likely to be intense and extended, especially when there is a preventable death of a close family member (Bugen, 1977; Gleser, Green, & Winget, 1981).

While most survivors of brief, natural disasters, such as tornadoes, do not suffer dysfunctional long-term effects, such effects have been noted in response to unusually destructive man-made catastrophes (Gleser et al., 1981; Lifton, 1967) or war (Blank, 1982; Figley, 1978; Segal, 1974). Man-made disasters appear more likely than natural events to provoke intense anger among survivors towards the perceived cause of the catastrophe (Boyts, personal communication, March 3, 1983; Vogel, personal communication, March 1, 1983).

When long-term emotional effects result from disaster, these effects can be pervasive and can dominate a victim's personality functioning. Long-term effects include chronic depression and loss of personal vitality (Hocking, 1970a, 1970b; Hoppe, 1971), survivor guilt (Krystal, 1968; Lifton, 1967), a narrowing of life interests to only material things (Ostwald & Bitner, 1968), and a rootless, loss-of-purpose orientation that may include antisocial behavior (Blank, 1982; Figley & Leventman, 1980). Of course, not all aversive environmental events qualify as disasters, just as not all apparently negative events will yield psychological damage for the victims. Berren, Beigel and Ghertner (1980) have hypothesized that the severity of psychological damage resulting from environmental events relates to a variety of distinguishing characteristics such as type (natural vs. man-made), duration, potential for a recurrence, degree of personal impact (e.g., death and destruction vs. inconvenience), and the amount of control the victim will have over future events. Thus, it appears likely that the extent of death and destruction personally experienced by victims and the impact of this on their immediate life circumstances are critical variables in producing stress following a disaster. Similarly, there may be a "gruesomeness factor" with the after-effect of disaster for survivors being modulated by the manner in which victims die, the number and condition of bodies witnessed by survivors, and the duration of contact with these horrifying details. For example, Gleser et al. (1981) were able to demonstrate relationships between the disaster experiences of survivors of the Buffalo Creek flood (a man-made catastrophe) and their later psychological functioning. Behavior patterns reported by these survivors "displayed to a substantial degree symptoms of anxiety, depression, somatic concerns, belligerence, agitation, social isolation, and changes in their daily routine and leisure time activities" (Gleser et al., 1981, p. 140). Gleser has noted that sleep disturbances were still being reported by three fourths of a sample of questionnaire respondents more than two years after this disaster occurred.

EMOTIONAL INJURY IN THE COURTS

The courts have traditionally been hesitant to award compensation to plaintiffs whose only injury was emotional (Comment Note - Right to recover, 1959). Thus, while victims have been able to recover for physical injuries to their person or property, emotional upset, anxiety, or fear has not typically merited compensation. Early court decisions noted that the law does not attempt to provide protection for a plaintiff's interest in tranquility (*Lynch* v. *Knight*, 1861). Rather, a plaintiff must show additional damages aside from the emotional injury before the courts would allow a compensatory judgment.

Several policy-based arguments have been used to justify the stubborn refusal of some courts to compensate victims for injuries to their emotional well-being (Magruder, 1935). First, there is the fear that compensation for those who have suffered only emotional injury will serve to encourage litigation. Under this theory, if victims expect to be compensated for emotional pain they will be encouraged to sue for every instance of unhappiness. This would open the courts to a flood of litigation. This argument, it should be noted, has little to do with the merits of providing compensation for psychological injury. The argument simply represents the hesitancy of judges to expand judicial jurisdiction into uncharted and potentially limitless areas of human conflict.

Aside from the administrative argument that compensation for emotional injuries will encourage litigation, there is the further concern that compensation for emotional injuries will also encourage fraudulent suits. The courts have feared that there are not adequate methods available to differentiate fraudulent from the justified claims of emotional injury since these injuries, unlike physically apparent injury or property destruction, are difficult to assess and can be fabricated with relative ease.

A related argument against allowing recovery for emotional injuries concerns the difficulty that the courts would have if they attempted to estimate the true value of an emotional injury (*Alsteen* v. *Gehl*, 1963). When property has been destroyed, for instance, its value can be easily determined by comparing the market value of the property both before and after the injury. But how much is bereavement worth? The courts have seemingly avoided the issue of emotional injury rather than attempt to award damages on a speculative weighing of the value of tranquility.

A strict rule against recovery for emotional injury would clearly serve to limit the number of fabricated claims. However, a strict rule against emotional damages would also produce considerable hardship and unfairness for those plaintiffs who have truly suffered. To prevent this type of inequity, the courts have developed a number of exceptions to the traditional rules against recovery for emotional injuries. For instance, plaintiffs who have suffered emotional injuries can seek compensation so long as they also suffered a physical injury, or if they were in a "zone of danger," and therefore could have suffered a physical injury (Annotation - Immediacy, 1981). The physical injury exception, sometimes called the "impact rule," has often been taken to tortured extremes to ensure that deserving plaintiffs do in fact receive compensation even if the "impact" was slight or nonsignificant. In one early case, for instance, a woman witnessed her husband being beaten by two men. She sued both men for emotional damages but was not allowed compensation from one attacker since he had avoided any physical contact with her. However, she was allowed compensation for her psychological injuries from the other attacker since he had brushed against her (*McGee* v. *Vanover*, 1912).

A second major exception to the rule against compensation for psychological injury allows recovery when the defendant's act, which led to the injury, was so malicious or wanton as to make it plain that the defendant actually sought out the emotional damages or willfully ignored the emotional harm which the plaintiff ultimately suffered (Annotation - Fright, 1968). This exception reinforces the concept that individuals must respect the emotional well-being of others, at least to some degree, since grossly negligent actions could yield compensable injuries.

The rules against compensation for psychological injuries serve as controls on litigation. However, the exceptions to these rules (gross negligence, impact, or threat of impact) have allowed the courts to apply sanctions which preserve a judicially defined social order. The rule against compensation, together with its exceptions, have allowed the courts to provide compensation to truly worthy complainants without also persistently intruding into routine interactions. These rules reflect the tension between a wish to compensate those who are injured and the need to limit litigation to those cases where real harm and meaningful claims do in fact exist.

LEGAL THEORIES OF EMOTIONAL DAMAGE
AND ENVIRONMENTAL USE

It appears that when use of the environment, as through construction or mining, has caused psychological injury the courts have rested their decisions about the desirability of compensation for psychological injury on the same legal theories which were used to resolve claims of emotional injury in other areas of litigation. That is, there continues to be the same hesitancy and the same exceptions which are used to circumvent these hesitancies. The tension between a wish to grant compensation for those who suffer real injury, as a result of environmental use, has competed with an effort to minimize the potential for fraudulant or nuisance claims while also avoiding judicial intrusions which would forestall effective use of natural resources. Sometimes these competing considerations had led to inconsistent results. This was demonstrated in decisions which arose from two nearly identical mining cases. In both cases the plaintiffs owned land adjacent to strip mining operations. Both mining operations used numerous unpredictable explosions which caused the land owners to suffer emotional difficulties and psychologically generated physical illnesses. However, while the facts in these cases are nearly identical, their results are at odds. One court (*Robert* v. *Peabody Coal Co.*, 1978) ruled that the vibrations from the explosions qualified as a sufficient "impact" so that the rule against compensation for psychological injuries was not a bar to recovery. In contrast, the other court (*Vaughn* v. *Peabody Coal Co.*, 1978), while noting the contrary result of the earlier case, still maintained that vibrations from the explosions were not of sufficient impact to justify compensation for psychological damage.

Litigation over a recent land use disaster again raised the issue of compensation for psychological trauma. In this case (*Prince et al.* v. *Pittston*, 1974), the collapse of three earthen dams owned by a coal company precipitated a massive flood in the Buffalo Creek Valley, destruction of several communities, the loss of over 100 lives, and severe psychological injury to the survivors. However, some of the residents of Buffalo Creek, the plaintiffs, claimed that they too had suffered psychological injury, even though they had neither experienced physical harm nor been within the area, or zone of danger, at the time of the flood. Under traditional rules, the plaintiffs could not have recovered damages since they were neither physically injured nor in the immediate vicinity of the flood. However, their claim was that they too had suffered emotional pain because of the destruction of their community and because they had lost friends and relatives. The court held that a showing of reck-lessness by the coal company, more than mere negligence but less than willful misconduct, would be sufficient to allow the plaintiffs to receive compensation for their psychological injuries. This holding was appar-ently sufficient to encourage the dam owners to settle the claim of these residents without further litigation. Included in the settlement was money paid in recognition of the plaintiffs' psychological damages.

The psychological condition of complainants has also been at issue in land use proposed by the federal government in projects which are, as a result, regulated by the National Environmental Policy Act (NEPA, 1976). In these cases, the plaintiffs claimed that federal construction projects should be stopped because the proposed projects would ad-versely affect the quality of an environment and therefore cause them anxiety and discomfort. The plaintiffs, typically citizen groups consisting of residents of neighborhoods surrounding proposed construction sites, have attempted to block the construction of low income housing (*Nucleus of Chicago Homeowners Association* v. *Lynn*, 1976), post office facilities (*Chelsea Neighborhood Association* v. *U.S. Postal Service*, 1975), detention centers (*Hanley* v. *Kleindienst*, 1973), and a Job Corp training facility (*Como-Falcon Community Coalition, Inc.* v. *U.S. Department of Labor*, 1980).

NEPA cases arise within a different context than the tort cases noted above. Tort suits are typically reactive, or in response to damages which have already occurred, while NEPA cases have been proactive, raised in anticipation of damages. A second difference between NEPA and tort cases is that the former cases have sought judicial application of a statute while the tort cases have largely depended on judicial interpretations of common law principles. However, despite these differences, it ap-pears that NEPA decisions on the issue of psychological damages have reflected the same conservatism which has characterized the awarding of damages for psychological injury in tort cases. Until the Three Mile Island case, to be described below, the courts were nearly consistent (*City of New York* v. *U.S. Department of Transportation*, 1982) in concluding that the anxieties and fears of citizens are not an environmental impact within the objectives of NEPA. Emotional injury to the plaintiffs, without other injury, could not cause the courts to curtail land use projects.

The legislative history and statutory language of the National Environmental Policy Act indicates that this act was intended to ensure that use of the environment by the federal government did not threaten the health and safety of the population. NEPA was intended to "promote efforts which will prevent or eliminate damage to the environment and biosphere and stimulate the health and welfare of man" (NEPA, 1976a). The act states that each person "should enjoy a healthful environment" (NEPA, 1976b). However, the act did not attempt to anticipate all of the factors which might affect health or to define the exact nature of the "health" concept. Does health include, for instance, the psychological well-being of those who might suffer intense fear because their property, after construction of a nearby low-cost housing unit, might diminish in value?

The difficult role of defining terms and filling interstitial gaps in statutory meaning is reserved for the courts. Most of the courts had concluded that the anxiety and psychological discomfort which might be caused to neighbors by new federal construction is not the type of health damage which was envisioned by Congress when it approved NEPA. The possibilities of increased noise, pollution, or crime are themselves conditions which affect the environment, and therefore require remediation before construction can be authorized, but the increased anxiety to plaintiffs arising from projects was not viewed, in and of itself, as sufficient to invoke concern over health issues. The federal courts concluded that labelling anxiety as an environmental health concern would require that the term "environment" be "stretched to its maximum" (*Maryland-National Capital Park and Planning Commission* v. *U.S. Postal Service*, 1973).

The federal courts, in evaluating NEPA claims, displayed the same type of hesitancy about awarding damages for psychological or emotional injuries which characterized the state courts. However, this precedent was challenged by the federal appeals court ruling which followed in the wake of the Three Mile Island (TMI) nuclear accident. Ultimately, changes suggested by the appeals court decision were reversed by a decision of the U.S. Supreme Court. However, the legal aftermath of TMI does provide an example of the theories and tensions which surround the status of legal claims of emotional damages which result from environmental use.

The next sections of this chapter will describe the nuclear accident at Three Mile Island and the research on the emotional impact of the event.

Also, the legal aftermath of TMI will be outlined. This latter summary will attempt to provide insight into the difficulties which might arise if emotional injuries which result from environmental use were given a more sympathetic legal status.

THE EMOTIONAL EFFECTS OF TMI ACCIDENT

There are two separate nuclear generating plants on Three Mile Island; TMI-1 was licensed in 1974 and TMI-2 was licensed in 1978. A misfunction occurred in Unit 2 in March, 1979, such that conditions inside Unit 2 went out of control for many hours. This prompted doomsday rhetoric in the media and a Governor's advisory that resulted in the temporary evacuation of 144,000 residents. At the time of the accident, TMI-1 was in cold shutdown status for routine maintenance. TMI-1 was not damaged in the accident but the Nuclear Regulatory Commission (NRC), at the request of Governor Richard Thornburgh of Pennsylvania, ordered the plant owner to keep TMI-1 in a nonoperational status until the operations could be safely resumed. This order directed that a restart of the unit should not cause harmful psychological reactions in the population around Three Mile Island.

Research into the TMI incident has included an extensive evaluation of the psychological aftereffects of this accident. For instance, soon after the accident, President Carter authorized a special commission to study the immediate reactions of male and female heads of households (Link & Dohrenwend, 1980). This study found that scores on a Demoralization Scale were greatly elevated in the first month after the accident and that these scores decreased sharply in the second month, May, 1979 (Dohrenwend, Dohrenwend, Kazl, & Warheit, 1979). This study also indicated that subjects expressed mistrust for authority, which declined only gradually, and that the subjects perceived threats to their physical health and reported psychosomatic distress.

Houts (1980a, 1980b) conducted telephone surveys of 2,748 area residents within the first year after the accident (July, 1979 and January, 1980). He compared responses on stress measures from residents living close to the island with responses from those living over 40 miles from TMI. The stress indicators included direct statements about how worried and upset respondents had been about the situation at TMI, the Langner Index of Psychological Stress (Langner, 1962), and respondents' reports of stress-related mental or physical symptoms. After controlling for demographic variables, Houts found a general tendency for distress to decrease with both greater geographic distance from Three Mile Island and with the passage of time after the accident. Houts concluded that the number of persons with severe distress decreased shortly after the crisis, but that 10% - 20% of respondents living close to TMI reported that they were still quite upset and experiencing higher stress-related symptoms nine months after the accident. The Langner Index, a scale of psychiatric symptoms, was the only measure that failed to distinguish between residents living close to TMI and those living further away. Results from the Langner Index suggested that the severity of the symptoms did not reach levels usually associated with mental illness.

Bromet, Parkinson, Schulberg, et al. (1980) investigated psychological effects caused by TMI in mothers of preschool children, nuclear power plant workers, and community mental health center clients. Each of the three experimental groups was matched with a control group living near another nuclear facility in Beaver County, Pennsylvania. Unlike the studies reviewed above, Bromet's procedure was designed to minimize possible response biases related to either pro- or anti-nuclear attitudes. Bromet and her colleagues used the Hopkins SCL-90 (Derogatis, 1977), a self-report measure of symptoms, and the SADS-L (Endicott & Spitzer, 1978), a psychological scale which provides criteria for clinical disorders of depression and anxiety. The results indicated that mothers of preschool children displayed high levels of subclinical stress following the accident, were five times more likely to have clinical episodes of anxiety or depression immediately afterwards, and maintained elevated but within-normal levels of symptoms up to a year after the TMI accident. However, the study yielded few significant differences for nuclear power plant workers or mental health system clients.

Baum, Gatchel, Fleming, and Lake (1981) attempted to study the stress caused by the venting of radioactive krypton gas in June and July, 1980, from the TMI-2 containment building. Baum et al. gathered data on TMI residents and control subjects from Frederick, Maryland, just prior to, during, and just after the venting, and again six weeks after the venting was completed. The dependent measures included catecholamine levels in urine (an indicator of stress levels), a proofreading task and an embedded-figures task, as well as other self-report symptom measures. The largest differences in distress measures between TMI and control groups appeared before the venting began, and gradually decreased during and after venting.

A confounding influence on TMI research has been the controversy over nuclear energy. To minimize the possible biasing effect of respondent attitudes about nuclear power (either pro or con), Mileti, Hartsough, and Madson (1982) compared archival data on behavioral stress indicators six months before the accident and six months afterwards. The unobtrusive indicators they used included alcohol sales, cardiovascular deaths, criminal arrests, psychiatric admissions, suicide, and automobile accidents. For each indicator, two TMI populations (within five miles and five to 10 miles away) were compared with a control group from Wilkes-Barre, Pennsylvania, which had been matched for selected demographic characteristics. For the days immediately following the accident, adjustments were made in daily indicators according to the population remaining in the area after evacuation. Data on crime, psychiatric admissions and suicide did not reflect observable changes. Traffic accident data showed some slight increases in the 5-10 mile ring several days after the incident occurred. There was a pronounced increase in the sale of alcoholic beverages in the first few days after the accident but this increase was only half of the increase seen at seasonal highs, such as Christmas. Finally, cardiovascular deaths seemed to increase slightly in a pattern one would expect if stress existed in the population. However, the incidence of cardiovascular deaths was so small as to make questionable any inferences about the TMI accident death rate. The authors concluded that the TMI incident did cause stress, but that the amount revealed by unobtrusive indicators of stress-induced behavior was slight, short-lived, and well within routine levels experienced by the population.

Several conclusions are suggested by the TMI studies:

1) Stress levels in the neighboring area to TMI increased sharply as a result of the accident;

2) There were differential effects such that the mothers of young children appear to have suffered the highest levels of psychological stress effects;

3) Although higher than normal, according to statistical findings, the stress levels resulting from the TMI incident did not reach the intensity typically associated with either severe trauma or with mental illness; and

4) The evidence for TMI-induced chronic stress was equivocal. Most studies showed a drop in reported effects over time, but even those studies which found long-term effects failed to also demonstrate the behavioral or clinical significance of these aftereffects. The major exception to this conclusion was the finding by Bromet, Schulberg, and Dunn (1982), which indicated that there was a greater likelihood of diagnosable clinical disorder among TMI mothers than among the controls.

TMI IN THE COURTS

During the summer of 1979, the Nuclear Regulatory Commission (NRC) established a hearing board to consider the restart of TMI-1 (Federal Register, 1979). The NRC ordered that several issues be reviewed, including the technical soundness of the plant, management capabilities of Metropolitan Edison, and the existence of a satisfactory emergency plan. A number of organizations accepted an invitation to become interveners in the restart hearings. One intervener, People Against Nuclear Energy (PANE), raised the issue of psychological stress. PANE contended that a restart of TMI-1 would cause severe psychological distress to persons living in the vicinity of the reactor, and that restart would seriously damage the stability, cohesiveness and well-being of the neighboring community. PANE argued that the original accident at TMI had already impaired the health and sense of well-being of residents, as evidenced by numerous psychological and physical symptoms, and that a restart of TMI-1 would severely aggravate existing problems thereby preventing Three Mile Island's neighbors from resolving and recovering from the trauma they had already suffered.

The NRC Licensing Board addressed the physical safety of the facility and concluded that TMI-1 was safe. It also concluded that psychological stress was probably not cognizable under the Atomic Energy Act (1976) and that the responsibility under this Act to protect the "public health and safety" did not extend to psychological health. Nor could the Board identify a source of evidence that would permit measurement of psychological stress with enough precision to allow the cost/benefit balancing characteristics of a complete environmental impact statement. However, the Licensing Board did conclude that the NRC should consider psychological distress and community fears under NEPA for the purpose of mitigating the effects of its TMI-1 licensing activity. This was the first indication that psychological stress would be considered as an environmental issue within the context of NEPA's regulations.

In December, 1980, the NRC rejected the recommendation of its own Licensing Board regarding psychological stress, and the hearings proceeded without this issue. One commission member concluded that the best way to minimize community fears was to ensure that the plant was technically safe before approving the restart. Another stated that "Congress had already decided that the country is to have a nuclear power program even if it makes some people uneasy" (Metropolitan Edison Co., 1980).

PANE appealed the NRC decision to the Second District Court of Appeals in Washington, D.C. The Court's judgment of January 7, 1982

(*People Against Nuclear Energy* v. *United States Nuclear Regulatory Commission*, 1982a) upheld the PANE position and ordered the Commission not to make a decision to restart TMI-1 until it had complied with the requirements of NEPA. In an interim judgment by the Appeals Court, the NRC was ordered to prepare an environmental assessment of the effects of the proposed TMI-1 restart on the psychological health of neighboring residents and the well-being of the surrounding communities (*People Against Nuclear Energy* v. *United States Nuclear Regulatory Commission*, 1982a). The Court's action thus clearly placed the psychological effects of operating the licensed nuclear plant within the purview of NEPA by relating these effects to general health. The Appeals Court later stated, "We conclude that, in the context of NEPA, health encompasses psychological health (*People Against Nuclear Energy* v. *United States Nuclear Regulatory Commission*, 1982b, p.228).

Subsequent to the Appeals Court decision, the NRC petitioned the U.S. Supreme Court to have the decision of the lower court overturned. The Supreme Court, in a unanimous decision, held that NEPA only requires an agency to assess the impact of environmental use projects on the "physical" environment (*Metropolitan Edison Co.* v. *People Against Nuclear Energy*, 1983). The Court held that the issue of psychological harm is too remote to be included in environmental impact statements. That is, the Supreme Court has now decided that, under present statutes, the existence of psychological stress among nearby residents cannot curtail federal environmental use projects unless the stress arises from a change in the physical environment.

The legal history of the TMI case can be summarized in the following steps:

1) The NRC decision to require hearings on the issue before allowing a restart of TMI Unit-1.
2) The recommendation of the NRC's Licensing Board that psychological stress be considered under NEPA.
3) The rejection by the NRC of the Licensing Board's recommendation that psychological stress be considered under NEPA.
4) The PANE appeal to the Second District Court of Appeals, and the Court's judgment to reverse the decision of the NRC.
5) The NRC appeal of the decision of the Appeals Court, and the subsequent unanimous decision by the U.S. Supreme Court to reverse the judgment of the lower court and exclude psychological effects, unless these result from physical changes in the environment.

BALANCING THE ISSUES

The TMI accident has raised many issues which are unique to the incident itself. In particular, this series of events has become synonymous with a growing national concern over energy production and the safety of nuclear power plants. However, this incident also served to raise traditional legal concerns about the proper role of psychological damages in litigation over environmental use. The TMI accident, and the series of court opinions and administrative decisions which followed it, have again revealed judicial concerns that credence for psychological damages will cause a flooding of the courts with fraudulent claims which could, in effect, disallow effective use of the environment and force the courts to continuously supervise land use projects.

Allowing psychological damage to be cognizable under NEPA could result in delay and complication for all federal construction projects. In particular, the construction and the operation of nuclear power plants may have been seriously curtailed by further judicial consideration of psychological effects. Indeed, one conclusion of the District of Columbia Appeals Court (*People Against Nuclear Energy* v. *United States Nuclear Regulatory Commission*, 1982b, p. 231) was that nuclear power plants, even those which had not suffered serious mishap, should continue to be subject to litigation if there were allegations that the running of the plant would result in psychological damage. It appears that there was a real possibility that the nuclear power industry could have been paralyzed by litigation ostensibly designed to forestall psychological harm but which actually attempted to delay the progress of nuclear power or to protect unique political or social interests.

Concern over "flooding" the courts with the issue of psychological damage was contained in the dissent to the TMI Appeals Court Decision (*People Against Nuclear Energy* v. *United States Nuclear Regulatory Commission*, 1982b, p. 248). The dissent noted that the majority opinion had the immediate effect of encouraging anti-nuclear groups to raise the issue of potential psychological damage in four separate nuclear power plant licensing and permit proceedings. In one instance cited by the dissent, a group of law students alleged that the operation of a nuclear plant would cause them enough anxiety to "detract from their studies" (p. 248). The dissent concluded that these follow-up cases made it "clear that today's decisions will not be considered limited or sui generis, but rather as inviting protest based on psychological stress to be raised in all nuclear proceedings" (p. 249).

If psychological stress is a real threat to the welfare of the population, then the fact that it will be frequently litigated and thereby slow the nuclear industry would seem to make little substantive difference. Real issues, even if frequent and annoying, deserve to have a forum for their resolution. But, of deeper concern is the belief that increased litigation will contain a disproportionate number of undetectable fraudulent claims. For example, were the anxiety-based study difficulties suffered by the law student litigants really the product of proximity to a proposed nuclear facility or the result of an effort to "make a case" and obtain a grade?

In essence judicial wariness about claims that allege that emotional damages have resulted from use of the environment can be understood as an effort to control the impact of these claims. If the courts recognize psychological damage as relevant to environmental use cases, how can this issue be kept in perspective and its relative weight ascertained? In other areas of litigation about psychological damage the control principles which were developed included the notion that claims for compensation which resulted from psychological damage were not awarded unless there was an impact, or at least the possibility of an impact, or gross negligence. Whether or not psychological damage can be included in environmental decisions seems to hinge on the ability of the courts or other administrative agencies to find similar kinds of controls. These controls are necessary so that concerns about psychological damage do not come to swallow all such projects.

The majority in the TMI Appeals Court decision seemingly acknowledged the difficulty in separating meritorious from frivolous claims of psychological injury. The Appeals Court noted, "We need not draw a bright line in this case" (*People Against Nuclear Energy* v. *United States Nuclear Regulatory Commission*, 1982b, p. 230). However, the majority opinion of the Appeals Court suggests that the TMI incident was different from other environmental use cases which had not allowed psychological damage to be considered. The nature of the stress raised by the TMI plant failure was considered by the Appeals Court to be more profound than the stress which might arise in more routine NEPA challenges. The stress associated with TMI, in the view of the Appeals Court, was different from routine stress in that this incident was of the degree that it would precipitate physical illness.

NEPA does not encompass mere dissatisfaction arising from social opinions, economic concerns, or political disagreements with agency policies. It does apply to post-traumatic anxieties, accompanied by physical effects and caused by fears of recurring catastrophe (*People Against Nuclear Energy* v. *United States Nuclear Regulatory Commission*, 1982b, p. 239).

The emphasis by the Appeals Court on the presence of stress-related physical illness among TMI residents seems to be analogous to the rule requiring an impact before damages for psychological injury are allowed. In other words, the notion that psychological damage should be considered because TMI caused residents to suffer physical injury suggests that the Appeals Court was using physical injury among residents as a test, a control, for when a court should consider the issue of emotional damages.

A second control for the issue of emotional damage offered by the Appeals Court was the belief that stress can be measured and quantified. If true, then fraudulent or spurious claims could be identified since the claimants would not be able to prove the existence of excessive levels of stress among nearby residents. This court, however, displayed more optimism about the validity of psychological testing than another court which rejected psychological issues from consideration in a NEPA case, noting "it is doubtful whether psychological and sociological effects upon neighbors constitute the type of factors that may be considered in making such a determination since they do not lend themselves to measurement" (*Hanley* v. *Kleindienst*, 1973, p. 833). Similarly, the Supreme Court in the TMI case was less willing to accept the ability of psychological testing to reliably measure stress. It noted that, "It would be extraordinarily difficult for agencies to differentiate between 'genuine' claims of psychological health damage and claims that are grounded solely on disagreement with a democratically adopted policy" (*Metropolitan Edison Co.* v. *People Against Nuclear Energy*, 1983, p. 11). If post-traumatic disorders can be reliably measured, then psychological measurements would serve to exclude spurious complaints and would discriminate claims which are based on mere discomfort from those claims which reflect severe levels of health-endangering anxiety. But the ability of psychological tests to do this appears questionable (Mischel, 1968).

The TMI Appeals Court did not draw "a bright line," but it did suggest two potentially valuable tests for determining when psychological stress should be a factor in an environmental impact statement. Stress, according to the Appeals Court, should be considered when it is: 1) severe enough to threaten physical health and 2) when it can be reliably measured. These broad principles suggest that psychological factors should be involved in environmental impact litigation only if these tests can be successfully applied.

Further consideration of the TMI accident, however, indicates that this incident itself was not ideally suited for the consideration of psychological factors. That is, the "tests" designed by the TMI Appeals Court may themselves have excluded psychological issues from the TMI controversy for two reasons. First, the research evaluation of the psychological aftermath of TMI did not indicate that there was, in fact, a level or duration of stress sufficient to cause debilitating physical or mental illness. There was intense stress, but apparently not widespread illness as a result of TMI. Second, there remains the problem of reliable measurement. The Appeals Court noted that PANE, the plaintiff, asserted that "post-traumatic neurosis . . . can be diagnosed with reasonable medical certainty on the basis of standardized quantitative tests" (*People Against Nuclear Energy* v. *United States Nuclear Regulatory Commission*, 1982b, p. 227). However, the Appeals Court did not mention which tests fit these exacting criteria. It appears, instead, that the measurement of post-traumatic stress, with enough certainty to fulfill the guidelines set out by the Appeals Court, may require further research and clinical progress.

Marshall (1982) has noted that the TMI Appeals Court decision may have created "an entirely new field: psycho-environmental law" (p. 481). Indeed, it does appear that this case has emphasized the fact that many feel a need to consider the emotional impact of projects that use the land or water. The decision of the Supreme Court may have limited the role of emotional factors under NEPA, but these factors are likely to continue to surface in litigation and social planning about environmental use. Society has not yet finalized a balancing of emotional needs with the wish for development of the environment. We continue to face a need to define the types and levels of stress that the public will tolerate before its policymakers conclude that some forms of environmental use are not worthwhile.

It is tempting to conclude that the emotional effects of an environmental use project always deserve intense consideration; that comfort and freedom from worry are essential environmental issues which far exceed the importance of other issues such as technological progress. The construction or operation of nuclear power generating plants is, for instance, certainly unwarranted if it results in widespread fear and panic. However, while this type of reasoning is certainly justified and convincing, enthusiasm for the psychological health of the populace must be tempered with the realities which surround the psychological sciences. Unless we can truly provide an objective assessment of the psychological effects of environmental use projects, we must be cautious to avoid the possibility that we have created unending, unanswerable, and potentially counterproductive controversies.

We must, of course, endeavor to provide the public with a safe and comfortable environment, but we should not allow concern over the presence of emotional stress to become the indirect impetus for making decisions which are, in the last analysis, political rather than psychological. We must not allow claims about psychological stress to become the vehicle of specialized political or technological interests. Research on the emotional effects of environmental use, or even nuclear energy, should continue. We must, however, reserve decisions about the significance of psychological research findings to an open and rational decision-making process.

REFERENCES

Alsteen v. *Gehl*, 21 Wis 2d 349, 124 NW 2d 312 (1963).

Annotation—Fright, shock, and mental disturbance. *American Jurisprudence* (2nd edition), 1968, *38*, 1-57.

Annotation—Immediacy of observation of injury as affecting right to recover damages for shock or mental anguish from witnessing injury to another. *American Law Review* (4th edition), 1981, *5*, 833-851.

Atomic Energy Act, U.S.C. 2133 (1976).

Baum, A., Gatchel, R.J., Fleming, R., & Lake, C.R. Chronic and acute stress associated with the Three Mile Island accident and decontamination: Preliminary findings of a longitudinal study. Bethesda, MD: Uniformed Services University of Health Sciences. 1981 (draft report).

Berren, M.R., Beigel, A., & Ghertner, S. A typology for the classification of disasters. *Community Mental Health Journal*, 1980, *16*, 103-111.

Blank, A.S., Jr. Stresses of war: The example of Viet Nam. In L. Goldberger, & S. Breznitz (Eds.), *Handbook of stress: Theoretical and clinical aspects*. New York: Free Press, 1982.

Bromet, E., Parkinson, D., Schulberg, H.C., Dunn, L., & Gondek, P.C. *Three Mile Island: Mental health findings*. Washington, DC: National Institute of Mental Health, 1980.

Bromet, E., Schulberg, H.C., & Dunn, L. The TMI nuclear accident and patterns of psychotherapy in mothers of infant children. Paper read at the American Psychological Association, Washington, D.C., 1982.

Bugen, L. Human grief. *American Journal of Orthopsychiatry*, 1977, *47*, 196-202.

Chamberlin, B.C. Mayo seminars in psychiatry: The psychological aftermath of disaster. *Journal of Clinical Psychiatry*, 1980, *41*, 238-244.

Chelsea Neighborhood Association v. *U.S. Postal Service*, 516 E. 2nd 378 (2d Cir. 1975).

City of New York v. *U. S. Department of Transportation*, 539 F. Supp 1237 (S. D. N.Y. 1982).

Comment Note—Right to recover for emotional disturbance or its physical consequences, in the absence of impact or other actionable wrong. *American Law Review* (2nd edition), 1959, *64*, 100-151.

Como-Falcon Community Coalition, Inc. v. *U.S. Department of Labor*, 609 F. 342 (8th Cir. 1979), cert. denied, 446 U. S. 936 (1980).

Derogatis, L.R. *SSCL-90 Adminstration, scoring and procedures manual for the revised version and other instruments of the psychotherapy rating scale series*. Baltimore: Johns Hopkins University School of Medicine, Clinical Psychometrics Unit, 1977.

Dohrenwend, B.P., Dohrenwend, B.S., Kazl, S.B., & Warheit, G.J. Technical staff analysis report on behavioral effects to President's Commission on the accident at Three Mile Island. Washington, DC: President's Commission on the Accident at Three Mile Island, 1979.

Endicott, J., & Spitzer, R.A. A diagnostic interview: The schedule for affective disorders and schizophrenia. *Archives of General Psychiatry*, 1978, *35*, 837-844.

Federal Register, 1979, *44*, 40461

Figley, C., & Leventman, S. *Strangers at home*. New York: Praeger, 1980.

Gleser, C.G., Green, B.L., & Winget, C. *Prolonged psychosocial effects of disaster: A study of Buffalo Creek*. New York: Academic Press, 1981.

Green, B.L. Prediction of long-term psychosocial function following the Beverly Hills fire. Doctoral dissertation, University of Cincinnati, 1980. (University Microfilms).

Hanley v. Kleindienst, 471 F. 2d 823 (2d Cir. 1972), cert. denied, 412 U.S. 908 (1973).

Hocking, F. Extreme environmental stress and its significance for psychotherapy. *American Journal of Psychotherapy*, 1970a, *24*, 4-26.

Hocking, F. Psychiatric aspects of extreme environmental stress. *Diseases of the Nervous System*, 1970b, *31*, 542-545.

Hoppe, K.D. Chronic reactive aggression in survivors of severe persecution. *Comprehensive Psychiatry*, 1971, *12*, 230-237.

Houts, P.S. Health-related behavioral impact of the Three Mile Island nuclear accident: Part I. Report to the TMI Advisory Panel on Health Research Studies, Pennsylvania Department of Health. Hershey, PA: Pennsylvania State University, College of Medicine, 1980a.

Houts, P.S. Health-related behavioral impact of the Three Mile Island nuclear accident: Part II. Report to the TMI Advisory Panel on Health Research Studies, Pennsylvania Department of Health. Hershey, PA: Pennsylvania State University, College of Medicine, 1980b.

Kinston, W., & Rosser, R. Disaster: Effects on mental and physical state. *Journal of Psychosomatic Research*, 1974, *18*, 437-456.

Krystal, H. (Ed.). *Massive psychic trauma*. New York: International Universities Press, 1968.

Langner, T.S. A 22-item screening score of psychiatric symptoms indicating impairment. *Journal of Health and Social Behavior*, 1962, *3*, 269-276.

Lifton, R.J. *Survivors of Hiroshima: Death in Life*. New York: Random House, 1967.

Link, B., & Dohrenwend, B.P. Formulation of hypotheses about the true prevalence of demoralization in the United States. In B.P. Dohrenwend, B.S. Dohrenwend, M.S. Gould, C. Link, et al. (Eds.), *Mental illness in the United States: Epidemiological estimates*. New York: Praeger, 1980.

Lynch v. Knight, 9 HL Cas 577, 11 Eng Reprint 854, 8 ERC 382 (1861).

Magruder, C. Mental and emotional disturbance in the law of torts. *Harvard Law Review*, 1935, *49*, 1033-1067.

Marshall, E. Fear as a form of pollution. *Science*, 1982, *215*, 481.

Maryland—National Capital Park and Planning Commission v. U. S. Postal Service, 349 F. Supp. 1212, 487 F. 2d 1029 (D.C. Cir. 1973).

McGee v. Vanover, 148 Ky 737, 147 SW 742 (1912).

Melick, M.E. Life changes and illness: Illness behavior of males in the recovery period of a natural disaster. *Journal of Health and Social Behavior*, 1978, *19*, 335-342.

Melick, M.E., Logue, J.N., & Frederick, C.J. Stress and disaster. In L. Goldberger, & S. Breznitz (Eds.), *Handbook of stress: Theoretical and clinical aspects*. New York: Free Press, 1982.

Metropolitan Edison Co., 12 N. R. C. 607, 612-618 (1980).

Metropolitan Edison Co. v. People Against Nuclear Energy, 75 L. Ed. 2d 534 (1983).

Mileti, D.S., Hartsough, D.M., & Madson, P. The Three Mile Island incident: A study of behavioral indicators of human stress. A report prepared for Shaw, Pittman, Potts, & Trowbridge, Washington, DC., 1982.

Mischel, W. *Personality and assessment*. New York: Wiley & Sons, 1968.

National Environmental Policy Act, 42 U. S. C. 4321 et seq (1976a).

National Environmental Policy Act, 42 U. S. C. 4331 (c) (1976b).

Nucleus of Chicago Homeowners Associations v. *Lynn*, 524 F. 2d 225 (7th Cir. 1975), cert. denied, 424 U. S. 967 (1976).

Oswald, P., & Bitner, E. Life adjustment after severe persecution. *American Journal of Psychiatry*, 1968, *124*, 1393-1400.

People Against Nuclear Energy v. *United States Nuclear Regulatory Commission*, 673 F. 2d 552 (D.C. Cir., 1982a) (order vacating NRC decision).

People Against Nuclear Energy v. *United States Nuclear Regulatory Commission*, 678 F. 2nd 222, (D. C. Cir., 1982b) (Wilkey dissenting in part).

Perry, R.W., & Lindell, M.K. The psychological consequence of a natural disaster: A review of research on American communities. *Mass Emergencies*, 1978, *3*, 105-115.

Prince et al. v. *Pittston*, 63 F. R. D. 28 (SD, W. Va., 1974).

Robert v. *Peabody Coal Co.*, 513 S. W. 2d 667 (1978).

Segal, J. *Long-term psychological and physical effects of the POW experience: A review of the literature.* Unpublished manuscript, Center for POW Studies, Naval Health Research Center, San Diego, 1974.

Vaughn v. *Peabody Coal Co.*, 375 N.E. 2d 1159 (Ind. App., 1978).

CHAPTER

17

From Victim to Survivor: Social Responsibility in the Wake of Catastrophe

CHARLES R. FIGLEY

*This chapter draws upon the observations made throughout the vol-
ume's 16 chapters to support a thesis regarding professional responsi-
bilities. It is argued that since 1) there is a critical mass of scientific
knowledge about the emotional consequences of traumatic events, which
2) enables professionals to anticipate traumatic and post-traumatic stress
in certain persons, and 3) to develop and implement intervention programs to ameliorate, if not prevent post-traumatic stress disorders, it
is unethical to maintain the status quo. It is the responsibility of everyone
in a position influencing the welfare of victims of traumatic events, the
chapter argues, to decrease the extraordinary emotional ordeal in the
wake of these events. The first section of the chapter presents a model
of the immediate and long-term consequences of traumatic events, drawing upon the empirical evidence presented throughout the volume and
elsewhere. The second section notes the implications of the model for
1) intervention programs focused on traumatic stress (both acute and
chronic types); 2) programs to prevent traumatic and post-traumatic
stress, including public information; 3) training programs for profes-*

sionals and paraprofessionals; and 4) social policies which recognize and address the consequences of traumatic events, especially those which are due to human errors or malice. The final section is a special plea for the plight of the victim of violent crimes and the victimized family: Their special struggles take place not only against the recognized victimizer, the criminal, but also those individuals and institutions responsible to the victim, such as law enforcement, criminal justice, and various social service systems.

We end this volume as we began: searching for the emotional by-products of catastrophes. It should be clear to even the most casual reader of the traumatic stress literature that human reactions to catastrophes are both common and predictable; that certain psychosocial factors account for certain emotional disabilities resulting from these catastrophes, such as post-traumatic stress disorder (PTSD). Equally obvious is the fact that the demographic profiles of those diagnosed with PTSD are as diverse as the catastrophes themselves.

BEING A SURVIVOR

The central theme of this chapter is that the process of recovering from traumatic events is the transformation from being a victim to being a survivor. Victims and survivors are similar in that they both experienced a traumatic event. But while the victim has been immobilized and discouraged by the event, the survivor has overcome the traumatic memories and become mobile. The survivor draws on the experiences of coping with the catastrophe as a source of strength, while the victim remains immobilized.

What separates victims from survivors is a conception about life, an attitude about the safety, joy, and mastery of being a human being. Being a survivor, then, is making peace with the memories of the catastrophe and its wake.

Authors throughout this volume, at least indirectly, have contributed to a description of the various processes by which catastrophes create victims and victims become survivors. As first noted in the introduction to this volume, there are six questions which address these fundamental processes. Their answers form the major subsections of this chapter:

1) What constitutes a catastrophe, one which may be viewed as a "traumatic event"?

2) Who will be traumatized by a catastrophe and who will not?
3) Among the traumatized, who will develop a post-traumatic stress disorder?
4) Among those with PTSD, how can we distinguish among those who are treatable, not treatable, and malingering?
5) Among the treatable, what clinical methods are most effective and why?
6) What are the parameters of societal responsibility to victims?

WHAT CONSTITUTES A CATASTROPHE?

Catastrophe is viewed here as an extraordinary event or series of events which is sudden, overwhelming, and often dangerous either to self or significant others. As illustrated throughout this volume, catastrophes come in many forms. According to Green, Wilson, and Lindy (Chapter 4), however, certain facets of the catastrophe experience are important: the role of the survivor in the catastrophe; the degree of life threat, warning, displacement, and exposure to the grotesque.

Based on research reported here and elsewhere, it appears that most "acts of God," create fewer victims, are less troublesome to overcome emotionally, than acts of man. For example, the latter is culpable for compensation (Trimble, Chapter 1) and destructive self-blame (Janoff-Bulman, Chapter 2). It is also clear from Quarantelli's analysis in Chapter 9, that natural disasters rarely lead to emotional destruction or debilitation. Yet those catastrophes which could be avoided, such as war (as noted in Chapters 5, 8, 10, 11, and 13), crime victimization (as noted in Chapters 6, 7, 8, and 15), rape (as discussed in Chapters 7, 8, and 15), industrial accidents (as discussed in Chapters 4 and 16), and other catastrophic events are especially troublesome to overcome emotionally. These experiences are not only unexpected, but the attribution of blame extends beyond simple fate and those who were caught in them, and can include, for example, a perpetrator, corporation employees, and government officials.

Some in this volume (c.f. Chapters 4, 5, 8, 10, and 13) have argued, as others have in the past (e.g., Figley, 1978; Figley & Leventman, 1980), that the Vietnam war was an extraordinary catastrophe for millions who fought in it, in contrast to past wars. Vietnam veterans not only endured the extraordinary, apocalyptic war many were forced to fight, but also were denied the normal support (moral, social, and material) for battle and were often ignored or mistreated upon return.

Perhaps the most emotionally devastating catastrophes, however, are those that not only are man-made, but also directly affect the intimacy and social support of the family. Catastrophes which affect children are especially impactive, such as the experiences of the children of Holocaust survivors (Danieli, Chapter 12), children of murdered parents (Pynoos & Eth, Chapter 3), and victims of childhood incest (Donaldson & Gardner, Chapter 15).

These catastrophes are troublesome not only because they affect children who are dependent and vulnerable, but also because, unlike natural disasters, crimes such as these are man-made, vicious, and their responsibility identified. Thus, violent crimes, including accidents caused by malicious malfeasance, such as drunk driving, are especially upsetting since they violate human justice.

WHO WILL BE TRAUMATIZED?

Reactions of those who experience a catastrophe vary widely depending on the circumstances of the catastrophe (i.e., man-made, age of the victims, duration). Moreover, there are individual variations in human reactions to the same catastrophe. These characterological traits account for the presence or absence of traumatic and post-traumatic stress.

Janoff-Bulman (Chapter 2), for example, drawing on the works of Epstein (1973; 1979; 1980), Parkes (1971; 1975), and Marris (1975), suggests that cognitive processes, including assumptions and personal theories about life experiences, account for emotional reactions to catastrophes. Extraordinary life experiences "force us to recognize, objectify, and examine our basic assumptions" (Janoff-Bulman, Chapter 2, p. 18). Janoff-Bulman suggests three separate, but highly related assumptions: 1) belief in personal invulnerability; 2) perception of the world as meaningful and comprehensible; and 3) the view of ourselves in a positive light. Thus, examining basic assumptions may predict subsequent reactions to catastrophic experiences.

Green, Wilson, and Lindy (Chapter 4) note that personality factors and their interaction with the situation account for emotional reactions to catastrophes, as have others (e.g., Hocking, 1970; Saul & Lyons, 1961). Similarly, the "coping mechanism," or characteristic patterns of dealing with stressful situations, also relates reactions to catastrophes (e.g., Anderson, 1976; Gleser, Green, & Winget, 1981; Silver & Wortman, 1980). Yet, it is difficult to clearly differentiate between stress reactions and coping which may be parts of the same mechanism.

Moreover, it is the position of the APA (1980) that PTSD is more likely to develop in persons with preexisting psychopathology. This predisposition thesis is supported by a few studies (Atkeson, Calhoun, Resick, & Ellis, 1982; Frank, Turner, Jacob, & West, 1981; Helzer, Robins, Wish, & Hesselbrock, 1979; McCahill, Meyer, & Fischman, 1979).

Irrespective of predisposition, be it personality or psychopathology, Kilpatrick, Veronen, and Best (Chapter 8) have found that initial traumatic stress immediately following a catastrophe (six-21 days) is the best predictor of post-traumatic problems (both three months and four years following a rape). Thus, reactions to catastrophe, as a thrill seeker, victim or survivor, can be determined by investigating responses immediately following the event. Their findings are at variance with other researchers who have found a delay phenomenon (e.g., Bard & Sangrey, 1979; Sutherland & Scherl, 1970) in the onset of post-traumatic stress disorders, which was classified in the DSM-III (APA, 1980).

Thus, irrespective of the specific findings, there appears to be a consensus among traumatic stress scholars that reactions to catastrophes vary greatly. These variations are due, in part, to individual differences (e.g., personality, coping styles, cognitive styles, life assumptions, previous emotional problems), characteristics of the catastrophe, and initial reactions to the catastrophe.

WHO WILL DEVELOP PTSD?

Given the special circumstances of a catastrophe which may lead to traumatic experiences, what are the processes by which a victim experiences the trauma and subsequently recovers and becomes a survivor? To answer this question requires considerable speculation. As noted elsewhere (Figley, 1979; 1983a), such an explanation based on empirical evidence requires a systematic epidemiological study. A set of working models of the process of trauma induction and recovery, however, can be based to an extent on scientific findings.

The model presented in Chapter 4 (Green et al.), for example, expands on earlier attempts at model building (Green, Wilson, & Lindy, 1982) and is similar to others (e.g., Figley, 1982). It provides a framework for viewing the psychosocial factors associated with experiencing, reacting to, and recovering from a catastrophic event.

Stages of Recovery

Another model, initially presented in 1979 (Figley, 1979), suggests five stages or phases whereby victims become survivors. This model rep-

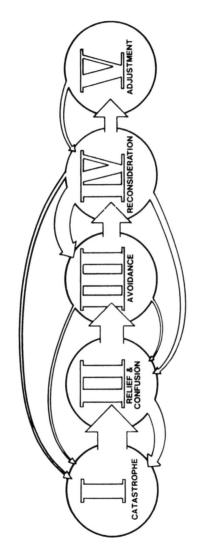

(THICKNESS OF ARROWS INDICATES APPROXIMATE % OF COHORT SHIFTS)

Figure 1. Stages of Recovery From Traumatic Events

resents the potential chronic nature of post-traumatic stress disorder. The circles represent general phases or stages of recovery and the arrows represent regression back to previous phases. This suggests, consistent with the research presented in this volume, that the recovery process rarely follows a sequential path. Rather, it follows a pattern of conscious processing, followed by periods of psychological withdrawal. Miller (1979), for example, uses the concepts of monitoring (cognitive processing of a stressful experience) and blunting (avoidance of these thoughts).

The *catastrophe* phase lasts as long as the victim believes it lasts; until there is a sense of safety. Stage/phase II, *relief and confusion,* is just that. It is a period of reflection immediately following the catastrophe: relief that it is over, but confusion about exactly what happened, why it happened, and what are the consequences of these events.

Avoidance is a method of coping which does reduce anxiety and stress symptoms, though only temporarily. *Reconsideration* is a point at which the victim is prepared to confront the trauma, to become a survivor. For some it is a lifelong struggle, which never reaches the final stage of *adjustment,* often remaining in the avoidance stage. For most others, however, adjustment is reached through adequate resources (e.g., personal, social, financial) and early intervention.

Elsewhere (Figley, 1979; 1980a; 1983a) I have noted that in the final phase victims become survivors by answering, to their satisfaction, five fundamental questions. The answers help them place their experiences in perspective and eliminate the trauma and subsequent stress. What emerges is a kind of "healing theory." The fundamental "victim questions" are: 1) What happened? 2) Why did it happen? 3) Why did I act as I did then? 4) Why did I act as I have since then? 5) What if it (the catastrophe) happens again?

Thus, the survivor emerges from being a victim by a gradual process of recapitulating and reconstructing the traumatic facets of the catastrophe. A new world emerges which incorporates catastrophes, traumata, and their wake.

Cognitive Processing of Traumatic Events

Figure 2 represents the cognitive processing of the traumatic event during and following the catastrophe.

The emergency (i.e., catastrophe) is, of course, the type of event, such as a fire, which may result in a trauma. Exposure to various stressors in an emergency leads to a certain level of traumatic stress, which is a

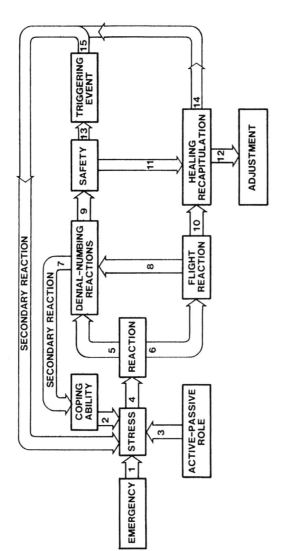

Figure 2. Reactions to Catastrophe

function of two major sets of variables: 1) The individual's *coping ability*, including, for example, utilizing social support (c.f. Burge, 1982; Burge & Figley, 1984; Figley & Burge, 1983), and viewing stressful adversities as opportunities for growth (c.f. Kobasa, 1979), and 2) the individual's *situation* within the catastrophe/emergency, which may be either passive (i.e., immobile, helpless, uncontrolled) or active (able to modulate the stressor or effectively cope with it). Thus, in every catastrophe there is a certain person-environment transaction in the extent to which the person was able to experience a sense of control and avoid a sense of helplessness.

Together, these two major sets of factors are associated with a certain level of stress. The stress subsequently leads to certain stress reactions (c.f. Cannon, 1929). The reactions take one of three forms: 1) momentary freezing (i.e., tonic immobility); 2) a flight reaction (e.g., surrender, compliance, learned helplessness) to cope with the emergency (and potentially end the catastrophe and begin the healing process); or 3) when the person must face prolonged exposure to the emergency, he or she adopts a mode of coping called the denial/numbing reaction (Figley, 1979; 1983a; Horowitz, 1976; 1979). It is a cognitive set which equips the person to withstand the constant threat of harm by either denying its existence (e.g., belief in invulnerability to harm [Janoff-Bulman, Chapter 2]) or becoming numb to it (i.e., a fatalistic or aggressive stance). This, in turn, increases the person's capacity to cope with the emergency.

Thus, a secondary reaction (i.e., feedback loop) enables a cycling between experiencing stress and building up more and more coping ability. This process is not unlike the process which occurs during the first year on the job for a fire fighter, police officer, combat veteran, emergency medical technician, or anyone working in highly stressful situations on a regular basis. This process continues throughout the catastrophe and beyond until a time that the person is convinced that the emergency has ended and the environment is safe.

Victims of traumatic events experience a sense of "safety" at varying points in time following the catastrophe. This was certainly true for the Iranian hostages released in 1981, for example. Some felt safe on the plane departing from Iran, others required nearly a year to sense such security. It is clear from the research on victims (c.f. Chapters 2, 3, and 8) that following a catastrophe the traumatic events tend to be reexperienced emotionally for months, years and, for a small number for the rest of their lives. In the process the survivor's experiences are recalled/triggered, as noted earlier, by a variety of environmental stimuli. Moreover, the experience is extremely emotionally upsetting since there is an involuntary recall of the traumatic facets of the catastrophe. These sudden flashbacks are assumed to be caused by sensory reminders of the more idiosyncratic facets of the traumatizing elements of the event (c.f. Keane, et al., Chapter 11).

These associations vary with each victim. For example, the triggering sensory stimulus for a rape victim could be the smell of an unusual aftershave lotion worn by the rapist; for the tornado victim, it could be seeing the same unusual type of motor oil can that he noticed when he hid in the basement from the storm; or for the combat vet, it could be the special taste of pound cake he had eaten just after his friend was killed.

Memories are also triggered when victims seek the support of others (e.g., family, friends, therapist) who invariably ask them to recall their experiences. We believe, as others do (c.f. Green et al., Chapter 4; Horowitz, 1979) that, in the process of recapitulation, victims are attempting to develop a "healing theory" in order to "work through" the memories and "let go" of the pain. Again, in the process, they will confront and answer the victim questions (i.e., What happened? Why did it happen to me? etc.) with both voluntary and involuntary triggering of recall. What occurs is a flooding back of memories.

While some of these traumatic memories are familiar, many have not been recalled since the event. During this time of recall victims relive one or more of the most traumatic facets of the catastrophe. Because the memories are so stressful, many victims become partially or completely dissociative and appear to be experiencing the catastrophe. This may last a few seconds or as long as several hours. During this period of time victims adopt the cognitive and behavioral repertoire of coping which was operative at the time of the catastrophe. For some, symptoms include depression; for others, violence. Most, however, experience the symptoms of acute PTSD.

PTSD symptoms are primarily associated with the anxiety of recalling an extremely stressful situation without adequate means of coping. Thus victims, convinced that they are unable to either make peace with or completely avoid these memories, develop both various strategies for *avoiding* the reminders of the catastrophe and effective tactics of cognitive management once they *are* reminded. All of this requires effort, especially soon after the catastrophe. In the process of "coping," victims may appear to be forgetful, withdrawn, moody, and tense.

It should be clear from this volume, however, that although most victims experience acute PTSD, most recover, becoming survivors. Acute PTSD is a normal reaction to an abnormal situation. But for some, the struggle with these memories can continue for a lifetime, especially if left unattended and untreated (Figley, 1978; 1983a).

These victims are especially vulnerable to traumatic recall when exposed to a pileup of various life stressors, as well as a triggering event which is especially extraordinary (e.g., sudden unemployment, death of a close friend, a heart attack). This time of crisis is when, unfortunately, the victim is least prepared to face and work through the traumatic memories.

Thus, a pattern of avoidance, recall, recovery, avoidance will continue, until there is an *adjustment:* an adequate working through of the traumatic experiences. An adequate working through is the extent to which a victim is able to answer the five victim questions and become a *survivor,* as noted earlier.

THE ROLE OF THE FAMILY IN RECOVERY

In the process of recovering from a traumatic event the role of the family is critical. As noted earlier, we have known for many years that social support is an important resource in both avoiding and recovering from emotional traumas (c.f. Burge & Figley, 1984; Figley, 1983b).

The "Family Treatment"

Elsewhere (Figley, 1983b) I have noted four separate ways in which family members facilitate recovery from traumatic stress. They are: 1) detecting traumatic stress; 2) confronting the trauma; 3) urging the recapitulation of the catastrophe; and 4) facilitating resolution of the trauma-inducing conflicts.

1) *Detecting traumatic stress.* The concept of the family is derived from the latin term *familia,* which means "household," including everyone who lives there (slaves, housekeeper, friends, mother-in-law, etc.). Anyone bound by a household—be they tied by blood or law—becomes well aware of the habits, dispositions, and patterns of behavior of others in the family. Add to this the similarities of inherited and acquired traits, and what emerges in most families is a remarkably sensitive "feel" for the normative behavior of fellow family members. Thus, when one member is having a "bad day" others know it immediately and, if appropriate, bring this observation to his or her attention. When a family member has experienced a catastrophe, for example, we *expect* variations in the pattern of behavior.

2) *Confronting the trauma.* Once the traumatic or post-traumatic stress is noticed, family members are in a key position to help the victim confront causes. The method selected is most often tailored to the individual needs and style of the victim in a way that only another family member can know. For some, the direct approach is best; for others, a more subtle method works better.

3) *Urging recapitulation of the catastrophe.* A third way that families provide social support and facilitate recovery from trauma is assisting the victim to reconsider the traumatic events; to recapitulate what happened. In the process, family members enable the victim to recall facets of the trauma which are critical in answering the other victim questions noted earlier.

4) *Facilitating resolution of the conflicts.* Finally, the family can be extremely useful in helping the victim work through his or her traumas and accompanying conflicts by answering the other five victim questions. Most importantly, the family member serves as a facilitator (e.g., active or passive, mutual self-disclosures or one-sided, confrontive or non-confrontive).

Another method of facilitating resolution is serving as a sounding board, such as (a) clarifying insights, (b) correcting distortions (placing blame and credit more objectively, and (c) offering or supporting new and more "generous" or accurate perspectives on the catastrophe.

Traumatized by Concern for Kin

As noted elsewhere, (Figley, 1982; 1983a) there are costs in providing social support. Indeed, as catastrophes affect individuals, so do they affect the families of these victims—they are the "families of catastrophe."

In addition to being directly affected by catastrophes as individuals, we are affected as members of families of catastrophe in four separate ways:

1) *simultaneous* effects, as when catastrophe directly strikes the entire family (e.g., fires, natural disasters, auto accidents);
2) *vicarious* effects, as when a catastrophe strikes a family member who is not in contact with the family (e.g., war, coal mine accidents);

3) *chiasmal* effects, as when the traumatic stress appears to "infect" the entire family after making contact with the victimized family member; and

4) *intrafamilial trauma*, as when a catastrophe strikes from within the family (e.g., incest, violence, divorce).

Simultaneous Effects

Perhaps one of the reasons natural disasters appear to leave so few emotional scars is that they often strike intact social support systems simultaneously: families, neighborhoods, communities. As a result *everyone* is a survivor and is able to appreciate and provide effective and knowledgeable support. There is no "blaming the victim," for example, because everyone is a victim. Families affected simultaneously by disaster are able to help each other to overcome the emotional horrors, rebuild, and recognize any valuable lessons which can be learned. Catastrophe-related pathology is rare in these situations.

Vicarious Effects

The emotional attachments to others through familial and friendship bonds enable us to feel safe, secure, and loved (c.f. Figley, 1973; Mc-Cubbin & Figley, 1983). When we learn by some medium (e.g., telephone, television, letter) that some catastrophe has affected in some way someone we love it is extremely stressful (Figley, 1983a; 1983b). The recent experience of a large group of Americans held hostage in Iran provides an illustration of this penomenon (Figley, 1980; Figley & McCubbin, 1983): The families experienced more stress than many of the hostages during the captivity.

Chiasmal Effects: "Infecting" the Family with Trauma

In the process of attending to the victimization of a family member, we ourselves are touched emotionally, though indirectly. As Kishur (1984) has recently noted, the phenomenon of the "transmission" of behaviors in general, and emotional experiences in particular, has been widely reported in the clinical literature for over 200 years. Such terms as *folie à deux* (Andur & Ginsberg, 1942; Gralnick, 1939); symbiosis (Bowen, 1960); copathy (Laughlin, 1970); identification (Brill, 1920; Freud, 1949); sympathy (Veith, 1965); couvade (Hunter & Macalpine, 1963); and most recently, secondary victimization (e.g., Symonds, 1980), indirect victimization (e.g., Knudten et. al., Meade, Knudten & Doerner, 1976), and vicarious victimization (Sparks, 1982) have been used to describe this topic.

Kishur (1984), drawing from human genetics, suggests the concept of the "chiasmal* effects of traumatic stressors" as a generic and unifying term to describe "the phenomenon of behaviors, impressions, actions, attitudes, or emotions which are first seen in one person following an emotionally traumatic event and subsequently observed in a supporter at a later time" (p.11). Recently, Kishur (1984) found empirical evidence for the existence of chiasmal effects. He noted that "as expected, the major predictor of *supporter distress* was *victim distress*" (p. 67). Moreover, he notes that:

> . . . It is clear that a pattern of effects emerge(s) in both victim and supporter. The crime victims as well as their supporters suffer from the crime episode long after the initial crisis has passed. Symptoms of depression, social isolation, disruptions of daily routine, and suspicion or feelings of persecution affect the lives of these persons. (p. 65)

Thus, in the process of abating traumatic and post-traumatic stress reactions, supporters are more susceptable to being traumatized themselves. This emphasizes and supports the notion that the treatment of a catastrophe victim should include the victim's entire family (Figley, 1983b).

Intrafamilial Abuse: Trauma Induction From Within the Family

A fourth way families are traumatized is *intrafamilial abuse*. These are, perhaps, the most potentially debilitating sources of trauma: spouse, parent, and child battering/neglect and incest and other sexual intrusions (Figley & McCubbin, 1983; McCubbin & Figley, 1983). Not only are all of the members of the family affected, but often the most traumatized members are denied minimal social support. Indeed, it is especially traumatizing because the source of comfort is simultaneously the source of pain and discomfort. However, these victims adopt the same basic cognitive processes for intrafamilial abuse as victims of other catastrophes outside the family system (Figley, 1983b).

---

*The Chiasma is the exchange of genetic material or "crossing-over" that takes place during meiotic cell division in which there is an exchange of genetic information between like pairs of chromosomes.

SOCIETAL RESPONSIBILITY TO VICTIMS

We conclude this volume with a question: Why in the last 10 years has the American public become interested in the plight of so many different victims? All who care about victims, including their families, rejoice at this recently emerging interest. To ponder its implications may provide some insight for the future of research and treatment in this area.

The subjugation and repression of blacks and other minorities has always been an unfortunate part of the country, including our treatment of Asian Americans during World War II. Why did it not become a national issue until the 1950s and 1960s?

Combat veterans usually return from war and are expected to accommodate to civilian life quietly and quickly without any recognition of their traumatic experiences. Why were Vietnam veterans the first to receive national attention for being victimized by their government and people?

The horror of the Holocaust could not be denied during and especially following World War II, yet not until the 1970s and 1980s were the lifelong and profound emotional struggles matters of national concern.

Women have been brutalized and raped here and in all parts of the world throughout history. But only within the last decade has it become an issue of national importance. Why?

Similarly, children have been abused and neglected everywhere, including such practices as infanticide. Why, in the 1970s, did we as a people become concerned enough about our victimized children to change public policy?

And only recently have we been concerned enough to stop wife and elderly parent battering, where before we turned our heads and said that it was a private "family matter." No longer.

In 1983 Congress began to consider a national crime victims' assistance program to help victims of violent crime recover financially and emotionally. Why now, why not years ago?

There is probably no single or simple explanation that accounts for this new appreciation of the plight of the victimized. Certainly, the concern over the morality of and opposition to war in Southeast Asia, the transition from an industrialized to a service economy, and the growing power and influence of electronic media all may account in some way for this trend.

What is important is the growing recognition of societal responsibility to the victims of catastrophe—especially those traumatic events in which the victim is held blameless, such as rape and other violent crimes. Each of us who has been victimized or who cares for those who have is part of a growing concern for the welfare of the trauma victim. And each of us in our own way can reinforce this sense of societal responsibility by insuring that the emotional upheaval of victims is neither minimized or forgotten. And each of us in our own way can work to enable those millions of victims and victimized families to recover and go on to live productive and happy lives, as survivors.

REFERENCES

American Psychiatric Association. *Diagnostic and statistical manual of mental disorders* (Third edition). Washington, D.C.: American Psychiatric Association, 1980.

Anderson, C.R. Coping behaviors as intervening mechanisms in the inverted U stress performance relationship. *Journal of Applied Psychology*, 1976, *61*, 30-34.

Andur, M. & Ginsberg, T. *Folie à Deux. Medical Bulletin of the Veterans Administration*, 1942, *14*, 230-263.

Atkeson, B.M., Calhoun, K.S., Resick, P.A., & Ellis, E.M. Victims of rape: Repeated assessment of depressive symptoms. *Journal of Consulting and Clinical Psychology*. 1982, *50*, 96-102.

Bard, M. & Sangrey, D. *The crime victim's book*. New York: Basic Books, 1979.

Bowen, M.A. Family concept of schizophrenia. In D. Jackson (Ed.), *The etiology of Schizophrenia*. New York: Basic Books, 1960.

Brill, A. The empathy index and personality. *Medical Record*, 1920, *97*, 131-134.

Burge, S.K. The social support scale: Development and initial estimates of reliability and validity of a measure of social support. Masters thesis, Purdue University, W. Lafayette, Indiana, 1982.

Burge, S.K., & Figley, C.R. The social support scale: Development and initial estimates of reliability and validity. Unpublished manuscript, 1984.

Burgess, A.W. & Holmstrom, L.L. *Rape: Crisis and recovery*. Bowie, MD: Brady, 1979.

Bennet, G. Bristol floods 1968. Controlled survey of effects on health of local community disaster. *British Medical Journal*, 1970, *3*, 454-458.

Cannon, W.B. *Bodily changes in pain, hunger, fear, and rage* (2nd ed). New York: Appleton, 1929.

Chamberlain, B.C. The psychological aftermath of disaster. Mayo Seminars in Psychiatry. *Journal of Clinical Psychiatry*. 1980, *41*(7), 238-244.

Dimsdale, J.E. *Survivors, Victims and perpetrators: essays on the Nazi Holocaust*. Washington, D.C.: Hemisphere, 1980.

Epstein, S. The self-concept revisited: Or a theory of a theory. *American Psychologist*, 1973, *28*, 404-416.

Epstein, S. The ecological study of emotions in humans. In P. Pliner, K.R. Blanstein, & I.M. Spigel (Eds.), *Advances in the study of communication and affect* (Vol. 5). New York: Plenum Press, 1979.

Epstein, S. The self-concept: A review and the proposal of an integrated theory of personality. In E. Staub (Ed.), *Personality: Basic issues and current research*. Englewood Cliffs, NJ: Prentice-Hall, 1980.

Figley, C.R. Child density and the marital relationship. *Journal of Marriage and the Family*, 1973, *35*,(2), 272-282.

Figley, C.R. The returning veteran and interpersonal adjustment: A review of the research.

Paper presented at the annual meeting of the National Council on Family Relations, Salt Lake City, August, 1975.

Figley, C.R. (Ed.). *Stress disorders among Vietnam veterans: Theory, research, and treatment.* New York: Brunner/Mazel, 1978.

Figley, C.R. Combat as disaster: Treating combat veterans as survivors. Invited address to the American Psychiatric Association, Chicago, 1979.

Figley, C.R. Treating the veteran as a survivor: Interview with C.R. Figley by Susan Salasin, *Evaluation and Change*, 1980, Special Issue, 137-139. (a)

Figley, C.R. The Iran Crisis: caring for families of catastrophe. *Family Therapy News*, 1980, 9:4-5. (b)

Figley, C.R. Traumatization and comfort: Close relationships may be hazardous to your health. Invited lecture, Texas Tech University, Lubbock, Texas, January, 1982.

Figley, C.R. Catastrophes: An overview of family reactions. In C.R. Figley & H.I. McCubbin (Eds.) Stress and the family, Volume II: Coping with catastrophe. New York: Brunner/Mazel, 1983 (a)

Figley, C.R. The family as victim: Mental health implications. In P. Berner (Ed.), Proceedings of the VIIth World Congress of Psychiatry. London: Plenum, 1983. (b)

Figley, C.R. & Burge, S.K. Social support: Theory and measurement. Paper presented at the Groves Conference on Marriage and the Family, Freeport, Bahamas, May, 1983.

Figley, C.R. & Leventman, S. (Eds.) *Strangers at home.* New York: Praeger, 1980.

Figley, C.R. & McCubbin, H.I. (Eds.). *Stress and the family, Volume II: Coping with catastrophe.* New York: Brunner/Mazel, 1983.

Frank, E., Turner, S.M., Steward, B.D., Jacob, M., & West, D. Past psychiatric symptoms and the response to sexual assault. *Comprehensive Psychiatry*, 1981, 22, 479-487.

Freud, S. *An outline of psychoanalysis.* New York: Norton, 1949.

Gleser, G.C., Green, B.L., & Winget, C. *Prolonged psychosocial effects of disaster: A study of Buffalo Creek.* New York: Academic Press, 1981.

Gralnick, A. Folie à Deux—The psychosis of association. *Psychiatric Quarterly*, 1939, 15, 277-279.

Green, B.L. Prediction of long term psychosocial functioning following the Beverly Hills fire, Doctoral dissertation, University of Cincinnati, 1980.

Green, B.L., Wilson, J.P., & Lindy, J.D. A conceptual framework for post-traumatic syndromes among survivor groups. Paper presented at the 33rd Institute on Hospital and Community Psychiatry, San Diego, September, 1982.

Grinker, R.R., & Spiegel, J.P. *Men under stress.* New York: Irvington, 1945.

Helzer, J., Robins, L.N., Wish, E., & Hesselbrock. Depression in Vietnam: Veterans and civilian control. *American Journal of Psychiatry*, 1979, 136, 526-529.

Hocking, F. Psychiatric aspects of extreme environmental stress. *Diseases of the Nervous System*, 1970, 31, 542-545.

Horowitz, M.J. *Stress response syndromes.* New York: Jason Aronson, 1976.

Horowitz, M.J. Psychosocial response to serious life events. In V. Hamilton & D.M. Warburton (Eds.), *Human stress and cognition.* New York: Wiley, 1979.

Huerta, F. & Horton, R. Coping behavior of elderly flood victims. *The Gerontologist*, 1978, 18, 541-546.

Hunter, R. & Macalpine, I. *Three hundred years of psychiatry, 1535-1860.* London: Oxford University Press, 1936.

Janoff-Bulman, R. Characterological versus behavioral self-blame: Inquiries into depression and rape. *Journal of Personality and Social Psychology*, 1979. 37,(10), 1798-1809.

Janoff-Bulman, R., & Frieze, I.H. Reactions to victimizaton. *Journal of Social Issues*, 1983 39(2), 1-17.

Kishur, G.R. Chiasmal effects of traumatic stressors: The emotional costs of support. Masters Thesis, Purdue University, West Lafayette, Indiana, 1984.

Knudten, R., Meade, M., Knudten, M., & Doerner, W. Victims and witnesses: The impact of crime and their experience with the criminal justice system. Report of the Marquette University/Milwaukee Co. Victim/Witness Project, August 15, 1976.

Kobasa, S.C. Stressful life events, personality and health: An inquiry into hardiness. *Journal of Personality and Social Psychology*, 1979. 7, 1-11.

Laughlin, H.P. *The Ego and its defenses*. New York: Appleton-Century-Crofts, 1970.

Marris, P. *Loss and change*. Garden City, NY: Anchor/Doubleday, 1975.

McCahill, T.W., Meyer, L.C., & Fischman, A.M. *The aftermath of rape*. Lexington, MA: DC Heath, 1979.

McCubbin, H.I., & Figley, C.R. *Stress and the family. Volume I: Coping with normative transitions*. New York: Brunner/Mazel, 1983.

Medea, A., & Thomspon, K. *Against rape*. New York: Farrar, Straus, & Giroux, 1974.

Miller, S. When is a little information a dangerous thing? Coping with stressful events by monitoring versus blunting. In S. Levine, & H. Ursin (Eds.), *Coping and health*. New York: Plenum, 1977.

Moore, H.E. *Tornadoes over Texas*. Austin: University of Texas Press, 1958.

Ochberg, F.M., & Soskis, D.A., (Eds.). *Victims of terrorism*. Boulder: Westview, 1982.

Parkes, C.M. Psycho-social transitions: A field for study. *Social Science and Medicine*, 1971, 5, 101-115.

Parkes, C.M. Unexpected and untimely bereavement. A statistical study of young Boston widows and widowers. In B. Schoenberg, I. Gerber, A Wiener, A.H. Kutscher, D. Peretz, & A.C. Carr (Eds.), *Bereavement: Its psychological aspects*. New York: Columbia University Press, 1975.

President's Task Force on Victims of Crime. Final Report. December, 1982.

Rich, R., & Cohen, D. Victims of Crime: Public policy perspectives and models for service. In C.R. Figley (Ed.), *Trauma and its wake, Volume II: Treatment programs*. New York: Brunner/Mazel, in press.

Saul, L.J., & Lyons, J.W. Acute neurotic reactions. In F. Alexander, & H. Ross (Eds.), *The impact of Freudian psychiatry*. Chicago: University of Chicago Press, 1961.

Segal, J., Hunter, E.J., & Segal, Z. Universal consequences of captivity: Stress reactions among divergent populations of prisoners of war and their families. *International Social Sciences Journal*, 1980, XXVII, 593-609.

Silver, R.L., & Wortman, C.B. Coping with undesirable life events. In J. Garber & M.E.P. Seligman (Eds.), *Human helplessness: Theory and applications*. N.Y.: Academic Press, 1980.

Sparks, R.F. *Research on victims of crime: Accomplishments, issues, and new directions*. U.S. Rockville, MD: Department of Health and Human Services, National Institute of Mental Health, 1982.

Steinmetz, S.K. *The cycle of violence*. New York: Praeger, 1977.

Straus, M., & Gelles, R.J. *Behind closed doors: Violence in the American family*. New York: Doubleday, 1980.

Sutherland, S., & Scherl, D. Patterns of response among victims of rape. *American Journal of Orthopsychiatry*, 1970, 40, 503-511.

Symonds, M. The second injury to victims of violent crimes. *Evaluation and change*, Special Issue on Services to Survivors, 1980, 36-38.

Trimble, M. *Post-traumatic neurosis: From railway spine to the whiplash*. New York: Wiley, 1981.

Trimble, M. Post-traumatic stress disorder: History of a concept (this volume, Chapter 1).

Veith, I. *Hysteria: The history of a disease*. Chicago: University of Chicago Press, 1965.

APPENDIX A

Patient Information Form A

Directions: Please complete the following questionnaire giving all the information requested.

I. DEMOGRAPHICS

Name: _____   Race: _____

Social Security #: _____   Religion: _____

Date of Birth: _____

Age: _____

Present Address: _____   How long have you lived

_____   here? _____

Present Telephone #: _____   _____

Name, address & phone number of person who will always know where you are: _____

_____

    1) How did you hear about our program?_____

       _____

    2) Have you ever been seen in the Jackson VA Medical Center before?
       What for?_____
       When? _____
    3) Have you ever been seen in any other VA Medical Centers before?
       What for? _____
       _____
       When? _____

II. MEDICAL HISTORY

1) Have you ever been diagnosed by a physician as having any of the following:

Problem	NO	YES	
		Past—not a problem now	Current problem
Diabetes			
Other sugar problems			
Epilepsy			
Head injury			
Ulcers			
Heart problems			
Kidney disorder			
Liver problems			
Hypertension			
Hearing loss			
Cancer			
Allergies			
Respiratory disease			
Skin problems			

2) Are any of the following problems frequent or severe for you:

Problem	NO	YES	
		Past—not a problem now	Current problem
Headaches			
Dizziness			
Blackout spells			
Ringing in ears			
Blurred vision			
Nose problems			
Shortness of breath			
Rapid breathing			
Racing heart			
Irregular heart beats			
Heart flutters			
Loss of interest in sex			
Difficulty getting erection			
Difficulty achieving orgasm			
Other sexual problems			
Specify:			
Constipation			
Diarrhea			

Nausea		
Buttererflies in stomach		
Gas		
Stomach cramps		
Muscle aches		
Nail biting		
Other aches or pains		
Specify:		
Backaches		

3) Please list previous hospitalizations for the following:

(a) Medical problems:

Diagnosis	Dates	Place
1.		
2.		
3.		
4.		
5.		

(b) Alcohol/drug problems:

Diagnosis	Dates	Place
1.		
2.		
3.		
4.		
5.		

(c) Emotional/nervous problems:

Diagnosis	Dates	Place
1.		
2.		
3.		
4.		
5.		

III. DISABILITY STATUS

1) Do you currently have a disability rating for any of the following:

Compensating agency	Yes	No	%	What for	Payment per month
VA					
Social Security					
Workmen's Compensation					
Other (please specify)					

2) Are you currently applying:

	Yes	No
A) for a disability?		
B) for a disability upgrade?		

3) If applying for disability or upgrade, please give the name of the advocacy agency handling your case _____

IV. EMPLOYMENT HISTORY

1) Current employment status:

    (a) Full-time _____ Part-time _____
    Place of employment _____
    Description of work _____
    Length of time at present job_____
    (b) Unemployed _____
    Length of time unemployed _____
    (c) Self-employed _____
    Description of work _____
    Length of time self-employed _____

2) Income:

	Amount per month
Your income	
Spouse income	
Other family member income	
(If applicable to household income)	
Welfare	
Aid to dependent children	
Food stamps	
Disability	
Retirement	
Unemployment compensation	
Other, specify	

3) Since separation from military:

    (a) How many jobs have you had? _____
    (b) How many times were you laid off? _____
    (c) How many times have you been fired? _____
    (d) How many times did you quit? _____
    (e) How much total time have you been unemployed? _____
    (f) How much total time have you been employed? _____
    (g) What is the longest time period that you have held a job?_____
    (h) What is the longest time period you've been unemployed?_____

4) Prior to your service entry:

    (a) How many jobs did you have? _____

    (b) How many times were you laid off? _____

    (c) How many times were you fired? _____

    (d) How many times did you quit? _____

    (e) How much total time were you unemployed? _____

    (f) How much total time were you employed? _____

    (g) What was the longest time period that you held a job? _____

    (h) What was the longest time period you had been unemployed?____

V. SOCIAL HISTORY

1) Current marital status:

    single _____

    married _____

    separated _____

    divorced _____

    widowed _____

    live-in partner _____

2) Have you been married more than once? ___Yes___ No

    How many times? _____

    Date(s) of marriage(s) _____

    _____

3) Number of children
    Please list children by sex, age, and marriage. Also, please indicate with whom the child resides: _____

    _____

    _____

4) List where you have lived during the past year, number of weeks you lived there, and with whom (include hospitals, jail and other temporary changes in residence):

Place	# Weeks	With Whom
1.		
2.		
3.		
4.		
5.		
6.		
7.		
8.		
9.		
10.		

5) How would you describe your current address (e.g., rent apartment, own home, trailer park, etc.): _____

VI. EDUCATION

1) Pre-military:

Dates

\# years high school _____
\# years vocational school _____
\# years college training _____
\# years post-college training _____

2) Post-military:

Dates

\# years high school _____
\# years vocational school _____
\# Obtained GED ____yes ____no
\# years college training _____
\# years post-college training _____

VII. MILITARY HISTORY

1) In which branch of the service did you serve? (circle)
   Army   Navy   Air Force   Marines   Coast Guard
2) Were you drafted or did you enlist?____enlisted____drafted
3) What type of discharge did you receive? (circle)
   Honorable   General   Dishonorable   Medical
4) Dates of entry and separation from military service: _____

5) Please list all overseas duty:

Date   Location

6) What was your highest rank in service? _____
7) What was your rank at time of separation? _____
8) What was your highest rank while serving in Vietnam? _____
9) Where did you do your basic training? Dates: From_____ To _____
   Place: _____
10) Did you receive advanced individual training? (check one)
    ____No   ____Yes   If yes, Type: _____
    Place: _____
    Dates: From _____ To _____

11) What was your MOS? Primary:_____
    Secondary:_____
12) How many tours of duty did you serve in Vietnam?_____
13) In or near what cities, corps, sectors, etc., of Vietnam did you primarily
    serve (e.g., Quang Tri, Camp Evans, MeKong Delta, Khe Sahn)?___
    _____

14) How would you describe your Vietnam duty? (check one)
    ____ mainly combat
    ____ mainly combat support (served in a unit directly supporting a
    combat unit)
    ____ mainly service support (service in noncombat-related duty)

Please give a brief description of duty performed in Vietnam:
    _____
    _____
    _____

APPENDIX B

Structured Interview for Post-traumatic Stress Disorder

EXPOSURE TO COMBAT

1) Did you ever go on combat patrols or have other very dangerous duty?
   __No__Yes, 1-3 times__Yes, 4-12 times__Yes, 13-50 times__Yes, more than 50

2) Were you ever under enemy fire?
   __Never__Yes, for a period of less than a month__Yes, for 1-3 months__Yes, for 4-6 months__Yes, for more than 6 months

3) Were you ever surrounded by the enemy?
   __No __Yes, 1-2 times__Yes, 3-12 times__Yes, more than 12 times

4) What percentage of the men in your unit were killed (KIA), wounded, or missing (MIA) in action in Vietnam?
   __No one__Between 1-25%__Between 26-50%__More than 50%

Please answer the following questions by circling the answer.

5) How often did you fire rounds at the enemy?

1	2	3	4	5
Never	1-2 times	3-12 times	13-50 times	50 or more

6) How often did you see someone hit by incoming or outgoing rounds?

1	2	3	4	5
Never	1-2 times	3-12 times	13-50 times	50 or more

7) How often were you in danger of being injured or killed (i.e., pinned down, overrun, ambushed, near miss, etc.)?

1	2	3	4	5
Never	1-2 times	3-12 times	13-50 times	50 or more

8) Which of the following, if any, describe your exposure to combat in Vietnam?
   —Stationed at a forward observation post
   —Received incoming fire from enemy (small arms, artillery, rockets, or mortars)
   —Encountered mines or booby traps while on patrol or at duty station

424

—Unit received sniper or sapper fire
—Unit patrol was ambushed
—Unit patrol engaged in Vietcong (or guerrilla troups) in a fire fight
—Unit patrol engaged NVA (organized military forces) in a fire fight
—Was part of a naval artillery unit which fired on the enemy
—Flew in aircraft over South Vietnam or North Vietnam
—Patrolled rivers in Vietnam
9) Were you wounded or injured in Vietnam?__No__Yes. If yes, please explain the nature of your injury. _____
10) Do you have a service-connected disability?
__No__Yes. If yes, what percentage are you?
What is it for? _____

COMBAT TRAUMA

List specific events (e.g., death of buddy, unit ambushed, perimeter overrun, direct hit with mortar, rocket, etc.)

1) _____

2) _____

3) _____

4) _____

5) _____

PTSD SYMPTOMS

Determine the degree to which the patient is experiencing the following symptoms:

I. Reexperiencing of the trauma:

A. Nightmares
1) Sleep disturbance

___ Trouble falling asleep

Freq: Times/Wk.
0 1 2 3 4 5 6 7

___ Waking up early in morning
Freq: Times/Wk.
0 1 2 3 4 5 6 7

___ Waking up in middle of night (nightmares)
Freq: Times/Wk.
0 1 2 3 4 5 6 7

___ Waking up in middle of night (fitful sleep)
Freq: Times/Wk.
0 1 2 3 4 5 6 7

___ Average # of hrs. sleep/night
___ Average # of hrs. sleep/daytime
___ Total hrs. sleep/24 hr. period

2) (a) Combat nightmares   (b) Non-combat nightmares
   ____ Freq: Times/Wk.   ____ Freq: Times/Wk.
   0 1 2 3 4 5 6 7   0 1 2 3 4 5 6 7
   ____ Times/Mo. 0 1 2 3   ____ Times/Mo. 0 1 2 3

Content of combat nightmares: _____

_____

_____

Non-combat nightmares: _____

_____

_____

3) Intrusive thoughts
   ____ Specific traumatic combat events
   ____ Ruminations of military service in general or of entire VN
   experience
   Specify _____

   _____

   (a) Specific   (b) General ruminations
      ____ Freq: Times/Wk.   ____ Freq: Times/Wk.
      0 1 2 3 4 5 6 7   0 1 2 3 4 5 6 7
      ____ Times/Mo. 0 1 2 3   ____ Times/Mo. 0 1 2 3

4) Hallucinatory flashback experience
   ____ Freq: Times/Wk.   ____ Times/Mo.
   0 1 2 3 4 5 6 7   0 1 2 3
   ____ Times/Yr.
   0 1 2 3 4 5 6 7 8 9 10 11

II. Numbing of Responsiveness or Reduced Involvement With External
World
   A. Markedly diminished interest in one or more significant activities
   ____ 1) Work
   Loss of interest in job, including feelings of incapacity, listlessness,
   perceived difficulty in attending work.

Rating:

0	1	2	3	4	5
Not at all	Mild		Moderate		Severe

____ 2) Social activities
   How often in the last year have you

   gone to the movies _____
   gone dancing _____
   played sports _____
   observed sports _____
   played cards _____

gone to parties _____

gone to picnics/outings _____

gone hunting/fishing _____

participated in church/social organization _____

gone visiting family/friends _____

_____ 3) Social motivation/willingness to socialize—makes efforts to join in activities with others; wants to have friends.

Rating:

0	1	2	3	4	5
Not at all	Mild		Moderate		Severe

Are there activities which interested you at one time but in which you no longer have interest?

List them:

1) _____

2) _____

3) _____

4) _____

5) _____

6) _____

7) _____

8) _____

9) _____

B. Estrangement and detachment from others:
Check if the patient expresses that he has experienced these feelings:

	Before VN	Immediately Past	Now
1) Wife/Girlfriend			
2) Children			
3) Mother			
4) Father			
5) Siblings			
6) Friends			

C. Constricted affect: Rate ability to experience feeling:

		Not at all	Somewhat	Moderately so	Very much so
1)	Happy	1	2	3	4
2)	Sad	1	2	3	4
3)	Angry	1	2	3	4
4)	Love	1	2	3	4
5)	Fear	1	2	3	4
6)	Hate	1	2	3	4
7)	Contentment	1	2	3	4
8)	Jealousy	1	2	3	4
9)	Suspicion	1	2	3	4

10. Are you able to cry? ___Yes___No

III. Six Miscellaneous Symptoms
   A. Exaggerated startle response
      1) Do loud noises bother you?
      Eliciting stimuli: _____

      Overall rating: 0   3   5
                          |_____|_____|
                       Not at all   Somewhat Extremely Bothersome

      2) Hyperalertness
      Do you repeatedly check the windows and/or door locks in your
      home? _____
      Where do you sit in a restaurant? _____

      Where do you sit in a movie?_____

      Are you uncomfortable with your back to the door?_____

      Do you try to be aware of everything around you?_____

      Overall rating: 0   3   5
                          |_____|_____|
                       Not at all   Somewhat   Extreme
                       Hyperalert   Hyperalertness

   B. Sleep disturbance (see nightmares)
   C. Survivor guilt: 0 - 5 rating
   _____Do you feel guilty about surviving VN?
   _____Do you feel guilty about behavior required for your survival?

                        0   3   5
                        |_____|_____|
                     Not at all   Extremely
                     Guilty   Guilty

D. Memory impairment
Do you have difficulty remembering things? 0 - 5 rating

_____ Recent events

_____ Remote events

0	3	5
No Difficulty		Extreme Difficulty

Administer Russell Wechsler Story Memory Test
(See Appendix Weschler Memory Paragraph Test)

Where were you living 5 years ago?
Where did you spend last Christmas?
What did you have for breakfast yesterday?
Who is U.S. President now?
Who was president before him?

# of errors 0 - 5 _____

E. Avoidance of activities that arouse recollection of traumatic event:
List activities:

_____

_____

0–5 subjective rating

0	3	5
No Avoidance		Extreme Avoidance

F. Intensification of symptoms by exposure to events
List examples:

_____

_____

0–5 subjective rating

0	3	5
No Symptom Intensification		Extreme Symptom Intensification

ASSOCIATED FEATURES

I. Depression   Rate the Following Symptoms on Severity:
  A. Crying spells _X per week; _X per month; _X per year.
  B. Suicidal potential
    1) Suicidal ideation _X per week; _X per month; _X per year.
    2) Suicidal plans _yes _no   Specify: _____

    _____

    3) Suicide attempts # pre-VN__; # post-VN__.

C. Appetite disturbance
    1) Do you lose your appetite___X per week; ___X per month.
    2) How long do you go without eating?_____

D. Anhedonia 1) ——absent
               2) ——mild
               3) ——moderate
               4) ——severe
               5) ——incapacitating

E. Subjective rating of depression:

0	3	5
Not at all Depressed	Moderately Depressed	Extremely Depressed

II. Anxiety
    A. Somatic anxiety: Physiological concomitants of anxiety, such as:
        gastro-intestinal—dry mouth, wind, indigestion, diarrhea, cramps,
        belching; cardio-vascular—palpitations, headaches; urinary fre-
        quency; sweating
        1) ____absent
        2) ____mild
        3) ____moderate
        4) ____severe
        5) ____incapacitating

    B. Subjective anxiety (non-combat–related thoughts)
        1) ____absent
        2) ____mild
        3) ____moderate
        4) ____severe
        5) ____incapacitating

    C. Subjective rating of anxiety:

0	3	5
Not at all Anxious	Moderately Anxious	Extremely Anxious

III. Aggression
    Rate the following behaviors on frequency:
    1) Destroying property

             _____ X per week
             _____ X per month
             _____ X per year

2) Threatening others with physical violence without a weapon

_____ X per week
_____ X per month
_____ X per year

3) Threatening others with physical violence with a weapon

_____ X per week
_____ X per month
_____ X per year

4) Physical fights with others

_____ X per week
_____ X per month
_____ X per year

5) Used a weapon against others

_____ X per year

6) Fear of loss of control

0	3	5
Not at all	Moderately	Extremely
Afraid	Afraid	Afraid

IV. Alcohol/drug use
  A. Current use:
    1) How many days in a month do you typically drink? _____
    2) How much do you typically drink at any one time?
      drink = 1 oz. liquor
      1 12 oz. beer

1	2	3	4	5
1 or 2	3–4	5–6	7–8	>8
drinks				
beer				

0 = No 3) Do you have binges of heavy drinking? _____
1 = Yes 4) How often do you have binges in a year? _____
    5) What nonprescribed drugs do you regularly use? _____
_____
    6) How often do you take these drugs? _____

B. Pre-Vietnam use:
1) How many days in a month do you typically drink?_____
2) How much do you typically drink at any one time?
   drink = 1 oz. liquor
   1 12 oz. beer

1	2	3	4	5
1 or 2	3–4	5–6	7–8	>8
drinks				
beer				

3) Did you have binges of heavy drinking?_____
4) How often did you have binges in a year?_____
5) What nonprescribed drugs did you regularly use?_____

_____

6) How many times per week did you take these drugs?_____

C. Use in Vietnam:
1) How many days in a month did you typically drink?_____
2) How much did you typically drink at one time?
   drink = 1 oz. liquor
   1 12 oz. beer

1	2	3	4	5
1 or 2	3–4	5–6	7–8	>8
drinks				
beer				

3) Did you have binges of heavy drinking? _____
4) How often did you have binges in a year?_____
5) What nonprescribed drugs did you regularly use? _____

_____

6) How many times per week did you take these drugs? _____

V. Legal Problems
A. Post-Vietnam:
1) Number of arrests: _____
List charges (including classification as misdemeanor, felony)
brought against veteran and length of incarceration: _____

_____
_____
_____

2) Number of DUIs/DWIs: _____
3) Is veteran currently: on probation _____
                         on parole _____
                         on bond _____
                         awaiting a court appearance_____
                         awaiting sentencing _____
                         have charges against him _____

B. Pre-Vietnam
1) Number of arrests: _____
List charges (including classification of misdemeanor or felony)

brought against veteran and length of incarceration:

_____

_____

_____

_____

2) Number of DUIs/DWIs: _____

VI. Marital/Relationship Discord
   1) How often do you have arguments with your spouse/partner?

   _____ X/week   _____ X/month
       0 1 2 3 4 5 6 7   0 1 2 3

   _____ X/year
   0 1 2 3 4 5 6 7 8 9 10 11

   2) How often do you have physical fights with your spouse/partner?

   _____ X/week   _____ X/month
       0 1 2 3 4 5 6 7   0 1 2 3

   _____ X/year
   0 1 2 3 4 5 6 7 8 9 10 11

   3) How would you rate your sex life with your spouse/partner?

   Not at all   Somewhat   Highly
   satisfying   satisfying   satisfying
       1   2   3   4   5

   4) Do you have sexual relations with your spouse/partner as frequently as you would like?
   _____ yes   _____ no

   _____ X/week   _____ X/month
       0 1 2 3 4 5 6 7   0 1 2 3

   _____ X/year
   0 1 2 3 4 5 6 7 8 9 10 11

   5) Do you have difficulty sharing or communicating with your spouse/partner?

0	1	2	3	4	5
Not	Very		Somewhat		Severe
a	little		of a		problem
problem	problem		problem		

6) Do you ever leave home without giving notice to your spouse/partner?

_____ Yes   _____ No

_____ X/week   _____ X/month
    0 1 2 3 4 5 6 7   0 1 2 3

_____ X/year
0 1 2 3 4 5 6 7 8 9 10 11

Duration ___(# of days, weeks, etc.)

7) How enjoyable is the free time that you spend with your spouse/partner?

1	2	3	4	5
Not at all enjoyable		Somewhat enjoyable		Very enjoyable

8) Overall, how would you describe the quality of your marriage/relationship?

1	2	3	4	5
Poor		OK, not particularly good or bad		Very good

PRE-MORBID ADJUSTMENT

I. High School Performance
  A. Grades: Above av.__av.__below av. __
  B. Extracurricular activities _____

  C. Suspended expelled _____
  D. Grades failed _____

II. Did You Enter the Service Immediately After High School? __Yes __No
If no, what did you do between the time you left/graduated high school and your time of service entry?
_____

III. Social Life: Pre-Vietnam
  A. Dating: _____
  B. Friends: Names _____

IV. Family Life: Pre-Vietnam
  A. Number of people in household: _____
  B. Number of brothers and sisters: _____

C. Did you live with your biological parents? ___ Yes ___ No
   If no, with whom? _____
   Why? _____
D. Emotional closeness to biological/adoptive parents:
   Circle one: Mother:

           0   3   5

   Not at all   Somewhat   Extremely
   Close   Close   Close

   Circle one: Father:

           0   3   5

   Not at all   Somewhat   Extremely
   close   Close   Close

E. Parents marital status:
   ___ divorced ___ separated ___ married ___ abandoned
F. Form of parental discipline used: _____
G. Were there family rules you were expected to follow when you
   were a teenager (e.g., curfew, allowance, driving a car, etc.)?
   _____
H. Number of residences while growing up? If more than 2–3, reason:
   _____

V. Family History of Mental Illness:
   Do any of your immediate family/or grandparents/aunts, uncles have
   any of the following psychological disorders? List who has them:
   A. Schizophrenia _____
   B. Depression _____
   C. Alcoholism _____
   D. Other psychological problems, specify: _____

Yearly progression of symptoms
   Severe

   Moderate

   Mild

   None

        D/C

Possible precipitating events _____
_____
_____
_____
_____

MENTAL STATUS EXAM

Orientation
1) What day of the week is this?
2) What month?
3) What day of the month?
4) What year?
5) What place is this?
6) Why are you here?
7) Have there been periods in which you've "blanked out," or suddenly realized you don't know what happened for the last few minutes?

Sensory
8) Do you ever see things others do not? (If yes, ask the person to describe these experiences.)
9) Do you ever wear glasses? (If not, ask "Do your eyes ever bother you?")
10) Have there been times when things looked "unreal," or distorted, or too small, or too big?
11) Have you any trouble hearing?
12) Have you had problems understanding what people say?
13) Do you hear things others don't seem to hear?
14) Do your hands or feet ever get numb?
15) Do you ever experience any unusual odors or tastes?
16) Does food still taste as good as it always did to you?
17) Have you had any unusual sensations in your body, such as tingling, "electricity," or pain?

Motor
18) Are the joints of your hands sore or numb?
19) Have you had any difficulty moving, e.g., walking, grasping and holding things, weakness?
20) Can you manage your normal work OK?
21) Do you notice any weakness in your body?

Emotional Tone
22) Do you lose your temper easily? (How long have you felt this way?)
23) Do you cry easily? (How long have you felt this way?)
24) Are you frightened easily? (How long have you felt this way?)
25) Do you feel sad or blue often?
26) Have you lost your get-up-and-go?
27) Do you have any trouble sleeping?
28) Have you ever thought of killing yourself? (If yes, have you recently considered killing yourself?)
29) Do you ever get excited or high for several days in a row?

Delusional Behavior
30) How do people treat you?
31) Does anyone ever talk about you?

32) Do you sometimes feel that people are plotting against you?
33) Do you feel you have any special powers?

Math
34) Do you have any trouble with calculations?
35) 9 + 3 is   _____
36) Add 6 (to the previous answer "to 12").   _____
37) Take away 5 ("from 18").   _____
38) Take away 7 from 100, then take away 7 from what is left and keep going: (If the patient makes a mistake, don't correct—just write down his or her answers.)
100 - 93 - 86 - 79 - 72 - 65 - 58 - 51 - 44 - 37 - 30 - 23 - 16 - 9 - 2
39) Beginning with Sunday, say the days of the week backwards.

Proverbs
Explain these old sayings in your own words.
40) No use crying over spilled milk.
41) Don't count your chickens before they're hatched.

Judgment
42) What should you do if while in the movies you were the first person to see smoke and fire?
43) Do a mistake and a lie differ?
44) What are your plans once you get over this problem?

Memory
45) Have you had any problems with your memory? (Tell me about them.)
45) Repeat these words after me and remember them. I will ask for them later.
HAT, CAR, TREE, TWENTY-SIX.
46) Who is the current president of the United States?
47) Who was the last president of the United States?
48) Who is the governor of Mississippi?
49) What happened on November 22, 1963?
50) What were those words I asked you to remember?

                             (HAT) _____
                             (CAR) _____
                           (TREE) _____
                    (TWENTY-SIX) _____

51) Please repeat these digits after I have given them to you. (Discontinue when patient has missed both trials in a number group.)

| 5–8–2 | 6–4–3–9 | 4–2–7–3–1 | 6–1–9–4–7–3 | 5–9–1–7–4–2–8 |
| 6–9–4 | 7–2–8–6 | 7–5–8–3–6 | 3–9–2–4–8–7 | 4–1–7–9–3–8–6 |

52) Please repeat these digits backwards after I have given them to you. For example, if I say 9–3, you say 3–9. (Discontinue when patient misses both trials in a number group.)

| 2–4 | 6–2–9 | 3–2–7–9 | 1–5–2–8–6 |
| 5–8 | 4–1–5 | 4–9–6–8 | 6–1–8–4–3 |

53) Listen to these numbers, 6–9–4. Count 1 through 10 out loud, then repeat 6–9–4. (Help if needed. Then use numbers, 5–7–3.)
54) Listen to these numbers, 8–1–4–3. Count 1 through 10 out loud, then repeat 8–1–4–3.

Visual-Spatial and Visual Memory
55) Please draw this figure without lifting your pencil.
     (Next ask the patient to point to the center of the figure.)
     (Next ask the patient to trace around the figure at an approximate distance of 3/6".)
     (Next ask the patient to reproduce from memory the figure on a blank sheet of paper.)

Anna Thompson/ of South/ Boston/
employed/ as a scrub woman/
in an office building/ reported/
at the City Hall/ Station/
that she had been held up/
on State Street/ the night before/
and robbed/ of fifteen dollars/.
She had four/ little children/ the rent/
was due/ and they had not eaten/
for two days/. The officers/
touched by the woman's story/
made up a purse/ for her/.

Number of Memories _____

Name Index

Subject Index

Abreaction, 244-245, 310
Accident neurosis, 11
Accidents, 8-13, 54, 197, 319, *see also*
    Disasters; Traumatic events
    compared to other survivor groups,
        153-171
    loss of meaning and, 21
    nuclear power plants and, 384-395
    self-blame and, 28
    victimization and, 15-16
Acting-out behavior, 47
Active/passive role, 230
Adjustment process, 404, 408
Adolescence, 47-48
Affect Balance Scale, 93, 96-97, 103-104
Affective states, 92-93, 101, 104
    memory and, 266
Aggression, 50, 265, 271, 343
    concentration camp survivors and, 301-
        302
Alcohol abuse, 153, 271, *see also* Substance
    abuse
Alienation, 92
Altruistic community, 201
Amnesia, 41
Anger, 146-147, 285-287, *see also* Rage
Anger control techniques, 283, 289-290
Anhedonia, 269
Anniversary dates, 48, 237, 305
Anomia, 152
Anorexia, 186
Antisocial behavior, 225
Anxiety, 38, 40, 64-66, 151, 153, 329, 343
    behavioral therapy techniques and, 277-
        278, 280, 282-283
    childhood incest and, 361-362
    chronic, 147, 269
    conditioned stimulus and, 263
    crime victims and, 93, 103-104
    Derogatis Symptom Check List 90-R
        and, 126-127

disasters and, 62, 186, 192-193, 196, 380-
    381, 387
negative reinforcement and, 266
potential for recurrence of trauma and,
    152
rape victims and, 117, 118-120
self-destructive behavior and, 47
State-Trait Anxiety Inventory and, 127
strangers and, 42
Subjective Units of Distress Scale and,
    277
victimization and, 16, 19
Appetite, loss of, 195-196
Approach-avoidance conflict, 106
Assertiveness training, 27, 289
Atomic Energy Act, 389
Atrocities, 74
Autonomic dysfunction, 39
Autonomic nervous system arousal, 151-
    152
Autonomy, 22, 30, 145
Aversive conditioning, 262
Avoidance behavior, 263, 269, 277, 404
    cognitive processing of the trauma and,
        147
    crime victims and, 91-92, 101, 110
    duration of the trauma and, 151
    Impact of Events Scale and, 158
    rape victims and, 117-120

Battering, 28
Beck Depression Inventory, 154, 157-158,
    160, 162, 165, 167-168, 273-274
Behavioral approach
    cognitive-behavioral approach, 342-347,
        350, 354
    treatment techniques, 277-290, 331
Behavioral changes, 26-27
Behavioral contrast, 267
Behavioral techniques, 244-245
Behavioral theory, 261-263, 274

449

self-blame and, 28-30
sense of safety and, 24
silent rape-reaction, 234
treatment for victims, 138-140
Rape Assault Characteristics Checklist, 125
Rape trauma syndrome, 12
Rational Emotive Therapy, 285, 344
Readjustment process, 231-232
Reality, 23-24, 56
  assumptions about, 17-18
Recovery environment, 60-62, 67
Redefining the event, 24-25
Reenactment of the event, 40, 42, 46, 147
Reexperiencing Disorder, 82
Reexperiencing the trauma, 147, 245-246, 269-270, 406-407
Regression, 145, 331
  as part of treatment, 245-246
  traumatic state of, 39
  traumatized children and, 43, 46
Reinforcement, negative, 266-267
Rejection, fear of, 281-282
Relaxation training, 278, 284, 288-289
Repetition compulsion, 56
Repression, 298
Resistance, 331
Role playing, 287
Role reversal, 300, 360

Scapegoating, 186
School problems, 44
School-age children, 44-46
Second-order conditioning, 118, 120, 139
Secondary disasters, 196
Secondary gain, 11, 220
Secondary victimization, 106, 374-375, 410-411
Self-blame, 26, 28-30, 91, 98-99, 326, 400
  community disasters and, 183
  rape victims and, 118
Self-control, 346-347
Self-defense training, 27
Self-destructive behavior, 47
Self-esteem, 21-22, 24, 335
  childhood incest and, 359, 361, 371
  identity diffusion and, 145
  obsessive/compulsive behavior and, 233
  rape victims and, 117, 138
  self-blame and, 30
  Self-report Inventory and, 126, 131, 133-134
  social support and, 27-28

Self-report Inventory, 126
Sensation seeking, 267
Sensation Seeking Scale, 154, 158, 160, 162-163, 165, 167-168
Sense of self, 146
Sensory system, 348
Separation, 42-43, 146
Serial conditioning paradigm, 262-263
Service medical record, 268
Sexual Assault Research Project, 114, 123
Sexual dysfunction
  childhood incest and, 359, 361-362
  precocious adolescent sexual activity, 47
  rape victims and, 117-118
Shame, 63
Shared fate, 153
Shell shock, 8
Situational variables, 143, 149-153
Sleep disturbances, 17, 62-64, 66, 269-270,
  see also Nightmares
  crime victims and, 92-93, 103, 110
  disasters and, 195-196, 380-381
  rape victims and, 118
  relaxation techniques and, 284
  traumatized children and, 43
Social disorganization, 179-180, 187
Social life, 183
Social problem model, 201-203
Social readjustment rating scale, 125
Social supports, *see* Support systems
Somatic complaints, 62-63, 300, 304
Startle reactions, 40, 55, 270
  environmental disasters and, 380
  problem solving technique and, 288
State-Trait Anxiety Inventory, 127, 274
Stimulus generalization, 118-120, 139, 264
Stimulus-response chain, 288-289
Stranger anxiety, 42
Stress, 406, *see also* Post-traumatic stress
  disorder
  childhood incest and, 358-360
  civilian wartime behavior and, 177
  collective, 174, 177-178, 183, 188
  environmental use and, 379-380
  families of trauma victims and, 410
  heart attack victims and, 342-343
  of human design (i.e. crime), 20
  Langner Index of Psychological Stress, 386-387
  perceived threat of misfortune and, 19
  personality characteristics, 60
  Three Mile Island and, 387-395
  Vietnam veterans and, 75-81
  war, 74-75